The Oppenheimer Hearing

The OPPENHEIMER HEARING

John Major

A SCARBOROUGH BOOK
STEIN AND DAY/*Publishers*/New York

To Eric, Elizabeth and Gerald

HISTORIC TRIALS SERIES
Editor: J.P. Kenyon, Professor of History, University of Hull

FIRST SCARBOROUGH BOOKS EDITION 1983
The Oppenheimer Hearing was originally published in hardcover by
STEIN AND DAY / *Publishers* in 1971.

Library of Congress Cataloging in Publication Data

Major, John, 1936-
    The Oppenheimer hearing.

    Reprint.   Originally published: New York: Stein and
Day, 1971. (Historic trials series)
    "A Scarborough book."
    Bibliography: p.
    Includes index.
    1. Oppenheimer, J. Robert, 1904-1967.   I. Title.
[QC16.062M3   1983]   353.0085'5397   82-22997
ISBN 0-8128-6179-5 (pbk.)

Contents

LIST OF ILLUSTRATIONS   6

PREFACE   7

ACKNOWLEDGMENTS   8

1   The News Breaks   9

2   The Hearing Opens   19

3   Communist Associations   43

4   The Hydrogen Bomb   91

5   Vista and Lincoln   147

6   The Verdicts   177

7   'An Inquiry and not a Trial'   211

8   Origins   238

9   Aftermath   276

REFERENCES   298

SELECT BIBLIOGRAPHY   320

INDEX   327

The Illustrations

1 Haakon Chevalier 96

2 Oppenheimer and General Groves, July 1945 96

3 Senator Bourke B. Hickenlooper 97

4 The Lilienthal Commission, 1949: Lilienthal,
Dean, Pike, Strauss 97

5 Oppenheimer opposes Strauss, June 1949 128

6 Edward Teller 128

7 William L. Borden 129

8 The FBI Director, J. Edgar Hoover 129

9 President Eisenhower 192

10 Senator Joseph McCarthy 192

11 Gordon Gray 193

12 Thomas A. Morgan 193

13 Ward V. Evans 193

14 General Kenneth D. Nichols 193

15 The Strauss Commission, 1953: Zuckert, Smyth,
Strauss, Murray, Campbell 224

16 Oppenheimer and his counsel Lloyd K. Garrison 225

17 President Johnson presents Oppenheimer with
the Fermi Award, 2 December 1963 225

Preface

This book is an excursion into what is known as 'contemporary history', that is to say, the history of our own times. One of the distinguishing features of this sort of history is often the lack of primary source material. In a book which treats a topic as sensitive as atomic energy, this deficiency is particularly marked. Official documents covering most aspects of the Oppenheimer case have not yet been released, and some may never be. Such things as the FBI records, and the reports of the General Advisory Committee of the Atomic Energy Commission, and of Project Vista and the Lincoln Summer Study are not available to historians. The same applies to private papers, and the added understanding which could be gained from the papers of Dr Oppenheimer or, among others, those of Mr Strauss, General Nichols and Mr Borden is self-evident.

Nonetheless it is possible to write history from what we already have, and I hope the result is not without interest. I also hope it will serve to clear the ground for a fully-documented account, if that should ever come to be written.

Department of History   JOHN MAJOR
The University of Hull

Acknowledgments

I should like to record the debts I owe on both sides of the Atlantic. I wish to thank Mrs Felicia Magruder, who introduced me to Mr Lloyd K. Garrison, and Mr Garrison for kindly lending me copies of the two briefs he submitted on behalf of Dr Oppenheimer. I should also like to acknowledge the exemplary help given to me by Mrs Lorna Arnold of the United Kingdom Atomic Energy Authority, and by Dr Richard G. Hewlett, chief historian of the United States Atomic Energy Commission. Finally, I should like to say how grateful I am to Professor John P. Kenyon, of my Department, and to B. T. Batsford Limited, for their immense forbearance.

JOHN MAJOR

The Author and Publishers would like to thank Harper & Row, Publishers, Inc., New York for permission to quote from R. J. Donovan, *Eisenhower: The Inside Story* (1956); H. Kissinger, *Nuclear Weapons and Foreign Policy* (1957); D. E. Lilienthal, *The Journals of David E. Lilienthal*. Vol. II (1964); D. E. Lilienthal, *The Journals of David E. Lilienthal*. Vol. III (1966); J. Mason Brown, *Through These Men* (1956); M. B. Ridgway, *Soldier*, (1956); W. W. Rostow, *The United States in the World Arena* (1960); P. M. Stern (with the collaboration of H. P. Green), *The Oppenheimer Case* (1969). Acknowledgments for the illustrations are also due to the following: Associated Press for figs 6, 7 and 16–17; Haakon Chevalier for fig. 1; Elton Lord, USAEC for fig. 15; United Press International (UK) Ltd. for figs 2–5 and 8–13; US Army for fig. 14.

The Oppenheimer Hearing

Chapter One

The News Breaks

On 6 April 1954 Senator Joseph McCarthy addressed the American people on television. For more than four years he had held the centre of the political stage as the self-appointed scourge of Communism in the United States, but now he himself was coming under fire. A month beforehand the commentator Ed Murrow had launched a detailed attack on him and the broadcast gave McCarthy the opportunity to make his rejoinder. Its main feature, however, was not the anticipated rebuttal of Murrow's charges but something quite unexpected—nothing less than an accusation that a pro-Communist faction in government circles had conspired to delay work on the hydrogen bomb.

'If there were no Communists in our government,' asked the Senator 'why did we delay for eighteen months, delay our research on the hydrogen bomb, even though our intelligence agencies were reporting day after day that the Russians were feverishly pushing their development of the H-bomb? And may I say to America tonight that our nation may well die, our nation may well die because of that eighteen-month deliberate delay. And I ask you, who caused it? Was it loyal Americans or was it traitors in our government?'[1]

Why had McCarthy suddenly broached this dramatic new issue? His initiative can only be understood against the background of the events of the past six months. By the autumn of 1953 McCarthy had established himself as a major political force, but although a Republican he was by no means happy with the direction taken by the Republican administration which had come to power under President Eisenhower the previous January. As the leader of the Republican right wing he was totally at odds with the moderates dominating the Eisenhower régime and in November he had gone so far as to voice public criticism of its policies. If he persisted in his challenge he was likely to damage many of the party's candidates in the forth-

coming mid-term elections in November 1954. The administration was therefore determined to eliminate the threat which
McCarthy posed, first by trying to reach an accommodation
with him, and then, when its overtures were rejected, by a
frontal attack.[2]

Its task was made easier by McCarthy's decision to begin
investigating so-called Communist activities in the Army, an
institution which not even he had so far dared touch. This was
a crucial blunder on McCarthy's part and from January 1954
onwards the government was concerting its plans to destroy him.
By the time of Murrow's broadcast on 9 March McCarthy was
in serious trouble. The same day he had been criticized in the
Senate by a fellow-Republican, Senator Flanders, and on 11
March the Army delivered its counter-stroke by accusing him of
trying to obtain preferential treatment for his aide, David
Schine, who had recently been called up for military service. He
had retorted by alleging that the Secretary of the Army had
made frequent efforts to impede his investigations. A public
hearing in which the two sides were to confront each other was
scheduled for 22 April and McCarthy had almost certainly
seized on the H-bomb question in an attempt to divert attention
from what was clearly going to be a major crisis in his career.

His bid was made at a moment when popular emotion was
running high on the issue of hydrogen weapons. On 1 March
the Atomic Energy Commission had tested a hydrogen bomb in
the Pacific, and the resultant radio-active fall-out had scattered
over a Japanese fishing-boat, *The Lucky Dragon*; one of the
crew was later to die of radiation sickness. On 31 March the
Chairman of the Commission, Mr Strauss, had been brought
forward to give an explanation of the incident, and on 5 April
Eisenhower himself had gone on television to reassure the
country that all was well. McCarthy's broadcast came the following evening.[3]

As might be expected, it raised an enormous flurry. On 7
April the Chairman of the Joint Congressional Committee on
Atomic Energy, Representative Sterling Cole, put out a statement. In it he admitted that there had been a lengthy debate
within the government following the explosion of a Soviet atomic
device in August 1949. One of the main questions had been
whether or not a hydrogen bomb programme should be under-

taken as part of the American response to the Russian achievement. A majority of the Atomic Energy Commission together
with the Commission's General Advisory Committee of scientists
had come out against it; the Congressional Committee, the State
Department and the Defense Department had been in favour.
Cole went on to list the various objections raised and to say that
the fact that there was considerable discussion 'is not of itself
sinister, nor does it imply that those who opposed the President's
final decision were motivated by a desire to lessen our military
strength'. The conclusion immediately threw doubt on this, however: ' . . . we cannot exclude categorically the possibility', the
statement ended, 'that a person or persons in our program
might have been motivated by interests other than those of the
United States.' Since Cole himself had opposed the H-bomb in
1949 and since the tone of this final paragraph ran counter to
that of everything that had gone before it, it seems probable that
it was added by another hand. At all events, it left the possibility
of treason very much in being, as no doubt it was intended to.[4]

Further light was thrown on McCarthy's outburst by the
columnist of *The New York Times*, James Reston. Reston's
article, which appeared on 8 April, was based on a long conversation with the first Chairman of the AEC, David Lilienthal,
who had been in office at the time of the hydrogen bomb debate.
It concentrated on the meetings held on 31 January 1950, the
day the decision to develop an H-bomb was taken by President
Truman, but, like Cole's statement, it asserted that there had
been no such eighteen-month delay as McCarthy had claimed.
At most the delay had lasted for just over four months, between
23 September 1949, when Truman announced the Soviet explosion, and the following 31 January. At that point the argument
came to an end.[5]

In view of subsequent developments, however, the most significant reaction came from President Eisenhower. Asked at his
news conference on 7 April to comment on McCarthy's accusation, Eisenhower declared that 'I never heard of any delay on
my part'. Moreover, Mr Strauss, whose duty it was to keep the
President informed on atomic energy matters, 'has never mentioned such a thing as you speak of . . . '. (In an interview given
in 1960 Strauss was to say that the hydrogen bomb was developed 'in about three years, which is certainly par for the

course. I think surely it was developed as soon as the most optimistic thought it could be done.')[6]

There the matter appeared to rest, but not for long. On 13 April it erupted once again in the disclosure of an astounding piece of news. Dr J. Robert Oppenheimer, the scientist who had directed the construction of the atomic bomb during the Second World War, had been suspended from his position as consultant to the Atomic Energy Commission and denied access to secret data on the basis of information that suggested he was a security risk. The previous day a hearing had begun in Washington before a tribunal of the Commission. It was to examine the allegations made against him and make a recommendation as to his security status to the Commission's General Manager.[7]

Thus was brought into the open one of the most sensational *causes célèbres* in recent history. The product of many years of venomous controversy, it epitomized the tensions which had accompanied American's post-war elevation to world power, and the wounds it inflicted were slow to heal. Even in the late 1960s it was clear that it was still regarded in official quarters as a highly sensitive matter, and it is doubtful whether anything approaching the full details will ever be known.

Much of the intensity of the Oppenheimer affair derived from the stature of its central figure. One of the ablest theoretical physicists of his generation, he had developed into a brilliant teacher, drawing to himself at the University of California many of the most promising students in the country. But Dr Oppenheimer's erudition ranged well beyond physics. He had a close knowledge of many aspects of literature, painting and music; he was competent in eight languages (including Sanskrit); and he was extremely well-read in philosophy and religion. In short, he appeared uniquely qualified to bridge the gap between the sciences and the humanities, and in the post-war years he had emerged as an outstanding spokesman for science, attempting to explain its relevance in terms which non-scientists might grasp. His most recent achievement in this direction had been the Reith Lectures, 'Science and the Common Understanding', delivered for the British Broadcasting Corporation at the close of 1953.

Oppenheimer's public record was equally impressive. Following his successful administration of the atomic bomb project at the Los Alamos laboratory in New Mexico, he was in constant demand as a government adviser. In 1945 he was among those who were consulted before the decision to use the bomb against Japan. In 1946 he was one of the principal authors of the abortive American proposals for the international control of atomic energy, and in 1947 he became chairman of the General Advisory Committee of the Atomic Energy Commission. In this capacity he played a major part in formulating nuclear policy in the period immediately after the war. Dr Oppenheimer was also employed from time to time by the State Department, the Defense Department and by the individual service departments. So great were the demands of government, in fact, that he had been compelled to give up his university teaching career. He was, however, able to keep in touch with the academic world as Director of the Institute for Advanced Study at Princeton, an appointment which he accepted in 1947 and which he was to hold for almost twenty years.

This, then, was the man whose reliability had been called in question. The information which had led to his suspension was catalogued in a letter to Oppenheimer from the General Manager of the AEC, General Kenneth D. Nichols, which had been sent on 23 December 1953 and which was now printed in *The New York Times* and *The New York Herald Tribune*. It fell under two broad heads. First came a long list of charges to the effect that Oppenheimer had been closely associated with the Communist Party in California between about 1936 and 1946. Among other things, his wife and brother had been members of the party, and he had joined several front organizations, attended party meetings and contributed to party funds. He had also brought Communists and pro-Communists to work with him on the atomic bomb project during the war. The second, much shorter list related to the hydrogen bomb, and here the full meaning of McCarthy's accusation seemed to become clear. In 1945, according to the Nichols letter, Oppenheimer had said that a hydrogen weapon was feasible and yet in 1949 he had opposed it at least partly on the grounds that it was not. What was more, his opposition had continued even after the presidential decision to go ahead, and that opposition, 'of which you are the most experienced, most powerful, and most effective member', had 'definitely slowed down its development'.[8]

Oppenheimer's reply of 4 March 1954 was also published. A

lengthy document of some 10,000 words, it sought to lay the groundwork for his defence at the hearing which he had chosen to have convened, and to do so by placing the statements Nichols had related in a large perspective. As Oppenheimer himself put it : 'The items of so-called derogatory information set forth in your letter cannot be fairly understood except in the context of my life and work.' Taken by themselves, the allegations seemed damning; looked at against the background of his service to the country over the past decade and more, they would assume much less disturbing proportions. It remained to be seen which view his judges would adopt.[9]

It was Oppenheimer, and not the AEC, who had given the correspondence to the press and disclosed what until then had been a well-kept secret. He was perfectly within his rights in doing so, and the letters were made public for a particular reason which will shortly be made clear. The Commission, however, felt the need for further explanation. In a statement put out during the afternoon of 13 April it declared that the case had been opened because of the requirements of a presidential Executive Order issued in April 1953 and cited in Nichols' letter. According to the Commission the Order stipulated that there must be a review of the dossiers of 'all employees and consultants concerning whom there was substantial derogatory information'. The object of the review was to determine whether or not their 'security clearance' (giving access to secret data) should be suspended. Dr Oppenheimer fell within the category of suspects, and in the summer of 1953 his file was scrutinized by both the Commission and the Department of Justice. By November it had been possible to come to a decision, and it was taken by the President himself, following a report from the Justice Department. In consultation with the Chairman of the Commission, the Secretary of Defense and the Director of the Office of Defense Mobilization, Eisenhower had ordered that, until the issue was finally resolved, 'a blank wall be placed between Dr Oppenheimer and any secret data'. Immediately afterwards the AEC's Security Clearance Procedures were set in motion, and the letter from General Nichols followed in due course.[10]

So the secret was out, yet why had Oppenheimer revealed it when silence while the matter was *sub judice* seemed in his own best interests? The answer was soon made plain. On the same day the correspondence was published, *The Christian Science Monitor* stated that Senator McCarthy had for some time been preparing 'a case' against Oppenheimer. According to the *Tribune* columnists Joseph and Stewart Alsop it had been expected that he would make his charges in a speech in Texas on 21 April, the eve of his hearing with the Army. Indeed, McCarthy had known of the affair from the start, and he apparently intended to use it to switch the spotlight away from his own embarrassments. To allow him to take such an initiative would obviously be more hurtful to Oppenheimer than for Oppenheimer to admit that the inquiry was under way, and already he had given the letters to Reston with instructions to publish if McCarthy seemed about to make a move. On the morning the hearing opened, Reston told Oppenheimer's lawyer that the story was about to break, and to forestall McCarthy's attack the decision to publish at once was taken.[11]

As it happened, McCarthy already seemed to have been effectively muzzled. Speaking from Arizona, where he was resting in preparation for his coming encounter with the Army, McCarthy described Oppenheimer's suspension as 'long overdue —it should have been taken years ago'. 'I think it took considerable courage to suspend the so-called untouchable scientist', the Senator declared, and went on to say that he gave Mr Strauss (the AEC Chairman) credit for doing so. The most remarkable feature of his reaction, however, was its modesty. Although he claimed to have affidavits which showed that Oppenheimer was an actual member of the Communist Party (a charge absent from the official indictment), he disclaimed any ambition to take a leading role and professed to be content to leave the matter in the hands of the administration. In other words, McCarthy was not prepared to challenge the right of the Executive Branch of the government to handle the issue and to insist that it fell within the scope of a Congressional investigation. Since he had so far made this challenge the basis of his claim to political power, this was an indication that his influence might well be on the wane and indeed it prefigured his eventual collapse.

McCarthy, in fact, had been excluded from considering the Oppenheimer case as early as May 1953. In that month the business magazine *Fortune* had published an anonymous attack on Oppenheimer and particularly on his attitude to the hydrogen bomb. According to McCarthy the Republican members of his Permanent Investigations Subcommittee had sought to launch an immediate inquiry but had been dissuaded by emissaries from the White House. They had been 'frankly convinced that it would not be wise to hold public hearings at that time because of the security measures involved'. Moreover, they had also 'received assurances ... from top Administration officials that this matter would be gone into in detail'. Much the same version of the episode was given by Senator Mundt, the acting chairman of the Subcommittee.[12]

To underline the fact that the affair was the responsibility of the Executive, Mundt stated explicitly that any investigation of the atomic energy programme was outside the Subcommittee's jurisdiction. At the same time, Representative Cole, speaking on behalf of the Joint Committee on Atomic Energy, maintained that while it alone could conduct a Congressional inquiry in the atomic energy field, in this instance it had left it to the AEC. Finally, as if to ram home the point emphatically, Senator Jenner, chairman of the Senate Internal Security Subcommittee, claimed that it had discovered 'voluminous information' on Dr Oppenheimer as far back as 1952 but had turned it over to 'the proper agencies of government'.[13]

Reactions within the government were mixed. On 16 April 'a high Administration official' (soon after identified as Vice-President Nixon) commented on the case in terms broadly favourable to Oppenheimer. 'Dr Oppenheimer', said Nixon, 'at least on the evidence I have seen, in my opinion is a loyal American. On the other hand the information in his file is voluminous and makes a prima facie case of security risk.' 'If the man is not a security risk,' he added, 'if he is not subject to blackmail, he should have a right to work for the government.' The fact that a government servant had an extremely left-wing background should not necessarily stigmatize him : each case, in Nixon's view, should be considered on its merits, 'particularly when dealing with an ideology which during the nineteen thirties had such an appeal among the intelligentsia and various other groups'.[14]

It is interesting to compare this with what was said by the Secretary of Defense, Mr Wilson. Whereas Nixon had spoken with the caution of a lawyer, Wilson appeared to have made up his mind before the hearing had barely started. Speaking after a press conference on 15 April, Wilson chose to talk hypothetically, as follows:

> ... It is a little bit like selecting a teller in a bank. If the man frequents gambling joints and has contacts with the underworld, you ordinarily don't hire him. Or if you found out after you did hire him that at one time he had been convicted of theft or something like that, maybe he is reformed and all, but you still don't expose him again. You don't wait until he has stolen money from the bank and then try to do something about it. You try to get people who are qualified and are not financial risks in that sense.
> ... I have great sympathy for people that have made a mistake and have reformed, but we don't think we ought to reform them in the military establishment. They ought to have a chance somewhere else.[15]

A great many people seem to have shared Wilson's prejudice and suspected the worst, especially in view of the fact that, as Reston put it, Oppenheimer 'carries around in his head as much top secret information as any man alive'. The country stood to lose a great deal if the government made a wrong decision about such a man as that, and it was not yet clear that the potential loss would be equally as great if clearance were denied as it would if it were upheld. Moreover, as Oppenheimer's lawyer later pointed out, 'the prestige of the Atomic Energy Commission was high, and the average person would be predisposed to credit any charges made by it'.[16]

Academics and scientists naturally rallied to Oppenheimer's defence. His suspension, in the view of Edward Shils, was 'a heavy-handed, stupid act of injustice'. 'It represents', wrote Shils, 'the triumph of the worst vices in American public life: vindictiveness toward political opponents, a bitter distrust of scientific and scholarly intellect, a crude unimaginativeness in the appraisal of the motives and attitudes, and a brutal eagerness to assert that all those who disagree with us must be Communists or in league with them.' More measured but no less forceful was the opinion of the editorial board of the *Bulletin of the Atomic Scientists*. 'It seems to us', they remarked, 'a breach of faith on the part of the government to call upon a man to assume such heavy responsibilities in full knowledge of his life history and then, after he has demonstrably done his best and given the most valuable services to the nation, to use the facts which were substantially known all the time to cast aspersions on his integrity. These charges required examination when they were first made; but to revive them now from the irrelevance to which a brilliant record of national service had finally relegated them, appears to us to be contrary to both decency and common sense.'[17]

Views such as these were exceptional however. Even Alistair Cooke, the correspondent of the left-of-centre *Manchester Guardian,* felt constrained to point out the magnitude of the risk involved. 'There remains, as a matter of judgment,' Cooke remarked, 'the proposition that the director of the most secret work at the government's disposal can accept a double standard whereby a man be tolerated as a Communist or former Communist and at the same time trusted as a loyal American and a man of integrity. The disillusioning history of the past nine years has so discredited this belief that it seems impossible the Government could employ anyone who still holds it.'[18] Although the hearing had scarcely got under way, Oppenheimer's fate already appeared to have been decided.

Chapter Two

The Hearing Opens

The hearing opened on 12 April and went on for almost four weeks, until 6 May. Its setting was prosaic—a converted office in an undistinguished building owned by the AEC, not far from the centre of Washington. It was also an extremely small-scale event. At no time were more than fourteen people present in the hearing room: Oppenheimer's three judges of the Personnel Security Board; himself and his four defence counsel; the two counsel representing the Commission; the witness currently testifying; a reporter; a transcriber; and, to maintain the strictest security in the proceedings, the AEC's Director of Classification, James G. Beckerley.

None of this could detract from its importance, however. The Oppenheimer hearing was a momentous occasion, and its significance can be gauged by the way in which it assembled so many of the outstanding figures in American political and scientific life. These were the witnesses, thirty-nine all told, apart from Oppenheimer himself, and at least half of them were men of the first rank in their respective fields. Taken together, their testimony built up a fragmentary but absorbing picture of the development of nuclear policy in the United States over the past decade, policy which most of them had had a major part in shaping.

There were, to begin with, two former chairmen of the Atomic Energy Commission: David E. Lilienthal and his successor, Gordon Dean. Accompanying them were General Leslie R. Groves, the officer in overall command of the wartime atomic bomb project; John J. McCloy, former President of the World Bank and at this time High Commissioner for Germany; and George F. Kennan, one of the chief architects of the post-war policy of containment and one of the country's foremost authorities on Soviet affairs.

Among the scientists were six of Oppenheimer's one-time colleagues on the General Advisory Committee of the AEC, including James B. Conant, who had recently retired as President of Harvard; Enrico Fermi, who had achieved the world's first self-sustaining chain reaction; and the Nobel Prize-winner, Isidor I. Rabi. In addition, there were Vannevar Bush, wartime head of the Office of Scientific Research and Development; Norris E. Bradbury, Oppenheimer's successor as director of the Los Alamos Laboratory; and Hans A. Bethe, who had played a crucial role at Los Alamos as head of the Theoretical Division. Finally, there were two men who had made vital contributions to the development of the hydrogen bomb : the mathematician John von Neumann, who had devised the computers which worked on the calculations for the programme; and the physicist Edward Teller who had elaborated the theoretical basis of the weapon and who was popularly seen as its 'father' (much as Oppenheimer was thought of as the progenitor of the atomic bomb).

All but one of those just mentioned (Teller) testified on Oppenheimer's behalf. His legal defence was in the hands of a team of a four lawyers : Lloyd K. Garrison; Herbert S. Marks; Samuel J. Silverman; and Allan B. Ecker. Garrison, who led, was the great-grandson of the celebrated abolitionist William Lloyd Garrison, a liberal Democrat who had served Roosevelt in the New Deal and who had also sponsored the Negro cause as President of the National Urban League. Marks had been the first General Counsel of the AEC in 1947, and since then had been in private practice in Washington. Silverman was a partner in Garrison's law firm in New York, Ecker an associate of the firm. Also involved was John W. Davis, Democratic candidate for President in 1924, who was too frail to take part in the hearing itself, but who assisted in preparing the second of the two briefs later filed on Oppenheimer's behalf.

The counsel for the Commission were Roger Robb and C. A. Rolander, Jr. Robb was a Washington lawyer in private practice, who, when the hearing began, had no more than a local reputation, but was soon to establish himself as a force to be reckoned with. His assistant, Rolander, was Deputy Director of the Security Division of the AEC.

Sitting in judgment on Oppenheimer was the Personnel Security Board of the Commission : Gordon Gray, the chairman of the Board; Ward V. Evans; and Thomas A. Morgan. Gray, a Democrat, had served in the Truman administration as Secretary of the Army and as a special assistant to the President. He had left the government in the autumn of 1950 to become President of the University of North Carolina. Evans was a professor of chemistry from Loyola University, Illinois. Morgan was a businessman, the former President of the Sperry Corporation, pioneers of the naval gyrocompass.

The process whereby Oppenheimer had come to appear before the Board had the following legal basis. His employment had been suspended in accordance with Public Law 733 of 26 August 1950 which authorized the Commission to do so 'when deemed necessary in the interest of national security'. The same Act gave the suspended employee the right to an administrative hearing in which to answer the charges against him, but in this respect it acknowledged that as far as the Atomic Energy Commission was concerned the governing legislation was the Atomic Energy Act of 1 August 1946. Section 1 of this Act had declared that its 'paramount objective' was that of 'assuring the common defense and security', and Section 10(a) stated that the Commission's policy would be to control the dissemination of restricted data in such a way as to attain this objective ('restricted data' being defined as 'all data concerning the manufacture or utilization of atomic weapons, the production of fissionable material, or the use of fissionable material in the production of power').[1]

According to Section 10(b) (5) (B) (ii), no individual was to be employed by the Commission until the Federal Bureau of Investigation should have made an investigation and reported to the Commission on his character, associations and loyalty. In the event that an employee's reliability was placed in question, Section 12 (a) (4) authorized the Commission to make adequate provision for an administrative review of any determination to dismiss him, that is, a hearing.

At the time of the Oppenheimer hearing the detailed rules and regulations covering security cases were contained in two documents, the Security Clearance Procedures of 12 September 1950 and the Personnel Security Clearance Criteria for Determining Eligibility issued on 17 November 1950.[2] The Procedures provided firstly that where eligibility for clearance was thrown in doubt, the Deputy General Manager should consult with appropriate staff members of the AEC and reach a decision on the individual's employment status. He was then to present the employee, if suspended, with a letter of notification outlining the charges and stating his right to appear before a Personnel Security Board appointed by the Manager. He would also have the right to challenge any members of the Board, to be present throughout the entire hearing, to be represented by counsel of his own choosing, and to present evidence on his own behalf, whether through witnesses or documents, or both.

All members of the Board were to have full clearance so as to have access to every item of information available and at least one was to be familiar with the employee's general field of knowledge. They were enjoined to 'avoid the attitude of a prosecutor' and always to 'bear in mind and make clear to all concerned that the proceeding is an inquiry and not a trial'. In this connection 'the utmost latitude' was to be given with respect to the relevance, materiality and competence of the evidence submitted and the normal rules applicable in a court were to be considerably relaxed. However, although 'every reasonable effort' was to be made to obtain the best evidence available, in cases where the source of information was confidential, the confrontation of accuser and accused mandatory in a court of law might not be possible. In no circumstances would it be possible to disclose any reports of the Federal Bureau of Investigation to the employee or his counsel.

The Board was to reach its recommendations on the basis of the FBI reports, witnesses' testimony, the evidence furnished by the employee, and the standards set out in the document on Criteria for Determining Eligibility. In doing so, the members, 'as practical men of affairs', were to be 'guided by the same consideration that would guide them in making a sound decision in the administration of their own lives'. They should also take into account 'the manner in which witnesses have testified..., their demeanor on the witness stand, the probability or likelihood of their testimony, their credibility, the authenticity of documentary evidence, or the lack of evidence upon some material points in issue'.

They were to make specific findings on the allegations in the letter of notification, and to give their reasons for doing so. Their recommendation as to whether or not clearance was to be denied was to be based on the findings and was also to be supported by a statement of reasons. It was to be determined by a majority vote, if need be, and transmitted to the Manager concerned. He in his turn was to make a recommendation, having first obtained 'all relevant data concerning the effect which denial of security clearance would have upon the atomic energy program'. (In other words, he was empowered to reach a judgment on the employee's value to the AEC which was beyond the scope of the Board.) This second recommendation along with the complete record of the case was then to be forwarded to the General Manager in Washington. In the event of a recommendation for denial of clearance, the employee had the right of appeal to the AEC Personnel Security Review Board and could submit a written brief in support of the appeal. Whether or not he appealed, the final decision rested with the General Manager, who was to consider the entire record together with all the recommendations made. He was then to inform the employee of his decision as soon as practicable.

The Criteria for Determining Eligibility may be summarized as follows. Those responsible for reaching a conclusion about an employee were instructed to consider a wide range of information besides that contained in the FBI reports, for example, 'whether the individual will have direct access to restricted data or work in proximity to exclusion areas, his past association with the Atomic Energy program, and the nature of the job he is expected to perform'. 'The judgment of responsible persons as to the integrity of the individual' was also to be borne in mind, and it was stressed that the final decision was 'an over-all, common-sense judgment, made after consideration of all the relevant information as to whether or not there is risk that the granting of security clearance would endanger the common defense and security'. Moreover, cases were to be 'carefully weighed in the light of all the information, and a determination must be reached which gives due recognition to the favorable as well as the unfavorable information concerning the individual and which balances the cost to the program of not having his services against any possible risks involved'.

Coming down to specifics, the Criteria listed two groups of

items of derogatory information which indicated a security risk.
Category (A) included information which established a presumption of risk, or 'grounds sufficient to establish a reasonable belief'
that the individual or his wife had:

1. Committed or attempted to commit, or aided or abetted
   another who committed or attempted to commit, any act
   of sabotage, espionage, treason, or sedition;
2. Established an association with espionage agents of a foreign
   nation; with individuals reliably reported as suspected of
   espionage; with representatives of foreign nations whose
   interests may be inimical to the interests of the United
   States. (Ordinarily this would not include chance or casual
   meetings; nor contacts limited to normal business or official
   relations.)
3. Held membership in or joined any organization which has
   been declared by the Attorney General to be Totalitarian,
   Fascist, Communist, subversive, or as having adopted a
   policy of advocating or approving the commission of acts
   of force or violence to deny others their rights under the
   Constitution of the United States, or as seeking to alter
   the form of government of the United States by unconstitutional means, provided the individual did not withdraw
   from such membership when the organization was so
   identified, or otherwise establish his rejection of its subversive aims; or, prior to the declaration by the Attorney
   General, participated in the activities of such an organization in a capacity where he should reasonably have had
   knowledge as to the subversive aims or purposes of the
   organization;
4. Publicly or privately advocated revolution by force or violence to alter the constitutional form of Government of the
   United States.

It also included cases where there were reasonable grounds for
believing that the individual alone had:

5. Deliberately omitted significant information from or falsified a Personnel Security Questionnaire or Personal History
   Statement. In many cases, it may be fair to conclude that
   such omission or falsification was deliberate if the informa-

tion omitted or misrepresented is unfavorable to the individual;

6. Violated or disregarded security regulations to a degree which would endanger the common defense or security;

7. Been adjudged insane, been legally committed to an insane asylum, or treated for serious mental or neurological disorder, without evidence of cure;

8. Been convicted of felonies indicating habitual criminal tendencies;

9. Been, or who is, addicted to the use of alcohol or drugs habitually and to excess, without adequate evidence of rehabilitation.

Category (B) included information such as to make it necessary to weigh the extent of the individual's activities, his attitudes or his convictions before deciding whether a presumption of risk existed. This category included cases in which there were reasonable grounds for believing that with respect to either the employee or his wife there was:

1. Sympathetic interest in totalitarian, fascist, communist or other subversive political ideologies;

2. A sympathetic association established with members of the Communist Party; or with leading members of any organization set forth in Category (A), paragraph 3, above. (Ordinarily this will not include chance or casual meetings, nor contacts limited to normal business or official relations.)

3. Identification with an organization established as a front for otherwise subversive groups or interests when the personal views of the individual are sympathetic to or coincide with subversive 'lines';

4. Identification with an organization known to be infiltrated with members of subversive groups when there is also information as to other activities of the individual which establishes the probability that he may be a part of or sympathetic to the infiltrating element, or when he has personal views which are sympathetic to or coincide with subversive 'lines';

5. Residence of the individual's spouse, parent(s), brother(s), sister(s), or offspring in a nation whose interests may be inimical to the interests of the United States, or in satellites

or occupied areas thereof, when the personal views or activities of the individual subject of investigation are sympathetic to or coincide with subversive 'lines' (to be evalu-
ated in the light of the risk that pressure applied through
such close relatives could force the individual to reveal
sensitive information or perform an act of sabotage);
6. Close continuing association with individuals (friends, relatives or other associates), who have subversive interests and
associations as defined in any one of the foregoing types of
derogatory information. A close continuing association may
be deeemed to exist if :
　(i) Subject lives at the same premises with such individual;
　(ii) Subject visits such individual frequently;
　(iii) Subject communicates frequently with such individual
by any means.
7. Association where the individuals have enjoyed a very close,
continuing association such as is described above for some
period of time, and then have been separated by distance;
provided the circumstances indicate that a renewal of contact is probable.

It also included cases where there were reasonable grounds
for believing that the individual alone had behaved as follows :

8. Conscientious objection to service in the Armed Forces during time of war, when such objections cannot be clearly
shown to be due to religious convictions;
9. Manifest tendencies demonstrating unreliability or inability
to keep important matters confidential; wilful or gross carelessness in revealing or disclosing to any unauthorized person
restricted data or other classified matter pertaining either
to projects of the Atomic Energy Commission or of any
other governmental agency; abuse of trust; dishonesty; or
homosexuality.

In addition it was possible for information to be considered
derogatory even though it might be at variance with or beyond
the scope of either category.

Finally, the Board was bound by the provisions of a presidential Executive Order, No. 10450, issued on 27 April 1953, which
laid down the security requirements for government employees.[8]

Here, the overriding criterion was that employment be 'clearly consistent with the interests of the national security'. Expressed in detail, this came down to the following eight items set out in Section 8 (a) of the Order, but, as in the case of the AEC Categories, they were not to be regarded as definitive, and other information not listed could also be considered derogatory.

1. Depending on the relation of the Government employment to the national security:

(i) Any behavior, activities, or associations which tend to show that the individual is not reliable or trustworthy.

(ii) Any deliberate misrepresentations, falsifications, or omissions of material facts.

(iii) Any criminal, infamous, dishonest, immoral, or notoriously disgraceful conduct, habitual use of intoxicants to excess, drug addiction, sexual perversion, or financial irresponsibility.

(iv) An adjudication of insanity, or treatment for serious mental or neurological disorder without satisfactory evidence of cure.

(v) Any facts which furnish reason to believe that the individual may be subjected to coercion, influence, or pressure which may cause him to act contrary to the best interests of the national security.

2. Commission of any act of sabotage, espionage, treason, or sedition, or attempts thereat or preparation therefor, or conspiring with, or aiding or abetting, another to commit any act of sabotage, espionage, treason, or sedition.

3. Establishing or continuing a sympathetic association with a saboteur, spy, traitor, seditionist, anarchist, or revolutionist, or with an espionage or other secret agent or representative of a foreign nation whose interests may be inimical to the interests of the United States, or with any person who advocates the use of force or violence to overthrow the government of the United States or the alteration of the form of government of the United States by unconstitutional means.

4. Advocacy of use of force or violence to overthrow the government of the United States, or of the alteration of the

form of government of the United States by unconstitutional means.

5. Membership in, or affiliation or sympathetic association with, any foreign or domestic organization, association, movement, group, or combination of persons which is totalitarian, Fascist, Communist, or subversive, or which has adopted, or shows, a policy of advocating or approving the commission of acts of force or violence to deny other persons their rights under the Constitution of the United States, or which seeks to alter the form of government of the United States by unconstitutional means.

6. Intentional, unauthorized disclosure to any person or security information, or of other information disclosure of which is prohibited by law, or willful violation or disregard of security regulations.

7. Performing or attempting to perform his duties, or otherwise acting, so as to serve the interests of another government in preference to the interests of the United States.

8. Refusal by the individual, upon the ground of constitutional privilege against self-incrimination, to testify before a congressional committee regarding charges of his alleged disloyalty or other misconduct.

Such was the basis on which the inquiry had come to be convened, and such were the criteria it was supposed to use in reaching its conclusions. What, then, was the material to which it had to apply these tests?

The answer is not so simple as it would seem. In a court of law the indictment is publicly stated, precisely framed and unchangeable. In a security hearing things are quite different. In the first place, the Board was duty-bound to consider the FBI reports, which, as has already been pointed out, could not be seen by Oppenheimer or his lawyers. In the second place, the Nichols letter of 23 December 1953, which constituted the open (and therefore contestable) segment of the allegations against Oppenheimer, was often loosely written and difficult to understand. In the third place, in section 4.15(j) of the AEC Security Clearance Procedures, it was stated that the notification letter could be amended so as to broaden the allegations and this was done several times (though without the formality of an amendment).

One extremely serious amendment was not allowed. From the day the news of the hearing broke, it had been rumoured that the immediate impetus behind the Commission's decision to initiate its procedures had come in the form of a letter of accusation from a former employee of the Joint Committee on Atomic Energy. It was not until a late stage in the hearing, however, that the truth of the rumour was admitted, and then only partially. On 30 April the writer of the letter, William L. Borden, was summoned as a witness for the Commission, and during his testimony, some—but far from all—of his role in the affair was revealed. Borden had been Executive Director of the Joint Committee between January 1949 and June 1953 and during that time had apparently become convinced that Oppenheimer was a critical threat to the country. The last thing he had done before leaving the Committee was to formulate no less than 400 questions about Oppenheimer's activities, and soon after leaving he had taken the matter a stage further by putting his conclusions down in writing, as a letter to the Director of the FBI, J. Edgar Hoover. Having first made his intention plain to the Committee, he sent the letter on 7 November 1953. This is what is said:[4]

Dear Mr Hoover,
This letter concerns J. Robert Oppenheimer.

As you know, he has for some years enjoyed access to various critical activities of the National Security Council, the Department of State, the Department of Defense, the Army, Navy, and Air Force, the Research and Development Board, the Atomic Energy Commission, the Central Intelligence Agency, the National Security Resources Board and the National Science Foundation. His access covers most new weapons being developed by the Armed Forces, war plans at least in comprehensive outline, complete details as to atomic and hydrogen weapons and stockpile data, the evidence on which some of the principal CIA intelligence estimates is based, United States participation in the United Nations and NATO and many other areas of high security sensitivity.

Because the scope of his access may well be unique, because he has had custody of an immense collection of classified papers covering military, intelligence, and diplomatic as well as atomic-energy matters, and because he also possesses a scientific background enabling him to grasp the significance of classified data of a technical nature, it seems reasonable to estimate that he is and for some years has been in a position to compromise more vital and detailed information affecting the national defense and security than any other individual in the United States.

While J. Robert Oppenheimer has not made major contributions to the advancement of science, he holds a respected professional standing among the second rank of American physicists. In terms of his mastery of Government affairs, his close liaison with ranking officials, and his ability to influence high-level thinking, he surely stands in the first rank, not merely among scientists but among all those who have shaped postwar decisions in the military, atomic energy, intelligence, and diplomatic fields. As chairman or as an official or unofficial member of more than 35 important Government committees, panels, study groups, and projects, he has oriented or dominated key policies involving every principal United States security department and agency except the FBI.

The purpose of this letter is to state my own exhaustively considered opinion, based upon years of study, of the available classified evidence, that more probably than not J. Robert Oppenheimer is an agent of the Soviet Union.

This opinion considers the following factors, among others:
1. The evidence indicating that as of April 1942—

(*a*) He was contributing substantial monthly sums to the Communist Party;

(*b*) His ties with communism had survived the Nazi-Soviet Pact and the Soviet attack upon Finland;

(*c*) His wife and younger brother were Communists;

(*d*) He had no close friends except Communists;

(*e*) He had at least one Communist mistress;

(*f*) He belonged only to Communist organizations, apart from professional affiliations;

(*g*) The people whom he recruited into the early wartime Berkeley atomic project were exclusively Communists;

(*h*) He had been instrumental in securing recruits for the Communist Party; and (*i*) He was in frequent contact with Soviet espionage agents.

2. The evidence indicating that—

(*a*) In May 1942, he either stopped contributing funds to the Communist Party or else made his contributions through a new channel not yet discovered;

(*b*) In April 1942 his name was formally submitted for security clearance;

(*c*) He himself was aware at the time that his name had been so submitted; and

(*d*) He thereafter repeatedly gave false information to General Groves, the Manhattan District, and the FBI concerning the 1939–April 1942 period.

3. The evidence indicating that—

(*a*) He was responsible for employing a number of Communists, some of them nontechnical, at wartime Los Alamos;

(*b*) He selected one such individual to write the official Los Alamos history;

(*c*) He was a vigorous supporter of the H-bomb program until August 6, 1945 (Hiroshima), on which day he personally urged each senior individual working in this field to desist; and

(*d*) He was an enthusiastic sponsor of the A-bomb program until the war ended, when he immediately and outspokenly advocated that the Los Alamos Laboratory be disbanded.

4. The evidence indicating that—

(*a*) He was remarkably instrumental in influencing the military authorities and the Atomic Energy Commission essentially to suspend H-bomb development from mid-1946 through January 31, 1950.

(*b*) He has worked tirelessly, from January 31, 1950, onward, to retard the United States H-bomb program;

(*c*) He has used his potent influence against every postwar effort to expand capacity for producing A-bomb material;

(*d*) He has used his potent influence against every postwar effort directed at obtaining larger supplies of uranium raw material; and

(*e*) He has used his potent influence against every major postwar effort toward atomic power development, including the nuclear-powered submarine and aircraft programs as well as industrial power projects.

From such evidence, considered in detail, the following conclusions are justified—

1. Between 1929 and mid-1942, more probably than not, J. Robert Oppenheimer was a sufficiently hardened Communist that he either volunteered espionage information to the Soviets or complied with a request for such information. (This includes the possibility that when he singled out the weapons aspect of atomic development as his personal speciality, he was acting under Soviet instructions.)
2. More probably than not, he has since been functioning as an espionage agent; and
3. More probably than not, he has since acted under a Soviet directive in influencing United States military, atomic energy, intelligence, and diplomatic policy.

It is to be noted that these conclusions correlate with information furnished by Klaus Fuchs, indicating that the Soviets had acquired an agent in Berkeley who informed them about electromagnetic separation research during 1942 or earlier.

Needless to say, I appreciate the probabilities identifiable from existing evidence might, with review of future acquired evidence, be reduced to possibilities; or they might also be increased to certainties. The central problem is not whether J. Robert Oppenheimer was ever a Communist; for the existing evidence makes abundantly clear that he was. Even an Atomic Energy Commission analysis prepared in early 1947 reflects this conclusion, although some of the most significant derogatory data had yet to become available. The central problem is assessing the degree of likelihood that he in fact did what a Communist in his circumstances, at Berkeley, would logically have done during the crucial 1939–42 period—that is, whether he became an actual espionage and policy instrument of the Soviets. Thus, as to this central problem, my opinion is that, more probably than not, the worst is in fact the truth.

I am profoundly aware of the grave nature of these comments. The matter is detestable to me. Having lived with the Oppenheimer case for years, having studied and restudied all data concerning him that your agency made available to the Atomic Energy Commission through May 1953, having endeavored to factor in a mass of additional data assembled from numerous other sources, and looking back upon the case from a perspective in private life, I feel a duty simply to state to the responsible head of the security agency most concerned the conclusions which I have painfully crystalized and which I believe any fairminded man thoroughly familiar with the evidence must also be driven to accept.

The writing of this letter, to me a solemn step, is exclusively on my own personal initiative and responsibility.

Very truly yours,

(Signed) William L. Borden,
(Typed) William L. Borden.

Robb's purpose in introducing this astonishing document is not clear. When Garrison protested that if it were to be considered at all (and he did not believe it should), it ought to be incorporated in the letter of notification, Gray assured him that it would not be added to the letter, while Robb stated that Borden's conclusions 'will not be allegations in any possible amendment of that letter'. After Borden had read his letter to the hearing, Gray even went so far as to say that the Board had no evidence before it—that is, in the classified material which Oppenheimer and Garrison were forbidden to see—which supported any of Borden's conclusions.[5]

The episode thus seemed no more than a disturbing aberration. Yet there was much more to it than that. It was not made clear then, or later, that the Borden letter was crucially important in instigating the Oppenheimer case. Indeed, when President Eisenhower ordered the 'blank wall' to be set up and when the members of the Commission voted to initiate their security clearance procedures, they did so largely on the strength of Borden's allegations, for the letter from Nichols had not even been drafted. Moreover, a close reading indicates that half of Borden's charges were reiterated by Nichols, often in somewhat modified versions, so as, presumably, to make them more credible.[6]

If it knew any of these things, the Board chose to ignore them, and to continue to focus its main attention on the indictment drawn up by Nichols. Since this formed the basis of their ultimate findings, it will be given in full. Nichols' letter read as follows:[7]

B

Dear Dr Oppenheimer,

Section 10 of the Atomic Energy Act of 1946 places upon the Atomic Energy Commission the responsibility for assuring that individuals are employed by the Commission only when such employment will not endanger the common defense and security. In addition, Executive Order 10450 of April 27, 1953, requires the suspension of employment of any individual where there exists information indicating that his employment may not be clearly consistent with the interests of the national security.

As a result of additional investigation as to your character, associations, and loyalty, and review of your personnel security file in the light of the requirements of the Atomic Energy Act and the requirements of Executive Order 10450, there has developed considerable question whether your continued employment on Atomic Energy Commission work will endanger the common defense and security and whether such continued employment is clearly consistent with the interests of the national security. This letter is to advise you of the steps which you make take to assist in the resolution of this question.

The substance of the information which raises the question concerning your eligibility for employment on Atomic Energy Commission work is as follows:

It was reported that in 1940 you were listed as a sponsor of the Friends of the Chinese People, an organization which was characterized in 1944 by the House Committee on Un-American Activities as a Communist front-organization. It was further reported that in 1940 your name was included on a letterhead of the American Committee for Democratic and Intellectual Freedom as a member of its national executive committee. The American Committee for Democracy and Intellectual Freedom was characterized in 1942 by the House Committee on Un-American Activities as a Communist front which defended Communist teachers, and in 1943 it was characterized as subversive and un-American by a special subcommittee of the House Committee on Appropriations. It was further reported that in 1938 you were a member of the Western Council of the Consumers Union. The Consumers Union was cited in 1944 by the House Committee on Un-

American Activities as a Communist front headed by the Communist Arthur Kallet. It was further reported that you stated in 1943 that you were not a Communist, but had probably belonged to every Communist front-organization on the west coast and had signed many petitions in which Communists were interested.

It was reported that in 1943 and previously you were intimately associated with Dr Jean Tatlock, a member of the Communist Party in San Francisco, and that Dr Tatlock was partially responsible for your association with Communist front-groups.

It was reported that your wife, Katherine Puening Oppenheimer, was formerly the wife of Joseph Dallet, a member of the Communist Party, who was killed in Spain in 1937 fighting for the Spanish Republican Army. It was further reported that during the period of her association with Joseph Dallet, your wife became a member of the Communist Party. The Communist Party has been designated by the Attorney General as a subversive organization which seeks to alter the form of Government of the United States by unconstitutional means, within the purview of Executive Order 9835 and Executive Order 10450.

It was reported that your brother, Frank Friedman Oppenheimer, became a member of the Communist Party in 1936 and has served as a party organizer and as educational director of the professional section of the Communist Party in Los Angeles County. It was further reported that your brother's wife, Jackie Oppenheimer, was a member of the Communist Party in 1938; and that in August 1944, Jackie Oppenheimer assisted in the organization of the East Bay branch of the California Labor School. It was further reported that in 1945 Frank and Jackie Oppenheimer were invited to an informal reception at the Russian consulate, that this invitation was extended by the American-Russian Institute of San Francisco and was for the purpose of introducing famous American scientists to Russian scientists who were delegates to the United Nations Conference on International Organization being held at San Francisco at that time, and that Frank Oppenheimer accepted this invitation. It was further reported that Frank Oppenheimer agreed to give a 6 weeks course on The Social Implications of Modern Scientific Development at the California Labor School, beginning May 9, 1946. The American-Russian Institute of San Francisco and the California Labor School have been cited by the Attorney General as Communist organizations within the purview of Executive Order 9835 and Executive Order 10450.

It was reported that you have associated with members and officials of the Communist Party including Isaac Folkoff, Steve Nelson, Rudy Lambert, Kenneth May, Jack Manley, and Thomas Addis.

It was reported that you were a subscriber to the *Daily People's World,* a west coast Communist newspaper, in 1941 and 1942.

It was reported in 1950 that you stated to an agent of the Federal Bureau of Investigation that you had in the past made contributions to Communist front-organizations, although at the time you did not know of Communist Party control or extent of infiltration of these groups. You further stated to an agent of the Federal Bureau of Investigation that some of these contributions were made through Isaac Folkoff, whom you knew to be a leading Communist Party functionary, because you had been told that this was the most effective and direct way of helping these groups.

It was reported that you attended a housewarming party at the home of Kenneth and Ruth May on September 20, 1941, for which there was an admission charge for the benefit of *The People's World,* and that at this party you were in the company of Joseph W. Weinberg and Clarence Hiskey, who were alleged to be members of the Communist Party and to have engaged in espionage on behalf of the Soviet Union. It was further reported that you informed officials of the United States Department of Justice in 1952 that you had no recollection that you had attended such a party, but that since it would have been in character for you to have attended such a party, you would not deny that you were there.

It was reported that you attended a closed meeting of the professional section of the Communist Party of Alameda County, Calif., which was held in the latter part of July or early August 1941, at your residence, 10 Kenilworth Court, Berkeley, Calif., for the purpose of hearing an explanation of a change in Communist Party policy. It was reported that you denied that you attended such a meeting and that such a meeting was held in your home.

It was reported that you stated to an agent of the Federal Bureau of Investigation in 1950, that you attended a meeting in 1940 or 1941, which may have taken place at the home of Haakon Chevalier, which was addressed by William Schneiderman, whom you knew to be a leading functionary of the Communist Party. In testimony in 1950 before the California State Senate Committee on Un-American Activites, Haakon Chevalier was identified as a member of the Communist Party in the San Francisco area in the early 1940s.

It was reported that you have consistently denied that you have ever been a member of the Communist Party. It was further reported that you stated to a representative of the Federal Bureau of Investigation in 1946 that you had a change of mind regarding the policies and politics of the Soviet Union about the time of the signing of the Soviet-German Pact in 1939. It was further reported that during 1950 you stated to a representative of the Federal Bureau of Investigation that you have never attended a closed meeting of the Communist Party; and that at the time of the Russo-Finnish War and the subsequent break between Germany and Russia in 1941, you realized the Communist Party infiltration tactics into the alleged anti-Fascist groups and became fed up with the whole thing and lost what little interest you had. It was further reported, however, that :

(*a*) Prior to April 1942, you had contributed $150 per month to the Communist Party in the San Francisco area, and that the last such payment was apparently made in April 1942, immediately before your entry into the atomic-bomb project.

(*b*) During the period 1942–45 various officials of the Communist Party, including Dr Hannah Peters, organizer of the professional section of the Communist Party, Alameda County, Calif., Bernadette Doyle, secretary of the Alameda County Communist Party, Steve Nelson, David Adelson, Paul Pinsky, Jack Manley, and Katrina Sandow, are reported to have made statements indicating that you were then a member of the Communist Party; that you could not be active in the party at that time; that your name should be removed from the party mailing list and not mentioned in any way; that you had talked the atomic-bomb question over with party members during this period; and that several years prior to 1945 you had told Steve Nelson that the Army was working on an atomic bomb. (c) You stated in August of 1943 that you did not want anybody working for you on the project who was a member of the Communist Party, since 'one always had a question of divided loyalty' and the discipline of the Communist Party was very severe and not compatible with complete loyalty to the project. You further stated at that time that you were referring only to present membership in the Communist Party and not to people who had been members of the party. You stated further that you knew several individuals then at Los Alamos who had been members of the Communist Party. You did not, however, identify such former members of the Communist Party to the appropriate authorities. It was also reported that during the period 1942–45 you were responsible for the employment on the atom-bomb project of individuals who were members of the Communist Party or closely associated with activities of the Communist Party, including Giovanni Rossi Lomanitz, Joseph W. Weinberg, David Bohm, Max Bernard Friedman, and David Hawkins. In the case of Giovanni Rossi Lomanitz, you urged him to work on the project, although you stated that you knew he had been very much of a Red when he first came to the University of California and that you emphasized to him that he must forego all political activity if he came to the project. In August 1943, you protested against the termination of his deferment and requested that he be returned to the project after his entry into the military service.

It was reported that you stated to representatives of the Federal Bureau of Investigation on September 5, 1946, that you had attended a meeting in the East Bay and a meeting in San Francisco at which there were present persons definitely identified with the Communist Party. When asked the purpose of the East Bay meeting and the identity of those in attendance, you declined to answer on the ground that this had no bearing on the matter of interest being discussed.

It was reported that you attended a meeting at the home of Frank Oppenheimer on January 1, 1946, with David Adelson and Paul Pinsky, both of whom were members of the Communist Party. It was further reported that you analyzed some material which Pinsky hoped to take up with the legislative convention in Sacramento, Calif.

It was reported in 1946 that you were listed as vice-chairman on the letterhead of the Independent Citizens Committee of the Arts, Sciences, and Professions, Inc., which has been cited as a Communist front by the House Committee on Un-American Activities.

It was reported in 1946 that you were listed as vice-chairmonths prior, Peter Ivanov, secretary of the Soviet consulate, San Francisco, approached George Charles Eltenton for the purpose of obtaining information regarding work being done at the Radiation Laboratory for the use of Soviet scientists; that George Charles Eltenton subsequently requested Haakon Chevalier to approach you concerning this matter; that Haakon Chevalier thereupon approached you, either directly or through your brother, Frank Friedman Oppenheimer, in connection with this matter; and that Haakon Chevalier finally advised George Charles Eltenton that there was no chance whatsoever of obtaining the information. It was further reported that you did not report this episode to the appropriate authorities until several months after its occurrence; that when you initially discussed this matter with the appropriate authorities on August 26, 1943, you did not identify yourself as the person who had been approached, and you refused to identify Haakon Chevalier as the individual who made the approach on behalf of George Charles Eltenton; and that it was not until several months later, when you were ordered by a superior to do so, that you so identified Haakon Chevalier. It was further reported that upon your return to Berkeley following your separation from the Los Alamos project, you were visited by the Chevaliers on several occasions; and that your wife was in contact with Haakon and Barbara Chevalier in 1946 and 1947.

It was reported that in 1945 you expressed the view that

'there is a reasonable possibility that it (the hydrogen bomb) can be made', but that the feasibility of the hydrogen bomb did not appear, on theoretical grounds, as certain as the fission bomb appeared certain, on theoretical grounds, when the Los Alamos Laboratory was started; and that in the autumn of 1949 the General Advisory Committee expressed the view that 'an imaginative and concerted attack on the problem has a better than even chance of producing the weapon within 5 years'. It was further reported that in the autumn of 1949, and subsequently, you strongly opposed the development of the hydrogen bomb; (1) on moral grounds, (2) by claiming that it was not feasible, (3) by claiming that there were insufficient facilities and scientific personnel to carry on the development, and (4) that it was not politically desirable. It was further reported that even after it was determined, as a matter of national policy, to proceed with development of a hydrogen bomb, you continued to oppose the project and declined to cooperate fully in the project. It was further reported that you departed from your proper role as an adviser to the Commission by causing the distribution separately and in private, to top personnel at Los Alamos of the majority and minority reports of the General Advisory Committee on development of the hydrogen bomb for the purpose of trying to turn such top personnel against the development of the hydrogen bomb. It was further reported that you were instrumental in persuading other outstanding scientists not to work on the hydrogen-bomb project, and that the opposition to the hydrogen bomb, of which you are the most experienced, most powerful, and most effective member, has definitely slowed down its development.

In view of your access to highly sensitive classified information, and in view of these allegations which, until disproved, raise questions as to your veracity, conduct and even your loyalty, the Commission has no other recourse, in discharge of its obligations to protect the common defense and security, but to suspend your clearance until the matter has been resolved. Accordingly, your employment on Atomic Energy Energy Commission work and your eligibility for access to restricted data are hereby suspended, effective immediately, pending final determination of this matter.

To assist in the resolution of this matter, you have the privilege of appearing before an Atomic Energy Commission personnel security board. To avail yourself of the privileges afforded you under the Atomic Energy Commission hearing procedures, you must, within 30 days following receipt of this letter, submit to me, in writing, your reply to the information outlined above and request the opportunity of appearing before the personnel security board. Should you signify your desire to appear before the board, you will be notified of the composition of the board and may challenge any member of it for cause. Such challenge should be submitted within 72 hours of the receipt of notice of composition of the board.

If no challenge is raised as to the members of the board, you will be notified of the date and place of hearing at least 48 hours in advance of the date set for hearing. You may be present for the duration of the hearing, may be represented by counsel of your own choosing, and present evidence in your own behalf through witnesses, or by documents, or by both.

Should you elect to have a hearing of your case by the personnel security board, the findings of the board, together with its recommendations regarding your eligibility for employment on Atomic Energy Commission work, in the light of Criteria for Determining Eligibility for Atomic Energy Commission Security Clearance and the requirements of Executive Order 10450, will be submitted to me.

In the event of an adverse decision in your case by the personnel security board, you will have an opportunity to review the record made during your appearance before the board and to request a review of your case by the Commission's personnel security review board.

If a written response is not received from you within 30 days it will be assumed that you do not wish to submit any explanation for further consideration. In that events, or should you not advise me in writing of your desire to appear before the personnel security board, a determination in your case will be made by me on the basis of the existing record.

I am enclosing herewith, for your information and guidance, copies of the Criteria and Procedures for Determining

Eligibility for Atomic Energy Commission Security Clearance and Executive Order 10450.

This letter has been marked 'Confidential' to maintain the privacy of this matter between you and the Atomic Energy Commission. You are not precluded from making use of this letter as you may consider appropriate.

I have instructed Mr William Mitchell, whose address is 1901 Constitution Avenue NW., Washington, D.C., and whose telephone number is Sterling 3–8000, Extension 277, to give you whatever further detailed information you may desire with respect to the procedures to be followed in this matter. Very truly yours,

K. D. Nichols, *General Manager*.

2 Enclosures. 1. Criteria and Procedures. 2. Executive Order 10450.

This, then, was the substance of the case which Oppenheimer had to refute. We shall now turn to see how the allegations were elaborated in the course of the hearing and how they were met by the man whose career they had put in jeopardy.

Chapter Three

Communist Associations

The first part of Nichols' indictment was concerned with Oppenheimer's alleged association with the Communist movement, not only before the Second World War, but during the war itself, and in the post-war years. What follows is the account of that association developed by the hearing in the course of its four-week session.

Like so many others of his generation, Oppenheimer was profoundly affected by the events of the 1930s, above all by the depression which paralysed the economy of the United States, by the Nazi accession to power in Germany, and by the transformation which Communism was bringing about in Soviet Russia. He also shared the view that the answer both to the collapse of *laissez-faire* economics and to the totalitarianism of the right had to be revolutionary change on the Soviet model.

Oppenheimer's involvement in the problems of his time came late in two respects, however. In the first place, it did not begin until 1936 and up to that point he had, in his own words, been 'almost wholly divorced from the contemporary scene'. He took no newspaper or magazine, he had no radio and no telephone. By his own admission he heard about the Wall Street crash of October 1929 only long after it happened. For almost seven years thereafter the drama of the political world passed him by, and his free time was almost completely taken up with that intense and wide-ranging exploration of the world of ideas which was to make him such a polymath. In the second place, it did not begin until he was thirty-two, and his previous isolation had not allowed him to pass through stages of experience which others who started earlier in life would have emerged from well before this time. Thus, when he did commit himself, it was with an uncritical abandon that would normally be expected of someone only half his age.[1]

Oppenheimer's introduction into left-wing circles seems to

have been effected by Jean Tatlock, the daughter of a professor of English at the university and a member of the Communist Party. They later became engaged. But the reasons for his new political awareness were not just personal. For one thing, he had observed the impact the depression was making on his graduate students, several of whom were unemployed or could not get jobs which fitted their talents. For another, as a Jew he could not help but be stirred by the persecution of the Jews in Germany, some of whom were his relatives. Then, as he later put it, there were many policies adopted by the Communist Party in which he himself fervently believed, among them the unionization of the academic community through the Teachers' Union, the organization of the unskilled migrants who had come to work in the Californian orchards, and, in particular, support for the Loyalist cause in the Spanish civil war. Therefore, although he did not go so far as to join the Communist Party, and although he did not subscribe to its doctrines, he was closely associated with it on issues which had a strong humanitarian and emotional appeal. In short, Oppenheimer was a dupe, and there is every indication that he was exploited as such in the period of his active association with the Communist movement.

In all, this lasted some five years and it can be said to have come to an end during 1941. As far as can be told (and the evidence is fragmentary in the extreme), the disengagement was protracted. Although he was aware of Stalin's purge and although in 1938 he had the Soviet Union described to him by three physicists who had lived there as 'a land of purge and terror, of ludicrously bad management and of a long-suffering people', he still continued to support Communist-sponsored causes. Moreover, he remained a fellow-traveller throughout 1939 in spite of the shocks of the Nazi-Soviet Pact and the Soviet invasions of Poland and Finland, which made so many others sever their ties. This does not necessarily condemn him. As one perceptive commentator has remarked, this could well emphasize the intermediate nature of his involvement; someone who had dedicated himself to the party from its earliest days would be more likely to suffer a sharp disillusion than someone who was a late-comer and who stood on its fringe. But it is undoubtedly a reflection on Oppenheimer's good judgment.[2]

The beginning of the end, in Oppenheimer's own view, came

with the fall of France in June 1940, and both Bethe and another physicist, Ramsey, testified to Oppenheimer's dismayed reaction to the turn events were then taking. From about this point his commitment 'tapered off' and, as he put it in 1943, he 'gradually disappeared from one after another of the organizations.' He made no dramatic public break, since he 'never had anything to break'. He also disliked the way some others 'came out and wrote letters to the Republic [*The New Republic*] saying they had seen the light', and he had strong feelings of loyalty to his friends.[3]

The tempo of his withdrawal may have been quickened as a result of his marriage on 1 November 1940. Mrs Oppenheimer had herself been a Communist Party member and her first husband had been killed fighting in Spain, but in one man's opinion this experience had made her determined to minimize Dr Oppenheimer's contacts with the movement. Lieutenant-Colonel John Lansdale, the chief security officer for the atomic bomb project, made it his business to interview Mrs Oppenheimer on several occasions during the early months of the project. As a result of these interviews he drew the conclusion that for Mrs Oppenheimer 'Dr Oppenheimer was the most important thing in her life and ... his future required that he stay away from Communist associations and associations with people of that ilk.'[4]

Whether or not Mrs Oppenheimer exerted such an influence, it is clear that by 1941 her husband's interest in Communism was waning and that quite other considerations were filling his mind. Although the United States was not directly involved in the war against Germany, it had been gearing itself for entry, and from the summer of 1940 onwards more and more scientists were being absorbed in the preparation. Oppenheimer in his letter to Nichols remarked on his envy of them, and his friend and colleague from the California Institute of Technology, Charles Lauritsen, testified that Oppenheimer had asked him whether there would be an opportunity of his joining in the work Lauritsen was doing there for the National Defense Research Committee.[5]

He had not long to wait. On 21 October 1941, at the insistence of Professor Ernest Lawrence of the University of California at Berkeley, he attended a scientific discussion of some of the main problems likely to be encountered in building an atomic bomb. In January 1942 he was assigned to the task of directing theoretical studies of fast-neutron reactions at Berkeley, and in May 1942 he took over responsibility for coordinating the basic experiments on fast-neutron reactions which were going on in various parts of the country, a job which carried with it the grimly humorous title of 'Co-ordinator of Rapid Rupture'. Within little more than six months he had taken on a key role in what was to be one of the most crucial—and most fateful—areas of the American war effort.[6]

No one could have foreseen what was to come, however. In June 1942 the Army had been given control of the programme to develop an atom bomb, and in September General Leslie R. Groves was placed in overall command of the project. One of Groves' first tasks was to select a scientist to run the laboratory in which the weapon would be built. Within a few weeks he had settled on Oppenheimer, and after consultation with Bush and Conant, the two leading scientists in the programme, he affirmed his choice. In mid-November 1942, at Oppenheimer's suggestion, Groves surveyed the remote area around Los Alamos, New Mexico, which Oppenheimer believed would be an ideal location for the weapons laboratory. Groves agreed. By the end of the month he had obtained authority to acquire the site, which was to be developed under Oppenheimer's leadership.[7]

Oppenheimer's new position was far from being assured, however. At the time of his appointment by Groves he had not been given security clearance, although he had applied for it as far back as 28 April 1942, when he filled in his personnel security questionnaire. The War Service Regulations of 16 March 1942 denied government employment in all cases where there existed 'a reasonable doubt as to loyalty to the Government of the United States', and the FBI was relaying reports on Oppenheimer's immediate past which, understandably, raised such a doubt. When Groves chose Oppenheimer he was well aware of the suspicions about him, 'that he had, you might say, a very extreme liberal background', but he was guided by two overriding considerations. There was first the fact that he believed Oppenheimer to be indispensable. In the second place he had to remember that Oppenheimer already knew an immense amount about the bomb and might conceivably be driven 'over to the other side' if he were dismissed from the project. Therefore he maintained his preference and, after a personal endorsement by Lawrence, Oppenheimer was given a formal letter of appointment in January 1943.[8]

There is no good reason to believe that Groves was not justified in what he did. All the evidence we have points to the extreme willingness of Oppenheimer to cut himself off from his left-wing past and prove his patriotism beyond any doubt. This was clear at least from the autumn of 1941 on, when he agreed to drop his attempts to unionize the members of staff on the Berkeley campus, attempts which Lawrence had consistently frowned on. In a letter to Lawrence of 12 November 1941, shortly after his introduction to the war effort, he wrote that 'I doubt very much whether anyone will want to start at this time an organization which could in any way embarrass, divide or interfere with the work we have in hand'. The anxiety to establish his good faith can only have increased after the summer of 1942 when he was told that there was a question-mark over him as regards clearance, and it is notable that it was he who advanced the idea of an isolated weapons laboratory which would minimize the chances of information leaking to the outside world. After his appointment he supported the plan to make Los Alamos a purely military organization, and even took the first steps towards becoming a commissioned officer. The plan was rejected owing to the vehement opposition of the scientists Oppenheimer began to recruit, but Oppenheimer, as Bethe described him, remained 'very security-minded compared to practically all the scientists'. According to Lansdale, he was always 'extremely cooperative' over security matters.[9]

The suspicions of the security agents were still very much alive, however. When Oppenheimer arrived at Los Alamos on 15 March 1943 he had still not yet been given clearance, and as construction began on the site disquieting reports from the FBI continued to come in. Lansdale in his testimony recalled several agonized conversations with Groves, but Groves stood firmly by his original decision. Nevertheless, Oppenheimer was kept under close scrutiny : he was followed whenever he left Los Alamos, his mail was opened, his telephone was tapped, and, in Lansdale's words, 'all sorts of nasty things' were done to keep watch on his activities.[10]

Even more concerned than Lansdale was Lieutenant-Colonel Boris T. Pash, chief of military counter-intelligence on the west coast. Pash's men had placed Oppenheimer under surveillance during a visit he paid to San Francisco on 12 June 1943. As a result of their report, which indicated that he had visited two known Communist Party members, his former fiancée, Jean Tatlock, and a certain David Hawkins, Pash raised the following possibilities, based on the assumption that Oppenheimer was still connected with the Party and might even be a member. Either he was transmitting secret information direct to the Party 'without submitting any phase of it to the United States Government', or he was doing so through 'his other contacts' and it was then sent to Soviet Russia.[11]

Pash then went on to urge three alternative courses of action. Firstly, a replacement for Oppenheimer should be found and as soon as he was trained Oppenheimer should be 'removed completely from the project and dismissed from employment by the United States Government'. Secondly, a second-in-command should be assigned to Oppenheimer who would share his knowledge of every aspect of the project. Thirdly, Oppenheimer should be summoned to Washington and reminded of the terms of the Espionage Act, told that his Communist affiliations were known, and informed that the government would not tolerate any leakage of secret data to the Communist Party.

'It is the opinion of this office', Pash concluded, 'that subject's personal inclinations would be to protect his own future and reputation and the high degree of honor which would be his if his present work is successful, and, consequently, it is felt that he would lend every effort to cooperating with the Government in any plan which would leave him in charge.' Therefore, the third alternative should be carried out, and Oppenheimer should have two men assigned to him, ostensibly as bodyguards to meet any attempt at assassination by Axis agents, but in reality to act as undercover agents for counter-intelligence.

Groves' response to this was not slow in coming. On 15 July he issued verbal instructions that Oppenheimer be given security clearance and he repeated this directive by letter on 20 July. Clearance was to be issued 'without delay, irrespective of the information which you have concerning Mr Oppenheimer. He is absolutely essential to the project.' As Groves later wrote in his memoirs : 'All procedures and decisions on security, including the clearance of personnel, had to be based on what was believed to be the overriding consideration—completion of the bomb. Speed of accomplishment was paramount.' 'I think we would have probably taken a convicted murderer,' said McCloy at the hearing. For, as Lansdale reminded the Board, America believed that it was engaged in a race with Nazi Germany for completion of the weapon, and that 'the nation which first obtained one would win the war'. The stakes were no less than that. Accordingly, the investigation of Oppenheimer was discontinued in mid-August on orders from Washington.[12]

Oppenheimer's troubles were far from over, however. Pash's report on him had been drawn up in connection with an investigation into a Soviet espionage attempt at the Radiation Laboratory at Berkeley. The Radiation Laboratory was important in so far as it was the mainspring of one of the two main efforts to produce quantities of the vital fissionable material, uranium 235. There, under the direction of Lawrence, the electromagnetic process of separating the 235 isotope had been devised, and although the other method of separation, gaseous diffusion, was widely believed to have the better chance of success, Lawrence was convinced that he would prove differently. At all events, Soviet intelligence was deeply interested and late in March 1943 succeeded in getting a piece of information from a young Communist physicist at Berkeley, Joseph Weinberg, who transmitted it through Steve Nelson, a leading member of the Party in California.[13]

The episode touched Oppenheimer in a number of ways. Weinberg was a former research student of his and gave Oppenheimer as a reference when he himself was taken on at the Radiation Laboratory on 22 April. Nelson was a fairly close acquaintance of Mrs Oppenheimer and had known her first husband well. Moreover, two of the other scientists under suspicion along with Weinberg, David Bohm and Giovanni Lomanitz, had also studied under Oppenheimer. As recently as March 1943 Oppenheimer had asked for Bohm to be transferred to Los Alamos and it was he who had persuaded Lomanitz to go to work at the Radiation Laboratory in June 1942. In July 1943, when an attempt was made to remove Lomanitz by cancelling the deferment of his military service, Oppenheimer entered a strong protest, following an outraged letter from the former associate director of Los Alamos, Dr Edward Condon.[14]

The security officers immediately drew the conclusion that Oppenheimer had interceded on Lomanitz's behalf because of his pro-Communist background. This did not necessarily follow. As Lansdale recalled at the hearing, it was the highly conservative Professor Lawrence who 'yelled and screamed louder than anybody else about us taking Lomanitz away from him'. Groves too remembered Lawrence's extreme reluctance to lose anyone he considered valuable simply because it was thought to be good for security. But a warning was held to be advisable, and early in August Lansdale was dispatched to Los Alamos, where he impressed it on Oppenheimer 'to avoid making any further requests for deferment for Lomanitz because he had been guilty of indiscretions which could not be overlooked or condoned'. He also made it clear to Oppenheimer that he should not press for the transfer to Los Alamos of any of the others implicated in the Radiation Laboratory affair. Oppenheimer, in reply, stated that he wanted no current members of the Communist Party working for him at Los Alamos, since their loyalties were bound to be divided. He also seemed to Lansdale to be trying to give the impression that he himself had made a decisive break with the Party when he entered the atomic project.[15]

There can be little doubt that Oppenheimer was badly shaken by what Lansdale had had to say. Shortly afterwards, on 25 August, during a visit to Berkeley, he confronted Lomanitz in a stormy interview. We have only Oppenheimer's version of what happened and that is somewhat contradictory. The following day, 26 August, he was to say to Colonel Pash that Lomanitz was doing work 'which he ought to continue', but in subsequent conversations with Groves and Lansdale his comments were sharply different. Then he made out that he had persuaded Lomanitz not to try to stay on the project, and he declared that he 'was sorry that he had ever had anything to do with him, and he did not desire any further connection with him'. This certainly corresponds with the cool and guarded tone of his letter to Lansdale of 19 October 1943, with which he forwarded a letter from Lomanitz (now in the Army) asking for his help in getting assigned back to Berkeley. Even though the suggestion had come from Lawrence, he told Landsdale he was 'of course, not able to endorse this request in any absolute way'. Thereafter he kept a file of his correspondence with Lomanitz, because Lomanitz had been 'in some kind of trouble' and 'I thought that . . . I might be asked about how I behaved'.

At the same time he dissociated himself from Lomanitz, Oppenheimer fended off Bohm and Weinberg, who also saw him at Berkeley on 25 August. In their view Lomanitz was being 'framed' for his politics and they too ran the same risk. They needed to know whether Oppenheimer thought they ought to get out of the project before they were punished as Lomanitz had been. Oppenheimer had replied that if they fulfilled three conditions, namely, dropped their trade union activities, severed their connections with Communists, and abided strictly by security regulations, then they should stay. If not, then they should leave. He did not, however, make it clear to Weinberg (as he soon afterwards did to Groves and Lansdale) that, although Weinberg expected to be transferred to Los Alamos, he would on no account have him there.[17]

Yet Oppenheimer's concern over the Weinberg-Lomanitz episode went much deeper than the indiscretions which they were alleged to have committed, even though they did involve him personally to a degree. Lansdale's revelation of the Berkeley espionage inquiry during his visit early in August 1943 did nothing less, indeed, than set off a chain of developments which contributed greatly towards his ultimate destruction.

During his conversation with Oppenheimer, Lansdale had pointed out that the suspects at Berkeley were all members of the Federation of Architects, Engineers, Chemists, and Technicians (FAECT), a union with decidedly left-wing sympathies. His mention of the Federation turned Oppenheimer's mind sharply back to an incident which had occurred several months before his arrival at Los Alamos. Some time before Christmas 1942, a friend and a colleague of Oppenheimer's at Berkeley, Haakon Chevalier, had spoken to him of a recent meeting with George Eltenton, an English chemical engineer working at the nearby Shell Development Company plant. Chevalier and Eltenton had both moved in the same pro-Communist circles which Oppenheimer had frequented, and as Oppenheimer later recounted it, at the hearing, Chevalier had said that Eltenton 'had told him that he had . . . means of getting technical information to Soviet scientists'. To this Oppenheimer (as he recollected) had said something like 'But that is treason' or 'This is a terrible thing to do'. Chevalier, he remembered, 'expressed complete agreement', and that was the end of the discussion. Nothing more had come of it.[18]

Nothing, that is, until Lansdale's visit to Los Alamos. It was then that Oppenheimer recalled that Eltenton was an active member of the FAECT. He knew that Lomanitz had revealed information by 'talking to unauthorized people who in turn would talk to other people'; in other words, that Lomanitz was almost certainly the source of the information which Weinberg had transmitted to Nelson in March. Lomanitz and Weinberg had been discovered, and it was entirely possible that the intelligence agents might be on to Eltenton as well. If they interrogated Eltenton, and then Chevalier, it was likely that his exchange with Chevalier would come to light. Blameless as it was, it could well be misinterpreted, especially in view of Oppenheimer's background and in view of the lingering suspicions about his reliability. It was not inconceivable that it might cost him his job as director of Los Alamos.[19]

It should be stressed that what has just been said is no more than an opinion as to what was going on in Dr Oppenheimer's mind in August 1943, but it is an opinion which is based largely on the available evidence and only slightly on reading between the lines. It also provides a reasonable explanation of the action he then decided to take.

It is clear that Oppenheimer now thought that Eltenton represented a serious threat to the security of the atomic bomb project. It is equally clear that he had no wish for his name to be associated with Eltenton's in any way whatsoever. Nor did he want Chevalier implicated, as he believed him to be innocent. Somehow the government had to be warned about Eltenton, but it had to be done without endangering himself or Chevalier.

The same day, therefore, that Oppenheimer saw Lomanitz at Berkeley he went to the resident security officer on the campus, Lieutenant Lyall Johnson, to tell him that Eltenton was 'somebody to worry about'. Then, to conceal his and Chevalier's part in the episode, he 'invented a cock-and-bull story'. This story he repeated the next day (26 August) to Colonel Pash, who had been telephoned at once by an agitated Johnson. In his testimony at the hearing Pash recalled that they both felt Oppenheimer's report was 'of considerable importance', and he evidently thought he now had the lead he had been seeking in vain during his investigation of the Radiation Laboratory.[20]

The account Oppenheimer gave ran as follows. He began by telling of the way in which Eltenton's approach had been presented. 'You know how difficult it is with the relations between these two allies,' it had been said. There were 'a lot of people who don't feel very friendly to Russia, so that the information—a lot of our secret information, our radar and so on, doesn't get to them, and they are battling for their lives and they would like to have an idea of what is going on. . . .' The details that were being sought were 'just to make up . . . for the defects of our official communication . . . for the fact that were a couple of guys in the State Department who might block such communications'.[21]

In reality, the request for secret data had come from Eltenton via Chevalier to Oppenheimer. In Oppenheimer's version, however, it had originated in the Soviet consulate in San Francisco and had passed through Eltenton to an unnamed intermediary at Berkeley and from him to three contacts working on the project, two at Los Alamos and one at the Radiation Laboratory. These three had come to Oppenheimer and told him they had been contacted with a view to giving information. The Russian at the consulate, who was 'a very reliable guy . . . and who had a lot of experience in microfilm work, or whatever the hell' was 'in a position to transmit, without any danger of a leak, or scandal, or anything of that kind, information, which they might supply'. An interview could be arranged with Eltenton for the purpose.[22]

It can be seen that Oppenheimer himself did not figure in the story, and although he glanced at the truth in saying that Eltenton had 'talked to a friend of his who is also an acquaintance of one of the men on the project', Pash had no means of knowing who this man was. Indeed, Oppenheimer was anxious to remove all doubts about his loyalty. 'I feel quite strongly', he told Pash, 'that association with the Communist movement is not compatible with the job on a secret war project, it is just that the two loyalties cannot go.' Moreover, he went on, 'I feel responsibility for every detail of this sort of thing [security] down at our place

[Los Alamos] and I will be willing to go quite far in saying that everything is 100 per cent in order. That doesn't go for this place up here [Berkeley]. . . . If everything weren't being done and if everything weren't proper, I think that I would be perfectly willing to be shot if I had done anything wrong.'[23]

At the same time, he refused to give the name of the intermediary—that is, Chevalier—and would say no more than that he was a member of the faculty at Berkeley. Nor did he say who the contacts were. 'To give more, perhaps, than one name', in his view, 'would be to implicate people whose attitude was one of bewilderment rather than one of cooperation.' He could not inform on men 'who are acquaintances, or colleagues and so on of whose position I am absolutely certain myself, and my duty is to protect them'. At the conclusion of the interview he apologized for his silence, but explained that it was 'because of my insistence on not getting people into trouble'.[24]

Pash, understandably, was seething. 'We will be hot under the collar until we find out what is going on there', he had said, but given Oppenheimer's unwillingness to talk, he was looking for a needle in a haystack. 'We could work a hundred years . . . and never get this information', he had burst out in his chagrin. He was to come across Chevalier's name a month or so later, but only in connection with general Communist activities in California, not in relation to espionage. He was therefore completely in the dark, and having sent a transcript of the interview to Lansdale on 28 August, on 2 September he addressed a memorandum to General Groves demanding that Oppenheimer be made to give the name of the Berkeley intermediary and, 'if disposed to talk', the names of the three contacts besides.[25]

Pash was also intensely suspicious of Oppenheimer himself, and in the memorandum he asked Groves if Oppenheimer had been approached since he came on to the project, whether by Eltenton, the unknown intermediary or someone else. This was a shrewd guess on Pash's part, and he felt sure that Oppenheimer had volunteered his information 'for the purpose of relieving any pressure that may be brought on him for further investigation of his personal situation'. This thesis he outlined in a second memorandum to Groves of 2 September, which ended by saying that in future Oppenheimer should not be 'taken fully into the confidence of the Army in ... matters pertaining to subversive investigations'.[26]

This view of Oppenheimer was elaborated in a further memorandum of 2 September, written by Captain Peer DeSilva, a member of Pash's staff; it was forwarded to Lansdale in Washington on 6 September. What DeSilva had to say showed that counter-intelligence's view of Oppenheimer had not changed since he had come under their scrutiny in June. 'J. R. Oppenheimer', Captain DeSilva alleged, 'is playing a key part in the attempts of the Soviet Union to secure, by espionage, highly secret information which is vital to the security of the United States.' Oppenheimer had 'allowed a tight clique of known Communists or Communist sympathisers to grow up about him within the project, until they comprise a large proportion of the key personnel in whose hands the success and secrecy of the project is entrusted. In the opinion of this officer, Oppenheimer either must be incredibly naive and almost childlike in his sense of reality, or he himself is extremely clever and disloyal. The former possibility is not borne out in the opinion of the officers who have spoken with him at length.'

Oppenheimer's disloyalty was evidenced, in DeSilva's view, by the fact that Nelson (Weinberg's contact) had 'visited him and solicited cooperation'; by his failure to report the Communist affiliations of 'some of his employees'; and by the timing of his disclosure about Eltenton. He had not made this disclosure until he knew that a full-scale investigation was under way at Berkeley, and he had done so to protect himself. By seizing the initiative, he evidently hoped to head off another survey of his own activities and establish the impression that he was a willing assistant of the security network, whereas in fact he was working against it. It was his opinion, DeSilva concluded, that

> Oppenheimer is deeply concerned with gaining a worldwide reputation as a scientist, and a place in history, as a result of the DSM project [Development of Substitute Materials, a codename for the atomic bomb project]. It is also believed that the Army is in the position of being able to allow him to do so or to destroy his name, reputation, and career, if it should choose to do so. Such a possibility, if strongly presented to him, would possibly give him a different view of his position

with respect to the Army, which has been, heretofore, one in which he has been dominant because of his supposed essentiality.[27]

In his covering memorandum of 6 September, Pash reiterated that his office was still convinced that Oppenheimer's loyalty was divided. As he put it: 'It is believed that the only undivided loyalty he can give is to science and it is strongly felt that if in his position the Soviet Government could offer more for the advancement of his scientific cause he would select that Government as the one to which he would express his loyalty.'[28]

This was essentially what Pash had been saying in June. His advice then had been discounted, but Groves could not afford to ignore this latest development. He had been in Berkeley for an important meeting on 2 September, and Oppenheimer accompanied him back to Washington on the train (key personnel on the project were not allowed to fly in case of accidents). During the journey Groves had a long conversation with him about his background and related the substance of it to Lansdale on his return to the capital. Lansdale was then assigned the task of interrogating Oppenheimer and the interview took place in Groves' office on 12 September. Like the Pash interview, it was recorded without Oppenheimer's knowledge.[29]

Lansdale began by explaining that counter-intelligence had known since February 1943 that several people were transmitting information about the bomb to the Soviet government. 'They know, we know they know,' he pointed out, 'about Tennessee, about Los Alamos, and Chicago [the sites of the uranium 235 separation plants, the weapons laboratory and the plutonium research centre respectively].' They also knew that the Radiation Laboratory was the headquarters of research on the electromagnetic process of separation, and about the likely production capability by that process. Here, then, was an instance 'in which there is an actual attempt at espionage against probably the most important thing we're doing', yet Oppenheimer had not only delayed reporting it but refused to tell the whole story. Now was the time for him to pass on everything he knew.[30]

Once more, however, Oppenheimer did not name any names. His own identity remained secret, although—surprisingly—

he revealed that he had spoken about Eltenton because he was afraid that he himself 'was being used or might be used for the provocation of leaks'. And his heart must have stood still when Lansdale said that he had reason to believe 'that you yourself were felt out, I don't say asked, but felt out to ascertain how you felt about it, passing a little information, to the party'. But this, and Lansdale's subsequent remark, that 'we have been fairly sure for a long time that you knew something you weren't telling us', was sheer bluff, and for the most part Lansdale concentrated on winning Oppenheimer's confidence. 'I've made up my mind that you yourself are O.K.,' he said reassuringly, 'or otherwise I wouldn't be talking to you like this. . . .' Oppenheimer could not have agreed more, and denied emphatically that he had ever been a party to industrial espionage and that he knew anything about it. Even so, Chevalier's name was not forthcoming.[31]

In other respects, Oppenheimer was disposed to collaborate. He was willing to dilate on the various degrees of commitment of his relations, his friends and his acquaintances, including his wife, his brother, Lomanitz, Weinberg, Nelson and Chevalier. Asked if Chevalier were a member of the Party he answered that 'I wouldn't be surprised . . . he is quite a Red'. If need be, he would be willing to get information as to who at Berkeley was and was not a Party member, but 'not in writing, I think that would make a very bad impression'. He would also help to discourage the FAECT if it tried to penetrate Los Alamos; indeed, he had already used his influence against it when he was at Berkeley. But he would still not identify Eltenton's intermediary, since 'I would regard it as a low trick to involve someone where I would bet dollars to doughnuts he wasn't involved'.[32]

Oppenheimer's behaviour over the Chevalier incident, as it came to be called, was to prove damning in 1954. The AEC's counsel, Robb, was later to describe it as 'probably the most important evidence' of what were held to be 'fundamental defects' in Oppenheimer's character, and during the course of the hearing he successfully extracted the maximum significance from it. Under Robb's relentless cross-examination, Oppenheimer was made to admit no less than fourteen times that he had lied to Pash, and finally to agree that he had told Pash 'not one lie . . .

but a whole fabrication and tissue of lies'. Asked why, he had no other answer than to say 'Because I was an idiot', a wretchedly inadequate reply which revealed his helpless awareness of the damage the episode had caused him. All he could add to this was that he was reluctant to mention Chevalier and 'no doubt somewhat reluctant to mention myself'. Later, towards the close of the hearing he was to offer the explanation that he had tried to give a tip to the security agents but had failed to realize that 'when you give a tip you must tell the whole story.' In fact, and not for the last time, Oppenheimer had been too clever by half, and in the long run it served to destroy him.[33]

As Cushing Strout has pointed out, Oppenheimer had three interests to protect: Chevalier; the government's project; and himself. If he had told the truth, he would have warned the government of the danger of espionage, but he would have jeopardized both Chevalier and himself. Indeed, if he had gone to the security officers at once, the chances are that he would have lost the directorship of Los Alamos. By lying, therefore, he hoped to reconcile all three interests simultaneously. The real source of danger, Eltenton, had been exposed, while his anonymity and that of Chevalier were preserved. What Oppenheimer did not appreciate was that he had to commit himself one way or the other, to the friend who symbolized his past, or to the government which could shape his future. By trying to maintain his loyalties to them both, he ended by losing the confidence of them both, and paid a terrible price for it.[34]

All Oppenheimer *had* succeeded in doing during the interview with Pash was to put himself in a trap from which there was no escape. He had lied and he was to be caught out in the lie. But what he had said was also, paradoxically, capable of being construed as the truth, and Robb was skilful enough to turn this possibility to his advantage, even at the very same time that he was branding Oppenheimer as a liar. Pash, for his part, declared that in 1943 he had believed Oppenheimer's story rang true, and he still believed that in 1954. For one thing, he considered that the detail was too circumstantial to have been invented. For another, the story Oppenheimer had told him at Berkeley was 'far more damaging to him and to any of his friends' than the account given in the reply to Nichols' allegations. This point was later taken up by Gray when he remarked that 'the story you told was certainly not calculated to lead to the conclusion of innocence on Chevalier's part'. It should be added that Oppenheimer had already lent a certain colour to this suspicion in his reply to Nichols. 'Nothing in our long standing friendship would have led me to believe that Chevalier was actually seeking information', he had written; 'and I was certain that he had no idea of the work on which I was engaged.' Again, under cross-examination by Gray, he declared that he had 'put an improper confidence in my own judgment that Chevalier was not a danger'. In both instances there was sufficient ambiguity to cast a doubt on his other assertions of Chevalier's innocence. Finally, as Gray pointed out in his examination of Pash, if Oppenheimer had not volunteered his information, and if the incident did only concern Chevalier and himself, the security officers would most likely not have found out about it and it would not have become part of the subject-matter of a hearing. Pash confirmed this supposition by saying that the detail of the story Oppenheimer had told him was so elaborate that it would have been bound to be uncovered and that he believed Oppenheimer knew this.[35]

These were ingenious theories, but they should have been demolished by the evidence of the sequel to the Lansdale interview. During the weeks that followed, Pash and his staff moved heaven and earth to find out the identity of the Berkeley intermediary. By 22 November they had produced a short list of nine (including Weinberg), but Chevalier's name did not appear on it, probably because he taught French and they were thinking it was a scientist. It was clear that they were getting nowhere, and their frustration is not difficult to imagine.[36]

It was not, however, shared by General Groves. In Groves' eyes, Oppenheimer had done what was essential, that is to say, had drawn attention to the man he considered the real danger, Eltenton. Whoever the intermediary was (and Groves apparently believed it was Frank Oppenheimer, not Chevalier), 'the man had made a mistake and he [Oppenheimer] had adequately taken care of that mistake and more or less warned this man off'. Oppenheimer had acted 'under the influence of what I termed the typical American schoolboy attitude that there is something wicked about telling on a friend'. This, to Groves, was not apparently a serious offence.[37]

Why did Groves, who was normally intensely security-conscious, adopt such a relaxed, not to say philosophical position? As it emerged during his testimony, it was because he considered the incident involved 'what after all was a minor point with respect to the success of the project'. This view of the electromagnetic process reads oddly in the light of what we now know from the official history of the Atomic Energy Commission. On 2 September 1943, at the very moment Oppenheimer's revelation was brought to his notice, Groves took the decision to give the process the same priority as gaseous diffusion, which had hitherto had the lion's share of available funds, and a week later more than $150 million were requested for an expanded programme. But as he described it at the hearing, 'while it was of extreme importance to us during the war, and we saved at least a year's time by doing it, ... it was not the process we would follow after the war. That is one reason why we put silver in those magnets, because we knew we could get it out.' Therefore, presumably, Weinberg's espionage had been allowed to proceed unchecked in the hope that Moscow would hurl the bulk of its resources into what could never be a project of lasting value. Therefore also there need be no hurry in obtaining the name from Oppenheimer. Groves already knew of the threat to the Radiation Laboratory and this latest disclosure had only served to confirm it, while to put pressure on Oppenheimer could well reduce his ability to get on with the job. As always at Los Alamos, the need to complete the bomb quickly was absolute.[38]

So Groves bided his time. During the train journey to Chicago at the end of the first week in September, Oppenheimer offered to give the name if Groves ordered him to, but Groves declined. It was, indeed, another three months before the order was given—Groves, as he cryptically put it, 'having then got the situation more or less adjusted'. On 12 December 1943 Oppenheimer revealed that his friend Chevalier was the man in question. He did *not,* however, speak of his own part in the affair; the secret telegrams which flashed the news to the nerve-centres of the project all mentioned that Chevalier had made three contacts, not one, that is, Oppenheimer himself. Yet twice during the hearing, Oppenheimer declared that he had told the whole truth and had admitted that it was he who had been approached. When Robb reminded him that the telegrams were still talking of three contacts, he could only say that he found this 'quite in-comprehensible'.[39]

What Oppenheimer said or did not say about the Chevalier incident in the winter of 1943 was certainly thought to be im-portant in the spring of 1954; at the time, however, it was not, judging from the available evidence. So far as we know, Eltenton had not been taken in for interrogation after 26 August; nor was Chevalier after 12 December. Nor again was any attempt apparently made to persuade Oppenheimer to divulge the names of the three contacts whom Chevalier was supposed to have ap-proached. This was understandable if the security officers ac-cepted the view that they must have been innocent if they had broached the subject to Oppenheimer, yet to have known who they were and to have interviewed them could hardly have been a complete waste of time.

Why was no action taken? Why was this further lead not followed up? Chevalier, in his book on the case, puts forward the hypothesis that counter-intelligence knew full well that Oppenheimer was lying all the time, and this knowledge gave them a weapon which they could use against him at some point in the future. Moreover, he probably guessed that they knew. When he went to Los Alamos, 'he had undoubtedly already made up his mind that he would pay whatever price was exacted in order to achieve what he wanted. A Faust of the twentieth century, he had sold his soul to the atom bomb.' Now, in December 1943, he was 'more than ever a prisoner of his superiors, and especially of his immediate superior, General Leslie R. Groves'.[40]

There is clearly an element of truth in Chevalier's view. Oppenheimer's lie *was* to be used against him with devastating effect, and if he did not guess that the government knew he had lied, he almost certainly feared it did, and this cannot have been easy to live with. What Chevalier misses, however, is the probability that the decisive factor was Groves' confidence that he had whatever threat there was to the Radiation Laboratory well under control, coupled with his belief that the electro-magnetic process had only a short-term significance. Groves without much doubt directed the situation, but not quite in the way Chevalier suspected.

It was also probably Groves' action which led to the revelation of the full truth about the incident in 1946. Although he knew of the existence of the left-wing group at the Shell Development Company (which, of course, included Eltenton), he said nothing to the management because 'I would rather have it there where I knew it'. After the war was over, however, he did draw it to their attention, 'and I believe that group was cleaned out in twenty-four hours'.[41]

It may be no more than a coincidence (but even so it is a remarkable coincidence) that early in June 1946 both Eltenton and Chevalier were simultaneously interrogated by the Federal Bureau of Investigation. Chevalier already had been touched by what Oppenheimer had said about him. In January 1944, immediately after Oppenheimer's disclosure, he had been refused clearance for a job with the Office of War Information, because of allegations in his dossier 'so fantastic as to be utterly unbelievable', in the words of the director of the OWI New York office. 'Someone obviously has it in for you', he had said. Nonetheless, in September 1945 Chevalier was employed by his government as an interpreter for the forthcoming Nuremberg war crimes trials. This may have been the reason why he was not interrogated earlier, but soon after his return from Europe he was taken by two agents to the FBI office in San Francisco.[42]

There, according to his own account, he was questioned for some eight hours, particularly about his relationship with Eltenton. During the course of the questioning, he was accused of having approached three scientists on the atomic bomb project to solicit information on behalf of Russian agents. Each scientist had testified by an affidavit (which Chevalier was not permitted to see) that Chevalier had come to him three times. He was asked to give their names, and when he could not (because they did not exist) he told the agents about his conversation with Eltenton and the subsequent meeting with Oppenheimer at the end of 1942.[43]

Eltenton had asked him to come round to his house. He told Chevalier that Soviet scientists felt that there should be close collaboration between them and their American counterparts, in particular 'exchanges of information as to strategically important research'. Oppenheimer was known to be in charge of a key war project and to be 'very much of a left-winger'. Would Chevalier sound him out 'as to how he felt about the possibility of such collaboration'? 'The answer that I gave', writes Chevalier, 'was of course an unqualified "No"; Eltenton appeared relieved to hear this.'[44]

Chevalier decided to tell Oppenheimer about the conversation because he was certain Eltenton was not acting on his own initiative. There were 'people behind him', in other words Soviet agents, and they might well be involved in a serious attempt to penetrate whatever work Oppenheimer was engaged in. So he told Oppenheimer one evening soon afterwards at his house in Berkeley. He mentioned Eltenton's name, but conveyed that he had 'let himself in for this rather naïvely and would now drop the matter'. Oppenheimer was 'visibly disturbed', but agreed that Chevalier had been right to tell him. With that, the incident closed.[45]

Although patently unsatisfied, the agents let Chevalier go. It was only several months later that he ran into Eltenton and discovered that they had both been taken in at precisely the same time, himself in San Francisco, Eltenton in Oakland, so that their accounts could be cross-checked by telephone during the interrogation. This was the first time that either of them had been questioned in the whole period since the incident came to light.[46]

Chevalier lost no time in telling Oppenheimer what had happened. Oppenheimer, needless to say, was extremely agitated. An entirely different version of the Chevalier incident was now in the hands of the FBI, and no doubt he would have a great deal of explaining to do. He did not, however, tell Chevalier about the story he had concocted but simply that he had reported their conversation of December 1942. Chevalier thus remained in ignorance of what Oppenheimer had done.[47]

The FBI were a different proposition. On 5 September 1946 they questioned Oppenheimer intensively, mostly about Chevalier, and Oppenheimer was constrained to give them the story which later appeared in his reply to the AEC's letter of accusation. That it was the truth (at last) there can be little doubt. Those who believed that the story given to Pash was true argued that Oppenheimer had only changed it *after* his talk with Chevalier in the summer of 1946, that they had devised a new version between them, and that it was therefore a lie. On the other hand, if there really had been three contacts, then

Chevalier would surely have been pressed into saying who they were, and there was never any suggestion in the evidence presented to the hearing that three such names had in fact emerged. Moreover, as we shall see, no less a figure than the director of the FBI himself was convinced that Oppenheimer had lied in 1943. No one was in possession of more detail on Dr Oppenheimer than he, and since his view was expressed in confidence, it is unlikely that he was being misleading.[48]

It is small wonder that Oppenheimer was shaken by the resurgence of the Chevalier affair: his left-wing past had come back to haunt him just when he must have considered it dead and buried. For there can be little doubt that he had moved decisively away from his pro-Communist background during the war years; the transition which had begun in 1941 was accomplished in 1945. From this point on, the evidence builds up a picture of a man who had become an accepted member of the American political establishment and who was perfectly happy to remain so.

One anecdote of the post-war years offsets this impression, but its significance lies in the fact that it is exceptional. On 24 July 1946 the first chairman of the AEC, David Lilienthal, met Oppenheimer 'in deep despair' at the likely failure of the American proposal for an international agency to control atomic energy. Such a failure, according to Oppenheimer, would 'fit perfectly into the plans of that growing number who want to put the country on a war footing, first psychologically, then actually. The Army directing the country's research; Red-baiting; treating all labor organizations, CIO first, as Communist and therefore traitorous, etc.' Here one can glimpse Oppenheimer of the period 1936–41, but it was a rare outburst.[49]

Heavily outweighing it is the evidence of someone decidedly anti-Communist, and expressing this new orientation in his attitude both to the issues of the post-war world and to his former friends and colleagues of the left. Thus, to take the first instance, as soon as he left Los Alamos in the autumn of 1945, he had testified in favour of the May-Johnson bill for an Atomic Energy Commission. In the eyes of its scientific critics, the bill would have left the atomic energy programme in the hands of the military, and it contained swingeing penalties for the disclosure of information. Then, in the following year, on the question of international control, Oppenheimer again diverged from many of his colleagues who believed that agreement between America and Russia was possible. He, on the other hand, saw an insuperable obstacle in the Soviet refusal to surrender sovereignty to the international authority. In March 1947, the hearing was told, Oppenheimer was actually in favour of breaking off negotiations with the Russians, while in the early 1950s, one of Oppenheimer's own witnesses believed he had even detected in Oppenheimer 'a certain tendency ... to be inclined toward a preventive war'. But perhaps the most glowing testimonial came from Conant. Writing in 1947 Conant had said of Oppenheimer: 'He is not sympathetic with the totalitarian régime in Russia and his attitude towards that nation is, from my point of view, thoroughly sound and hard headed ... any rumor that Dr Oppenheimer is sympathetically inclined toward the Communists or toward Russia is an absurdity.' This opinion he still held when he testified on Oppenheimer's behalf in 1954.[50]

At the same time, Oppenheimer dissociated himself emphatically from the left. In October 1946 he resigned from the Independent Citizens' Committee of the Arts, Sciences and Professions on the grounds that it was taking up positions on international policy which did not correspond with American interests. His action was symptomatic of his growing estrangement with the people whose views he had once so enthusiastically shared, and they were bitterly aware of it. Jungk, in *Brighter Than A Thousand Suns,* quotes a former pupil as saying that he thought 'his sudden fame and the new position he now occupied had gone to his head so much that he began to consider himself God Almighty, able to put the whole world to rights'. Chevalier, in the immediate post-war years, began to hear not only that he had 'let many of his closest collaborators down', but that he had 'denounced some of them as communists and been responsible for getting them into difficulties and for their losing jobs'. He was even accused of sheering away from his brother, presumably for ideological reasons.[51]

The most solid (and unpleasant) confirmation of these rumours came in June 1949. On 7 June Oppenheimer gave testimony to the House of Representatives Committee on Un-

c

American Activities in connection with its inquiry into the Communist attempt to penetrate the Radiation Laboratory. Among other things, he was asked to give his opinion of a former graduate student of his, Bernard Peters, a German who had been put in Dachau by the Nazis and had succeeded in escaping to the United States with his wife. Late in 1942 Oppenheimer had invited Peters to come to Los Alamos, but he had not done so; instead, he worked with Lawrence at Berkeley.[52]

In reply, Oppenheimer recalled that he had once described Peters as 'a dangerous man and quite Red'. This had been early in January 1944, shortly after his disclosure of Chevalier's name. DeSilva, who only four months before had accused Oppenheimer of disloyalty, had asked him which of the men at Berkeley he considered 'truly dangerous'. Oppenheimer named Bohm and Peters; the latter, he believed, was a 'crazy person' and 'quite a Red'. At the hearing in 1949 he elaborated on these opinions and stated into the bargain that he knew Peters had been a member of the German Communist Party.[53]

The testimony before the Committee had been delivered in secret, but on 15 June extracts from it were printed in a local paper in Rochester, New York, where Peters was teaching at the university. Immediately there was uproar. Oppenheimer was overwhelmed with protests from Peters himself, from his brother, from Condon (who had also protested against the treatment of Lomanitz in 1943), and from the eminent theoreticians Bethe and Weisskopf. Condon believed Oppenheimer had turned informer to buy immunity for himself and pointed out that if his file were ever made public, 'it would be a much bigger flap'. On 30 June Oppenheimer tried to make amends in a letter sent to the Rochester *Democrat and Chronicle*. In it he regretted profoundly that anything he had said 'should have been so misconstrued, and so abused' as to damage Peters personally and threaten his career. At the same time, he made the same plea which his defenders were to make on his behalf five years later, namely, that America should avoid the example of the totalitarians and refuse to apply 'criteria of political orthodoxy . . . to ruin scientists, and to put an end to their work'.[54]

The Peters episode brought out the worst in Oppenheimer, and his behaviour before the Committee was yet one more illustration of his determination to cut himself off from his old associates and to prove himself anxious to cooperate with authority. (Moreover, it should be noted that his letter of 30 June did not explicitly retract his testimony and that in particular he did not say he believed Peters' denial of Communist party membership.) But this was not the aspect which Robb fastened on. The subtleties of Oppenheimer's explanations of his position could well be taken for sophistry and it was not difficult to present his letter as a volte-face brought about by pressure from the left. In Oppenheimer's own view he had modified his statements because 'it was an overwhelming belief of the community in which I lived that a man like that ought not to be fired either for his past or for his views, unless the past is criminal or the views lead him to wicked action.' But, as he himself admitted, he should have kept that belief in mind when he testified to the Committee. All he had succeeded in doing was to leave the chairman of his tribunal with the distinct impression that he had said 'one thing in executive session, and another thing for public consumption', in other words, that he had spoken the truth about Peters in confidence and lied about him at the instigation of his friends. It was to prove a costly mistake.[55]

The Peters incident stood out in sharp relief because it was one of the few instances where Oppenheimer's past impinged on him. If there were more, then the AEC did not bring them forward, and if there had been, then we can be certain it would have done so. It was pointed out that Oppenheimer had helped Bohm to get a teaching post at Princeton in 1946 or 1947, and in May 1949, he had a brief conversation with Bohm and Lomanitz in the main street of Princeton. Both were scheduled to appear before the Un-American Activities Committee in connection with the hearing on the Radiation Laboratory, and they had spoken to Oppenheimer about it. This was a chance encounter, according to Oppenheimer, and he said he had simply advised them to tell the truth. Later, however, when they testified to the Committee, both invoked the fifth amendment and refused to answer when asked whether or not they knew Steve Nelson, the man who had committed espionage with Weinberg in March 1943. The inference which the AEC was attempting to draw was clear: they had been influenced by Oppenheimer, who was presumably trying to protect himself against being involved, since, of course, he and his wife had known Nelson quite well.[56]

Apart from this, the most serious evidence of continuing association with the left was his relationship with Chevalier. During the post-war years, until Chevalier left the country to live in France in November 1950, he and Oppenheimer met intermittently, and during 1950 Oppenheimer tried to help him out in several ways. Since his interview with the FBI, Chevalier had run into great difficulty in finding a university job, and he believed, with some justification, that the reason lay in his political background. He had been particularly hard hit by an account of the December 1942 incident given on 30 October 1947 by a former FBI investigator, Louis J. Russell. Chevalier, according to Russell, had 'approached' Oppenheimer at Eltenton's request after Eltenton had told him he wanted 'some research data' related to 'a highly destructive weapon'. Oppenheimer had reacted by saying that he 'considered such attempts treasonable and would have nothing to do with them'. When asked to comment, Oppenheimer had not dispelled the suggestion that Chevalier had made a real bid for information. Instead he had put out the remarkably opaque statement that he 'would like to withhold comment, either confirmation or denial, of the statements in general or detail in order not to interfere in any manner with the activities of the agencies of the United States Government concerned'.[57]

Chevalier, summoned before the California Senate Fact-Finding Committee on Un-American Activities on 7 November, had denied the charge. In his own words, he 'did not approach Dr Oppenheimer in order to obtain information of any kind ... but merely related to him a conversation I had had with Mr Eltenton ... Dr Oppenheimer immediately dismissed the subject. That was all there was to it.' His denial made no difference. On 28 September 1948 the Un-American Activities Committee in Washington issued a report in which it said, among other things, that Oppenheimer 'declined to cooperate with Eltenton in the attempt to secure information regarding the atomic bomb and told Chevalier that he considered such acts or such attempts to obtain information on this subject as constituting treason'. There was no reaction from Oppenheimer.[58]

On 7 June 1949, however, during his appearance before the Committee, Oppenheimer gave the version of the incident which he subsequently claimed to be the truth. Chevalier, he said, had been 'terribly disturbed' over his talk with Eltenton, and he had come to Oppenheimer 'clearly embarrassed and confused'. 'I, in violent terms, told him not to be confused and to have no connection with it. He did not ask me for information.' These remarks, like Oppenheimer's simultaneous comments on Peters, leaked to the Press and early in 1950 Chevalier learned about them. On 21 February he wrote to Oppenheimer to get his confirmation. Oppenheimer replied that he had said that, as far as he was aware, Chevalier had known nothing about the bomb until after Hiroshima. Moreover, 'I said that you had never asked me to transmit any kind of information, nor suggested that I could do so, or that I consider doing so. I said that you had told me of a discussion of providing technical information to the USSR which disturbed you considerably, and which you thought I ought to know about.' Although he wrote that he had been 'deeply disturbed by the threat to your career which these ugly stories could constitute', he did not explain why he had so far neglected to publicize his concern.[59]

However, Oppenheimer *had* come to Chevalier's aid, and he did so again in the autumn of 1950. During the summer Chevalier's marriage had broken up, and in October he spent two weekends with the Oppenheimers at Princeton pouring out his troubles. By this time, Chevalier had decided to leave America and settle in France, but he was experiencing great difficulty in getting a United States passport (this, it should be remembered, was a moment when anti-Communist discrimination was reaching unprecedented heights). Oppenheimer recommended a Washington lawyer, Joseph Fanelli, and Chevalier also used Oppenheimer's letter of February to further his application. It was to no avail, and he was compelled in the end to get a French passport—to which he was entitled by virtue of the fact that his father was French—and with it he left the country on 2 November.[60] Oppenheimer and he were not to meet again for more than three years.

In the autumn of 1953 Oppenheimer came to London to record the Reith Lectures for the British Broadcasting Corporation. According to Mrs Oppenheimer, Chevalier and his wife (he had re-married in 1952) had read about this and wrote to the Oppenheimers asking them to look them up if they should visit Paris where they were now living. She had telephoned to arrange a meeting, and on 7 December the reunion took place over dinner in the Chevaliers' flat in Montmartre.[61]

Once again, Oppenheimer's behaviour was held suspect. In one view, he even 'took the chance that, like many other nuclear scientists, he might have been forced at gun-point into a plane and taken behind the Iron Curtain'. This aspect of the visit did not emerge at the hearing, however. What did was the fact that Chevalier had once more asked Oppenheimer's aid in the continuing difficulties arising out of his political past. A great deal of his income came from translation work for UNESCO, but if he wished to go on with this work as an American citizen he would have to submit himself for investigation, and he was doubtful whether in the current atmosphere he would be granted clearance. One possible way of keeping his job was to renounce his American citizenship, but he did not want to do this. Oppenheimer's response was to give him the name of a Harvard classmate, Dr Jeffries Wyman, the science attaché at the Paris embassy. On 23 February 1954 Chevalier wrote to Wyman and on 1 March Wyman replied inviting him to lunch to discuss the problem.[62]

As will be seen, high significance was attached to the dealings between Chevalier and Oppenheimer from 1946, when they saw each other for the first time since Oppenheimer had left for Los Alamos, to 1953, the year of their last meeting. Yet by Chevalier's own reckoning, in all these years they came together only eight times, three times in 1946, twice in 1949, twice in 1950, and once in 1953. Moreover, if Mrs Oppenheimer is to be believed (and the AEC did not contradict her), between 1950 and 1953 Chevalier had written to them only three or four times. And it was unlikely that in 1953 Chevalier was active any longer in left-wing politics. He was, for instance, sufficiently well-acquainted with André Malraux to take the Oppenheimers to meet Malraux at his house in Boulogne-sur-Seine on 8 December, and although Malraux had been pro-Communist in the thirties, he was by then an ardent Gaullist. It is doubtful whether such a man would associate with a known Communist sympathizer. As for the fear that Oppenheimer might be kidnapped during his visit to Chevalier, he was well aware that he was shadowed wherever he went and that the secret service were close at hand in case of emergency.[63]

Nonetheless, Oppenheimer behaved with characteristic circumspection. He had recommended Wyman to Chevalier not as a confidential source of help (as Chevalier appeared to think), but in his capacity as a government official, 'because anything that was said would be reported to the Government and would be quite open'. Wyman himself, in an affidavit that was not, oddly enough, produced at the hearing, testified that neither at the time he met Oppenheimer in Paris nor later did Oppenheimer 'mention or endorse Chevalier'. Oppenheimer could not have done so when he saw Wyman since this was before his meeting with Chevalier, but it is significant that he took no positive action to follow up his reference. Finally, it is worth pointing out that although in his letter to Nichols he said that he still thought of Chevalier as a friend, and although he affirmed this early in the hearing, towards the close he maintained that their friendship was over (unlike his wife, who testified to the contrary the next day).[64]

This, then, was the case made out against Dr Oppenheimer on the grounds of past and continuing association with Communists, or rather, since a great deal of the classified FBI material remained undisclosed, that part of the case which the AEC chose to reveal. There may have been worse things in the FBI file, but if there were, then the AEC did not bring them out, and in the light of its overall conduct of the proceedings there can be no doubt that it would have done so without hesitation.

As Garrison pointed out at the very beginning of the hearing, the bulk of the charges in this part of the indictment dated from the years before 1945. A great many of these in turn made up the basis of the suspicions which formed around Dr Oppenheimer when he entered the atomic project in 1942. They had been discounted by General Groves when he issued his order for clearance in July 1943, but, as Groves himself testified, the exigencies of war had considerably influenced his decision and it could not be expected to stand once the war was over. As he wrote early in 1947, shortly after he relinquished command of the project and handed it over to the Atomic Energy Commission, he did not believe that everyone he had cleared was automatically to be cleared by the Commission. Indeed, at the end of 1946 he had urged the AEC to remove all the remaining employees taken on during the war despite the 'considerable doubt' hanging over them. Although Oppenheimer did not fall within this category since he had left the project in October 1945, if he had still been a member of the project, Groves would have placed him in it.[65]

Oppenheimer was not removed, but his case was periodically brought up for examination in the post-war years. It is in the nature of a security system that the status of government employees should be kept under frequent review, and Oppenheimer was no exception. Between November 1946 and July 1953 the issue of his clearance arose certainly on three occasions and probably on four, and in each instance clearance was recommended after a careful study of all the existing information in his dossier.

The first clearance is the one which is least well-documented. The only available reference to it comes from Mr Strauss, a member of the original Commission and its Chairman at the time of the hearing. One of the Commission's first tasks after its appointment on 28 October 1946 was to recommend nine men to the President as members of the General Advisory Committee provided for under Section 2 of the Atomic Energy Act. Their function was 'to advise the Commission on scientific and technical matters relating to materials, production, and research development'. Oppenheimer was among those whose names were submitted to Truman on 9 December, but not before all five Commissioners had reviewed his file and taken into consideration Groves' warning about the doubtful cases he had engaged during the war. It was almost certainly on the basis of this review that the Commission authorized formal clearance for Oppenheimer in February 1947.[66]

This, however, was only the prelude to a furore in which Oppenheimer's entire future as a government adviser was once again placed in question almost immediately after it appeared to have been settled. The backdrop to this was the Senate hearing to confirm Truman's nomination of the commissioners, and particularly of the Chairman, David E. Lilienthal. Lilienthal had come to the AEC after more than thirteen years as director of the Tennessee Valley Authority, a New Deal project set up during Roosevelt's 'First Hundred Days' in the spring of 1933. From the outset it had been one of the most controversial agencies of New Deal policy, claiming, as it did, to be the spearhead of a social revolution in the states in which its programmes operated. Lilienthal, as its chief, had become identified in the eyes of conservative critics of the New Deal (Democratic as well as Republican) as the archetype of the bureaucrat who would stop at nothing to extend governmental power. To them, he was a dangerous man who was paving the way for Socialism or even for Communism in the United States. As it worked in practice, the TVA was a good deal less radical than its opponents (or it itself) asserted. Nonetheless, Lilienthal was branded as a ruthless left-wing idealist, and it was to be expected that his enemies in Congress would do their utmost to deny him this new responsibility. He for his part was well aware what lay in store. As he confided to his diary shortly after the appointment as AEC Chairman, 'the throat-slitters will soon be at us in volume'.[67]

Lilienthal was not mistaken. Bitter attacks were launched on him as soon as the confirmation hearing opened on 27 January 1947, and they were not confined to him alone. Not content with being head of the AEC, it was said, he was bent on filling it with officials and advisers of a similar political persuasion. Among them was Oppenheimer.

Oppenheimer was not mentioned by name, but on 6 March the complaint was raised that various men with left-wing backgrounds had been given influential positions, and 'someone else had a brother who was a Communist'. FBI reports on the people in question were, apparently, being discussed in secret session, and there was a distinct possibility that the subject might be leaked to the press. On Saturday, 8 March, Lilienthal was telephoned with the news that J. Edgar Hoover, the FBI director, had sent over two short summary memoranda prepared by his staff, one on Oppenheimer and one on his brother Frank.[68]

Why had Oppenheimer's reliability been put in doubt again so soon? Lilienthal's immediate reaction was to wonder whether Hoover's initiative was part of a 'scare campaign' designed to undermine him by discrediting his advisers. At the hearing, however, he did not speak of this possibility but said he assumed that it was taken in accordance with the routine prescribed by the Atomic Energy Act. Section 10 of the Act stated that no one was to be employed by the Commission until the FBI had investigated his character, loyalty and associations and reported to the Commission on them. Pending such a report any clearance given during the war would continue to obtain. The files on war-time personnel had been transferred to the FBI at about the time of the passage of the Act on 1 August 1946. Oppenheimer's dossier had therefore been in Hoover's possession for seven months and he had not previously drawn the information in it to Lilienthal's notice. The mandatory investigation would surely have taken place earlier than this, and the obvious time for a report to be transmitted would have been November 1946 when the Commission was considering Oppenheimer for the General Advisory Committee. One can say no more than that the co-incidence in timing between the veiled allegations in the Senate and Hoover's report to Lilienthal is extraordinary.[69]

Whatever the truth of the matter, it is clear that certain figures in the United States government were gravely suspicious of Oppenheimer's trustworthiness. At least one other was not. On the very day the FBI sent across its reports the Under Secretary of State, Dean Acheson, was showing Oppenheimer the latest draft of the President's epochal speech on the Truman Doctrine, which four days later formally committed America to the Cold War with Russia. Moreover, Oppenheimer had just flown to Washington from San Francisco to urge the government to break off negotiations with the Soviet Union over the international control of atomic energy. To go on negotiating, as Oppenheimer saw it, would 'give the Soviets chances to stall, to seek com-promises that would dilute the strength of the [American] plan without yielding their own position, and to win propaganda victories'. As Frederick H. Osborn, Oppenheimer's political superior on the UN Atomic Energy Commission, recollected it, Oppenheimer had been certain the Russians had no intention of accepting international control, since to do so would mean they had to lift the Iron Curtain and that in turn would entail the end of the régime. He was also concerned that the United States might accept an agreement which included the prohibition of atomic weapons (in other words, the cancellation of the advantage of its nuclear monopoly) without getting any comparable concession in return—such as the breakdown of Russia's closed society. Oppenheimer's advice was overridden, but he stayed on as consultant; as Osborn pointed out, 'this is not always the case when you cross a man at the beginning'.[70]

Both this loyalty and the recommendation Oppenheimer had

put forward were scarcely consonant with the idea that he was in league with Communism. Those who claimed he was were either out of touch with reality or utterly careless of it, but they had succeeded in setting the machinery of the security system in motion and there was no alternative to carrying through the fullest possible inquiry.

There can be no doubt that the inquiry was undertaken with extreme thoroughness. On 10 and 11 March, for example, the Commission met to discuss the case no less than four times. In the morning of 10 March each of the Commissioners read the summaries and noted that they gave an incomplete account which 'either . . . did not reflect the results of a full investigation or did not contain all information bearing on the matter'. What was there could 'seriously impeach' Oppenheimer, however, and it was decided to bring in Bush and Conant, who had both been closely associated with him during the war.[71]

At the end of the meeting Lilienthal telephoned Bush, who had already had wind of the FBI's action. He told Lilienthal that 'he and General Groves had known all about that [Oppenheimer's left-wing background], had decided it was no reason not to use the man, and had never regretted it'. At the second AEC meeting that afternoon, Bush reiterated this view, and he was joined in his opinion by Conant, who, although he had not seen Oppenheimer's file, considered that his record of service since 1942 cancelled out whatever was in it. It was unanimously agreed that Oppenheimer was so valuable to the atomic energy programme that his dismissal would not only be 'a very serious blow to our progress in this field' but would also trigger off a hostile reaction among his colleagues upon whom the success of the programme ultimately depended. Even the disclosure of any of the information in the dossier, or of the fact that it existed, would be likely to produce uproar in the scientific community. This was not to mention the probability of a contrary but equally violent response from the general public. As one of the Deputy General Counsel to the Commission, Joseph A. Volpe, Jr, remarked to Commissioner Strauss, 'if anyone were to print all the stuff in this file and say it is about the top civilian adviser to the Atomic Energy Commission, there would be terrible trouble. His background is awful.'[72]

On 11 March the AEC met yet again and came to some

preliminary conclusions. First, Oppenheimer's loyalty was 'prima facie clear' in spite of the evidence in the FBI summary. Second, he was probably now the best-informed scientist in the country as far as atomic secrets were concerned. Third, while there is no immediate danger to security, a complete evaluation of the case was essential so that a final decision might be reached quickly. As a first step towards this, Bush, Conant and Groves were to be asked to give their views on Oppenheimer in writing. Secondly, since Oppenheimer was a presidential appointee, Lilienthal and Bush were to confer with the White House with a view to having a board of jurists set up to make the evaluation. This latter approach was adopted as the result of a proposal by Herbert S. Marks, the Commission's General Counsel and in 1954 one of Oppenheimer's team of lawyers.[73]

In the afternoon of 11 March Lilienthal and Bush met at the White House with Truman's special counsel, Clark Clifford, who said that he would place the suggestion for a review board before the President and report back to them the following day. Their discussion was retailed to the Commission at five o'clock the same day, and the AEC waited for the presidential response. There was none. Unlike Eisenhower in December 1953, Truman took no action. In a telephone conversation with Lilienthal on the morning of 12 March, Clifford said that he had put the issue to Truman and that Truman was thinking it over; nothing further came of it, however. One possible reason is that Truman was preoccupied with the details of the momentous policy change —the Truman Doctrine—announced that very day, and had no time to spare for anything else. Another is that he did not consider the case of sufficient importance to justify his intervention, and this is certainly the impression which Clifford gave over the 'phone. Whatever his motive, he did nothing.[74]

By this time, Lilienthal was even more concerned about the episode. His confirmation had still not come through after more than seven weeks of hearings, and he was convinced the country was on the verge of an anti-Communist witch-hunt. The Republicans had made security one of the main issues in the recent mid-term elections in November 1946, as the result of which they had seized control of both houses of Congress, and Truman had been compelled to forestall a Republican initiative by setting up a comprehensive loyalty programme covering all employees in the Executive branch. His Executive Order putting it into effect was issued on 21 March. The criterion for refusing employment was that 'reasonable grounds exist for belief that the person involved is disloyal to the Government of the United States'. This was generous as compared with the standards later used, but for Lilienthal it was a disaster. 'In effect,' he wrote in his diary, 'it makes service in the Government subject to the risk that some malevolent or crazy person may accuse you of being leftist. The accusation for most people, in the present temper of things, would be so injurious, however the hearings came out, that it might prejudice their chances of employment in the Government or elsewhere. In practical effect, the usual rule that men are presumed innocent until proved guilty is in reverse.' If applied to the atomic energy programme, as it seemed to have been applied in Oppenheimer's case, 'our position of leadership in science ... could be swept away by a wild nightmare of fear leading to drastic limitations on scientific men and standards of "personal clearance" that are impossible and that assume that scientists can function behind barbwire compounds.' This he was determined to prevent.[75]

Accordingly, on 25 March Lilienthal went to see Hoover with the aim of clarifying the situation and moving closer towards a decision. He was accompanied by the General Manager, Carroll L. Wilson, Volpe and the acting Security Officer, Thomas O. Jones. It was an important meeting, primarily because Hoover took a charitable view of the Oppenheimer brothers' background. Thus, he declared that there was no question of Frank Oppenheimer's 'undesirability', while 'in the case of J. Robert', although he 'may at one time have bordered upon the communistic, indications are that for some time he has steadily moved away from such a position'. Hoover's one reservation was extremely significant, namely, Oppenheimer's failure 'to report promptly and accurately what must have seemed to him an attempt at espionage in Berkeley'. In other words, he believed that Oppenheimer had lied to security in 1943 (and not in 1946), and yet he was, apparently, ready to allow his clearance to go forward. Technically, of course, Hoover was the head of an agency which merely collected and distributed information on suspected persons, and did not evaluate it, but there can be little doubt that his opinion counted for a very great deal and if he had felt very strongly that clearance must be denied to Oppenheimer he would almost certainly have said so.[76]

The Commission therefore felt able to continue the clearance it had already authorized, and Lilienthal no doubt thought himself in a stronger position to do so after his confirmation was given by the Senate on 9 April, more than ten weeks after the hearings had opened. The actual decision was not recorded until 6 August. The delay may be accounted for by the fact that the AEC was in a state of administrative chaos, starting from scratch in a multitude of fields and groping its way through to established procedures. Security was no exception to this situation, and in the absence of the highly formalized security system which came into being shortly afterwards, the main load in clearance cases fell on the five Commissioners themselves, and they were grievously overburdened as it was. It does not seem to have been until 18 July that the Assistant General Manager noticed that the Commission had not come to a final decision, but it was reached soon after that. Throughout the last week of July and the first week of August, Lilienthal and his colleagues wrestled with more than a dozen of the most intractable cases bequeathed to them by Groves, and among them was Oppenheimer's.[77]

Lilienthal hated what he was called on to do. As he wrote in his diary:

> This afternoon's [meeting] was punishing as hell. And again, the worst part of the job, in wear and tear on the soul: the passing on FBI reports about people. There is an accumulation of these, men and women who were in the Manhattan District and who have been reinvestigated. There are really no cases of 'disloyalty'. These are usually cases of people who have a mother or a brother or wife who is, or is reputed to be, a Communist or the equivalent, and the 'evidence' to confirm these conclusions is only some FBI agent's rendition of what someone has said, or a conclusion from some very flimsy, thin stuff indeed. And so we sweat and agonize about the injustice to these people by such a travesty as our examination of these files must be. And against this is the risk that some of these people may indeed turn very bad or that the whole project will be badly hurt by ballyhoo and prejudice

aroused over these cases if we 'clear' them; or by a feeling that we are spending too much time and energy on such matters because of our concern about individual justice, while the major interest committed to us suffers—as indeed it already has.

He was, however, reassured to see how 'humane, balanced, decent, sensible' his four colleagues were in this trying situation. Clearly, they had gone into the problem as thoroughly as anyone could have expected. Most of the cases they considered did not pass this exhaustive test. Oppenheimer's did, and with the confirmation of clearance on 6 August he was through yet another major crisis in his career.[78]

The third and fourth clearances were minor affairs compared with the second, but they were nonetheless significant and they were based on much the same evidence. The third clearance took place in 1950, and it came about as follows. On 9 May 1950 a Mrs Paul Crouch testified before the California Senate Fact-Finding Committee on Un-American Activities in Oakland. In July 1941, she said, she had attended a closed meeting of a special section of the Communist Party at which her husband had explained changes made in the party line following the German invasion of the USSR in June. The house where the meeting was held was 10 Kenilworth Court, Berkeley, and Oppenheimer's name entered into the situation because this was a house which he had leased for a year from a colleague at the university. Moreover, he had not only allowed the Party to use the house, but, according to Mrs Crouch, he was present at the meeting together with Weinberg (she identified them later from photographs). Subsequently, she saw them both at social gatherings arranged by the Party.[79]

Oppenheimer had already been questioned by the FBI shortly before Mrs Crouch's allegation, and so he was forewarned. His denial was issued to the press the same day. It ran as follows: 'I have never been a member of the Communist Party. I never assembled any such group of people for any such purpose in my home or anywhere else. I am unable to recall any gathering in my house that could reasonably have been mistaken for such a meeting. Neither the name Crouch nor the accounts of Mr and

Mrs Crouch recall to me anyone I have ever known.' This he repeated at the hearing.[80]

Still the accusation persisted. On 10 May Mr Crouch explained just what the meeting signified. The special section, he pointed out, consisted of people whose identity had to be protected, that is, public office-holders, professional men, academics, employees of the Radiation Laboratory and those working for the Shell Development Company. It was, in short, 'a secret, closed meeting of top ranking Party members', and no one with a knowledge of the Chevalier incident could fail to notice the juxtaposition of the university, the Radiation Laboratory and the Shell Development Company. Nor could he fail to suspect that Oppenheimer had been deeply involved in the espionage said to have been fomented there.[81]

Oppenheimer was thus placed in an extremely bad light and he had been given no advance opportunity to defend himself. The interview with the FBI had taken place only a few days before the Crouchs' appearance, and the Committee had given him no warning of what they were going to say. Nor was he invited to tender an affidavit which could be produced as soon as they had testified. Nor was he asked to come and appear himself until after the allegations had been made, and his failure to do so could easily be construed as an unwillingness to confront his accusers.[82]

It is clear that the object of this episode was to damage Oppenheimer, but it did not produce the intended effect. On 12 May the San Francisco *Chronicle* condemned 'the careless spreading of confusion and distrust through the undermining of confidence in those in whom we have placed the utmost trust, and for the soundest reason'. The previous day Representative Richard M. Nixon, who, as a member of the Un-American Activities Committee in Washington, was well-acquainted with Oppenheimer's background, stated that he was 'convinced that Dr Oppenheimer has been and is a completely loyal American and further, one to whom the United States owe a great debt of gratitude for his tireless and magnificent job in atomic research'. On 18 May General Groves sent him a letter incorporating a statement of confidence which he was free to make public 'if at any time you should feel that it were wise'.[83]

At the same time, the matter was brought to the attention of

Gordon Dean, Lilienthal's successor as AEC Chairman. Dean at once instructed Volpe, now General Counsel, to talk to Oppenheimer about the incident. Volpe reported back that Oppenheimer denied that such a meeting had ever taken place, and Oppenheimer himself repeated this when Dean asked him to discuss the incident with him. Prior to this confrontation Dean had gone through Oppenheimer's file in person, and on the strength of his review and of the discussion he concluded that Oppenheimer was loyal. Moreover, in Dean's opinion, he was not a security risk: if he had considered him a risk, said Dean, when he testified, he would have initiated a hearing such as the one in process. But he had not, and none of the subsequent FBI reports which had come in up to the time of his resignation in July 1953—and which he had specifically demanded to see— had done anything to shake his confidence in Oppenheimer.[84]

The last recommendation for clearance came less than a fortnight after Dean's departure from the Commission. It was made by Walter G. Whitman, then special assistant to the Secretary of Defense for research and development. Whitman had known Oppenheimer well for some three years, both as a colleague on the General Advisory Committee and as chairman of the Research and Development Board at the Pentagon. Oppenheimer had served on the Board's Committee on Atomic Energy since 1947, and it was this appointment which was under review.[85]

Whitman's examination of Oppenheimer's file (or rather of a long FBI summary of the material therein) was made on 11 July 1953, and it used the more stringent security criteria established by President Eisenhower's Executive Order of 27 April (see pp 26-28). Even given these stricter terms of reference, and even on the assumption that all the derogatory information in the summary could have been true, Whitman concluded that Oppenheimer was not a security risk. He reached this conclusion 'rather prayerfully', as he put it, but he was ready to recommend without qualification that Oppenheimer be reappointed as a consultant to the Defense Department. His recommendation was upheld by a Pentagon security review board.[86]

In spite of the fact that these successive affirmations of Oppenheimer's loyalty had been made, however, there still remained a doubt as to the significance which should be attached to them in

1954. For in a security system the legal principle of double jeopardy does not apply. A man's integrity may be questioned not just twice but time after time, and on the basis of the same evidence. This Oppenheimer's lawyers were bound to admit, and when Gray raised the point during his summation Garrison agreed that the 1947 clearance, to which he attached the highest importance, in no way foreclosed the issue. Nonetheless, he believed it should carry great weight with the Board when it came to make its recommendations.[87]

A good deal, of course, depended on whether or not the conclusions reached on all these occasions had been derived from a survey of all the available evidence. Robb's purpose was to show they had not. Thus he tried to cast doubt on Dean's assertion that he had seen the complete file on Oppenheimer, while in the case of the 1947 clearance his questioning was directed towards establishing the impression that all the Commission had seen was the FBI summary and not the entire file. This did not, however, agree with the recollection of the three members of the 1947 Commission who testified at the hearing. Lilienthal remembered it as 'a very substantial file', 'a big file', 'a typical FBI personnel file'. Pike recalled 'a pretty thick file'. Bacher spoke of 'first a summary of information from the FBI, and later a quite voluminous file', 'a very much thicker file', 'a fairly thick document'. Moreover, a memorandum from Jones of 18 July 1947 transmitted 'a complete investigative file on J. Robert Oppenheimer' and stated that 'each Commissioner and the General Manager have seen every report in this file with the exception of a summary of July 17, and my memorandum for the file dated July 14, 1947'. Ironically enough, this was a document which Robb himself read into the record.[88]

Equally important was the nature of the 1947 clearance. Was the decision recorded on 6 August merely a retrospective formality, rectifying an omission from the minute-book and tidying up the record; or was it something much more significant? The AEC, to judge by its actions, was anxious to minimize the importance of what took place in 1947. Thus on 15 January 1954 it had given Garrison the following stipulation: 'On August 6, 1947, the Commission recorded clearance of Dr. J. Robert Oppenheimer, which it noted had been authorized in February 1947.' This had been perfectly acceptable, and it was read into the record when the hearing opened on 12 April. By 26 April, however, after Robb's questioning of Lilienthal, Pike and Bacher, Garrison's suspicions were aroused and he asked to see the minutes of the 6 August meeting. He was refused by Robb's assistant, Rolander, but Gray agreed to forward the request to the Commission, and on 28 April the full text of the minutes relating to the clearance was produced. It read:

> Mr Belsley called the Commission's attention to the fact that the Commission's decision to authorize the clearance of J. R. Oppenheimer, chairman of the General Advisory Committee, made in February 1947, had not previously been recorded. The Commission directed the secretary to record the Commission's approval of security clearance in this case and to note that further reports concerning Dr Oppenheimer since that date had contained no information which would warrant reconsideration of the Commission's decision.

As Garrison was quick to point out, the stipulation had given a totally misleading impression of what actually happened in 1947. It had, indeed, done nothing less than conceal the whole sequence of events touched off by Hoover's transmission of the FBI summaries on 8 March. Above all, it had obliterated the fact that the Commission had come to its decision on 6 August as the result of exhaustive inquiry into the Oppenheimer file. So far as the stipulation was concerned that inquiry might never have taken place.[89]

To make the picture of the 1947 situation clear beyond doubt Garrison was concerned to know still more. He had already (on 20 April) asked for a copy of the FBI summaries sent on 8 March 1947 and been refused on the grounds that they were FBI documents and therefore might not be disclosed to Oppenheimer or his counsel. On 30 April he tried again. In the first instance, he asked for a list of the items of derogatory information taken into account by the Commission in 1947, and then, when this was refused by Gray, he asked to be told which of the items before the Board had been considered by the Commission. This request too was turned down, and Garrison remained in the dark.[90]

So too, apparently, did Gray. Several times during the hearing Gray had spoken of the difficulty he felt in grasping exactly what had happened in 1947. For one thing, thanks to Robb's skilful obfuscation, he was not sure whether or not the full FBI file had indeed been reviewed, although the evidence on that score was plain enough. For another, he did not even seem to think that clearance had actually been granted. Right at the very end of the hearing he observed that 'it is not yet clear to the board that the full file was before the Commission in 1947', and during Garrison's summation he revealed his uncertainty over the issue of the clearance itself in his remark that Garrison was prepared to argue it was clearly established (he, by implication, was not). Thus one of the most telling points in Garrison's case for the defence was nullified, and Oppenheimer suffered accordingly.[91]

The debate over the past clearances was closely related to the argument over the significance of Oppenheimer's political associations as a whole. Here, there were several issues to be considered. In the first place, as Gray asked Rabi, was security relative or absolute? In other words, was what was acceptable in, say, 1943, necessarily unacceptable in 1954? His question was put in relation to the Chevalier incident, which had by this time emerged as the touchstone of Oppenheimer's trustworthiness. Naturally, all of the defence witnesses stressed its uniqueness. Rabi believed that while it had been 'a great mistake in judgment' and 'a very foolish action', he would not 'put a sinister implication to it' and he was confident that Oppenheimer would not repeat his error. For Lilienthal it was 'the only thing ... in the whole record ... that would give the gravest concern'; Lansdale considered that this was the only occasion when Oppenheimer had lied to security personnel. To Conant the incident 'stood by itself' and there was no question that Oppenheimer continued to have divided loyalties. On the other hand, the suspicion obviously lingered in Gray's mind that Chevalier had continued to influence Oppenheimer's actions, and no account seemed to have been taken of the fact that in December 1943 Oppenheimer had lied not to save Chevalier but to damn him; if he had saved anyone then, it was himself.[92]

The incident crystallized the broader controversy over this question, and once again Oppenheimer's witnesses took the view that his left-wing politics were only an episode in an evolving career. As Lansdale, the most eloquent exponent of this view, put it: 'I have never ... adopted the assumption, once a Communist sympathizer, always a Communist sympathizer.... It would be a terrible mistake to assume that, once having had sinister associations, a man was forever thereafter damned.' This could lead, as Lansdale had already pointed out, to the dangerous habit of 'looking at events that transpired in 1940 and prior in the light of present feeling rather than in the light of feeling existing then'. 'You can hardly put your finger on a scientist or a university professor or people who tend to get into civic affairs, you can hardly find one anywhere who is now in his fifties or so that has not been on at least one list of an association which was later determined to be subversive or have leanings that way.' Moving from the thirties to the war years he pointed out that no less a personage than Mrs Roosevelt had insisted that known Communists be given Army commissions, and he could have also mentioned the fact that during the war the Civil Service Commission had forbidden inquiry into many left-wing organizations, including some Oppenheimer himself had contributed to, such as the Spanish Relief groups and the Harry Bridges Defense Committee. Yet, as Gray remarked, the Board was bound by its regulations to take all these associations into account and could not set them on one side.[93]

A further consideration, in the opinion of a good many pro-Oppenheimer witnesses was the stature of the individual concerned. Here, the argument was most forcefully taken up by Kennan. 'It seems to me', said Kennan, 'that the exceptional people are often apt not to fit into any categories of requirements that it is easy to write into an act or a series of loyalty regulations.' The background of such people should not therefore be given too much weight. 'Had the Church applied to St Francis the criteria relating solely to his youth, it would not have been able for him to be what he was later ... it is only the great sinners who become the great saints'. There was a need for considerable flexibility in judging both the individual and his relationships. 'I suppose most of us have had friends or associates whom we have come to regard as misguided with the course of time, and I don't like to think that people in senior capacity in Government should not be permitted or conceded maturity of judgment to know when they can see such a person or when they can't.' This, of course, was open to the criticism that it brought a double standard into operation, and Evans reminded Kennan that the Atomic Energy Act (by which the Board was bound) said nothing about outstanding ability. Gray, for his part, asked Kennan whether the gifted man he postulated could ever 'reach a stability on the basis of which there can be absolute predictability as to no further excursions', and though Kennan maintained that there could be enough predictability to warrant government employment, the form of Gray's question indicated that he was looking for more than this.[94]

The question of high ability was related to the issue of what weight should, or could, be given to a man's service to the country. Of all Oppenheimer's witnesses, it was, perhaps, Rabi who raised the point most graphically. During wartime and in the post-war years Oppenheimer had established a 'real positive record'. His achievement was 'tremendous' and so, he asked the Board, 'what more do you want, mermaids?' DuBridge later agreed. Oppenheimer's early associations were 'quite irrelevant' in view of his subsequent 'devoted interest to the welfare, security and strength of the United States'.[95]

This again was one of the major elements in Garrison's case for the defence, and he emphasized it on two notable occasions. In the first instance he drew the Board's attention to the wording of the opening passage of the AEC Criteria for Determining Eligibility. Here, it was stated that among the things to be borne in mind were the individual's 'past association with the Atomic Energy program, and the nature of the job he is expected to perform'; 'the judgment of responsible persons [that is, witnesses] as to [his] integrity'; 'all the information presented whether favorable or unfavorable'; and the need to balance 'the cost to the program of not having his services against any possible risks involved'. The second reminder came as Garrison finished his examination of McCloy, who had claimed that there two sides to security, positive as well as negative. Even if Oppenheimer's past connections had been dubious, 'you have to balance his affirmative aspect against that, before you can finally conclude in your own mind that he is a reasonable security risk'.[96]

The Board, and counsel for the AEC, took a very different view. Garrison's first reading of the Criteria was allowed to pass unchallenged, but his second reading was not. Robb immediately pointed out that the passage in question referred to the decision to be made by the General Manager and not to the recommendation to be made by the Board. It was purely 'an administrative matter in determining whether the subject is to be kept on'. This was, to say the least, an extremely narrow and legalistic interpretation, and it was rebutted by Section 4.16 of the Security Clearance Procedures which, among other things, enjoined the board to 'carefully consider... the standards set forth in "AEC Personnel Security Clearance Criteria for Determining Eligibility".' Garrison had had made this point already, but after Robb's intervention, Gray told McCloy that 'the discussion you have is by no means conclusive as to the duties of this board'. 'That', Robb remarked, 'is all I wanted to point out.'[97]

Gray, indeed, appeared to take the view that it was the duty of the Board to consider only the unfavourable aspects of Oppenheimer's past, and Garrison's first citation of the Criteria was prompted by Gray's reading of extracts from Category A to one of Oppenheimer's witnesses, Harry A. Winne. These were Number 1, relating to espionage, Number 3, relating to membership of subversive organizations, and Number 6, concerning the violation or disregard of security regulations. Gray seemed here to be making the point that a finding against Oppenheimer on any of these counts would place him in the category of security risk, although Garrison reminded him that it would only establish a presumption of risk which could, in his view (the Criteria did not say so) be rebutted by other evidence.

Time and again, moreover, Gray stressed the importance of the procedures which governed the Board, and made it clear that he gave them priority over the testimony of Oppenheimer's witnesses. 'There has been an inclination to be impatient with procedures and regulations and things of that sort', he observed, and asserted that 'men of great stature and eminence ... have been inclined to treat very lightly these matters which we have been discussing here, I think with sincerity and conviction, on the ground that what they think they know of Dr Oppenheimer ... washes out anything that happened in the past.' His position was perhaps best summed up in the question he put to McCloy, namely, 'when the paramount concern is the security of the country ... can you allow yourself to entertain reasonable doubts?'[98]

In the face of such an attitude of mind it was extremely

difficult for Oppenheimer's counsel to minimize the significance of the associations. The difficulty was aggravated, however, by the strategy they adopted. As has already been indicated, this was to devote comparatively little attention to the associations and instead to concentrate attention on Oppenheimer's record of achievement since 1942. Thus, almost half the references to associations volunteered by Oppenheimer were contained in his letter of 4 March 1954 and Garrison pointed out at the start that this represented about all they had to say on the matter. More was, in fact, added during Garrison's questioning of Oppenheimer, but this amounted to no more than 7 out of a total of 59 pages in the transcript. Similarly, only 4 out of the 19 pages of Garrison's summation covered the issue, and only 25 of the 128 pages of his brief submitted to the Board on 17 May.[99]

Garrison was right to point out in this brief the salient features of Oppenheimer's previous associations. These were first that they were all formed in the years 1936–41 and that few remained in being (those with his brother and his sister-in-law, with Chevalier, and with the physicists Serber and Morrison). In the second place, they only represented a fraction of his total relationships, and in the third place, they must be seen in the light of a personal evolution from the unconstrained atmosphere of Berkeley to the climate of power and responsibility in Los Alamos and Washington; during that evolution he had been learning all the time.[100]

What he should also have done, however, was to examine Oppenheimer's relationship to Communism closely and to demonstrate its essential innocence. DuBridge had pointed out that Oppenheimer's political involvement in the 'thirties sprang from deep humanitarian concern and not from anything that could be described as treasonable. As Oppenheimer himself had said of his activity in an interview published in November 1948 : 'I'm not ashamed of it; I'm more ashamed of the lateness. Most of what I believed then now seems complete nonsense, but it was an essential part of becoming a whole man. If it hadn't been for this late but indispensable education, I couldn't have done the job at Los Alamos at all.'[101]

Equally, he could have brought out Oppenheimer's post-war anti-Communism more tellingly by summoning witnesses whose loyalties were still to the left than, as he did, by invoking the testimony of men who themselves were resolutely anti-Communist. Chevalier or Lomanitz or Peters would almost certainly have indicated their distaste for Oppenheimer's post-war alignment and this would in turn have created a powerful impression. Yet such a bold stroke was beyond Oppenheimer's team. So too was the readiness to focus in depth on the associations of the Berkeley period.

This meant, however, that the ground was left for the prosecution to take, and Robb exploited his advantage to the full. It is worth pointing out that of the 114 pages of the transcript given to his cross-examination of Oppenheimer no less than 92 are taken up with the issue of the associations. The result was to remove any possibility that Oppenheimer would be given the benefit of the doubt as far as his past was concerned. If Garrison had covered the subject with the same thoroughness, this would most likely not have happened.

In this situation Oppenheimer did little or nothing to help himself, moreover. During his questioning by Garrison, the general tone of his replies was easy and confident, as might be expected. Robb's progressive revelation of what he himself described as 'a long record of folly' seemed to undermine him, however. This is very understandable. It must have been unnerving to be faced continually with proof that his prosecutor knew more about his past than he could possibly remember, down to the smallest detail. It is almost as though Robb had seized control of his identity, and nothing can be more psychologically damaging than that. Particularly eerie must have been the experience of listening to the sound of his own voice, recorded more than a decade before in the security office at Berkeley during his interview with Pash and Johnson.[102]

The deterioration produced in him was marked. As Robb remembered, 'it turned out that Oppenheimer was his own worst witness' and in the celebrated reply 'Because I was an idiot', he was convinced that Oppenheimer had destroyed himself. In the words of one commentator, Oppenheimer 'made it too easy for Robb'. Chevalier gained a similar impression from his reading of the transcript. Oppenheimer came out of it as 'hesitant by turns. There is no trace of the strong personality, the commanding intellect, the assertive will. He has become limp and docile.'[103]

This was not the man he had known, a towering figure, the natural centre of every circle he had moved in. In September 1954, some months after the hearing ended, he discussed Oppenheimer's performance with Malraux. In Malraux's view, Oppenheimer should have refused categorically to answer questions about his political background, and should have stood resolutely on the ground that he was the builder of the atomic bomb. He had been trapped because he accepted the prosecution's terms of reference and had consistently allowed them to retain the initiative. Oppenheimer's diffidence is intelligible, given the fact that the raging hysteria of McCarthyism had still not been quelled, but it was a crucial flaw in his defence. He was equally vulnerable on the issue of the hydrogen bomb, to which we now turn.[104]

Chapter Four

The Hydrogen Bomb

The second part of Nichols' allegations turned on Oppenheimer's attitude to the hydrogen bomb. In so far as we know it—and there is still a great deal that has not been disclosed—the story of the bomb and of Oppenheimer's relationship to it is as follows.

The possibility of bringing about an explosive reaction through the thermonuclear fusion of the heavier isotopes of hydrogen, deuterium and tritium, was first discovered by a group of theoreticians which met under Oppenheimer's direction at Berkeley in June 1942. Such a reaction would be much more powerful than nuclear fission, so much so, indeed that when the group dispersed in July Oppenheimer made a special journey to Michigan to give the news to Arthur H. Compton, his immediate superior on the project.[1]

When the Los Alamos Laboratory was set up in March 1943, work on thermonuclear reactions went ahead side by side with work on the atomic bomb. As Oppenheimer himself pointed out at the hearing, one of the first projects started there was the measurement of the properties of tritium. Among those scientists most interested was Luis Alvarez, who testified that Oppenheimer had used the possibility of thermonuclear work as 'the primary incentive' to persuade him to come to Los Alamos. But the man who quickly emerged as the leading figure in the field was Edward Teller. Teller had participated in the Berkeley conference in the summer of 1942 (after Oppenheimer had interceded to have him cleared), and he went on with his calculations at Los Alamos. In fact, he became so preoccupied with them that he refused to cooperate on the work on the atomic bomb, according to Hans Bethe, the head of the Theoretical Division. As Bethe pointed out, this was a considerable blow to the programme since there were very few men sufficiently qualified to take Teller's place. However, there was no alternative but to allow him and his group to pursue their own research entirely independently of the main line of development.[2]

Teller and his apologists have presented the situation somewhat differently. The authors of the book, *The Hydrogen Bomb,* for instance, have said that 'because Oppenheimer did not like him personally—a fact that was perhaps traceable to their differing political views—Teller was denied a special job in connexion with the development of the atomic bomb'. Teller himself has stated that it was only at Oppenheimer's urging that he stuck to thermonuclear work, since 'every one of us considered the present war and the completion of the A-bomb as the problems to which we wanted to contribute most'.[3]

Teller here was speaking of the moment in February 1944 when it became clear that the difficulties of reaching the stellar temperatures necessary for the fusion of deuterium—some 400 million degrees!—were so great that the hydrogen weapon had to be ruled out as a wartime possibility. The atom bomb, on the other hand, was now known to be feasible and quantities of uranium 235 were beginning to come in from the production centre in Tennessee. Even so, Teller maintained, Oppenheimer and others 'continued to say that the job at Los Alamos would not be complete if we should remain in doubt whether or not a thermonuclear bomb was feasible'.[4]

Teller's assertion is borne out by two letters from Oppenheimer to Richard C. Tolman, one of Groves' two chief scientific advisers. In the first letter of 20 September 1944 he recommended that once the war was over, 'the subject of initiating violent thermonuclear reactions be pursued with vigor and diligence, and promptly'. In the second, dated 4 October 1944, he argued that 'no government can adequately fulfill its responsibilities as custodian if it rests upon the wartime achievements of this project, however great they may temporarily seem, to insure future mastery in this field'.[5]

Yet in view of the problems encountered at Los Alamos, how long would it take before a hydrogen weapon was proved feasible? Bush and Conant in a memorandum sent to the Secretary of War, Stimson, on 30 September 1944, spoke of it as 'not far in the future', and seven months later Oppenheimer estimated that it would take three years to develop. Oppenheimer's forecast was made at a meeting on 31 May 1945 of the so-called Interim

Committee of the War Department, set up earlier that month to consider a wide range of questions. Among them were the use of the atomic bomb against Japan, the future shape of the atomic energy programme in the United States, and the creation of an international atomic energy authority. Oppenheimer had been selected to sit on a scientific panel formed to advise the Committee, together with Arthur Compton, Lawrence and Fermi. On 16 June 1945 the panel issued three reports. As far as the atom bomb was concerned, it saw no acceptable alternative to its direct military use against Japan. On the issue of the hydrogen bomb, it expressed the belief that 'the subject of thermonuclear reactions among light nuclei is one of the most important that needs study. There is a reasonable presumption that with skillful research and development, fission bombs can be used to initiate the reactions of deuterium, tritium, and possibly other light nuclei.' Either in this report or in the more comprehensive prospectus which followed it in September came the phrase in Nichols' letter, namely, that 'there is a reasonable possibility that it [the hydrogen bomb] can be made'. This Oppenheimer accepted as a fair statement of his views at the time.[6]

It was at this juncture, according to the men who later became Oppenheimer's opponents on the hydrogen bomb issue, that he altered his views. Teller, their leader, testified that after the successful test of the first atom bomb at Alamogordo on 16 July, it was generally assumed at Los Alamos that thermonuclear development would be pushed 'in a vigorous fashion'. Very shortly after the dropping of the second and third bombs on Japan, however, this plan was changed, 'and to the best of my belief it was changed at least in good part because of the opinion of Dr Oppenheimer that this is not the time to pursue this program any further'. In a book published some years later, Teller was more precise. On the day of Hiroshima, he wrote, Oppenheimer 'told me he would not develop a hydrogen bomb' and before Nagasaki he 'made it clear to me that he would have nothing further to do with thermonuclear work'.[7]

Oppenheimer's version of events differs sharply from this. Some time between Alamogordo and Hiroshima, that is, between 16 July and 6 August, he saw Groves in Chicago and asked him how he felt about the hydrogen bomb programme. Groves replied that he was 'unclear whether his mandate and therefore mine extended to fiddling with this next project'. Shortly after the Japanese surrender on 15 August, the subject had come up again when Oppenheimer was in Washington. Groves said that he had been told by Byrnes, the Secretary of State, that 'with things as they were' the work at Los Alamos ought to go on. This account is supported by the official history of the Atomic Energy Commission, where Byrnes is described as taking a pessimistic view of future relations with Russia and as demanding that since an international agreement was not practicable, Oppenheimer 'and the rest of the gang should pursue their work [on the hydrogen weapon] full force'.[8]

Groves, however, while he believed that atomic bomb development should go ahead, differed when it came to the hydrogen bomb, and it was he, after all, who was still in charge of the atomic project. His reasons have been described by the chief historian at the AEC. Groves, in his words, 'was not willing to authorize new projects which would significantly commit the new Commission [the AEC-to-be]. Extensive research on a thermonuclear weapon surely would have done that.' This again is in line with what Oppenheimer said at his hearing. In other words, the decision rested with Groves and Groves alone. It was not determined by Oppenheimer, nor, apparently, was the question considered by the President, crucial as it was. So work on a hydrogen bomb programme was not begun, and there the matter lay until the Commission took over on 1 January 1947.[9]

The advocates of the H-bomb kept up their pressure nonetheless. In the autumn of 1945, at about the time when Oppenheimer was succeeded as director of Los Alamos by Norris E. Bradbury, Teller approached Bradbury. He told him that he wanted to stay on at the laboratory, but that he would do so only either if it would launch a series of fission weapons tests or if it would get a thorough investigation of the thermonuclear problem under way. But although Bradbury had on 1 October said that he was in favour of 'fundamental experiments' to see whether or not the hydrogen bomb was feasible, he told Teller that both of his suggested programmes were out of the question. In fact he was having his work cut out to hold Los Alamos together in the hectic demobilization which had begun as soon as the war was over. Oppenheimer, when approached in his turn, refused to support Teller's campaign. Teller and Alvarez may have been right when they said at the hearing that if work on the bomb had started on a large scale at the end of 1945 then the country would have had one in 1948, but it was not, and all they and their colleagues could do was to wait their opportunity.[10]

Meanwhile they went on trying. Early in 1946, for example, Teller went before Senator Brien McMahon's Special Committee on Atomic Energy to say that he was 'convinced that it will not be very difficult to construct atomic bombs which will dwarf the Hiroshima bomb in the same way that that bomb has dwarfed high explosives'. In April he managed to convene a conference at Los Alamos (attended, among others, by Klaus Fuchs) which aimed to show that a thermonuclear weapon was feasible, and a report was issued in June. But although the enthusiasts did not waver in their conviction that the bomb could be built given the necessary support, and although in September 1946 Teller suggested a new approach to the problem, the odds were heavily stacked against the project. For one thing, feasibility was a long way from being proved, and for another there was no sense of urgency when the country had a monopoly of the atomic bomb. So the Los Alamos studies on the H-bomb were severely curtailed and the research team there dwindled to a handful of dedicated men.[11]

This was the position when the Atomic Energy Commission took over in January 1947. Much of the responsibility for framing the Commission's policy fell on the General Advisory Committee, which immediately elected Oppenheimer as its chairman. The Committee faced two broad problems. First, it had to raise morale throughout the programme, and especially at Los Alamos, which, in the words of one of Oppenheimer's witnesses, 'was in a state where there was a real question as to whether or not it could survive'. Second, it had to lay out an order of priorities for future work. 'Without debate—I suppose with some melancholy,' Oppenheimer testified, 'we concluded that the principal job of the Commission was to provide atomic weapons and good atomic weapons and many atomic weapons.' By this he meant fission weapons.[12]

The emphasis laid on the fission programme signified a continued low status for work in the thermonuclear field. At its first business meeting on 2 February, the GAC agreed almost unanimously that the first aim of the AEC should be 'to revitalize

Los Alamos and accelerate weapon research, especially on thermonuclear models'. But the requirement for atomic bombs was overriding, particularly as the United States moved deeper into the Cold War. The encouragement given to the hydrogen bomb work at Los Alamos was only to the 'efforts which were then directed toward modest exploration of the super [the colloquial term for the H-bomb] and of thermonuclear systems'. Research into fusion went on, as one commentator has put it, 'only to the extent possible without interference with the main work'. Bradbury was exaggerating when he testified that 'interest continued after the war in a very active way'. In the words of Bethe, 'it was definitely a matter of very minor priority'.[13]

There were manifold reasons why this should have been so. First, there was the doubt as to feasibility. As Oppenheimer stated in his letter to Nichols, the GAC in 1947 and 1948 had to recognize 'the still extremely unclear status of the problem from the technical standpoint'. It was a situation where, as he later put it, 'the unknowns overwhelmed the knowns'. Second, as both Bethe and Bradbury pointed out, advances in the fusion field depended greatly on advances in fission, in the sense that a sophisticated atomic bomb was needed as the trigger for the thermonuclear reaction. In the late 1940s such atomic bombs were not available, so that even if the hydrogen weapon had been feasible (which it was not) it would still have had to wait on developments in the nuclear sphere. Third, thermonuclear success also depended, to a lesser but still to a significant extent, on the development of high-speed computers. Such a machine was the MANIAC (Mathematical Analyzer, Numerical Integrator and Computer), the brain-child of Oppenheimer's colleague at the Institute for Advanced Study, John von Neumann. But, as von Neumann and Bradbury indicated in their testimony, the MANIAC was only started in 1946 and not completed until 1951. Last, there was the fact that during the immediate post-war period, the armed forces had their hands more than full adapting to the atom bomb. As a senior Air Force officer, General McCormack, remarked at the hearing, the forces could not develop tactics suited to nuclear weapons until they had some idea of their characteristics. This was difficult enough in respect of the rapidly evolving atomic arsenal; it was impossible in the case of

1 Haakon Chevalier, the symbolic figure of Oppenheimer's pro-Communist period

2 The war years: Oppenheimer and General Groves congratulate each other at the site of the world's first atomic explosion, July 1945

3 Senator Bourke B. Hickenlooper, one of the most persistent critics of the AEC

4 The Lilienthal Commission answers Hickenlooper's charges of 'incredible mismanagement': (l to r) Lilienthal, Dean, Pike, Strauss (Smyth absent)

the unknown quantity which was the hydrogen bomb. There was, therefore, no military demand for it.[14]

Even so, the advocates of the H-bomb were convinced that there was more to it than this. Their leading spokesman at the hearing was Wendell M. Latimer, professor of chemistry at the University of California. In about 1947, Latimer testified, he became more and more certain that the Russians would not only get the atom bomb but that when they had got it, they would 'shoot immediately for the super weapon'. Latimer was right on this, as we now know. His other speculations were less intelligent. As it appeared to him, the American response to the probable Russian challenge was negligible. In his own words, 'we seemed to be twiddling our thumbs and doing nothing', making no progress in the production of fissionable materials, in uranium production, or in reactor development.[15]

These were grave charges, and they echoed almost exactly what Borden had had to say in his letter of 7 November 1953. But they were easily refutable, and this is no doubt why they were not put in Nichols' allegations the following month. As the Chairman of the AEC pointed out in 1968, there was an abundance of uranium 235 and plutonium in the period 1947–49. As for reactors, they were still in a primitive stage of development (like the hydrogen bomb, he might have said) and the breakthrough had not yet come.[16]

Latimer went even further than this, however. The cause of the trouble, in his opinion, was none other than Oppenheimer. Oppenheimer's influence was at work everywhere. Young scientists had returned to Berkeley from Los Alamos as 'pacifists', and 'it looked to me like a certain amount of indoctrination had taken place'. Oppenheimer had deployed 'various arguments' for not working on the hydrogen bomb; he had even 'wanted to disband Los Alamos'. Groves, it seemed to him, had been 'following the Oppenheimer line'; so too, later on, had the members of the General Advisory Committee. All told, it seemed clear that Oppenheimer was responsible for the 'inaction' of the immediate post-war years, and this caused Latimer 'considerable worry about his judgment as a security risk'.[17]

Latimer's appraisal of the atomic energy programme in the late forties corresponded only marginally with reality. One thing,

D

however, was certain: the hydrogen weapon was not considered to be of high importance. In the summer of 1949, however, this situation was transformed by an almost totally unexpected development. On 29 August 1949 the Soviet Union exploded its first atomic device.

It had, of course, been accepted that Russia would acquire a nuclear capability sooner or later, but few had believed it would happen so soon. Bethe and his colleague Frederick Seitz had predicted late in 1946 that 'any one of several determined foreign nations could duplicate our work in a period of about five years', but this was an exceptionally accurate forecast. Groves had said it would take at least twenty years for the Russians to accomplish the bomb, and the most usual estimate was in the region of ten years. As late as April 1948 Oppenheimer himself had ventured that Russian would not obtain 'a significant atomic armament ... for a long time to come'.[18]

The Russians had, in fact, been working on their project since the summer of 1942 under the direction of the nuclear physicist Kurchatov. They had achieved their first self-sustaining chain reaction on 25 December 1946, that is, four years after the Americans, and their rate of progress thereafter matched the American rate almost exactly. The United States had taken some two-and-a-half years from chain reaction to a fission explosion, and Russia's performance followed approximately the same time-scale.[19]

Evidence that a Soviet explosion might have taken place reached Washington during the first weekend in September. It came in the form of reports from an aircraft on patrol between Japan and Alaska and carrying filter papers to pick up signs of radioactivity. As yet, however, this evidence was by no means conclusive and it had to be submitted to a rigorous examination before it could be accepted. Accordingly, a scientific advisory panel was set up under the chairmanship of Dr Bush. Here again, the suspicions about Oppenheimer came into play, and it was at this point that the hostility of at least certain elements in the Air Force became manifest. As we shall see, that hostility was to be a prime factor in the development of the Oppenheimer case over the next four years.[20]

In the view of Oppenheimer's Air Force critics, he had shown a distinct lack of drive in respect of the programme for the long-range detection of a Soviet explosion. The man identified as the instigator of the programme was Lewis L. Strauss, then a member of the AEC. It was Strauss, according to a statement put out by the Joint Committee on Atomic Energy on 19 October 1951, who had brought it into being and 'averted the disaster that might have ensued had the United States remained ignorant of Russia's success'. This view was repeated some eighteen months later by Charles J. V. Murphy, a colonel in the Air Force Reserve. Strauss, wrote Murphy, had been disturbed that neither the AEC nor the military was using the various techniques available for surveillance, but at his insistence, the necessary action was taken.[21]

The position was not quite like this. At the close of the hearing, Oppenheimer described the support he had given to long-range detection as early as 1945, when the Hiroshima burst had been identified and described by flights made over the continental United States. His main critic at the hearing on this issue, General Roscoe C. Wilson, was, however, not aware of Oppenheimer's contribution. Nor, apparently, was General Hoyt S. Vandenberg, in September 1949 the Air Force Chief of Staff. According to Alvarez, Bush had told him that he thought he and not Oppenheimer had been appointed chairman of the assessment panel because President Truman did not trust Oppenheimer. Bush later denied this, but two days after a sworn affidavit from Lawrence was presented to the Board which stated that Bush had said that Vandenberg had insisted that he [Bush] must be chairman since he [Vandenberg] distrusted Oppenheimer. The solidity of this evidence was somewhat undermined by the fact that Robb's assistant, Rolander, had elicited it after Bush's testimony, but the feelings attributed to Vandenberg were certainly in line with what subsequently emerged as the official Air Force view on Oppenheimer and his activities.[22]

Whatever the truth of this episode, it was soon clear to the panel that the USSR had exploded an atomic device, if not a deliverable bomb. It was not so clear to Truman. To the end of his presidency, and beyond, Truman was convinced that what had happened was the accidental explosion of a plant producing radio-active materials, and less than a week after leaving office he declared publicly that he did not believe Russia had the atomic bomb. Therefore in his statement issued on 23 September

Truman spoke only of 'an atomic explosion', but his reference to the Washington Declaration of 15 November 1945, which had said that no nation could have a monopoly of atomic weapons, left the issue in little doubt.[23]

It was generally accepted, then, that the Soviet Union had become a nuclear power. The question then immediately arose: what was the American response to be? Truman himself appears to have had no doubts. As he wrote in his memoirs, 'I believed that anything that would assure us the lead in the field of atomic energy development for defense had to be tried out.' By this he meant the hydrogen bomb.[24]

A considerable number of people both in and out of government shared Truman's view. They included scientists such as Lawrence, Teller, Alvarez and Latimer; members of the Atomic Energy Commission such as Strauss and, later, Dean; the majority of the Joint Committee on Atomic Energy, notably its chairman Senator McMahon and its executive director William L. Borden; and military figures such as General Kenneth D. Nichols. These men were convinced that, as Latimer put it, 'the very existence of the country was involved and you can't take odds on such things'. The only possible answer in such circumstances was to manufacture a large number of thermonuclear weapons.[25]

The reasons advanced for the adoption of this policy were as follows. The critical factor was the demonstration that Russia possessed the atomic bomb and was therefore capable of using it as the trigger for a fusion reaction, if that were technically feasible. It was therefore held to be essential that it be proved whether or not fusion was possible. If not, then the world would be spared a weapon which promised to be unimaginably devastating. Also, or so Alvarez believed, the United States could preserve its lead over the USSR simply by ensuring that it held a bigger stockpile of atomic bombs. If it were possible, then America had no alternative but to produce the H-bomb on a large scale.[26]

In military terms, the hydrogen bomb had a number of attractions. At the hearing, a former member of the AEC, Sumner Pike—himself an opponent of the bomb—pointed out two of them. There was, first of all, the much greater margin of error in a weapon which could lay waste an area a hundred times more extensive than that which could be destroyed by an atomic bomb. Second, it meant that if they could get through, it would take only a handful of planes to eliminate a large target; with fission weapons, whole squadrons would be needed. This, as Bernard Brodie has written, was an important consideration at a time when both bombers and their crews were scarce and expensive, and it was reinforced by the poor intelligence on Soviet targets as well as by the wish to reach a decision in the shortest possible time.[27]

McMahon agreed wholeheartedly. He was a firm believer in the H-bomb. In the summer of 1952 (when in fact he was dying of cancer) he sent a message to the Connecticut Democratic Convention which was intending to nominate him for the presidency as a 'favourite son'. If elected President, he promised the convention, he would direct the AEC to manufacture hydrogen bombs 'by the thousands'. In a letter to Truman on 21 November 1949 he argued that they would release atomic bombs for other targets, would have a much higher cost-effectiveness, and could be used against isolated tactical targets as well as against the strategic objective of the cities. Strauss, in a letter and memorandum sent to Truman four days later, also claimed that the thermonuclear had great tactical possibilities, and discounted the danger of radioactive fall-out from fission products. 'The number of such weapons necessary to pollute the earth's atmosphere', he stated, 'would run into many hundreds.'[28]

The advocates of the hydrogen bomb also rejected the proposition that it was inherently immoral. As Strauss later remarked —and it was a telling point—it was no less moral than the atom bomb. The difference between them was a difference of degree, not of kind. He went further than that, however. There was a moral argument in favour of thermonuclear weapons if they ended war more quickly or prevented defeat. Moreover, in Strauss' view, it was 'certainly immoral to concede to an atheistic and unscrupulous enemy the sole possession of such weapons. It is not only immoral—it makes no sense.'[29]

The scientists, for their part, believed that they had a duty to respond to the intellectual challenge with which the problem of fusion presented them. Teller was the most forceful exponent of this view. Scientists, he said, resented the implication that 'as long as you people go ahead and make minor improvements and work very hard and diligently at it, you are doing a fine job, but if you succeed in making a really great piece of progress, then you are doing something immoral'. The year after the hearing he wrote that 'some may think it would have been better never to develop this instrument.... I ... believe that we would be unfaithful to the tradition of Western civilization if we were to shy away from exploring the limits of human achievement. It is our specific duty as scientists to explore and explain. Beyond that our responsibilities cannot be any greater than those of any other citizen of our democratic society.'[30]

In the end, however, it came down to the issue of how America was to be placed *vis-à-vis* Russia in the global balance of power, and for the supporters of the bomb, this is what counted most. Some believed that once it had been acquired, the country would regain the lead it had lost when Russia drew level on the atomic plane in August. This view was put by Vandenberg when he appeared before the JCAE on 14 October. As Vandenberg saw it, 'having the super weapon would place the United States in the superior position that it had enjoyed up to the end of September 1949 by having exclusive possession of the weapon.'[31]

Most members of the H-bomb lobby, however, chose to stress the danger to America of allowing Russia to secure a thermonuclear capability before it had acquired one itself. Earlier in the year, before the Soviet explosion, a fervent believer in air power had written this:

> By far the greatest peril is ... that another nation will be able to develop genuine long-range, high-speed strategic air power *before* the United States. ...
>
> Security for the United States lies, above all, in its technological superiority. This superiority ought to be pushed farther and farther. Leadership in the atomic and aeronautical fields should never be lost. ... If by misfortune another strong nation should acquire ... an atomic air force first, it will become the master of the skies.[32]

The Russian success seemed to reinforce the argument still further. As Alvarez put it in his testimony, for the Russians to beat America to the hydrogen bomb would have been 'one of the most disastrous things that could possibly happen to this country ... if they did make it, that would give them a great jump ahead of us and essentially nullify our stockpile of atomic weapons.' The director of the Radiation Laboratory was equally emphatic. It was not criminal to be wrong (about the hydrogen bomb), said Lawrence; it would be worse than criminal for the United States to be confronted with an H-bomb, having none itself. 'If we let Russia get the super first,' McMahon wrote to Truman on 21 November, 'catastrophe becomes all but certain—whereas, if we get it first, there exists a chance of saving ourselves.' Strauss, in his letter to Truman of 25 November, proclaimed that it was 'the historic policy of the United States not to have its forces less well armed than those of any other country'.[33]

The opponents of the hydrogen bomb denied all these arguments. The main centres of opposition lay in the Atomic Energy Commission. Three of the five Commissioners were against producing the bomb—Lilienthal, Pike, and Henry D. Smyth. Eight of the nine members of the General Advisory Committee took up the same position—Oppenheimer, Conant, Lee A. DuBridge, Hartley Rowe, Enrico Fermi, Isidor I. Rabi, Cyril S. Smith, and Oliver E. Buckley. The ninth, Glenn T. Seaborg, was in favour, even if reluctantly. Of these twelve men, nine testified at the hearing, all, that is, except Smyth, Smith and Seaborg. Smyth could not appear as a witness as he was still a member of the Commission and therefore an interested party. All nine, understandably, testified on Oppenheimer's behalf. So too, however, did six of the eleven witnesses who had supported launching into a vigorous thermonuclear programme in 1949—Bradbury, Karl T. Compton, Dean, General James McCormack, Norman F. Ramsey and von Neumann.[34]

The arguments levelled against the H-bomb were numerous. In the first place, there was the question of feasibility. In his memoirs, Truman asserts that 'by the early fall of 1949, development of the "super" ... had progressed to the point where we were almost ready to put our theories into practice'. This was not so. In a letter written to Conant on 21 October, Oppenheimer stated that he was 'not sure the miserable thing will work ... it appears to be singularly proof against any form of experimental approach.' As Rabi put it, 'it was a field where we really did not know what we were talking about'. It is important to remember that Oppenheimer never claimed the bomb was not feasible (as

Nichols had alleged). As he stated in his testimony, 'the objection was that we did not like the weapon, not that it couldn't be made'. The uncertainties were very great, but not so great as to rule out the possibility of fusion entirely.[35]

A second important consideration was the impact which a stepped-up effort on thermonuclear development would have on the existing atomic weapons programme. The difficulty here was that both required large supplies of neutrons. The heavy-hydrogen isotope tritium was best made by exposing lithium to neutron bombardment, while the fissionable material plutonium was manufactured by bombarding uranium 238 with neutrons from uranium 235. Any concentration on tritium would therefore be at the expense of plutonium, and the problem was aggravated by the fact that more neutrons were needed to make tritium than to make an equal amount of plutonium, and that the half-life of tritium was not much more than twelve years—a tiny fraction of the half-life of plutonium.[36]

The issue was doubly serious in that at the onset of the debate over the hydrogen bomb, a vast expansion in plutonium production was being contemplated. In July 1949 Truman had appointed a special committee of the National Security Council to study the expansion of production facilities, and in September it had reported in favour of a big increase. A large body of opinion within the Commission felt strongly that this programme should not suffer for the sake of an H-bomb which was as yet unproven, and at the hearing Pike, Rabi, Winne and Bush all remembered their misgivings on this score. As it happened, the expansion was approved by Truman on 19 October, and in the words of the official history, it 'certainly took precedence over plans for a new type of weapon which would not be available for years, if ever'. At the same time, this did not mean that discussion of the thermonuclear project was foreclosed.[37]

The conviction that the expansion in plutonium must not be impaired was largely based on the view that the atomic bomb was a weapon of much greater military value. There was firstly the fact of its superior deliverability. At a secret hearing before the Joint Committee on 29 September General McCormack pointed out that the hydrogen bomb as then contemplated was almost certainly too cumbersome to be carried in an aircraft and that it would probably have to be delivered by ship or by train! Oppenheimer, in his letter of 21 October, stated that he was not sure it could be 'gotten to a target except by ox cart'. Recent work on the atom bomb, on the other hand, held out hopes of weapons that were comparatively small in size and weight, and which could be mass-produced into the bargain.[38]

Moreover, it was argued that the H-bomb was an inefficient weapon. Although the energy release of the bomb was a thousand times greater than that of the earliest fission weapons, the radius of its destructive power was not proportionate to this. Bethe, in an article published early in 1950, claimed that where the radii of destruction by blast and heat radiation at Hiroshima were one mile and three miles respectively, those of a fusion bomb would be ten miles and twenty miles. In other words, its range of devastation was very much smaller than its explosive power, and this made atomic bombs a more worthwhile proposition. Pike made this point during the hearing, and Lilienthal attempted to reinforce it by reminding the Board that by 1949 the AEC was developing a fission bomb of 500 kilotons, that is, forty times more powerful than the weapon which had destroyed Hiroshima. 'We were advised', he said, 'that one such bomb would take out almost any target in the world, and two would take out any target.' Given an arsenal of weapons such as these, the H-bomb seemed superfluous.[39]

Indeed, the number of suitable targets for the H-bomb seemed extremely limited if it were to be used only against very large cities and if it were only to be used against the Soviet Union. For Russia contained only a handful of vast urban concentrations and even these could be covered by the 500-kiloton A-bomb. The United States, conversely, had many more conurbations, as Bethe and Bush both pointed out, and this made America much more vulnerable to thermonuclear attack. If both countries should possess the H-bomb, then America would be in the weaker position, far from impregnable, as the devotees of the bomb supposed.[40]

The dubious military worth of the bomb was underscored, moreover, in the eyes of its opponents, by the apparent lack of interest shown by the armed forces. As of September 1949, Lilienthal pointed out, the AEC had received no request from the Pentagon for a weapon 'of unlimited size or destructive power'; nor did it have a military evaluation of such a weapon. As

Oppenheimer recollected, 'there had been no great expression of interest on the part of the military in more powerful weapons . . . no suggestion that large weapons would be very useful. The pressure was all the other way; get as many as you can.' General Wilson, an ardent supporter of the bomb, admitted that it was probably the announcement of the Soviet A-bomb which sparked off military interest in a still bigger weapon. Even then, seemingly, there were reservations. Norman Ramsey, who was a member of the Air Force Science Advisory Board at the time, testified that, as presented to the Air Force, the hydrogen bomb was 'a pretty dismal proposition', especially from the delivery point of view. General Bradley, when he appeared before the General Advisory Committee on 29 October, described its advantages as 'purely psychological'. Although the Joint Chiefs of Staff had by then written to the Commission criticizing it for its apparent inactivity, they had not stated how much they were prepared to lose in the way of atomic bombs in order to get it, and they had still not done so when the AEC sent its opinions to Truman on 9 November. Nor had they even put in a formal statement of their need for the weapon. Strauss himself was compelled to admit this at a Commission meeting on 3 November, and Pike reiterated the point in his memorandum on the bomb submitted on 28 November. In the circumstances, it was an extraordinary omission, and one which the opposition could not fail to capitalize on.[41]

The crux of the matter, however, as far as the military value of the fusion bomb was concerned, was the relation of the bomb to overall American strategy. It was Kennan who brought this out most clearly at the hearing. As an opponent of the H-bomb in 1949 he had seen the situation as follows. If United States nuclear strategy were simply deterrent and retaliatory, then an atomic capability was all that was needed. This was sufficient to prevent an all-out Soviet attack on the United States or its allies, or to strike back against the USSR if such an attack took place. This would hold good even if Russia alone had the hydrogen bomb.[42]

The only case that Kennan could see for American possession of the bomb was if American strategy went beyond this—and he believed it did—and envisaged launching a strike against Russia regardless of whether the Russians themselves had used nuclear weapons against the West. Here, presumably, Kennan was thinking of the position which did obtain at the time, in which the response to a full-scale attack by the Red Army on western Europe was to be the immediate nuclear devastation of Russia's major cities. The hydrogen bomb would no doubt accomplish this more quickly, but the prospects of its introduction were so horrific that it had to be resisted.[43]

In short, the only use for the H-bomb was as a weapon of indiscriminate mass destruction and this, for the opponents of the bomb, was totally unacceptable. 'We built one Frankenstein', said Rowe. For Oppenheimer himself, it was the main reason behind his decision to come out against it. There can be little doubt that he and many other nuclear physicists were appalled at having helped to promote the atomic bomb when they knew what it had done to Hiroshima and Nagasaki. Late in 1947 he had said: 'In some sort of crude sense which no vulgarity, no humor, no over-statement can quite extinguish, the physicists have known sin; and this is a knowledge which they cannot lose.' As he put it at the hearing, 'I felt, perhaps quite strongly, that having played an active part in promoting a revolution in warfare, I needed to be as responsible as I could with regard to what came of this revolution.' Bethe remembered that in the days after the Japanese surrender, 'there was a general belief that this was a tremendous weapon that we had brought into the world and that we might have been responsible for incredible destruction in the future'. It was thoughts like this which had preoccupied him in the autumn of 1949, and he had found Oppenheimer 'equally undecided and equally troubled in his mind about what should be done'.[44]

Bethe's concern was genuine, and it prevented him from agreeing to work on the hydrogen bomb in the first instance. Yet he was to do so later, and Oppenheimer displayed a similar ambivalence. Under cross-examination by Robb, for example, he declared that his moral qualms about the H-bomb sprang from that fact that America had 'freely used the atomic bomb'. Almost immediately afterwards, however, he was to state that he would not have supported dropping an H-bomb on Hiroshima because 'the target is too small'. During the same dialogue he agreed that he would have discovered the H-bomb at Los Alamos if it had been possible. This undoubtedly vitiated the force of his moral objections, just as the fact that they were prepared to speak in favour of a more 'efficient' 500-kiloton A-bomb undermined the position of the opponents of the H-bomb as a whole. Their argument in this respect was untenable, and their critics, as we have seen, were not slow to point it out.[45]

The final arguments in favour of a decision not to produce thermonuclear weapons turned on the positive results which might flow from it. These were twofold: first, it was hoped that it would serve to minimize the country's dependence on a nuclear strategy; second, that it might open the way forward to a disarmament agreement with the Soviet Union.

As Oppenheimer saw it, by the autumn of 1949 the United States had come to a crossroads. Either the reliance on atomic weapons would increase still further or it would begin to be reduced. One of the most alarming features of the H-bomb, he wrote to Conant on 21 October, was that it seemed likely 'even further to worsen the unbalance of our present war plans. What does worry me is that this thing appears to have caught the imagination, both of the congressional and of military people, as the answer to the problem posed by the Russian advance ... that we become committed to it as the way to save the country and the peace appears to me full of dangers.' Kennan said much the same in 1954. Popular opinion, he pointed out, tended to equate security with military strength, and possession of an absolute weapon would cultivate the illusion that absolute security was possible, when it was not. Lilienthal felt equally strongly, and pointed to a speech by General Bradley to support his argument. Speaking in Chicago in November 1949, Bradley had said, according to Lilienthal, that America 'had no reserve except the A-bomb in the event of aggression against us any place in the world'. This to Lilienthal was harrowing, and he was determined that a full examination of the place of nuclear weapons in American strategy should precede any decision on manufacturing the thermonuclear bomb.[46]

At the same time, the occasion was to be used to promote disarmament negotiations with the USSR, leading to a Soviet-American agreement not to produce the weapon. Here, it was believed, was the best opportunity to control a nuclear arms race since the collapse of the proposals for an international atomic energy authority in 1946, and Kennan in the State Department urged the attempt strongly. Bethe, in his obituary on Oppenheimer, compared it in importance with the current effort to reach a similar self-denying ordinance in the field of anti-ballistic missiles. From Oppenheimer's point of view, it was essential to avoid competition in H-bomb production because 'we were infinitely more vulnerable and infinitely less likely to initiate the use of these weapons, and because the world in which great destruction has been done in all civilized parts of the world is a harder world for America to live with than it is for the Communists to live with'. 'I think we were right', he said, 'in believing that any method available consistent with honor and security for keeping these objects out of the arsenals of the enemy would have been a good course to follow.' He had been encouraged to support this policy by the mistaken belief that the Soviet régime would take its cue from Washington and would be less likely to undertake a thermonuclear programme if the United States took the lead in abstaining. (In fact, as we now know, Soviet physicists began on their H-bomb work immediately after their success in the atomic field and it was under way even while the American debate was going on.) Later, however, under questioning by Gray, Oppenheimer changed his story and stated that 'we were always clear that there might be a Russian effort whatever we did.' Hence the need for a hard-and-fast disarmament treaty. This, coupled with Lilienthal's subsequent assertion that it had been generally assumed in 1949 that the Russians were capable of going ahead, threw some doubt on his earlier testimony. In view of the closeness of Gray's cross-examination, this cannot have escaped his notice.[47]

While the opponents of the bomb were discussing the issue among themselves, its advocates were busy promoting their cause. Since secrecy was paramount, they could not take the issue to the country and their activities were confined to governmental circles in Washington and to the scientific centres of the atomic energy programme, particularly Los Alamos, Berkeley and Chicago. In all these places they propagated their views with zeal.

The first positive reaction we know of came in the form of a memorandum drafted by Strauss on 30 September and presented to the Commission when it met on 5 October. In this, Strauss declared that the time has now come for a quantum jump in our planning (to borrow a metaphor from our scientist friends)—that is to say, that we should now make an intensive effort to get ahead with the super. By intensive effort, I am thinking of a commitment of talent and money comparable, if necessary, to that which produced the first atomic weapon. That is the way to stay ahead.

Casting around for allies, Strauss at once thought of Lawrence, Teller, McMahon and Borden, and he spoke of his proposal to Admiral Souers, the executive secretary of the National Security Council. Souers, according to the official history, found that Truman apparently knew nothing about the hydrogen bomb, but reported back to Strauss that Truman wanted Strauss 'to force the issue up to the White House and to do it quickly'. Strauss went ahead immensely encouraged.[48]

Meanwhile, the interested scientists in Berkeley—Lawrence, Alvarez and Latimer—were conferring with each other, and in the evening of 6 October Lawrence and Alvarez flew to Los Alamos to discuss plans with Teller. Teller explained that there was still a great deal of research to be done before fusion could be proved feasible, but that in the interim precious time could be saved by building a neutron-producing reactor for the manufacture of tritium. This project they immediately took to Washington, where they spent the best part of three days lobbying the AEC, the Pentagon and the Joint Committee. On 11 October they moved up to New York and visited Rabi at Columbia University. He, they found, was also in favour of the project; his attitude was described by Oppenheimer at the hearing as 'one of somewhat quizzical enthusiasm'.[49]

Lawrence and Alvarez had also gone to New York in the hope of flying from there to Canada to inspect the experimental heavy-water reactor at Chalk River, but they were unable to get a seat on a flight to Ottawa. They therefore split up, Alvarez returning to Berkeley and Lawrence going back to Washington, where he continued to move the idea along. On 12 October he visited the Armed Forces Special Weapons Project in company with Bradbury and urged the thermonuclear programme on its director, General Nichols. Nichols in turn saw Vandenberg the following day and asked him, in the words of General Wilson, 'as the No. 1 bomber man to express again the military's interest in a large weapon'. This Vandenberg did before the Joint Committee on 14 October. It was the military view, he said, that the H-bomb should be 'pushed to completion as soon as possible'. On 17 October the Joint Chiefs of Staff wrote to the AEC expressing concern that it had not asked for funds for H-bomb development, and the same day McMahon requested a special report on what was currently being done.[50]

In Berkeley meanwhile, plans for a heavy-water reactor were rapidly taking shape, although they had not yet been given government approval. Lawrence proceeded to move ahead entirely on his own authority. He informed the university that the Radiation Laboratory was thinking of 'embarking on a large-scale construction program' and secured the approval of one member of the Board of Regents. A site for the reactor was picked out just north of San Francisco and Alvarez was told that he had been 'elected' to be its first director. Since he and Lawrence were self-confessed amateurs in the field, experts on reactors were called in. Lawrence R. Hafstad, director of the Reactor Development Division of the AEC was present at a meeting in Berkeley on 14 October, and the promoters were also in touch by telephone with Walter H. Zinn, head of the Argonne Laboratory in Chicago.[51]

Teller too was hard at work on behalf of the project. His commitment to it was fervent and total. As Pike said at the hearing, Teller was 'never one to keep his candles hidden under bushels. He was kind of a missionary.' He was convinced that most scientists shared his views. 'At Los Alamos', he later wrote, 'there was a widespread feeling that the laboratory should turn to the development of the hydrogen bomb', and he believed that the opposition was confined to a very small minority. To maintain the pressure and win over any waverers he flew east on 19 October. His main target was Bethe, whom he was extremely anxious to attract back to Los Alamos. Bethe, apparently, agreed to come, but changed his mind some two or three days later, much to Teller's regret. Yet Teller pressed on. On 24 October he was at Chicago airport to greet Fermi on his return from a trip to Italy and attempt to enlist him in the crusade. He then flew back to Los Alamos to meet a delegation from the Joint Committee sent out by McMahon to be briefed on the latest developments. As

he did so, Alvarez left for Chicago to discuss reactor design
with Zinn and his staff. From there he flew on to Washington,
where what was to prove a momentous meeting of the General
Advisory Committee was due to take place.[52]

The Committee had been summoned at the request of Strauss.
In his memorandum of 5 October, Strauss had asked that the
GAC be consulted 'to ascertain their views as to how we can
proceed with expedition'. In other words, he was assuming that
when the Committee met, the question of whether or not the
H-bomb should be built would already have been settled. This
was not, however, the assumption behind the letter sent by
Lilienthal to Oppenheimer on 11 October. In this, Lilienthal
asked Oppenheimer to bring the Committee together to consider 'if the present, and presently planned, program constitutes
doing everything that it is reasonably possible for us to do for
the common defense and security'. 'We would welcome your
advice and assistance', he added, 'on as broad a basis as possible.' Here, the issue was clearly left open, and it was equally
clear that Lilienthal expected the Committee to range beyond
strictly technical considerations.[53]

The AEC's instructions to the Committee were elaborated in a
another letter to Oppenheimer, this time from Pike. Here the
GAC was enjoined to see 'whether the Commission is now doing
things which might well be curtailed or stopped, and also what
further things we ought to do to serve the paramount objective
of the common defense and security'. The first items on the
agenda were to be plans for civil defence and the expansion of
production facilities. As regards the hydrogen bomb, the Commission wished to know whether America would use it if it could
be built and what its military value would be relative to atomic
weapons. The AEC was also keenly interested in an immediate
expansion of heavy-water production and in a reactor which
would yield a surplus of neutrons as well as manufacture plutonium.[54]

It should be noted that in neither of these letters was there
any mention of Strauss' proposal for an 'intensive effort' on
thermonuclear weapons. Yet Oppenheimer remembered in his
letter of 4 March 1954 that the GAC had been asked to advise
on 'two related questions'. The Commission had wanted to know

'first, whether in view of the Soviet success the Commission's program was adequate, and if not, in what way it should be altered or increased; second, whether a crash program for the development of the super should be a part of any new program.' He repeated this in his testimony, and he was confirmed by Lilienthal when he took the stand.[55]

Just how the issue of a 'crash program' was raised was never made clear. Lilienthal believed that he might have brought it up when the Commissioners met with the GAC during their weekend conference. Pike's impression was that it 'crept into the discussion.' DuBridge recollected that Oppenheimer himself had broached the subject when the Committee assembled. In all probability, Pike's explanation is the most acceptable. Even though the question was not made explicit it was undoubtedly in the forefront of everyone's mind and had been since Truman's announcement on 23 September. 'The first problem to decide', wrote Truman in his memoirs, 'was how much of the AEC's energies and resources should be devoted to an early test that might show us whether or not the H-bomb would work.' Like so much else of Truman's account of the debate of autumn 1949, this was neither a complete nor an accurate statement of the situation, but it went to the heart of the matter, and this, in fact, is what the GAC discussion was to turn on. It would have been astonishing if it had not.[56]

The GAC meeting took place in Washington on 28, 29 and 30 October. On the first day, the Committee heard the views of Kennan, Bethe and Robert Serber, who had been sent by Lawrence to put the case for a heavy-water reactor. On the second day, it met with the Joint Chiefs of Staff, the Commissioners and the AEC division directors. On the final day— Sunday—it drew up its conclusions, which were put into written form by Oppenheimer and Manley, the GAC secretary. There were three documents in all: a report representing the views of all eight members present; a majority annex; and a minority annex.

One member of the Committee was absent—Glenn T. Seaborg. He had already given his views to Oppenheimer in a letter of 14 October, and they were broadly in favour of going ahead, as Alvarez later affirmed. Seaborg was firmly behind the proposal for a neutron-producing reactor and on balance inclined to support a thermonuclear programme. 'Although I deplore the prospects of our country putting a tremendous effort into this, I must confess that I have been unable to come to the conclusion that we should not. . . . I would have to hear some good arguments before I could take on sufficient courage to recommend not going toward such a program.'[57]

In this, Seaborg was at variance with all his colleagues, who opposed the bomb unanimously. Their report, which was essentially technical, fell into two sections, as Oppenheimer pointed out in his letter of 4 March 1954. The first 'recommended a number of measures that the Commission should take to increase in many ways our overall potential in weapons'. It addressed itself to the questions posed in the letters from Lilienthal and Pike. The recommendations were threefold. First, the Committee urged a further expansion in the production of fissionable materials, that is, plutonium and the isotopes of uranium. Second, it gave high priority to the development of tactical atomic weapons and declared that it favoured a 'booster' programme to increase the explosive power of fission weapons in general. Third, it supported building a neutron-producing reactor, but only on the understanding that this was 'not intended as a step in the super program'. In other words, it was not to serve as a source for tritium for a fusion weapon.[58]

The second section of the report, in Oppenheimer's words, expressed 'unanimous opposition to the initiation by the United States of a crash program of the kind we had been asked to advise on'. It pointed out that the basic theoretical studies of fusion were still incomplete and that they would have to be ratified by a programme of tests. Only then would the AEC know whether it could engineer a thermonuclear bomb or not. The ultimate feasibility of the weapon was therefore unknown, but the Committee was prepared to forecast that 'an imaginative and concerted attack on the problem has a better than even chance of producing the weapon within five years'.[59]

Yet even assuming it was feasible, the GAC did not wish to see the programme undertaken. The bomb's relative inefficiency meant, as Oppenheimer put it, that 'for anything but very large targets, this was not economical in terms of damage per dollar, and then even for large targets it was uncertain whether it would be economical in terms of damage per dollar.' Whatever the case, it was clear that it was a weapon which would only come into its own if used against cities, and it could only lead to an extension of 'the policy of exterminating civilian populations'. This the GAC believed must not happen. 'We all hope', the report ended, 'that by one means or another, the development of these weapons can be avoided. We are all reluctant to see the United States take the initiative in precipitating this development. We are all agreed that it would be wrong at the present moment to commit ourselves to an all-out effort toward its development.'[60]

The majority annex was signed by Oppenheimer, Conant, DuBridge, Rowe, Smith and Buckley. It proposed a complete and unconditional renunciation of the bomb, which could only be 'a weapon of genocide'. Its existence would be an intolerable threat to the very future of the human race. To develop it would not prevent the Soviet Union from doing so, and even if the Russians launched an H-bomb attack, America had enough atomic weapons to make its reprisal. 'We believe', the majority declared, 'a super bomb should never be produced. Mankind would be far better off not to have a demonstration of the feasibility of such a weapon until the present climate of world opinion changes.' 'In determining not to proceed to develop the super bomb,' they concluded, 'we see a unique opportunity of providing by example some limitations on the totality of war and thus of eliminating the fear and arousing the hope of mankind.'[61]

The minority annex came from Fermi and Rabi. The bomb, in their view, was so devastating that it could not be justified 'on any ethical ground which gives a human being a certain individuality and dignity even if he happens to be a resident of an enemy country'. 'The fact that no limits exist to the destructiveness of this weapon', they went on, 'makes its very existence and the knowledge of its construction a danger to humanity as a whole. It is necessarily an evil thing considered in any light. For these reasons we believe it important for the President of the United States to tell the American public and the world that we think it is wrong on fundamental ethical principles to initiate the development of such a weapon.' America should invite other nations to join in a pledge to renounce it, even if no effective international control system were brought into operation to underwrite the bargain. They did not say what the

American response should be if the invitation were rejected, but it was clear to Lilienthal at the time that they meant it to be understood that 'if the other fellow refused to agree not to go ahead, we would'. This was confirmed at the hearing by both Fermi and Rabi. Fermi described the proposal as an attempt 'to outlaw the thing before it was born', while Rabi saw it as a political gesture which would strengthen America's moral standing if the decision were taken to go ahead.[62]

These, then, were the positions taken by the Committee on 30 October. Its opposition to the bomb had been stated emphatically, but was it categorical? Gray appeared to think so, and he fastened on the sentence in the majority annex: 'We believe a super bomb should never be produced.' Was not this, he asked Oppenheimer, a statement of opposition not just to a crash programme but to any thermonuclear programme whatsoever? It was not, but the phraseology was undoubtedly much less equivocal than that of the conclusion of the unanimous report, and it bred an understandable confusion in Gray's mind.[63]

Oppenheimer did his best to dispel it. Under cross-examination by Robb, he had said that the sentence had to be interpreted as meaning that 'it would be a better world if there were no hydrogen bombs in it'. It was, as he later said to Gray, 'an exhortation . . . to the Government of the United States to seek to prevent the production of super bombs by anyone'. Moreover, three things would have qualified this position. One would have been an indication that the Russians were working on the bomb themselves: 'Nothing in what we had said was meant to obtain should it be clear or should it be reasonably probable that the enemy was on this trail.' A second would have been a theoretical breakthrough. 'I think if we had had that technical knowledge,' he told Garrison, 'then we should have recommended that we go ahead full steam, and then or in 1948 or 1946 or 1945.' A third would have been the failure of the bid for international renunciation of the weapon—'a serious and persuasive conclusion that the political effort to which we referred in our annexes could not be successful'. Rabi, when he testified, stated that at the end of the October meeting Oppenheimer had said he would be willing to sign either or both of the annexes, that is, he would have agreed to go ahead if the proposal for an international pledge fell through. It is also worth pointing out that Rabi had the distinct impression that Oppenheimer was 'not unalterably opposed' to the bomb, while Lilienthal identified not him but Conant as the mainstay of the opposition. On 31 October he made a personal telephone call to Conant to congratulate him on the result of the meeting. On the second day, as he noted in his journal, it had seemed that as many as five of the Committee were for going ahead all-out, and, as the official history puts it, 'without Conant's unswerving opposition to the proposal, he thought the committee's report might well have favored it'.[64]

None of this, however, appeared to be clear to Gray. Nor was he able to understand exactly what the GAC had recommended in the way of a thermonuclear programme. Looked at in the simplest terms, there were four differing levels of effort which could be decided on. First, there might be no work at all on the bomb. Second, research could continue at the low pitch which had been maintained since 1945. Third, research could be stepped up and pursued much more intensively. Fourth, a full-scale production effort could be mounted.

It was evident that the Committee had not recommended the first alternative, and they had come out decisively against the fourth. What was not evident from its report was that it had supported the third, that is, a programme falling well short of a crash development but considerably more energetic than that carried out since the war. Thus Pitzer—who declared that the crash programme was 'largely what we called a strawman'!— and General McCormack both believed that such an intermediate programme could have been adopted, and that it had not been recommended by the GAC. In Pitzer's opinion, the recommendations in the report were in fact 'almost entirely negative in character'.[65]

The Committee had not, apparently, meant their report to be taken in this way. DuBridge testified that 'we did not feel at the time that the time 1950 was ripe for the production effort, but we always advocated the research and development effort'. Oppenheimer, in his letter to Conant of 21 October 1949, had said that 'it would be folly to oppose the exploration of this weapon. We have always known it had to be done; and it does have to be done. . . .' He refused, however, to plunge headlong into a crash development. It *was* folly, to him, that 'on the basis of what was then known, plant be built, equipment be procured and a commitment be made to build this thing irrespective of further study and with a very high priority.' In such a development 'alternatives would not have an opportunity to be weighed because one had to get on and because we were not going to sacrifice time'. This was what the Committee had opposed, but that did not mean, Oppenheimer told Gray, that it 'would not have been sympathetic to studies and clarification'.[66]

This was not brought out clearly enough in the report of 30 October, as indeed, Oppenheimer's careful conditional admitted. One of his colleagues, Buckley, had realized this at the time, and realized too that it laid this section of the report open to misinterpretation. At the next GAC meeting on 3 December he had submitted a memorandum, which, he believed, would put the GAC position beyond dispute. In it, he argued for a complete and detailed study of all aspects of the bomb so that the ultimate policy decision could be made on the basis of research by the best mathematicians and scientists in the country. This would show, he hoped, that the Committee was by no means opposed to any activity in the thermonuclear field, as its critics were suggesting it was.[67]

What the GAC had done, then, was to advocate a 'less precipitous approach' to the bomb, as Smith later put it; in his view, it was 'the proper recommendation to be based on the technical information that was then available'. This was the very same moderate and gradualist programme which McCormack and Pitzer had said they favoured. It was, indeed, closely akin to the programme sanctioned by President Truman on 31 January 1950! But the damage had been done in not making this clear at the outset, and the effects were lasting. Not even after all the clarification provided at the hearing was Gray able to grasp that Oppenheimer and his colleagues had not opposed the hydrogen bomb point-blank. This was an error comparable with his misunderstanding of the circumstances of the 1947 clearance, and it was to cost Oppenheimer equally dear.[68]

The nuances of the GAC position were no clearer to the supporters of the crash programme in 1949 than they were to Gray in 1954. They had demanded a total commitment, and when the Committee turned its face against it, they felt utterly defeated. The prestige of the GAC was extremely high, and the report of

30 October was seen, for the moment at least, as a crushing blow to their hopes. As Alvarez put it, 'the program was dead'. They were certain the AEC would uphold the Committee's recommendation.[69]

They were equally certain that it was Oppenheimer who had been mainly responsible for what had happened. It was his influence which, as over the past four years, had moulded policy and been brought to bear on his colleagues to persuade them to fall in line with his views. This was, of course, the burden of Nichols' charges with respect to the H-bomb, and in Nichols' letter Oppenheimer had been described as 'the most experienced, most powerful, and most effective member' of the opposition to the bomb. Robb took up this point during his cross-examination and elicited the reply from Oppenheimer that he 'was not the most powerful, ... the most experienced, ... and the most influential'. If all three factors were taken together, however, 'perhaps I combined a little more experience, a little more power, and a little more influence than anyone else'. This was probably a very accurate description of Oppenheimer's authority in the scientific and political communities. Whether it had been exercised in quite the way his critics alleged was another question.[70]

For Teller the first danger sign had come the day Truman made his announcement of the Soviet test. He had immediately telephoned Oppenheimer to get his reaction, and according to Teller, Oppenheimer had merely said, 'Keep your shirt on'. 'This answer', Teller later wrote, 'worried me even more than the Russian explosion.' Latimer recounted that, when he accompanied Lawrence and Alvarez to Washington on 8 October, there was a favourable start, but that opposition quickly set in, and 'the source of it was Dr Oppenheimer'. Alvarez, at least when he testified, was disposed to believe that 'Dr Oppenheimer is quite free and should try to persuade people of his convictions', but Lawrence felt otherwise. According to his official biographer, Lawrence 'had no doubt that the country's defense would be in bad shape defensively if Oppie's advice and that of those others Ernest felt were under his influence, had prevailed. It was, he thought, unfortunate that it had prevailed for so long ... his persuasive, almost hypnotic influence made it dangerous, particularly in the halls of power where decisions had to be made realistically—not mystically.'[71]

What seemed most remarkable was the number of people who appeared to have changed their views on the thermonuclear programme after talking to Oppenheimer. Alvarez raised this point during his testimony. The men he had in mind were Du-Bridge and Bacher of the California Institute of Technology, Rabi and Serber. All had been enthusiasts until, apparently, they had spoken to Oppenheimer. DuBridge, when Alvarez met him on 19 October, had supported his ideas, but when Borden saw him a week later, he 'seemed to be speaking virtually as Oppenheimer's puppet'. Rabi had promised his support in New York on 11 October, but he had gone on to vote against a crash programme. Serber had been sent to Oppenheimer to present the case for a heavy-water reactor, but when he appeared before the GAC on 28 October he was careful to dissociate himself from the hydrogen bomb campaign. When Alvarez had lunch with him and Oppenheimer on 29 October, he surprised Alvarez by agreeing wholeheartedly with what Oppenheimer had to say.[72]

Alvarez could also have mentioned Bethe. As we have seen, Bethe had originally agreed to take up thermonuclear work when he saw Teller at Cornell, but he had changed his mind following a conversation they had with Oppenheimer at Princeton on 21 October. Bethe had not refused immediately, but when he did, Teller could not help feeling that Oppenheimer had been the cause. In fact, as Bethe testified, it was his friends Weisskopf and Placzek who had persuaded him that after a hydrogen-bomb war, 'the world would not be ... the world we want to preserve'. It was as a result of this discussion, and not the meeting with Oppenheimer, that he had reversed his attitude. Teller was thus mistaken, and it is likely that Alvarez was similarly mistaken about the position taken up by Bacher, DuBridge and Serber, who may all have been prepared to support a reactor programme but unquestionably drew the line at putting it at the service of the bomb. With Rabi there was less excuse for error, since he had been ready to go ahead with the bomb if the conditions which he and Fermi put forward were not met.[73]

The implication, as far as DuBridge and Rabi were concerned, was that Oppenheimer had imposed his own opinion on them at the GAC meeting of 28–30 October. At an early stage in the hearing, however, Oppenheimer maintained that 'it was not a committee that regarded itself as subject to manipulation, or . . . was subject to manipulation'. This was corroborated by both the men in question. Oppenheimer, as Rabi put it, was 'not one of those chairmen who sort of takes it their privilege to hold the floor; the very opposite. Generally he might express his own view last and very rarely in a strong fashion, but generally with considerable reservations.' In the words of DuBridge, 'at no time did he dominate the group or did he suppress opinions that did not agree with his own. In fact, he encouraged a full and free and frank exchange of ideas throughout the full history of the Committee.'[74]

As his opponents saw it, this was precisely the reverse of the truth. In their view, Oppenheimer had done his utmost to stifle the expression of views which did not coincide with his. During the hearing, for example, it was insinuated that he had not shown Seaborg's letter to the GAC October meeting. At the same time, he was accused of having told the Joint Committee on 30 January 1950 that he had not had an opinion from Seaborg before the October meeting. On the first point, the evidence is conflicting. At the hearing, none of the then members of the GAC could recall the letter being brought to their notice, but Oppenheimer in 1957 and Smith in 1967 said they believed that it had been presented. On the second point, there is no such room for doubt. What Oppenheimer told the Joint Committee was that Seaborg had not expressed himself in person at the October meeting because he was abroad. This was made clear by Gray, and indeed, when Robb first brought the matter up, he described Oppenheimer as saying that 'Dr Seaborg was not heard there', that is, at the GAC conclave.[75]

As Oppenheimer himself pointed out, his motivation throughout this episode could hardly have been suspect when he stood to gain nothing from lying. On 30 January the decision to go ahead with the bomb was virtually made, as we shall see, and the Joint Committee was the last body of men to be dissuaded from supporting the programme. Again, what could he possibly hope to achieve by concealing the existence of the letter, when he knew that since the end of 1953 it had been in the possession of the AEC? These were compelling arguments, but they were to carry no weight with his judges, and the Seaborg incident was to do him serious damage when the final verdicts came to be considered.[76]

Following on from this, Teller was convinced that Oppenheimer was behind what he called 'an effort . . . to keep congressional leaders from knowing that scientists close to the problem might disagree with the GAC report'. This, at least, was his interpretation of Manley's behaviour on 1 November when he was on his way east to see McMahon. Teller was in Chicago to try to discover from Fermi what had happened at the GAC meeting; he himself had not been there, and it is in keeping that he felt he had been prevented from appearing before the Committee. During their conversation Manley had telephoned to ask him not to call on McMahon. Manley's version of the incident differs sharply from this, apparently, but since it is not available, it is not possible to say how. The official history says merely that Manley suggested the meeting 'would only confuse the situation'.[77]

Teller was also sure that when the GAC report was made available at Los Alamos, it was with the intention of undermining support for a thermonuclear programme. He even went so far as to say that the report stopped work at the laboratory 'because we were instructed not to work', an extraordinary view to take of something which could only be advisory. Later, he was to complain that the report was 'not communicated immediately' to Los Alamos. In Nichols' indictment, the charge took a somewhat different form. There, Oppenheimer was accused of having the majority and minority annexes to the report distributed 'separately and in private, to top personnel at Los Alamos . . . for the purpose of trying to turn such top personnel against the development of the hydrogen bomb'.[78]

All this was denied in an affidavit from Manley, later confirmed by Bradbury. The GAC report, Manley stated, had not been despatched to Los Alamos until the Commission's views were sent to the President on 9 November. He had shown it, together with the annexes, to Bradbury and seven other leading figures at the laboratory (including Teller) on 12, 13 and 14 November. In addition, he had shown them to several members of the laboratory's Technical Board, in preparation for a visit by McMahon on 15 November. He had done so on the authorization of the General Manager of the Commission, Carroll L.

Wilson, and of Bradbury. Everything was done in accordance with established procedures, and Oppenheimer had nothing whatever to do with the matter.[79]

This would almost certainly have cut no ice with Oppenheimer's opponents in the autumn of 1949. They were furious at what he and the Committee had done, and they laid much of the blame at his door. At a later stage in the debate over the bomb, on 20 January 1950, Senator McMahon was to state his belief that the GAC 'had gone far beyond their area of competence in opposing the Super on moral and political grounds and for that transgression they would suffer in the judgment of history'. When Lilienthal saw him on 31 October to discuss the report, the Senator was in an explosive mood. War with Russia was inevitable, Lilienthal understood him to say, and there was only one solution : 'blow them off the face of the earth, quick, before they do the same to us—and we haven't much time'. This (one hopes) was a misreading of McMahon's rhetoric; what could not be in doubt was that he was still passionately in favour of the hydrogen bomb, and he intended to rally its supporters after the setback they had just suffered.[80]

McMahon, indeed was to act as the spearhead of the counter-attack which was now launched against the General Advisory Committee's findings. On 1 November, he fired off the first of a series of letters to Truman, urging him not to give way to the pressure to renounce the bomb. On 2 November he received Teller in the Capitol building; the GAC report, he said, 'just makes me sick'. They both reaffirmed their determination not to admit defeat. The following week he left for a tour of the Commission's major facilities in the west, in the course of which he took the opportunity to confer with Strauss, who had withdrawn in deep depression to Beverly Hills. McMahon comforted him with the news that Dean had definitely come over to their side and that most of the Joint Committee were united behind him. On 15 November, he and Borden met Manley at Los Alamos for an up-to-the-minute briefing. Brushing aside Manley's arguments against the bomb, he proposed that the government should present an ultimatum to the Russians, telling them that it would go ahead with its development until they 'behaved'. On 21 November he sent a second letter to the President, rehearsing the case for the bomb at considerable length. By now he could feel much more confident. He had the support of his committee. He had the backing of such distinguished physicists as Teller and Lawrence, who by this juncture was 'very intolerant of anything that would obstruct or delay fusion'. Above all, perhaps, he was in alliance with the Defense Department, and even General Bradley, who had been so sceptical before the GAC meeting, was persuaded to write to Louis A. Johnson, the Secretary of Defense, on 23 November, reporting that the Joint Chiefs had concluded that if the bomb were feasible, American possession of it was imperative.[81]

McMahon was also greatly helped by the relative lack of forcefulness displayed by the opposition. Strauss, in his memoirs, asserts that 'those opposed to the development were more numerous and more articulate' and that they mounted 'a powerful campaign . . . in the various media of information'. Quite what this latter statement means it is difficult to understand, when one remembers that the debate was conducted almost wholly in secret, but even setting that aside, the picture conveyed is misleading. The most striking feature of the opposition in the period after the GAC meeting was its passivity. As Rabi put it : 'We just wrote our report and then went home, and left the field to others.' In the words of Schilling, 'equally qualified scientists differed greatly in the time and energy they spent circulating their views of the technical (and political) prospects'. As Oppenheimer recalled it, the GAC had made its recommendation as challenging as possible so as to bring about a breathing-space for reflection and ease the pressure for a hasty decision. This was not the result. The pro-H-bomb faction was allowed to seize the initiative and its pressure was immediately renewed. Had the Committee followed through, 'history might have been different', as Rabi later remarked. But it did not, and its inertia, in Schilling's somewhat laboured understatement, was to be 'by no means without consequence for the judgments of others'.[82]

The indecisiveness of the GAC was reflected in the Commission itself. Here, one of the main difficulties lay in Lilienthal's position. There was no doubt as to where Lilienthal stood on the issue of the bomb : he was utterly opposed, and on 30 October he described the scientists such as Lawrence and Teller as 'drooling with the prospect and "bloodthirsty" '. But he had come under heavy fire during a congressional investigation of the AEC the previous summer, and his authority was undermined. Several members of the AEC staff thought they detected a loss of grip on Lilienthal's part, and in Manley's view he was not capable of leading a fight on the H-bomb issue. Their fears were no doubt confirmed after 7 November, when Lilienthal placed his resignation before Truman; he agreed to stay on until a decision on the thermo-nuclear programme was reached, but as a 'lame-duck' chairman he was in no position to set his mark on events.[83]

The division of opinion within the Commission was therefore left as sharp as before. It was manifest as soon as the members came together on 3 November. Lilienthal alone was ready to propose an unconditional renunciation of the hydrogen bomb. Smyth joined him in opposing the bomb, but wanted to reserve the right to reverse a decision against it within six months or a year. Pike was uncommitted, and Dean was now aligned with Strauss in rejecting the GAC report. It was clear that as things stood, no single recommendation could be sent to the White House.[84]

One possibility of breaking the deadlock was for the GAC to take the issue straight to the President. At a further AEC meeting on 4 November, Lilienthal reported that Oppenheimer had suggested this to him. But a proposed meeting between the GAC and Truman on 30 October had not taken place, and this one did not either. Instead, the AEC (Strauss excepted) met with the Committee on 7 November in an effort to reach an agreed position.[85]

It was not successful. The report that went to the President on 9 November revealed no change in the situation. It was based on a number of technical considerations formulated by the AEC staff. Among them were the facts that the H-bomb was a mass-destruction weapon of unlimited power and relatively cheap to build. The Russians were believed to be well capable of developing it, and to beat them in a race for possession would entail an all-out effort which would derange the existing pro-gramme and which could not be kept secret. On this basis, Lilienthal, Pike and Smyth believed that the President should announce that he had decided not to proceed with the bomb at that time. Smyth added that he thought Truman should use the occasion to propose a renewal of negotiations on the inter-national control of atomic energy. Strauss and Dean recommended a secret approach to Moscow to sound the Russians out on the possibility of a control agreement. If it failed, Truman —with the approval of the Defense Department—could announce a decision to go ahead.[86]

This was to be the last time the Atomic Energy Commission alone was given the opportunity of pronouncing on the issue. Up to this point, it had been left almost entirely to the Commission, but with the failure to reach consensus it was taken out of AEC hands. On 19 November Truman revived the special committee of the National Security Council, set up earlier in the year and consisting of the Secretary of State, the Secretary of Defense and the Chairman of the AEC. Its mandate was to serve the President with a recommendation 'as to whether and in what manner the United States should undertake the development and possible production of "super" atomic weapons'. The ultimate decision was still unknown, but the AEC would no longer have the exclusive privilege of shaping it, and this, as far as the advocates of the bomb were concerned, was an important gain.[87]

The transfer of advisory power meant, among other things, that the GAC had been effectively removed from the decision-making process. It met again on 3 December to clarify and elaborate its position, but by that time its thoughts were not of decisive interest. Its impotence was perhaps most starkly revealed soon after 13 January, when Bradley sent another letter to Johnson, which was primarily a critique of the findings of the meeting of 3 December. Lilienthal received a copy on 20 January, but when he asked Truman's permission to show it to the Committee, it was refused. The debate approached its conclusion without further reference to the GAC, except for a short hearing before the Joint Committee on Atomic Energy on 30 January, which merely served to tidy up the record. By then, the decision was as good as made, and it was to be a victory for the hydrogen bomb school.[88]

In other words, the coalition of congressional, scientific and military opinion welded together early in October had come out on top. The scientists now had Los Alamos behind them, for on 9 December Bradbury had written to the Commission urging a thermonuclear test 'at the fastest practicable rate'. The Pentagon, for its part, was unshakeably committed, and coordinating them both stood McMahon, whose committee had now emerged as the hub of the pro-H-bomb movement. On 9 January, as Congress opened its new session, McMahon began hearings designed to step up the pressure on the White House. By 20 January the JCAE was ready to call for production plants to be built even before the results of a feasibility test were known.[89]

McMahon's confidence was doubtless fortified by the awareness that the State Department was moving in his direction. On 24 January, a departmental working paper expressed the view that for the Russians to secure a monopoly of thermonuclear weapons 'would cause severe damage not only to our military position but to our foreign policy position'. Acheson felt bound to agree with this assessment. The continuing Soviet threat to western Europe, as most recently evinced in the Berlin blockade, and the establishment of a Communist régime in China made it almost impossible to resist the demand for an ultimate weapon. Moreover, Acheson strongly suspected that negotiations on international control, as advocated by Kennan, would only be spun out by Moscow so as to give the Soviet programme time to come to fruition. He also took very seriously the possibility that the Russians might use a thermonuclear monopoly to attempt political blackmail in the 'grey areas' just beyond the Soviet borders. For all these reasons, he and the Department felt the country could not forgo the bomb.[90]

The pressure for the bomb was also intensified by the fact that news of the debate was leaking to the press. Considering the time it had taken, it was a minor miracle that this had not occurred before. It is true that on 1 November Senator Edwin C. Johnson of Colorado had disclosed the secret during a broadcast put out by a local New York television station, and this was reported in *The Washington Post* on 18 November. Truman, however, had managed to prevent any further revelations. By the second week in January it was becoming more and more difficult to do so, and references to the fact of the debate were sprouting in all the news media. Truman finally admitted that the issue was under consideration at his press conference on 27 January.[91]

All these developments progressively undermined the opposition. When Smyth and Pike appeared before the Joint Committee on 27 January they had lost heart and were not even prepared to defend their position in the face of a barrage of aggressive questioning. They were defeated, and they knew it.[92]

The outcome was already decided, but as if to place it absolutely beyond doubt, an unexpected and shattering piece of news was given to the President. On 27 January, the British nuclear physicist, Klaus Fuchs, confessed that he had passed atomic secrets to the Russians. Fuchs had worked at Los Alamos during the war, and he had attended the conference on thermonuclear problems in the spring of 1946. Whether that had given the Soviet government any great insight into fusion was doubtful, but the possibility could not be ruled out entirely. If any further proof were needed of the dangers of an American renunciation of the bomb, this appeared to be it.[93]

Therefore when the special committee of the National Security Council met to draft its recommendation to the President on the morning of 31 January, its discussion was little more than a formality. The fullest account we have of the meeting comes from Lilienthal, who dictated it a few hours after it took place. The recommendation as originally drafted envisaged three things. First, the AEC was to be directed 'to proceed to determine the technical feasibility of a thermonuclear weapon'. By this, an actual test was understood, and here, the committee accepted the proposal of Bradbury, put forward on 9 December. The rate and scale of the effort were to be determined jointly by the AEC and the Defense Department, while ordnance developments and a carrier programme were to go forward concurrently.[94]

In the second place, the Secretary of State and the Secretary of Defense were to be instructed to carry out 'a reexamination of our objectives and of the effect of these objectives on our strategic plans' in the light of Soviet achievements. In other words, this was to be a full appraisal of the diplomatic and military consequences likely to flow from American possession of the bomb. The General Advisory Committee, Acheson promised, would be consulted here, 'particularly since they had taken a strong and critical view about our present policies in this whole matter'.[95]

Thirdly, pending this re-examination, the President would defer a decision 'as to whether thermonuclear weapons should be produced beyond the number required for a test of feasibility'. In other words, the project was not to aim immediately at

5 Oppenheimer opposes Strauss before the Joint Committee on Atomic Energy, 13 June 1949

6 Edward Teller, the leading scientific advocate of the hydrogen bomb

7 William L. Borden, whose distrust of Oppenheimer drove him to lay an accusation of treason before the FBI

8 J. Edgar Hoover, the FBI Director, who forwarded Borden's allegations to the White House

quantity production, as the Joint Committee had urged on 20 January.[96]

As the meeting progressed, certain modifications were introduced into this draft. At Johnson's suggestion, the third item was deleted, although this did not turn the first recommendation into a recommendation for quantity production, as we shall see. Nonetheless, Smyth, who was also present, objected to the deletion on the grounds that it weakened the proposal for a policy review contained in the second section. Lilienthal, who was the originator of the idea of the review, also felt, understandably, that a decision to mount a test programme would set the terms of reference for the review and prejudice its outcome. To this, Acheson replied that a decision to go ahead could not be deferred because of the rapidly growing pressure from Congress. Johnson agreed : 'the heat was on in the Congress,' he said, 'and every hour counted in getting this matter disposed of.'[97]

Accordingly, the committee went straight to Truman. Admiral Souers, who accompanied them, is reported to have told the President that he did not think he had a choice : 'It's either we make it or wait until the Russians drop one on us without warning.' Truman, however, had almost certainly made up his mind long before. As he signed the press statement, he remarked that three years ago, when the Truman Doctrine was being formulated, everybody had predicted the end of the world if America threw down an open challenge to Russia. But the world had not come to an end, and he felt the same would happen this time. So the AEC was enjoined 'to continue ... work on all forms of atomic weapons, including the so-called hydrogen or super-bomb'. This, as Truman interpreted it, was an order 'to take whatever steps were necessary to determine whether we could make and set off a hydrogen weapon'.[98]

It is important to remember that this was *not* a decision to go into production of the bomb. The Defense Department was keenly aware of this and pressed hard for as broad as possible a construction of Truman's directive (although it had still not established a formal requirement for the weapon !). Thus Robert LeBaron, Johnson's deputy secretary for atomic energy affairs and the chairman of the Military Liaison Committee of the AEC, called on 2 February for the production of enough tritium to make it possible to go into production at once if a test were

E

successful. Pike, who was acting Chairman of the Commission (Lilienthal left on 15 February), was ready to accept this. As he testified at the hearing, the country 'could be in no more miserable position than to have a successful development on our hands and then have to spend 3 or 4 years in building factories to produce the thing'. On 10 February he outlined plans for a programme which would go beyond the need for testing alone.[99]

This was still not enough for Johnson, however. On 24 February, intensely alarmed by the possibility that Fuchs had given Russia a long lead in the race for the bomb, he and the Joint Chiefs appealed to Truman for a crash programme. The Joint Chiefs had explicitly discounted this in their study of 13 January, but now nothing less was demanded than 'immediate implementation of all-out development of hydrogen bombs and means for their production and delivery'. On 1 March LeBaron declared that the Pentagon would readily accept a cutback in fission weapons to speed up the thermonuclear project, but the AEC replied that it needed a further directive from the White House before it could prepare for stockpile production of thermonuclear materials.[100]

Truman once again referred the issue to the special committee of the National Security Council. On 9 March the committee reported that there were 'no known additional steps which might be taken for further acceleration of the test program', and that the earliest possible date for a full test was late in 1952 (an extremely accurate forecast). Even then, it pointed out, success could not be guaranteed, but the production reactors could be turned to the manufacture of plutonium if fusion was impossible and tritium could not be put to use. Nonetheless, the following day Truman issued the order the Defense Department had asked for. Research on the hydrogen bomb was proclaimed to be a matter 'of the highest urgency' and the AEC was instructed 'to plan at once for quantity production'. If the bomb were feasible, the possibility of assessing its value in the broad framework of a policy review was foreclosed, as Lilienthal had feared; the first draft of the review reached Truman on 7 April, four weeks *after* his new fiat to the Commission. The die was cast, but it still remained to be seen whether the gamble on feasibility would come off.[101]

The outcome of the hydrogen bomb debate is not surprising.

What is, is the fact that it took nearly six months to reach it. This is, admittedly a tribute to the democratic process, and it is worth remembering that the Soviet government allowed no such hesitation, yet it is inconceivable that the argument could have ended in a decision to renounce the bomb. In many ways, it was an argument conducted in unreal terms. As both Kennan and Lilienthal pointed out, the problems confronting the United States in the mid-twentieth century were not necessarily soluble by possession of the latest means of mass destruction. There had been considerable restrictions on America's freedom of action in the years of atomic monopoly, and these restrictions would not be removed simply by obtaining a thermonuclear striking force. Again, as Kennan remarked, the H-bomb was not all-important when one called to mind the existence of biological and chemical weapons.[102]

Both men sought other answers. For Kennan they lay in 'plans that envisage the constructive and peaceful progress of humanity'. In other words, it was America's primary interest to foster economic and social development and make this its response to the Communist challenge. For Lilienthal, the need was to step up the country's conventional capability, that is, its capacity to fight a non-nuclear war if such a war should break out (as it soon did in Korea). Neither policy, however, was acceptable in the circumstances. The hydrogen bomb appeared to offer a definitive reply to the Communist threat; their solutions seemed arduous, expensive and uncertain. Moreover, their appraisal of the situation was much too sophisticated for those whose reaction to a crisis was what Dean rightly called 'visceral', and in this instance, as in so many others, instinct prevailed over reason.[103]

Truman's decision had wide repercussions, as was only to be expected. As far as the General Advisory Committee was concerned, it signalled the beginning of the end of its influence within the AEC, which had been supreme since its foundation. The Committee itself was immediately aware of this. When Lilienthal broke the news to them on leaving the White House, he described the occasion as 'like a funeral party, especially when I said we were all gagged. Should they resign? I said definitely not, on the contrary. This would be very bad. Though before long a number of them may, just because they feel their standing is impaired.'[104]

Here, Lilienthal touched on an issue which was to assume considerable importance in the development of the Oppenheimer affair. It was Pitzer who raised it at the hearing. He had been very surprised, he said, that after 31 January Oppenheimer should have retained his position as chairman of the GAC. He should have resigned, and, at the most extreme, all his colleagues with him. Alternatively, a new advisory panel should have been set up.[105]

In fact, as we have just seen, he—and the entire GAC—had offered to resign at once, and Lilienthal's answer had been an emphatic 'no'. Oppenheimer nonetheless persisted, together with Conant, but they got an equally negative response from Acheson. Later, during the summer, Oppenheimer thought of resignation yet again, and in about August tendered it to the new Chairman, Dean. Once more, the offer was turned down. It could easily have been accepted. For one thing, Dean and Oppenheimer had disagreed over the hydrogen bomb, and this would have been an ideal opportunity for Dean to rid himself of an adviser who had opposed him on such a fundamental issue. For another, whereas a resignation in February would have been an acute embarrassment to the administration, six months later Oppenheimer could have gone without any fuss. That he was not allowed to do so testifies to the high value which was still placed on him. At the same time, however, it deepened the chagrin of his enemies, and in the view of Pitzer and of Bethe, it was one of the main reasons why he was brought to judgment at the end of 1953.[106]

As Oppenheimer's opponents understood it, he was clinging to office in a determined bid to preserve his influence. As we have seen, this was already extremely suspect, and their suspicions remained even after the announcement of Truman's decision. Oppenheimer, they believed, was not prepared to accept the decision. He had made a last-ditch effort to counter it, via his 'mouthpiece' Lilienthal, at the meeting of 31 January, and he was going to do everything in his power to minimise its consequences. Thus, at a party thrown by Strauss in the evening of 31 January to celebrate both the H-bomb victory and his resignation from the AEC, Oppenheimer was supposed to have remarked that, 'as Woodrow Wilson said, "A battle is never won or lost" '. In other words, he was not going to give up his struggle against the thermonuclear programme.[107]

The first evidence adduced in support of this view related to his reaction to Teller's attempt to activate the programme. In an article entitled 'Back to the Laboratories', published in the *Bulletin of the Atomic Scientists* in March, Teller issued a call to action. 'To my mind', wrote Teller, 'we are in a situation not less dangerous than the one we were facing in 1939 [when the proposal for American development of an atomic bomb was first put forward], and it is of the greatest importance that we realize it. . . . The holiday is over. Hydrogen bombs will not produce themselves. Neither will rockets nor radar. If we want to live on the technological capital of the last war, we shall come out second best.'[108]

In Teller's view, Oppenheimer responded to this summons with a marked lack of enthusiasm. A few days before Truman's announcement he had refused an invitation from Teller to join the programme, and so in the spring Teller asked him not for his direct participation but for help in recruitment. Oppenheimer, according to Teller, had replied that he was neutral, but gave Teller a list of men working at the Institute for Advanced Study. None of them had come to Los Alamos. As Dean recollected at the hearing, Teller had told him thought he would not get much help out of Oppenheimer, and even feared that Oppenheimer might discourage people from going to the laboratory. The official history recounts that on 23 February Teller declared that the hesitation of some of the older scientists had deterred some of their younger colleagues from entering the project, and on 3 March he disclosed his anxieties about recruitment to a hearing of the Joint Committee. He later wrote to Borden that he felt the attitude of the GAC was at the root of the difficulties. 'A man like Conant or Oppenheimer can do a great deal in an informal manner which will hurt or further our efforts.' According to the authors of *The Hydrogen Bomb*, a request by the Committee to the AEC for its support in the matter was rejected by Pike after consultation with Oppenheimer. Teller, or so it seemed to his partisans, was being blocked at every turn. 'It took guts for Edward to go ahead', one of them was reported as saying. 'You don't fight God, you know, and Einstein [an arch-opponent of the bomb] was God and Oppie was His only begotten Son.' As a result, 'the climate at Los Alamos was at least indifferent, more often hostile', although there was no evidence that Oppenheimer 'took overt action to persuade the scientists at the weapons laboratory to strike against the President's decision'.[109]

Again, Oppenheimer denied these charges. As he wrote in his letter of 4 March 1954, 'we never again raised the question of the wisdom of the policy which had now been settled, but concerned ourselves rather with trying to implement it'. This was confirmed by a supporter of the bomb, von Neumann. Oppenheimer and all those who had opposed the development 'took this decision with very good grace and cooperated'. As Bethe pointed out, he was extremely careful to observe Truman's injunction to the GAC not to air the controversy over the bomb in public, and in fact he made only two public references to the subject. One was in a radio broadcast with Mrs Roosevelt on 12 February, in which he deplored the secrecy in which the debate had been conducted. The other was an address to secondary-school boys on 6 March, when he told them that unless attitudes to the hydrogen bomb were different when they came of age, 'you will have reason to reproach your elders for your inheritance'.[110]

Bethe, on the other hand, had openly criticized the decision. So too had Bacher who, according to Alvarez, had supported the bomb the previous October. Speaking in Los Angeles on 27 March, Bacher described it as a weapon 'on which we can place relatively little reliance for the future. Quantities of hydrogen bombs will not contribute very much to the security of the United States.' It could be pointed out that neither man bore public responsibilities. Bethe was a private citizen and Bacher had left the AEC in May 1949. The same, however, could not be said of Representative W. Sterling Cole who, as *The New York Times* remarked a week after the hearing opened, had on 17 July 1950 expressed 'very grave doubts as to whether such a weapon would be a very useful addition to our arsenal.' Congressman Cole was then a member of the Joint Committee on Atomic Energy, and in spite of his speech a member he remained.[111]

At the same time, Oppenheimer denied Nichols' charge that he had been 'instrumental in persuading other outstanding scientists not to work on the hydrogen-bomb project'. Both Teller and Bradbury mentioned the fact that he had given the physicist Conrad Longmire leave of absence from the Institute for Advanced Study to go and work at Los Alamos before the Soviet test and he had made no objections when Longmire stayed there. Von Neumann also pointed out that Oppenheimer had made no difficulties about releasing him from the Institute to work on the calculations for the thermonuclear programme, and that the MANIAC computer (which was of the utmost importance in the final stage of the programme) was built at the Institute, needless to say with Oppenheimer's approval. Moreover, Willard F. Libby, a supporter of the bomb whom Pitzer believed he had succeeded in getting appointed to the General Advisory Committee in August 1950, also turned out to have been recommended by Oppenheimer. Strauss in his memoirs noted that 'contrary to predictions, the Commission experienced no difficulty in finding dedicated scientists who were willing to work on the H-bomb', and by the close of the hearing not one name of a man dissuaded by Oppenheimer had been brought forward.[112]

As for his alleged refusal 'to cooperate fully in the project', Oppenheimer explained that he did not give 'active support' after 31 January 'in the sense that I rolled up my sleeves and went to work'. Nor did he do so in the sense of attracting people to the job as he had attracted them to Los Alamos in the winter of 1942–43. It might have been, he said, that he could have stimulated activity simply by being at Los Alamos again, but he believed that it was impossible to be a real source of inspiration 'unless you are doing something about it yourself'. Here, perhaps, Oppenheimer put his finger on the ambiguity of his position. He was not opposing the programme outright—that would have been stupid and dangerous. Instead, he was lending it his formal support, but no more, and given his enormous prestige, this was tantamount to weakening it. Probably the most accurate description of Oppenheimer's attitude and its consequences was provided by an anonymous physicist who chose to call himself a 'neutral observer'. 'There was a feeling at Los Alamos', he said, 'that Oppenheimer, just by being inert at the time of the Truman decision, had put a damper on the hydrogen program.' It was an uncomfortable situation for a sensitive man to be in, and that is why he asked Dean to let him relinquish the chairmanship of the General Advisory Committee late in the summer of 1950. As we have seen, he was not allowed to do this.[113]

Oppenheimer's dilemma could only be ended by the discovery that the bomb could or could not be made, and it was prolonged as long as feasibility remained questionable. This was the case throughout the remainder of 1950. Fusion did not yield its secrets easily and the programme continued to mark time. Meanwhile the GAC supported developments on other fronts. The first task was to expand facilities for the production of vast quantities of neutrons. One possible approach was Lawrence's 'Materials Testing Accelerator' (or MTA), a huge linear accelerator which he hoped would do at least as much for the hydrogen bomb as the electromagnetic process had done for the atomic bomb during the war. The main engine of production, however, was to be a complex of heavy-water reactors to be constructed at Savannah River, South Carolina. Presidential approval was given on 8 June, and almost immediately afterwards, under the impact of the Korean War, yet more production plant was called for. This was authorized by Truman on 9 October.[114]

All these facilities were to be dual-purpose, that is, they could turn out either plutonium for atomic weapons or tritium for the hydrogen bomb. This was just as well as long as the H-bomb remained hypothetical, and it was especially important since there were prospects of immediate improvements in the fission weapons field. These improvements came to light in the summer of 1950, and as Dean remarked in his testimony, they were very significant indeed. A new bomb had been designed which required only a fraction of the critical mass of fissionable material hitherto needed to bring off an explosion. Once it had been successfully tested, the stockpile of atomic bombs would be enormously increased. At a meeting on 10 September the GAC took note of this remarkable progress and it was positive in the view that it should not be jeopardized by the preparations in hand for a test of thermonuclear principles in the spring of 1951.[115]

The importance which the GAC attached to these developments was shared by the Pentagon. In the summer of 1948 a panel of the Committee on Atomic Energy of the Research and Development Board of the Defense Department had attempted a military evaluation of atomic weapons, and it was clear that a further appraisal was now needed. This was especially so in view of the

Korean War, and it was not difficult to see how the smaller fission bombs which were now feasible could be put to tactical use and so relieve the strain on American conventional forces in both Europe and the Far East. Accordingly, LeBaron brought together a second panel, which met for the first time on 21 November. Oppenheimer, who had headed the first, was once again in the chair.[116]

The main concern of the panel was atomic weapons, but it was expected to take the hydrogen bomb programme into account as well. LeBaron, knowing Oppenheimer's attitude towards the bomb, believed that it was 'not inconceivable' that he might use the panel's report to curtail any increase in thermonuclear work. He therefore made sure that four of the ten members were known supporters of fusion—Alvarez and the three generals, Nichols, Wilson and McCormack. They would counterbalance Oppenheimer, Bacher and Charles C. Lauritsen, of the California Institute of Technology, who had all opposed it.[117]

The report was issued on 29 December 1950, and it urged that a major effort be put into fission development. Progress in this area was so immediately important that not even the work on fusion must be allowed to divert attention from it. As the report obliquely put it, 'we believe that only a timely recognition of the long-range character of the thermonuclear program will tend to make available for the basic studies of the fission weapon program the resources of Los Alamos Laboratory.'[118]

These words, it should be remembered, were written at a time when, as Oppenheimer testified, 'technical prospects on the thermonuclear program were quite bleak'. In the fine phrase of the official historians, the project seemed to be 'aground upon the unyielding rock of natural phenomena'. Indeed, the future of the hydrogen bomb then seemed so dark that the panel devoted very little of its time to discussing it, so little that one member who testified on Oppenheimer's behalf, Mervin J. Kelly, could not remember any exchanges on the subject.[119]

Alvarez, testifying for the AEC, remembered a great deal. Oppenheimer and Lauritsen, he said, had argued that the H-bomb programme 'was going to interfere seriously with the small-weapons program by taking away manpower at Los Alamos which could otherwise be put on the hydrogen bomb'. Oppenheimer had also said this : 'We all agree that the hydrogen bomb program should be stopped, but if we were to stop it or to suggest that it be stopped, this would cause so much disruption at Los Alamos and in other laboratories where they are doing instrumentation work that I feel we should let it go on, and it will die a natural death with the coming tests [scheduled for the spring] when those tests fail. At that time will be the natural time to chop the hydrogen bomb program off.'[120]

Alvarez signed the report, although he could not possibly have agreed with what he credited Oppenheimer with having said. As he rationalized it later, he had been unaware of the urgency of the report—although it had been written at a time when President Truman had declared a state of national emergency and when the country was in turmoil over the Chinese intervention in Korea. As the official history points out, the possibility of a general war with Russia in the near future underlay the whole discussion, and it was recognized that victory might well hinge on the ability to bring atomic weapons into play 'in several military situations'. The panel was not a long-range panel, as Alvarez maintained. Its predecessor of 1948 had been, but it most surely was not. Nor was its report 'anything more than a document to go into the files to be looked at in two or three years', as Alvarez described it. Its significance was immediate, and Alvarez himself admitted that the weapons primarily under discussion could be produced in less than two years.[121]

None of this, Alvarez stated, became clear to him until later. The implications of the report were not lost on Teller, however. 'Luis,' he raged, 'how could you ever have signed that report, feeling the way you do about hydrogen bombs? . . . it has caused me no end of trouble at Los Alamos. It is being used against our program. It is slowing it down and it could easily kill it.' Someone in the AEC, Teller was convinced, had read the report and had apparently tried to use it to re-orientate work at Los Alamos to the detriment of the H-bomb. Alvarez felt a fool, exactly, in his view, like the hapless Secretary of the Army, Stevens, after his unwitting capitulation to Senator McCarthy at their celebrated luncheon meeting on 24 February 1954.[122]

At the hearing Oppenheimer denied Alvarez' allegations, and particularly his supposed remarks about the spring 1951 test, but they showed how the suspicions of his behaviour had persisted. Indeed, early in February 1951 Dean was informed that he had 'effectively dampened enthusiasm over the Super'. The real cause of the lack of progress lay elsewhere, however, in the inability to discover a formula which would produce a workable bomb. On 9 February, Strauss visited Dean and read to him a long memorandum advocating still more effort on the problem. This was almost certainly a counsel of near-despair. A year after Truman's directive, the researchers on the thermonuclear project were still groping for an answer.[123]

Yet although Dean and Strauss did not know it, that answer was in fact emerging. Two weeks after their meeting, the mathematician Stanislaw M. Ulam, who was working on thermonuclear calculations at Los Alamos, wrote a letter to von Neumann. In it, he outlined a scheme for a hydrogen bomb which immediately superseded all previous approaches. As Oppenheimer correctly pointed out at the hearing, 'with the hydrogen bomb ... the pacing factor was ideas'. Here, at last, was the critical idea, and Teller, whom Ulam had spoken to about it, was full of excitement about the vistas it opened up.[124]

In the months that followed, Ulam and Teller elaborated the new concept and by the late spring they were ready to present it to the AEC. At the instance of Oppenheimer, a meeting was held at the Institute for Advanced Study on 16 and 17 June 1951. In attendance were, among others, the full Commission, the General Manager, McCormack, Bradbury, six of the nine members of the GAC, Teller, Bethe, and von Neumann. After Teller's presentation, no one could doubt that the bomb was now a possibility. The meeting, in the words of the official history, was 'a turning-point in the quest for a thermonuclear weapon'. 'Everyone clearly recognized', as Teller later wrote, 'that with a little luck, only a great deal of hard work stood between us and final success.'[125]

Oppenheimer, it should be noted, shared in the general enthusiasm. The discovery was, in his words, 'technically so sweet that you could not argue about that. . . . it is my judgment in these things that when you see something that is technically sweet, you go ahead and do it and you argue about what to do about it only after you have had your technical success.' He could not easily imagine, he added, that if he had known in October 1949 what he knew in June 1951 the tone of the GAC report would have been the same. When questioned by Robb about his alleged lack of support for the H-bomb, he was quick to say that he had 'certainly helped to make the decision which I believe got the thing started in the right direction'. It was Bradbury's opinion that Oppenheimer and the GAC as a whole were willing to go even farther than Los Alamos in support of the new approach.[126]

To left-wing commentators such as Robert Jungk, this 'macabre enthusiasm' was only further confirmation of their belief that Oppenheimer was infatuated with power and would accommodate himself to anything in order to stay close to it. Others did not see things this way. Not long after the Princeton conference, reports were still circulating 'that the GAC was not facilitating thermonuclear work, and even that scientists both within and without the GAC were actively working to prevent the success of the H-bomb'. As late as October 1951, John Walker, a new employee of the Joint Committee and a close friend of Borden, could find no more than a dozen important scientists in favour of the bomb, and this situation he ascribed to Oppenheimer.[127]

There is no evidence that Teller shared these views, but he was becoming increasingly doubtful about the capacity of Los Alamos to give the work on the thermonuclear programme the necessary impetus. He was sure that Bradbury's approach was far too conservative, and differences between them were apparent from at least the beginning of 1951. By the spring, Teller had come to the conclusion that the issue could only be resolved by setting up a second weapons laboratory quite separate from Los Alamos, and on 20 April he made a formal proposal to Dean for a new establishment at Boulder, Colorado. Borden and Strauss, apparently, offered their help, and the Air Force indicated that it was interested in the project if the test of thermonuclear principles scheduled for 1 May proved a success.[128]

The idea of a second laboratory had already been aired before the GAC in September 1950, but nothing had come of it. Teller's proposal did not bring it up again immediately as a problem for the Committee to consider since he did not press it. He was ready to stay at Los Alamos on certain conditions, above all, if one of Bradbury's key men were replaced. Early in September 1951, at a conference in Chicago, he told Oppenheimer that he would be happy to work under him or Bethe or Fermi. Oppenheimer promised he would consult Bradbury and, as he expected, Bradbury rejected the idea. He himself was not comfortable about it either. As he said in his testimony, he did not think he could repeat his wartime exploit: 'you can't make an omelette rise twice. . . . I would have been ancient and not on my toes anymore.' Moreover, success would have depended decisively on a high degree of personal commitment on the part of the man involved, and this he did not possess. At the end of September, therefore, Teller made the final break with Bradbury and left Los Alamos for good. 'I felt', he later wrote, 'that the safety of our country could not be entrusted to a single laboratory, even though that laboratory were as excellent as Los Alamos.'[129]

On 11 October, he put his proposal for a second laboratory to the GAC; it was turned down. On 13 December he made a personal appeal to the Committee, but this time the proposal was rejected by the AEC itself. On 19 December, one of the Commissioners, Thomas E. Murray, joined with Teller in submitting a memorandum urging the scheme on the AEC. At the same time, McMahon and the Joint Committee entered a plea. Neither was successful. On 9 January 1952 Dean wrote to the JCAE to say that 'the division of talent between Los Alamos and a competing laboratory would at this time retard rather than accelerate the development program'.[130]

As usual, the fountain-head of the opposition was identified as Oppenheimer. This was the opinion of Murray, given in a conversation with David T. Griggs, who had recently taken up the post of Chief Scientist of the Air Force. Griggs had met Teller and, like him, was convinced that a second laboratory was the only way of ensuring the H-bomb was pushed as hard as possible. Early in February 1952 he arranged a meeting between Teller and Thomas K. Finletter, the Air Force Secretary. Shortly afterwards, on 21 February, McMahon indicated that the Joint Committee's interest was still strong by holding a hearing on the subject. Nothing, he averred, could be permitted to stop the United States being the first to have thermonuclear weapons.[131]

At this stage, the Air Force was even prepared to set up the laboratory under its own auspices, if need be, since the Atomic Energy Act did allow the armed forces to carry out work on nuclear weapons if authorized by the President. Preliminary negotiations were entered into with the University of Chicago, which already had a contract with the Air Force. At the same time, Griggs arranged for Teller to brief the Secretary of Defense, Robert A. Lovett, who had recently said that he saw no reason to move thermonuclear development from Los Alamos at that juncture. Borden, likewise by-passing the AEC, made a 'final appeal' to LeBaron. On 27 March the three service secretaries petitioned Lovett to take the issue to the National Security Council. By the time Dean went to the Pentagon on 1 April for yet another briefing by Teller, the decision had been made over his head: a second laboratory would, after all, come into being, and it would be the responsibility of the Commission.[132]

By common consent, it was to be sited at Livermore, where Lawrence's gigantic Materials Testing Accelerator had been constructed. Lawrence himself had suggested this to Teller during a visit he had paid to Berkeley on 2 February, and the suggestion was adopted by the AEC as the least disruptive of the several available alternatives. It was confirmed by the demise of the MTA during the following months. Lawrence's project did not expire for technical reasons: tests carried out in April were successful. It was brought to an end because the AEC considered there was no economic justification for it. The heavy-water reactors were a much more efficient way of producing neutrons, and so the MTA succumbed to them much as the electromagnetic process gave way before gaseous diffusion in 1945. In this way, the field was left clear for Teller and his new laboratory. Teller moved in on 14 July and by September he had more than a hundred scientists and technicians working under him on fusion weapon research. Within two years, it was believed there would be a thousand.[133]

The controversy over the second laboratory by no means closed the story of Oppenheimer's attitude to the bomb, as developed during the hearing. As we shall see, many more considerations were to be opened up than had already been touched on. As far as the bomb *per se* was concerned, however, there was only one more short chapter to be added. It concerned the first test, to be carried out at Eniwetok Atoll in the Pacific on 1 November 1952, local time. On 14 April, Oppenheimer had been appointed chairman of a State Department panel on disarmament, and in that context it had discussed the forthcoming test. Sometime in June, Oppenheimer raised the possibility of postponing it, as did Bethe. The test was due just a few days before the presidential election, and they feared it might become a political issue if the news leaked to the public. It would also confront a new President—Truman was not running again—with an accomplished fact for which he was not responsible but for which he would never the less have to bear the full responsibility. Bush, who was also serving on the panel, went directly to Acheson to put this view, and to argue that the test might also be postponed as part of an attempt to reach a test-ban agreement with Russia. At the hearing, Lauritsen also testified that he was concerned that the government should not let slip the opportunity to try for a test-ban treaty and also for an agreement on limiting the use of thermonuclear weapons. Oppenheimer was associated with these ideas, although not, apparently in his capacity as chairman of the disarmament panel.[134]

His opponents once again read highly sinister implications into his views. During his cross-examination on this point, Robb insinuated that Oppenheimer had really wanted to postpone the test because without it, it would be impossible to tell whether or not a thermonuclear device would work. In other words, he was trying to stall for time in the hope that the government would change its policy and decide not to manufacture the bomb after all. Robb did not go so far as the anonymous writer in *Fortune* magazine a year before. There, the disarmament panel was credited with generating a proposal that the President 'should announce that the U.S. had decided, on humanitarian grounds, not to bring the weapon to final test; and that it would regard the detonation of a similar device by any other power as an act of war.' The drift of his questioning, however, was clear enough. Oppenheimer's bid to prevent the test was all of a piece with the attitude he had shown since 1945. He had opposed the bomb throughout, *and* he had opposed it covertly but powerfully even after the presidential order to step up the programme. Ultimately, he had been unsuccessful. The test was carried out on schedule, and the country had been made secure, but if Oppenheimer had had his way, things would have been very different.[135]

This, then, was the substance of the case in so far as it bore on Oppenheimer's attitude to the development of the hydrogen bomb. What was its significance for the prosecution and the defence?

It was twofold. In the first place, the allegations relating to the H-bomb could be considered in their own right. If they were, however, the AEC was at once open to the criticism that it was putting Oppenheimer on trial for his opinions. This was the view of the scientists in particular. Rabi, who had succeeded Oppenheimer as chairman of the GAC, told how he had spoken to Strauss in January 1954 about his 'very grave misgivings as to the nature of this charge', and there was no doubt that he was talking about this section of the indictment. Even Pitzer, who testified against Oppenheimer, said that he felt 'very strongly that scientists should feel free to advise the Government and not be held to account if their advice proves not the best afterward'.[136]

The most formidable protests came from Conant and Bush. Nichols' letter, said Conant, 'would indicate that anybody who opposed the development of the hydrogen bomb was not eligible for employment on atomic energy work later'. If that were so, then it would apply to himself since he had opposed the bomb in 1949 as strongly as anyone else on the GAC (most strongly of all, in all probability). Moreover, if one accepted this interpretation of the charge, it could be extrapolated to mean that anyone who gave advice to the government on any subject could later be dismissed as a security risk on account of the views he had put forward.[137]

Bush was even more emphatic. The Board, he said, should have asked for Nichols' letter to be re-drafted in such a way as to remove all implication that Oppenheimer was being tried for his opinions. Although he did not say so, he clearly believed that this part of the indictment should not have been considered at all. When Gray pointed out that there was another range of items as well—those relating to Communist associations—Bush agreed, and declared that 'the case should have been tried on those'. As it was, 'this has gotten into a very bad mess [and] I don't see how you can get out'.[138]

Garrison, however, dissociated himself entirely from what Bush had to say. He and Oppenheimer were quite willing for the H-bomb allegations to stand. The question was not whether Oppenheimer had expressed opinions, but whether they had been expressed in good faith or not. Garrison's defence was therefore dedicated to the proposition that the advice Oppenheimer had tendered had been offered honestly, and, as he later put it, 'if Dr Oppenheimer's motives were honorable, his recommendations were irrelevant'.[139]

This was the second way of looking at the hydrogen bomb charges. Instead of being considered independently, they had to be related to the first half of the indictment. It was Bush's contention that this link between the two parts had not been made clear, as it should have been. Indeed, the connection had not been spelled out, but it was very strongly implied and apparent to most. Conant brought out the implication in his testimony. It was that 'Dr Oppenheimer's association with alleged Communist sympathizers ... somehow created a state of mind in Dr Oppenheimer that he opposed the development of the hydrogen bomb for what might be said reasons which were detrimental to the best interests of the United States, because they were interests of the Soviet Union which he in one way or another had at heart.' As Garrison put it in the brief he submitted to the Board on 17 May, Oppenheimer was being accused of having been 'motivated by a sinister purpose to aid Russia at the expense of our own country'. This was the instinctive reaction on most people's part when the charges were first published. Mrs Trilling has written that she immediately believed 'that Dr Oppenheimer, once an admitted fellow-traveler, had favored the fiercest possible weapon which would presumably be used against Germany or Japan but had opposed the fiercest possible weapon which would presumably be used against Russia'.[140]

Robb, needless to say, took this second view of the charges, as he made clear in his questioning of Bush, and just as Garrison based his defence on the innocence of Oppenheimer's motivation, so he did his utmost to discredit it. It was for this reason that he spent so much of his time building up the impression that Oppenheimer's associations went on exerting a continuing influence on his actions during his years of government service. Once he could establish that Oppenheimer's relations with Chevalier, Peters, Bohm and Lomanitz were suspect, it was not difficult to transfer the suspicion to Oppenheimer's attitude to the H-bomb. At the outset of the Cold War, the director of the FBI had warned the country against 'subversive or disloyal persons' in the government who would attempt to influence policy so that it 'will either favor the foreign country of their ideological choice or will weaken the United States Government ... to the ultimate advantage of the above indicated foreign power'. Seven years later, with the Mc-Carthyist fears of such subversion at their peak, public opinion was receptive even to the idea that the administration's top-ranking adviser in this crucial field had betrayed his trust and failed to put the interests of his country first. It remained to be seen whether Robb could persuade the Personnel Security Board to accept such a view or whether Garrison could convince them that it was beyond possibility.[141]

Chapter Five

Vista and Lincoln

In its exhaustive examination of Oppenheimer's political past and his attitude to the development of the hydrogen bomb, the hearing had covered the two main sets of allegations raised in Nichols' letter of notification. It went beyond the letter, however, and broke new ground in addressing itself to two further major items. These were related to the hydrogen bomb, but to its military application and not to its development as such. They concerned the use of tactical atomic weapons and the air defence of the United States. Oppenheimer was involved by reason of his participation in two study groups set up to explore the problems, Project Vista in 1951 and the Lincoln Summer Study in 1952.

Both were considered germane to the inquiry by the terms of Section 4.15(j) of the AEC Security Clearance Procedures, which allowed for the broadening of the notification letter. At the start of the hearing, Garrison had indicated that he would not insist on the formal amendment of the letter, but that he would like adequate notice of new items if they were to be brought up. He was therefore surprised when, half-way through, Robb began to direct his attention to both questions and he queried their relevance immediately. Robb contended that they did have a bearing on the case, and pointed out, rightly, that Garrison had already introduced testimony on tactical atomic weapons (and, he could have added, on air defence). Up to this point, however, neither topic had taken on any great significance. Thereafter, both came well into the foreground, and towards the close of the proceedings, Gray was anxious to point out that the Board considered them 'material to the matters under consideration'. Garrison had no choice but to accept this view. Clearly, there were serious allegations on both subjects in Oppenheimer's secret dossier, and 'the more they were brought to the surface and answered, the better'.[1]

The significance of tactical atomic weapons and air defence derived from the challenge which they both presented to the doctrine of strategic air power, and it cannot be fully understood without some reference to the importance of that doctrine in current American defence policy.

The idea of strategic air power grew out of the experience of the First World War, and its first influential exponent was the Italian, Giulio Douhet. In 1921 Douhet published *Il Dominio dell' Aria,* usually translated as *The Command of the Air.* In this book he argued that in the next great-power conflict it would be possible to avoid the stalemate which had marked so much of the war of 1914–18. A quick victory could be won, and it would be won in the air. The secret of success lay in a swift penetration by an aerial bombing force deep into enemy territory. The targets would be air bases, factories and cities, and the objective would be to destroy the enemy's air force on its own ground, to wipe out his industrial capacity and to shatter the morale of his civilian population. Since there was no defence against such an attack, the war would be over in a matter of weeks, at most.[2]

Douhet's concepts were taken up with enthusiasm in flying circles. In the United States their most sensational advocate was Brigadier-General 'Billy' Mitchell, who was court-martialled after he had accused the upper echelons of the military establishment of treasonably disregarding them, but many others besides Mitchell found them irresistible. Like him, they called for an Air Force which would take the biggest share of the defence budget, and an Air Force which would give overwhelming priority to its offensive arm. Moreover, their belief that bombing would force a decision in the next war was widely shared. As Stanley Baldwin stated to the House of Commons on 10 November 1932 : 'The bomber will always get through. . . . The only defence is in offence.' When war broke out, it was generally expected that cities would be demolished at once, bringing huge casualty figures and a complete breakdown of normal life.[3]

The experience of the Second World War did not bear out these forecasts. The outbreak of war did not lead to the anticipated exchange of 'knock-out blows', and when the initial stalemate was broken it was broken by the application of tactical, not strategic air power, acting in close conjunction with highly mobile, mechanized units of infantry and armour on the ground. It was one of the ironies of the war that this *Blitzkrieg* gave its name to city bombing, a purely strategic conception. At the same time, defensive measures in the form of radar and fighter aircraft had the edge over the bomber for the greater part of the war and were able to reduce the threat it posed to acceptable proportions. Thus German war production did not flag until the second half of 1944, and German civilian morale did not crack at all, to judge by the country's spirit of resistance which remained high until the very last moment.

The significance of the war for strategic air power was distorted, however, by the way it came to an end. The German capacity to put up an effective defence in the air was destroyed by the fact that after June 1944 the armed forces were fighting on two major fronts simultaneously as well as having to cope with air attack on Germany itself. Japan for its part was placed in the stranglehold of an ever-tightening naval blockade and was similarly over-committed on land. In both cases, a defence was not offered not so much because it was technically impossible as because there simply were not the resources to construct it from. The result was that both countries were laid wide open to air attack, and it was driven home with impunity. Hence the holocausts of Dresden, Tokyo, and, ultimately, Hiroshima and Nagasaki.

The devotees of strategic air power could therefore point to the war as proof that their claims had been vindicated. Moreover, their position was reinforced by several factors in the immediate post-war period. For one thing, the United States held a monopoly of the atomic bomb which had come to symbolize the triumph of the strategic air offensive. For another, conventional forces were unpopular; quite apart from their expense, losses in a ground war were almost certain to be high. For another, the American atomic stockpile was still too small and its components still too bulky for nuclear weapons to be used against any other than strategic objectives. For all these reasons, strategic bombing was given pride of place in the American response to the Soviet challenge which began to develop not long after 1945.

In addition, there were two peculiarly American elements in the situation which enhanced the attractiveness of the doctrine.

The first was the still-powerful fear of a second Pearl Harbor. Among those who believed that another surprise attack was all too likely, especially when the enemy was a Communist dictatorship unfettered by the constraints which bound a democracy, was William L. Borden. In 1946, shortly after he left the Air Force, Borden published a small book entitled, significantly, *There Will Be No Time*. 'Tomorrow,' he wrote, 'the enemy will prepare at his leisure and then strike, when, where, and how he chooses.' The only thing capable of preventing such an attack or of delivering a crushing counter-blow was strategic air power, and Borden believed that if a reprisal were necessary, the Air Force should be authorized to take it regardless of opinion in the Senate and regardless of the level of international tension.[4]

The second specifically American factor favouring the strategic air force was its appeal to isolationism. The force was exclusively American and it was believed to have taken the place of the 'Big Navy' urged by Mahan in the 1890s and championed by Theodore Roosevelt in the 1900s. The days of sea power had gone, but the concept of 'the fleet in being', unseen but omnipresent and always ready to be brought devastatingly into play, could easily be applied to the *corps d'élite* entrusted with the nuclear mission, the Strategic Air Command. As one commentator has put it, 'A preponderant Strategic Air Command—like the Great White Fleet—appeared a device for performing as a world power without getting too deeply enmeshed in the complex, dangerous, interior affairs of Eurasia.' In view of America's decisive commitment to the defence of western Europe after 1947, this was wishful thinking, but although it bore little relation to reality (or, perhaps, because it did so) it was still capable of stimulating a powerful emotional response.[5]

So strategic air power was given the central place in American security policy in the years after 1945, and the Air Force alone had the privilege of deploying what few nuclear weapons the United States possessed. The Strategic Air Command was thus made the possible instrument of greater destruction than the world had ever known, and it is not surprising that its leaders and its admirers developed a grand concept of its role and its potentiality. Thus, writing late in 1946, the former Chief of Air Staff, General H. H. Arnold, proclaimed that the purpose of the post-war world was 'to make the existence of civilization subject to the good will and the good sense of the men who control the employment of air power'. In July 1949, Senator McMahon wrote that strategic bombing with nuclear weapons was 'the keystone of our military policy and a foundation pillar of our foreign policy as well'. In the same year, one of Douhet's disciples asserted that:

> Once war comes American air power will be the decisive factor, the kingpin on which victory or defeat will hinge. The preservation of political, economic and religious freedom and the rights of the individual, and of cultural, social and economic progress will ultimately depend on the strength and bombing power of the Air Force of the United States. . . . The global air dominion must be held securely by a technically superior, all-weather, 24-hours-a-day, high-altitude, fast and accurate United States Air Force of overwhelming bombing and fire power. In the words of Milton: 'They who seek nothing but their own just liberty, have always the right to win it, whenever they have the power, be the voices ever so numerous that oppose it.'[6]

The Commander of the SAC between 1948 and 1956 was General Curtis E. LeMay. In his memoirs he reminisced about the years of the American atomic monopoly. 'We in SAC were not saber-rattlers', he wrote. 'We were not yelling for war and action in order to "flex the mighty muscles we had built." No stupidity of that sort. We wanted peace as much as anyone else wanted it.' But he and his colleagues 'knew for a fact' that it would be possible to stem Russian expansion if Washington presented Moscow with an ultimatum (backed up by its nuclear strike force) while the Soviet Union was without either offensive or defensive capacity. 'Some of us thought it might be better to do so then, than to wait until later. . . . That was the era when we might have destroyed Russia completely and not even skinned our elbows in doing it. We could have pushed them back within their own borders, and freed some other smaller nations from a hideous infliction.'[7]

In short, as Kissinger has pointed out, the SAC believed that it had realized 'the secret dream of American military thought: that there exists a final answer to our military problem, that it is possible to defeat the enemy utterly, and that war has its own rationale independent of policy'. This being so, it demanded recognition. In November 1947, for example, Arnold's successor, General Carl A. Spaatz, called for an Air Force of no less than seventy combat groups, 'the barest minimum necessary for our security'. This plea was endorsed two months later by the report of the presidential Air Policy Commission, chaired by Thomas K. Finletter, later to become Secretary for the Air Force. But although the Air Force's unique position as wielder of the deterrent was confirmed by the Key West agreement of March 1948, recognition in the shape of increased funds was not immediately forthcoming. In the budget then before Congress, the Air Force was allocated only twelve per cent of military appropriations. Two years later, its share had gone up to thirty per cent, but this was not considered enough either. Nothing less than two-thirds of the defence budget would satisfy the extremists, and they made it clear that the bulk of this money should go on the further reinforcement of the strategic capability.[8]

Oppenheimer was not persuaded by any of these arguments. Indeed, he believed the country was running a dreadful risk if it accepted them. It was extremely dangerous, in his view, to think that nuclear weapons had only heightened the scale of destruction in war; they had, in fact, opened a new era. Writing in the same symposium as Arnold at the end of 1946, he disputed the claim that the atom bomb had brought 'merely an extension and consummation of the techniques of strategic bombing'. 'It is clear that in a very real sense the past patterns of national security are inconsistent with the attainment of security on the only level where it can now, in the atomic age, be effective.' In other words, far from reinforcing the doctrine of strategic air power, the atom bomb had thrown it very much in question.[9]

His answer to the problem was the international control of atomic energy, but by the time the symposium was published it was evident that the Soviet Union would never agree to the scheme which Oppenheimer had helped to draft. The solution had therefore to be found on the national plane, within the framework of American defence policy alone.

The fullest expression of Oppenheimer's thinking at this time is to be found in a letter written on 14 April 1948, that is, at the beginning of the Soviet blockade of Berlin, and less than two months after the Communist seizure of Czechoslovakia. He began by accepting the premiss that America had to possess a strategic capability: 'we must ... be prepared, if need be, to engage in total war, to carry the war to the enemy and attempt to destroy him.' But one of the primary purposes of American policy should be 'not to engage in a total war aimed at destroying the sources of Soviet power', because 'the consequences, even in victory, of a total war carried out against the Soviet Union would be inimical to the preservation of our way of life'.[10]

What Oppenheimer no doubt had in mind was the Defense Department's current definition of strategic air warfare. It read as follows:

> air combat and supporting operations designed to effect, through the systematic application of force to a selected series of targets, the progressive destruction and disintegration of the enemy's war-making capacity to a point where he no longer retains the ability or the will to wage war. Vital targets may include key manufacturing systems, sources of raw material, critical material, stock piles, power systems, transportation systems, communications facilities, concentration of uncommitted elements of enemy armed forces, key agricultural areas, and other such target systems.[11]

Given this definition, and the fact that the United States had just developed a bomb of some 50 kilotons—more than twice as powerful as the weapon which annihilated Nagasaki—it is not difficult to appreciate the force of his conclusion. 'There is to my mind', Oppenheimer said, 'little doubt that were we today, with the kind of provocation which the Soviet Union almost daily affords, to attack the centers of Soviet population and industry with atomic weapons, we should be forfeiting the sympathy of many potential allies on whose cooperation the success of our arms and the fundamental creation of a stable peace may very well depend.'[12]

Oppenheimer was not alone in this. Speaking before the House Committee on the Armed Services in October 1949, Admiral Ralph A. Ofstie stated that the Navy considered that 'strategic air warfare as practiced in the past and as proposed for the future, is militarily unsound and of limited effect, and is morally wrong, and is decidedly harmful to the stability of a postwar world'. In his memoirs, General Matthew B. Ridgway declared that 'this country could not adopt a more dangerous doctrine, nor one more likely to lead us down the path to war'. It may well be that these declarations had more to do with inter-service rivalry than with matters of high principle, and Ofstie's statement was made expressly to counter the charge that the Navy was only opposing the Air Force demand for the B-36 bomber (the subject of the hearing) in order to obtain funds for a 'super-carrier' equipped to take nuclear bombers. It is also notable that the Navy did not demur when it was assigned to operate the Polaris submarine force ten years later. But whatever their motives, others besides Oppenheimer were prepared to dissent from the Air Force orthodoxy and to do so openly.[13]

What the United States needed to do, as Oppenheimer saw it, was to develop a wide range of defence options and avoid an excessive concentration on strategic response. As he put it in his letter, 'we must surely be prepared, both in planning and in the development of weapons, and insofar as possible in our "force in being", for more than one kind of conflict'. The alternatives could take many forms. Lilienthal, as we have seen, favoured a build-up of conventionally-armed ground forces. Oppenheimer, however, pinned his hopes on tactical atomic weapons. Conventional armies were expensive, and difficult to recruit and maintain, and it was doubtful whether the West could ever match Russia in this respect. Small-scale atomic bombs purely for use in the field might make up for this deficiency by giving Western troops a weight of fire-power out of all proportion to their numbers. They would also serve to rescue the West from the predicament of having no choice but to bomb Russia's cities if the Red Army moved west in strength.[14]

At the hearing Oppenheimer revealed that General Groves had asked for such a bomb when the seaborne invasion of Japan was being contemplated, but it was not technically possible to make one until 1948. In April and May of that year, however, the *Sandstone* series of tests in the Pacific had achieved the necessary breakthrough. Immediately after the tests, Oppenheimer had been appointed to chair a panel for the Research and Development Board of the Pentagon on the long-range military applications of nuclear weapons. His co-members were Admiral William S. Parsons, who had primed the Hiroshima bomb, and the three generals, Nichols, Wilson, and McCormack. Their job was to sort out the various possible military uses of atomic energy—for submarine and aircraft propulsion as well as for tactical weapons—and to make recommendations as to their relative priority.[15]

This they did, but there were no immediate and dramatic results, since all the projects under review had to be explored at length. As far as tactical nuclear weapons were concerned, although the *Sandstone* tests had transformed the situation, a great deal still remained to be done, and they remained a hope for the not too distant future. They continued to have their advocates, notably General Bradley, in an article published only a few weeks before his conversion to the hydrogen bomb in November 1949. But it was not until the second great post-war advance in fission development in the summer of 1950 that the position became really promising and tacticals could be considered as something attainable within the next two years. Hence the Defense Department's decision to reconvene the panel that autumn.[16]

As we have already seen, it focussed almost entirely on the possible uses of the new acquisition. The range of atomic weapons, as a member of the panel, Mervin J. Kelly, pointed out, could now be extended 'well beyond that of the large free-falling bombs'. The new weapons were suitable for a wide variety of military purposes, and Oppenheimer, in the view of another panel-member, Whitman, felt he had to press hard for governmental recognition of this fact. This was because he was operating 'in a climate where many folks felt that only strategic bombing was a field for the atomic weapon'. This was an attitude of mind bred in the days of a small stockpile, when there was 'a strong feeling that the bomb was the peculiar and sole property of the Strategic Air Command'. It died hard, however, even with the coming of atomic plenty and, in Whitman's words, 'it was very necessary to open the mind of the military as to the other potential uses of this material'. This was especially so in view of the fact that 'if and when the atomic weapon is really loosed in a strategic campaign, which would be on both sides, it is the end of civilization as we know it', and Oppenheimer recognized 'as practically everybody else has that the strategic use was being pushed with utmost speed'.[17]

Oppenheimer spelled out his ideas in an address delivered on 11 January 1951, some two weeks after the panel's report had gone in. The atom bomb, he said, was most usually thought of 'as an instrument of strategic bombing, for the destruction of lives and of plants, essentially in cities'. The question facing the world was whether it was to go on being thought of in this way. Oppenheimer believed it should not. He accepted a strategic role for the bomb as a deterrent but *not* as a weapon. It was clear that atomic bombs

> can be used only as adjuncts in a military campaign which has some other components, and whose purpose is a military victory. They are not primarily weapons of totality or terror, but weapons used to give combat forces help that they would otherwise lack. They are an integral part of military operations. Only when the atomic bomb is recognized as useful in so far as it is an integral part of military operations, will it really be of much help in the fighting of a war, rather than in warning all mankind to avert it.[18]

This was not to the liking of the Air Force. In his testimony, Whitman remarked that he thought 'there was some resentment at the implication that this was not just the Strategic Air Command's weapon'. He was right. In the view of General Roscoe C. Wilson, who also sat on the panel, Oppenheimer had displayed 'a pattern of action that was simply not helpful to national defense'. He therefore went to the Air Force Director of Intelligence 'to express my concern'.[19]

Wilson had no evidence that Oppenheimer was either disloyal or indiscreet. His objections were all over policy issues. Four things worried him. First, 'my awareness of the fact that Dr Oppenheimer was interested in what I call the internationalizing of atomic energy'. Second, Oppenheimer's lack of interest in some methods of long-range detection of nuclear tests. Third, his opposition to the project for a nuclear-powered aircraft, and fourth his 'conservatism' over the H-bomb.[20]

On the first issue, as Oppenheimer's counsel at once reminded the general, international control of atomic energy was a policy which had also been espoused by others, not least the government of the United States, and could hardly be described as a merely personal enthusiasm. On the second, as we have seen,

Oppenheimer had in fact approved the detection system which discovered the Soviet test of August 1949. As for the third, this was a scheme which never really got off the ground between its launching in 1946 and its cancellation by the Kennedy administration in 1961. In the words of Eisenhower's Defense Secretary, 'the atomic-powered aircraft reminds me of a shite-poke—a great big bird that flies over the marshes, that doesn't have too much body or speed to it, or anything, but can fly'. Oppenheimer was thus not alone in his attitude. As for the hydrogen bomb, the Air Force was fully entitled to dislike Oppenheimer's approach, but unless there were a question of disloyalty involved —and by Wilson's own admission there was not—then it was simply a matter of opinion, and there could be no cause for alarm. Moreover, this was still the time when the feasibility of the bomb had not been established, and it was doubtful whether the Air Force would ever be able to have it.[21]

As Wilson no doubt knew, all these things were peripheral. The crux of the issue was the Air Force's conviction that Oppenheimer was doing his utmost—as, indeed, he was—to take away its primary function and deprive it of the glory of obliterating Russia's heartland. It must be remembered that the report of the panel was issued during the Korean War and shortly after a particularly critical moment in the war, the Chinese intervention. For the Air Force, Korea was a frustrating experience. Soon after the outbreak of the war in June 1950, Wilson's predecessor as Commandant of the Air War College, General Orville Anderson, stated in public that the service was ready and awaiting orders to bomb Moscow; he was retired immediately. General LeMay has written of his anguish at being restricted to tactical operations against ground units and at having the industrial cities of Manchuria placed out of bounds. To be in possession of weapons more powerful than anything yet devised and to be forbidden to use them in war requires self-discipline of the highest order, and it was a self-discipline which had to be kept up for three years. The Air Force would have been more than human if it had not found an outlet for its fury, and it vented it on the man who, so it believed, stood between it and the fulfilment of its destiny.[22]

Feeling in the Air Force was doubtless heightened by the rapid progress of tactical atomic weapons during 1951. On 27 January the test site at Yucca Flats, Nevada, was opened with a series of low-yield explosions mostly of either 1 or 8 kilotons. This was followed by a further series in the autumn, by which time the bombs were a proven success. They were taken up enthusiastically by Senator McMahon, who, in a major speech on 18 September, called for an American strategy based unequivocally on the widest possible range of nuclear and thermonuclear bombs. They also were given open support by Dean. Speaking on 27 September, Dean said that the atom bomb could now 'definitely' be used as a battlefield weapon, and on 5 October he spoke of the advent of 'a new concept of warfare . . . much less fearsome as far as non-combatants are concerned and much more promisng than city bombing as a means of halting aggressors'. The concept of atomic warfare in terms of inter-continental bombers striking at great cities and industrial centres was no longer 'the whole truth'. In other words, a tactical capability had come into being to challenge the dominion of the SAC.[23]

This was the background to the study of tacticals then under way at the California Institute of Technology in Pasadena. Named after the small town at the southern end of the state, Project Vista was an inquiry sponsored by all three services and directed by the President of the Institute, DuBridge, Oppenheimer's colleague on the General Advisory Committee. Also taking part was Charles Lauritsen, professor of physics at the Institute. Oppenheimer entered the project at a late stage to help in drafting the final report.

Oppenheimer's contribution was to chapter five of the report, which was concerned with the way nuclear weapons might be used to support ground operations. As Lauritsen described it, they were to be brought into play to destroy mass attacks by large numbers of men and they had to be 'suitable for precise delivery at close range from our troops and in all kinds of weather'. For Oppenheimer, the significance of the report lay in its attempt to draw guidelines for a situation which no one then knew a great deal about. It showed that a wide range of nuclear options could and must be made available, and that it was essential to be able to switch from one to another at high speed during the course of battle.[24]

It is exceptionally difficult to write about the Vista report since the text has not yet been released and what was disclosed at the hearing was sparse to say the least. It was, however, clear that the Air Force was displeased about it, and about three features in particular. These were its position on the hydrogen bomb, its recommendation for a division of the stockpile of fissionable materials, and its attitude to the strategic use of the bomb.

On the first issue, the Air Force was angry that the project had excluded the H-bomb from its deliberations. Teller had visited Pasadena and tried to persuade DuBridge that the bomb could be studied as a tactical weapon, but the idea was rejected and with obvious reason. How Teller could believe that a gigantic device such as the thermonuclear could be placed in the same category as the weaponry Vista was considering is almost beyond comprehension. Moreover, although the feasibility of the fusion reaction was no longer in doubt, there had still not been a test and a deliverable thermonuclear weapon still lay some years in the future. An evaluation of its military worth was therefore impossible. Teller may have been convinced that the H-bomb was paramount, but DuBridge was not. 'It was not my understanding then or now', he testified at the hearing, 'that President Truman's decision [of 31 January 1950] meant that no other military program should go forward other than the H-bomb program, or even that the H-bomb program would have overriding priority over all others.' For him, fission development was the most immediately important item, and so the hydrogen bomb did not feature in the report when it was drawn up in November.[25]

The second Air Force objection was to the recommendation in the draft that the stockpile should be divided into three, one third to be allocated to the sac, one third to be assigned to the tactical defence of western Europe, and one third to be held in reserve. This was now possible, thanks to the abundance of weapons-grade material, but it was not acceptable to the Air Force. It was made still less so by the fact that the recommendation also sought to bring changes in the kind of weapons which made up the stockpile, since hydrogen bombs and 500-kiloton atomic bombs were obviously unsuitable for tactical use. What percentage of the stockpile was to consist of tactical weapons is unknown : we have no means of telling, for example, how much of the reserve was to be tactical. But it was clear that the proposal would end the monopoly which the SAC had so far enjoyed, and this was the purpose behind it. As Lauritsen remarked, 'we felt that [classified material deleted from the transcript] it would not be wise to devote all of our stockpile to strategic weapons'. As Oppenheimer saw it, the report represented a change in 'a healthy direction', and Robb spoke for the Air Force when he took immediate issue with this judgment. To his mind, it stood for a restriction on the Air Force's freedom of action 'if the Air Force could use its atomic weapons in any way it chose'. Oppenheimer rightly answered that 'we were not given an Air Force which could use its atomic weapons in any way it chose'. The Air Force, however, apparently believed it could.[26]

It was the third item which aroused most controversy. According to Griggs, the report had advocated that the President should announce that the United States would not launch a strategic attack on Russian cities except in retaliation to a Russian strike against American cities. A similar allegation had been made in the anonymous *Fortune* article in May 1953. Oppenheimer, in the words of this writer, had

> proposed that the US should announce that, if war were to come, it would withhold SAC from action.
>
> The assumption was that if the Kremlin knew that its cities would be spared, it would spare those of Western Europe and the US. This mutual forswearing of strategic air warfare would, in a Vista phrase, have the effect of 'bringing the battle back to the battlefield'.
>
> SAC was no longer essential to national survival ... its replacement by short-range air forces limited to offsetting other military forces would lift from the world the fear of an insensate trading of mass-destruction weapons.[27]

Such a policy had, in fact, been pressed on the State Department by Kennan during the debate over the H-bomb in the months after September 1949. It was clear to him, wrote Kennan, that the atomic bomb was 'something we would ... expect to use deliberately, promptly, and spontaneously in any major encounter, regardless of whether it was first used against us'. He proposed that the government should publicly abandon first use and say that it did not envisage ever using nuclear weapons unless compelled to do so by a nuclear attack launched from the USSR.[28]

Kennan's proposal was secret, but it was made openly very soon after Truman's announcement that the H-bomb would go forward. On 4 February 1950, twelve scientists—including Bethe and Lauritsen—urged the government to 'make a solemn declaration' never to use the hydrogen bomb first. The only circumstances in which it might be used would be 'if we or our allies were attacked by *this* bomb'. There could be only one justification for developing the H-bomb, and that was to prevent it from being used. This statement, of course, left open the question of whether the strategic use of high-yield atomic weapons was to be allowed, but on the hydrogen bomb it was categorical enough. A thermonuclear Hiroshima or Nagasaki must not be permitted to happen, for reasons which Bethe soon made terrifyingly clear in his article on the H-bomb.[29]

Under close questioning by Gray, Oppenheimer denied that he had recommended a public renunciation of a first-strike policy, and this denial was repeated in the brief which his lawyers submitted to the Board on 17 May. Soon after the hearing closed Oppenheimer came across a copy of the draft report. In it there was no recommendation for a presidential announcement or for any governmental announcement by the United States. This cannot yet, of course, be verified, but it certainly accords with Oppenheimer's position at the time of the GAC meeting of October 1949. Then, unlike Fermi and Rabi, he and his five colleagues subscribing to the majority annex had not proposed that the government should publicly forswear H-bomb development, and in his reply to Gray, Oppenheimer made it clear that he considered statements of this kind extremely dangerous.[30]

This did not mean that he and the others involved in Vista had not contemplated the possibility of such a statement being made. Lauritsen's testimony on this point was cautious, but he thought it was possible 'that we pointed out that we felt that the tactical support should be available if such a statement was made'. As Oppenheimer remembered it, the report had focussed on the contingency of a conventional Soviet attack on western Europe and had put forward a policy to meet that contingency. It believed that the nuclear response in such circumstances should be entirely tactical. Strategic retaliation should be ruled out,

F

since it could only bring about a strategic counter-strike by Russia against the United States and its allies. As far as this particular situation was concerned, any nuclear exchange should be held at the tactical level if at all possible, and a public commitment to this effect might be necessary. However, the report had not gone so far as to make a firm recommendation in favour of it.[31]

For Oppenheimer, then, the report had primarily been an opportunity to explore possibilities and he was by no means certain as to precisely what form the American reaction to a major Soviet thrust would take. He was, for example, sure that 'the very first thing we would do against the USSR is to go after the strategic air bases and to the extent you can the atomic bases of the USSR. You would do every thing to reduce their power to impose an effective strategic attack upon us.' This was hardly keeping the battle in the area of confrontation in central Europe, and, as Gray asked, once that step had been taken, where did you draw the line? Could you then abstain from hitting cities and industrial concentrations? Oppenheimer could not give an answer, but, as he pointed out, it was just this kind of question the Vista report was raising. Its function was to stimulate thought rather than to provide ready-made solutions, and this was urgently needed at a time when very few people had addressed themselves to the problem.[32]

Taken as a whole, there was nothing in the Vista report to suggest that the Strategic Air Command should forfeit its role, as Griggs, Oppenheimer's chief critic on this item, was bound to admit. He agreed that the aim of the report was to introduce an element of flexibility into American policy, and this meant that either strategic or tactical air power could be used according to circumstances, and that neither was excluded from contingency planning. As Oppenheimer put it, 'the main emphasis was that whatever you thought, you should be able to convert from one to the other at a minute's notice'. At the very end of the hearing, in reply to a question from Robb, he stated that the SAC 'must obviously be capable of destroying everything on enemy territory' and that it should do so if Russia struck the United States.[33]

The SAC, however, appeared to believe that any encroachment on its prerogatives was tantamount to its liquidation, and for men accustomed to thinking in absolute terms this was, perhaps, understandable. It seemed, or so the authors of *The Hydrogen Bomb* put it, 'as if some US scientist, unable to stop Teller and his hydrogen bomb, had seized on the invitations to study the Air Force as an opportunity to make political war against SAC.' The commander of the SAC was, apparently, particularly disturbed. 'Before LeMay would relinquish one bomb,' Shepley and Blair have written, 'he wanted to see the Soviet Union destroyed three times.' Finletter's reaction was to summon Oppenheimer to the Pentagon and discuss the matter with him. Oppenheimer, according to this account, 'questioned the morality of a strategy of atomic retaliation'. The Air Force Secretary, however, was certain 'than the greater immorality would be for the US to discard its strongest weapon while conditions for world disarmament were still absent'.[34]

The Air Force therefore did everything in its power to minimize the impact of the report. Early in December Oppenheimer, DuBridge, Lauritsen and Whitman took the draft to General Eisenhower in Paris. They did so under the auspices of the Research and Development Board of the Defense Department of which Whitman was chairman, and the study had, after all, been sponsored by all three services. The Air Force, however, felt that its interests were supreme here, and that it was being circumvented. As the Vista party left for Europe, General Norstad, the commander of the American and allied air forces, was recalled to Washington by Finletter and ordered to object to the report. He did so when Oppenheimer and his companions met him at his Fontainebleau headquarters, and changes were made in the draft. The group then returned to the United States.[35]

Since we have neither the draft nor the final report it is impossible to say how important the changes were. In his replies to Gray, Oppenheimer tried to play them down. As he recollected it, he and the others told Norstad that they had rewritten their views 'in a form which will be as little irritating to you as possible and still keep them our views'. Norstad had replied that he now thought it was 'a fine report and very valuable'. Under cross-examination by Gray and Robb, however, Oppenheimer testified that the final report contained an admission that strategic deterrence was one of the factors involved in the protection of European cities against a conventional Soviet attack. In other words, although the arguments for tactical defence remained untouched, they were counterbalanced to a very great extent by the concession which Norstad had succeeded in exacting.[36]

Even so, the Air Force had not managed to suppress the report completely, and it still worried them. 'They were afraid', one of Oppenheimer's witnesses recalled, 'that Vista would carry too much weight with higher authorities that did not understand their problems, and would hurt their program.' In an article in *The New York Times* shortly after the report was finally issued, Hanson Baldwin wrote that 'its conclusions are interpreted by the Army, by the Navy and by some in the Air Force as a definite blow to the "big bombers" school of thinking that dominated the Air Force and our strategic concepts for some time after World War II'. For this reason, 'considerable criticism' was being heard from officers who described the project as ' "theoretical" and the work of "long-haired scientists" '.[37]

As it turned out, Vista *had* made inroads into strategic air power dominance, but it was only the first of two major clashes between Oppenheimer and the SAC. By the time Baldwin wrote his article, another storm was already brewing, this time over the issue of the defence of the United States against Soviet air attack.

American control of the western hemisphere, and the vast barriers of the Atlantic and the Pacific, had so far kept the United States free from the danger of aerial bombardment, except for one brief moment in June 1942 when the Japanese seized a foothold in the Aleutians. The emergence of Russia as an enemy and the development of heavy bombers of very high endurance transformed this situation after the Second World War, however. Both the United States and Canada were then open to attack from Siberia, coming in either across the Bering Strait or over the North Pole, and there was no defence against it.

In the years just after the war the Soviet threat was not immediate, and few called attention to it. Among those who did was Borden who, in *There Will Be No Time,* urged a policy of cooperation with Canada over the defence of the northern latitudes. Bush, in a book written in 1949, pointed out that America's atomic monopoly had led to a neglect of air defence and asked for research into a system which would give the country adequate coverage. In his opinion, 'the spectre of great fleets of bombers, substantially immune to methods of defence, destroying great cities at will by atomic bombs, is a spectre only. There is a defence against the atomic bomb. It is the same sort of defence used against any other type of bomb.'[38]

Bush's book was in the press when the news of the first Soviet nuclear test broke and triggered off the demands for the hydrogen bomb. Truman's decision to go ahead with the bomb meant, for some, that the need for air defence was paramount. One of the foremost spokesmen for this view was the physicist Leo Szilard, one of the small company who had drawn the possibility of the atomic bomb to Roosevelt's attention in October 1939. 'If we are building H-bombs,' said Szilard in a broadcast on 26 February 1950, 'and if the arms race is on, what will cost us most is not making H-bombs but rather the defense measures which we shall be forced to take. . . . If we go into this arms race at all, it will be lunacy not to take defense measures.'[39]

In fact, the subject was already being studied at the Massachusetts Institute of Technology, which was under contract to the Air Force to explore it. Moreover, shortly after Szilard spoke, the policy review which Truman had instigated in January came out in favour of high priority being given to an air defence system for the continent. It was not until after the outbreak of the Korean War in June, however, that more action was taken. In December 1950 the Federal Civil Defense Administration was set up, and in January 1951 the Air Force commissioned a full study of the problem from the MIT, which was given the name Project Charles. It was at this moment that Oppenheimer publicly urged intensive work on possible counter-measures against attack, because as Lauritsen testified, it was known 'that the Russians had, or very soon would have, a very considerable capability of striking us [deletion from transcript on classification grounds]. We knew they had an air force that was capable of coming over here and delivering those weapons.'[40]

As an interim measure, seventy-three radar stations were built in the northern United States and Alaska, and two new Air Force commands were set up—the Antiaircraft Command and the Air Defense Command. All-weather interceptor fighters were allocated to the latter, and an agreement was reached with Canada on the co-ordination of policy. But these were make-shifts, and air defence was by no means given the same priority as Korea or German rearmament. Its deficiences were made even more apparent by a study of civil defence, Project East River, started in August 1951. During the course of the study, its director, Lloyd V. Berkner, became convinced that the 'pas-sive defence' precautions of the Civil Defense Administration would be useless without the 'active defence' provided by an efficient system of early warning and interception. Deep shelters and evacuation would be nothing but a mockery if most of the Soviet strike force was allowed to penetrate as far as the cities. He therefore urged still further study of the problem.[41]

Here, however, the supporters of air defence ran head-on into the devotees of strategic air power. As one of the authorities on British strategic air doctrine has pointed out, its practitioners were dedicated to the offensive above everything else, and 'main-taining the offensive meant not being diverted from' it by auxi-liary demands or the needs of air defence'. The only defence, to their way of thinking, was counter-attack, the delivery of the celebrated 'knock-out blow'. In Britain, these attitudes had largely been formed by the experience of the First World War, in particular by the devastating raids mounted on England by the huge German *Gotha* bombers in the summer of 1917. As we have seen, throughout the inter-war period the bomber was considered invulnerable, and the concentration on the develop-ment of Fighter Command in the 1930s was bitterly resisted by Bomber Command on the grounds that it 'amounted virtually to losing the war before it started'. They were proved wrong, of course, by the outcome of the Battle of Britain, won by the combination of radar and the fighter and not by any massive counter-strike against Germany, but they were extremely reluctant to admit it.[42]

Bomber Command in Britain naturally had its counterparts elsewhere. The diversion of the *Luftwaffe*'s main effort from the fighter bases and radar stations to London in September 1940 was a classic example of the (misguided) application of strategic bombing methods. So too was the American insistence on sending 'self-defending' formations of B-17 bombers on daylight raids over Germany during 1942 in the confident belief that they could meet any fighter attack the Germans sent up. It took many months of terrible losses to persuade them that the bomber was not, in fact, impregnable, but even then belief in the offensive survived, and daylight raids continued with fighter escort. To a 'big-bomb man', the fighter was a mere adjunct to the bomber force, clearing the path for it to sweep majestically along, and the attitude was maintained in the post-war period.

It was, perhaps, most strenuously expounded by General Le May's predecessor as commander of the SAC, General George C. Kenney, writing at the end of 1950. The United States, avouched General Kenney,

> *must never set up the radar and the fighter airplane as a Maginot Line to hide behind....* Only the offensive will smash [the Russian] attempt to dominate the world, will remove the threat to civilization, will bring peace—real peace, lasting peace, security.
>
> The offensive means the right hand, the punching hand, the one that gains the decision—the long-range bomber striking force that carries *our* bombs in retaliatory attacks against the key points of the enemy war-making system.
>
> This force must be the number one air power of the world with a heavier punch than any possible opponent and *capable of operating immediately the emergency is known.* If we are going to pay the huge bill for a modern bomber force, we want to buy a winner. They don't give out any prizes for second place in war.[43]

To counter this argument, the advocates of air defence put forward several reasons for embarking on the sort of programme they wanted to see. Rabi gave three of them at the hearing. First, it would serve to protect American lives. Second, it would place the country in a strong position if war actually broke out, since the fighting would be taking place 'from a protected citadel, rather than just being open and just a slugging match with no defense guard put up'. Third, the existence of such a system 'would make us less liable to intimidation and blackmail' on the political plane. He could also have mentioned the psychological advantage of avoiding a feeling among the public at large of total exposure to attack, which could well lead to mass hysteria.[44]

Looked at in purely military terms, the gains seemed to be

considerable. If the damage from a Soviet attack were mini-
mized, then enough industrial capacity would remain to operate
a war economy. At the same time, it would clearly be better for
the Strategic Air Command to have its bases well-screened than
for it to expose its aircraft to the risk of being caught helpless and
immobile, as the Pacific Fleet had been caught at Pearl Harbor.
As the supporters of air defence saw it, the risk was becoming
more and more serious, since defensive techniques were not keeping pace with developments in delivery systems, and action had
to be taken soon before the offensive gained a decisive lead.[45]

The impetus for taking an initiative came from two sources.
Berkner was anxious to have an investigation of early warning,
while Lauritsen and Jerrold R. Zacharias, a physicist at the
MIT, wanted a wide-ranging study of the whole air defence
problem. Early in 1952 Zacharias and Berkner both approached
Dr Albert G. Hill, director of the Lincoln Laboratory at the
Institute. The Laboratory had been set up the previous summer
under the auspices of all three services to provide an institu-
tional framework for the research on air defence which had been
going ahead less formally for the past two years or so, and it was
the natural centre for the inquiry they had in mind. Hill agreed
on condition that Zacharias took charge of it, and when
Zacharias said he would, preparations got under way for what
was to be called the Lincoln Summer Study.[46]

As Zacharias described it at the hearing, the defensive system
envisaged by the study was as follows. It was to consist of four
concentric rings. The innermost ring would hold anti-aircraft
guns and ground-to-air missiles. The second would be provided
with short-range interceptor aircraft. The third ring, 'further out
away from our shores, and away from our borders' was, presumably, the distant early-warning line, backed up by more
interceptors. Last, in terms of distance but not of priority, there
was to be the destruction of Soviet air bases by the Strategic Air
Command. By all these means it was hoped that the country
could be made reasonably secure against attack, particularly
against a surprise attack launched in secret.[47]

The Air Force refused to believe it. Its main spokesman at the
hearing was Griggs, the leading Air Force witness on Project
Vista. For Griggs, as for the Air Force as a whole, both Vista and
the Lincoln Summer Study were complementary aspects of the

same policy. Both were designed to place tight curbs on strategic air power, if not to eliminate it altogether. Both also had in common the evil genius of Dr J. Robert Oppenheimer, or so, at least, it seemed. 'I think it is a fair general observation', said Griggs, 'that when you get involved in a hot enough controversy, it is awfully hard not to question the motives of people who oppose you.'[48]

Shortly after he became Chief Scientist on 1 September 1951, Griggs testified, both Finletter and Vandenberg had told him they had serious doubts as to Oppenheimer's loyalty. Late that autumn he had learned that Oppenheimer, Rabi and Lauritsen had formed an informal committee 'to work for world peace or some such purpose'. In order to attain world peace, Zacharias was alleged to have suggested, the government should 'give up ... the Strategic Air Command, or more properly ... the strategic part of our total air power, which includes more than the Strategic Air Command'. He had done so 'after considerable discussions ... with Dr Oppenheimer'. Oppenheimer himself, at the meetings of the State Department disarmament panel, was alleged to have proposed that the government should consider giving up 'strategic missiles'.[49]

At the same time, Griggs said, the trio had taken the position that 'many things were more important than the development of the thermonuclear weapon', in particular the air defence of the United States. This, coupled with the supposed attitude to the SAC, had made him fearful of what might come out of the Lincoln Summer Study. Three things stood out. First, it threatened to destroy the general effectiveness of the Lincoln Laboratory. Second, it seemed to be based on an over-optimistic assessment of the rate of attrition which might be achieved against attacking aircraft, and if a national policy flowed from the study's report, 'we could be in terrible trouble'. Third, the study appeared to intend recommending changes in budgetary allocations, that is, to increase the funds for air defence at the expense of the SAC.[50]

In making these last two points, Griggs was touching on familiar themes. In *The Hydrogen Bomb,* Shepley and Blair emphasize that the Air Force 'believed the *best* way to stop an enemy bomber fleet was to destroy it on the ground in the Soviet Union. It considered efforts to down it while flying across Canada and into the United States as a last ditch and largely ineffective strategy.' To the anonymous writer of the article in the May 1953 issue of *Fortune,* 'the whole panoply suggested a jet-propelled, electronically hedged Maginot Line'. Both were echoing the words of General Kenney, quoted above, and he in turn was only repeating what was a truism for the strategic air power school of thought. As for the complaint about the probable effect on Air Force appropriations, this again was a staple feature of the American military scene. Each winter the three armed services jostled for fiscal supremacy, and the Air Force had had to fight particularly hard to expand its share of military expenditure from 12 per cent in 1948–49 to 32 per cent in 1952–53. The Lincoln Summer Study proposals were expected to cost (according to Air Force estimates) between $50 billion and $150 billion, and even spread over several years, this was a huge sum in view of the fact that the military budget for 1952–53 was just over $44 billion. The Strategic Air Command believed, as Shepley and Blair put it, that 'the US, Congress or no, would not buy this . . . and SAC as well'.[51]

There were flaws in both arguments. On the question of the relative merits of offence and defence, the Air Force was forgetting for one thing that the Maginot Line had held firm along almost its entire length in 1940, and if it had been extended to the Channel, the outcome for France might well have been different. Again, it failed (or refused) to see that air defence, far from detracting from the SAC's deterrent and retaliatory power, would actually enhance it. Furthermore, it did not appear to be aware that Oppenheimer did not believe a near-perfect attrition rate was attainable. Nor did it seem to know that he accepted that the SAC did have an important role and that one of its most vital functions was to strike against Soviet air bases. As Kelly recollected in his testimony, Oppenheimer's view, as related to him by General McCormack, was that 'while the country had not given proper emphasis to continental defense relatively, . . . our chief deterrent was strike, and . . . nothing should be done in bringing up to a proper level a continental defense effort that would weaken our strike'. Rabi described the two as complementary, like the arms of a boxer. One was 'the punching arm and the other the guard. You have to have both in my opinion.' What the Summer Study wished to do, as

Zacharias saw it, was to reach a situation in which no single element of defence policy would have absolute priority. In other words, as with Project Vista, the scientists were aiming at a balanced response to the Soviet threat, not a complete switch to another supposedly comprehensive solution.[52]

On the budgetary issue, the SAC was subscribing to a principle which had become one of the corner-stones of the Republic, that is, that government spending must be kept to the minimum. While this had been critically undermined by the Depression and the Second World War, it still retained its hold over the mind of the generation which had come to maturity before the 1930s. It posited a fixed, or better still, a shrinking expenditure, and so a new interest could only establish its claims by encroaching on those of others. Thus de Seversky, a fanatical believer in strategic air power, was prepared to accept air defence, but only if funds were transferred to it from Army and Navy appropriations. He would not have agreed with Zacharias' proposition that the overall defence budget could and should be higher (although the cost of an air defence system was put at no more than $20 billion). In this way, Zacharias maintained, no aspect of policy need suffer at another's expense. The SAC rejected this notion, not, perhaps, without a certain disingenuousness. That the budget could be expanded was unquestionable, but if retrenchment meant that air defence could be set aside, it would obviously do no good to admit it. Yet whatever its motivation, it was adamant: in no way was its position to be infringed upon.[53]

The two sides were thus poles apart, and the gulf between them became wider in the weeks leading up to the start of the Summer Study. On 30 April, for example, DuBridge and Rabi had lunch in Washington with Griggs and Garrison Norton and William Burden, two of Finletter's aides. Norton and Burden had gone to Whitman on the eve of his departure to Europe with the Vista report to express Air Force concern at its findings. They were no less disturbed at the probable implications of Lincoln, and during the meal a furious argument began, or, to use DuBridge's euphemism, 'a very vigorous discussion'. Griggs accused Oppenheimer of persuading the General Advisory Committee to soft-pedal the development of the H-bomb, and Rabi and DuBridge angrily denied it. According to Robb, who was questioning DuBridge about the meeting, Rabi had said that anyway there were two things more important than the bomb. The first was a nuclear disarmament agreement with Russia, and the second was a determined effort to improve air defence. The confrontation broke up with Rabi promising to introduce Griggs to Oppenheimer so that his suspicions about the GAC's attitude to the thermonuclear programme could be laid to rest.[54]

Griggs saw Oppenheimer at Princeton on 23 May. It was, to say the least of it, an unhappy encounter. Griggs began by taxing Oppenheimer with using a story that was going the rounds 'as an illustration of the dangerous warmongers who rule the Pentagon, and who are going to precipitate this Nation into a war unless a few scientists can save it'. The story was that at a briefing on 19 March 1952 Finletter had said : 'If only we could have [number deleted from transcript] of those [hydrogen bombs] we could rule the world.' Oppenheimer told Griggs he believed the incident had actually happened, and then went on to show him the recommendations which the GAC had made on the H-bomb at the end of 1949. When Griggs exclaimed that it would have been a disaster if they had been accepted, Oppenheimer asked him 'if I thought he were pro-Russian or just confused'. Griggs replied that he wished he knew. Oppenheimer then asked Griggs if he had impugned his loyalty to high officials in the Pentagon. Griggs said he had. Oppenheimer said he thought Griggs was paranoid. 'After a few more pleasantries,' wrote Griggs in a memorandum reporting the occasion to Finletter, 'our conversation came to an end.'[55]

By this time, the start of the Summer Study was fast approaching—it was due to begin during the last week in June—and Finletter told Griggs to discover whether it was going to be run 'in such a way as to result in a net gain to the effectiveness of Lincoln or a net loss'. The Air Force was disturbed about two main possibilities. First, it was concerned that the Study would place too much emphasis on the distant early-warning line and that this would lead to a 'diversion of effort' in the Laboratory. Since the Air Force was providing from 80 to 90 per cent of the Laboratory's funds, it was not prepared to countenance such a programme. In the second place, Finletter did not want the findings of the Study reported to a higher authority such as the National Security Council; they were to be kept strictly under

Air Force control. Griggs made inquiries of both the Provost and the President of the Institute and received assurances on both scores. If he had not, then Finletter would have cancelled the Study out of hand.[56]

This was Griggs' testimony. Zacharias and Hill saw things differently. In Zacharias' view, Griggs had been doing everything in his power to prevent the Study from getting under way; he even went so far as to accuse him of trying to sabotage it. Zacharias felt very deeply about Griggs' behaviour. He had no wish to bring formal charges of disloyalty against him, he said, but 'it is a bit of a pity that dueling has gone out of style. That is a very definite method of settling differences of opinion between people than to try to bring out all the detail in a hearing.' Hill denied that the Summer Study was setting out to weaken the SAC, and he pointed out that Griggs had never come to see him about it. He believed that Griggs had tried to destroy morale inside the Laboratory and to undermine the confidence of the MIT authorities in it. At the annual conference of the American Physical Society late in April, he said, Griggs had questioned the wisdom of allowing Oppenheimer to participate in the Study for security reasons and this had made some scientists think twice about joining. This, presumably, is what Zacharias meant when he mentioned that Griggs had spoken about Oppenheimer 'in a very derogatory way', and it was no doubt the same incident that was reported to Dean when he was told that Oppenheimer had been 'viciously attacked ... on patriotic grounds' at the conference. Oppenheimer, as usual, was the principal target, and it is noticeable that Griggs' attacks on him coincided with the preparation of an indictment against Weinberg which was expected to involve Oppenheimer. Weinberg was accused of perjury in denying that he had ever attended Communist meetings in California, among them the meeting which the Crouchs said had taken place in Oppenheimer's house in July 1941. If Oppenheimer's name were dragged into the case, it would clearly do him a great deal of harm.[57]

Oppenheimer survived the episode. When the indictment was published on 23 May (the day of his interview with Griggs at Princeton), he did not figure in it. The Summer Study, moreover, went ahead as planned, and he took a small, but active part in it. The accusations of conspiracy lingered, however. The prime movers of the Study, Oppenheimer's enemies were still convinced, were the men who had gathered round him the previous autumn. They now called themselves by the acronym ZORC—Z for Zacharias, O for Oppenheimer, R for Rabi and C for Charles, that is, Lauritsen. The first public mention of this sinister-sounding group was made in the *Fortune* article of May 1953, but Griggs had come across it before this. His evidence was as follows. Zacharias, he said, had written the initials on the blackboard during a presentation of the findings of the Study to a meeting of the Air Force Science Advisory Board in September 1952, before an audience of between 50 and 100 people. Later, he said that he had first heard of the name in a telephone conversation half-way through the Study.[58]

This was, on the face of it, one of the crasser pieces of evidence put forward by AEC witnesses, and it seemed to rank alongside Professor Latimer's allegation that Oppenheimer had turned young physicists at Los Alamos into pacifists and General Wilson's testimony that he had been troubled about Oppenheimer because he had supported an international atomic energy authority. As Oppenheimer pointed out early in the hearing, there was no room for conspiracy in tendering advice to the government since he and his colleagues were working under 'a very intensive searchlight of scrutiny'. And even if there really were such a group as Griggs had described, it is unlikely that it would have publicized itself in such a blatant way at a large gathering of Air Force officers, and it may be significant that not one other witness was brought in to support what Griggs had alleged. Zacharias, needless to say, denied both the existence of the group and the act of writing on the blackboard. Both he and Griggs were testifying under oath, and clearly one of them was lying. It was up to the Board to decide which, and, as Robb pointed out, if Griggs' story were true, it would add considerable weight to the proposition that Oppenheimer was doing everything he could to cut down America's offensive capability.[59]

The discussion of the ZORC episode ended the testimony on Oppenheimer's attitude to strategic air power, and with it, that part of the hearing devoted to his role as a policy adviser. What was its significance? Had his government service cancelled out his dubious left-wing past, as his defence counsel maintained? Did the advice he had given, whether on the hydrogen bomb, tactical atomic weapons or continental air defence, have any bearing on the issue of security clearance if the opinions he had offered were honestly based? Was his work for the United States a real contribution towards its welfare and its safety?

One witness had no doubts. To his mind, Oppenheimer's contribution was minimal. In answer to a question by Robb as to the effect on the atomic energy programme 'if Dr Oppenheimer should go fishing for the rest of his life', Teller said this. 'I should say that committees could go fishing without affecting the work of those who are actively engaged in the work . . . . the general recommendations that I know have come from Oppenheimer were more frequently, and I mean not only and not even particularly the thermonuclear case, but other cases, more frequently a hindrance than a help.' Therefore, concluded Teller, 'if I look into the continuation of this and assume that it will come in the same way, I think that further work of Dr Oppenheimer on committees would not be helpful'.[60]

This opinion was not based on a supposition that Oppenheimer was disloyal. 'I have always assumed,' said Teller, 'and I now assume that he is loyal to the United States. I believe this, and I shall believe it until I see very conclusive proof to the opposite.' At a later stage of his evidence, he declared that 'I believe, and that is merely a question of belief and there is no expertness, no real information behind it, that Dr Oppenheimer's character is such that he would not knowingly and willingly do anything that is designed to endanger the safety of this country.' However equivocally phrased, this was a positive enough statement as far as Oppenheimer's character was concerned, and so two of the basic security criteria appeared to have been met. Moreover, since he did not mention the third criterion of associations, it might seem that for Teller there was no question of Oppenheimer being a security risk.[62]

Not so. 'In a great number of cases', said Teller in reply to Robb, 'I have seen Dr Oppenheimer act—I understand that Dr Oppenheimer acted—in a way which for me was exceedingly hard to understand. I thoroughly disagreed with him in numerous issues and his actions frankly appeared to me confused and complicated. To this extent I feel that I would like to see the vital interests of this country in hands which I understand better, and therefore trust more.' Later, when Gray asked him to state specifically whether he meant by this that Oppenheimer was a security risk, he replied as follows. 'To the extent . . . that your question is directed toward intent, I would say I do not see any reason to deny clearance. If it is a question of wisdom and judgment, as demonstrated by actions since 1945, then I would say one would be wiser not to grant clearance.'[62]

In other words, Teller was condemning Oppenheimer purely for the opinions he had expressed. This was not the line Robb had taken; as we have seen, he had concentrated on throwing doubt on Oppenheimer's motivation. But, as Bush had so forcefully pointed out, it was perfectly possible to reach this finding from a reading of the indictment as framed by Nichols. The question which still remained unanswered was whether the Board would do the same when it came to consider its verdict.

Chapter Six

The Verdicts

The hearing closed on 6 May with Garrison's summation; Robb did not choose to give one. In this long speech, which took up the greater part of the morning, Garrison set out the essence of the case for Oppenheimer. The basic question which the Board had to decide, he believed, was whether Oppenheimer was to be trusted in the handling of classified material. In reaching an answer, they had to make up their minds largely on their opinion of Oppenheimer's loyalty. The other two criteria laid down in the Atomic Energy Act—character and associations— were unimportant by comparison.[1]

Garrison supported this contention by referring to the Commission's decision to grant clearance to Dr Frank Graham, President of the University of North Carolina. Graham had been a member of several civil rights organizations in the South, some of which were said to have been Communist-influenced. In 1948 the AEC Review Board, headed by the former Supreme Court Justice Owen J. Roberts, had recommended that clearance be denied, but the Commission had voted unanimously to disregard the recommendation. It had done so on the grounds that 'it is the man himself the Commission is actually concerned with, that the associations are only evidentiary, and that commonsense must be exercised in judging their significance'. 'Our long-range success in the field of atomic energy', the Commission had concluded, 'depends in large part on our ability to attract into the program men of character and vision with a wide variety of talents and viewpoints.'[2]

If the Board used this decision as their model, Garrison argued, they could not fail to come to the conclusion that Oppenheimer was not a security risk. Moreover, they must bear in mind the indisputable fact of his discretion. 'The most impelling single fact that has been established here', Garrison declared, 'is that for more than a decade Dr Oppenheimer has created and has shared secrets of the atomic energy program and has held them inviolable . . . . for more than a decade Dr Oppenheimer has been trusted, and . . . he has not failed that trust.' In the light of considerations such as these, the derogatory information set out by Nichols and elaborated by Robb fell into its true perspective.[3]

Thus, they made nonsense of the allegations that hinged on Oppenheimer's advice on the hydrogen bomb, tactical atomic weapons and air defence. At least they did, said Garrison, 'unless you are willing to believe to me the unthinkable thought, and I am sure to you, that in spite of everything he has done to help this country from 1945 on, he suddenly somehow becomes a sinister agent of a foreign power.' Likewise, they reduced to its real proportions the Chevalier incident, which to the prosecution was the most tell-tale evidence of where Oppenheimer's loyalties really lay. This was an episode which should not be judged by the standards of 1954, and it had taught Oppenheimer an important lesson. He did not deserve to be damned for that alone.[4]

Finally, Garrison emphasized the previous clearances which Oppenheimer had been given, by Groves and Lansdale in 1943, by the AEC in 1947, by Dean in 1950. The most significant of these he believed was the 1947 clearance, partly because it had been granted in the full knowledge of the Chevalier incident and partly because it had been based on an exhaustive study of all the available information. Neither it nor the others could be controlling, but they were a weighty factor in Oppenheimer's favour. Moreover, the decisions to grant clearance had been reinforced both by the extremely meagre evidence of continuing association with the left and by Oppenheimer's record as a public servant. 'Once a man has been cleared,' maintained Garrison, 'unless there are serious things that have happened since, it ought to stick.' The Board should also remember that even given the stricter criteria of Eisenhower's Executive Order, Whitman had been prepared to recommend clearance in July 1953, and Rabi had seen no reason to proceed with the case after reading the file Strauss had shown him the following January.[5]

The Board, he concluded, faced a grave decision, made even graver by the fact that if Oppenheimer's clearance were to be denied, it would almost certainly never be restored. A clearance could be questioned repeatedly, in the absence of a principle of double jeopardy, but 'if a man's clearance is taken away from him, that action probably is final for all time . . . . that is the end of that fellow for the rest of his life.' But, Garrison pointed out, 'it is the end of the country's chance to use him, too'. The issue was not only personal. 'There is more than Dr Oppenheimer on trial in this room', Garrison proclaimed. 'The Government of the United States is here on trial also. Our whole security process is on trial here, and is in your keeping as is his life—the two things together. . . . There is an anxiety abroad that these security procedures will be applied artificially, rigidly, like some monolithic kind of a machine that will result in the destruction of men of great gifts and of great usefulness to the country by the application of rigid and mechanical tests. America must not devour her own children.' If, however, the Board judged Oppenheimer 'the whole man', as he had urged it to at the outset, then a positive finding could not be in doubt, and that, he was certain, would be the outcome.[6]

With this, the hearing came to an end and the Board dispersed for a short holiday. It re-convened on 17 May to consider its verdict on the basis of the transcript of the hearing (which ran to more than 3,300 pages of typescript), an equivalent amount of secret file material, and a long brief from Garrison, Marks and Silverman which amplified the arguments Garrison had made in his summation. On 27 May it sent its findings and recommendation to General Nichols. Both were adverse to Oppenheimer by a majority of two to one: Gray and Morgan versus Evans, who believed that clearance should be renewed.

The majority report was by no means an outright condemnation of Oppenheimer. In the first place, it concluded that he was in no way disloyal. 'Indeed,' the majority found,'we have before us much responsible and positive evidence of [his] loyalty and love of country.' At the same time, there could be no doubts on the score of his discretion. 'It must be said', they remarked, 'that Dr Oppenheimer seems to have had a high degree of discretion reflecting an unusual ability to keep to himself vital secrets.' It was also clear that he had an excellent record of service to the country. 'The Nation', said Gray and Morgan, 'owes these scientists . . . a great debt of gratitude for loyal and magnificent

service. This is particularly true with respect to Dr Oppenheimer."[7]

In respect of the allegations listed in Nichols' letter, the
majority were also remarkably favourable. On the issue of Communist associations, they found that almost all the charges listed
by Nichols were true—with the notable exception of the Crouch
incident, on which the evidence was held to be inconclusive.
Moreover, their report stated, 'the Board takes a most serious
view of these earlier involvements. Had they occurred in very
recent years, we would have found them to be controlling and,
in any event, they must be taken into account in evaluating
subsequent conduct and attitudes.' But, as the statement indicated, they were not thought to be controlling, and they did not
figure in the four considerations which led the majority to their
conclusion.[8]

As regards the allegations over the hydrogen bomb, Gray and
Morgan found that Oppenheimer was not responsible for distri-
buting the annexes to the GAC report of 30 October 1949 at Los
Alamos; nor had he urged other scientists not to work on the
thermonuclear programme. More importantly, they believed that
Oppenheimer's opposition to the bomb was honourably motivated, and not by 'lack of loyalty to the United States or attachment to the Soviet Union'. They had concluded that 'any
possible implications to the contrary which might have been
read into the second part of General Nichols' letter are not
supported by any material which the Board has seen'. This, by
definition, included the secret information withheld from Oppenheimer and Garrison.[9]

In reaching these conclusions, the majority had effectively
undermined the AEC's case, which had rested on the supposition
that Oppenheimer's attitude to nuclear weapons had been
moulded largely by his pro-Communist past. This was what
Robb had consistently implied and what Garrison had done his
utmost to disprove. It did not follow, however, that Oppenheimer was not a security risk. In the opinion of Gray and
Morgan, he was, and for four main reasons.

The first rose out of the H-bomb controversy. 'We cannot
dismiss the matter of Dr Oppenheimer's relationship to the
development of the hydrogen bomb simply with the finding that
his conduct was not motivated by disloyalty,' said Gray and

Morgan, 'because it is our conclusion that, whatever the motivation, the security interests of the United States were affected.' In other words, Oppenheimer was being judged for his opinions alone, as Bush had feared and as Teller had supposed he would be.[10]

As with the allegations on Communist associations, the majority found that most of the H-bomb allegations were true, including the version of Oppenheimer's reasons for opposing the bomb, which Conant had described as 'rather a caricature of the type of argument which was used'. The only exception to this was that Oppenheimer was not held to have claimed that the bomb was not feasible, but instead to have questioned its feasibility until the late spring of 1951 (there was no mention of the fact that so too had the vast majority of scientists in the atomic energy programme). In addition, they ranged beyond the original allegations in commenting on the period between 1945 and 1949, when, they said, Oppenheimer was 'aware that the efforts being put forth in this endeavor were relatively meager and he knew that if research were conducted at the same pace, there would be little likelihood of success for many years'.[11]

They concluded that, after Truman's decision, Oppenheimer did not oppose the government's new enterprise 'in a positive or open manner'; nor did he refuse to cooperate in it. But although he did not urge other scientists not to participate, 'enthusiastic support on his part would perhaps have encouraged other leading scientists to work on the program'. Oppenheimer's attitude, in the majority's view, 'undoubtedly had an adverse effect on recruitment of scientists and the progress of the scientific effort in this field . . . . if Dr Oppenheimer had enthusiastically supported the thermonuclear program either before or after the determination of national policy, the H-bomb project would have been pursued with considerably more vigor, thus increasing the possibility of earlier success in this field.' It was impossible to say categorically that the opposition to the bomb had 'definitely slowed down its development', as Nichols had alleged, but it did 'delay the initiation of concerted effort which led to the development of a thermonuclear weapon'.[12]

The significance of all this did not lie in Oppenheimer's motivation, but in the impact on national security. Oppenheimer's opinions had been motivated by moral concern and a sense of guilt at having helped to bring nuclear weapons into the world, and this was understandable, but he had allowed his feelings to get the better of his technical judgment. Given the issues at stake, this was inadmissible. 'Emotional involvement in the current crisis', declared Gray and Morgan, 'like all other things, must yield to the security of the nation. . . . In evaluating advice from a specialist which departs from the area of his specialty, Government officials charged with the military posture of our country must also be certain that underlying any advice is a genuine conviction that this country cannot in the interest of security have less than the strongest possible offensive capabilities in a time of national danger.' This presumably referred to tactical atomic weapons and air defence as well as to the development of the hydrogen bomb, but there was no explicit mention of these issues, in spite of the amount of time devoted to them at the hearing. At all events, the conclusion was that Oppenheimer's conduct over the H-bomb had been 'sufficiently disturbing as to raise a doubt as to whether his future participation, if characterized by the same attitudes in a Government program relating to the national defense, would be clearly consistent with the best interests of security'.[13]

The second major reason for denying clearance was that 'Dr Oppenheimer's continuing conduct and associations have reflected a serious disregard for the requirements of the security system'. Here, seven items were listed: the Chevalier incident; Oppenheimer's relationship with Chevalier after 1943; his refusal, in 1946, to discuss a meeting said to have been held in Chevalier's house; his refusal, in 1950, to discuss people he had known to be Communists; his disclosure, during the hearing, of 'pertinent details' about meetings and individuals, which he had not revealed before; his part in getting Bohm a post at Princeton and his continued relations with Bohm; and his discussion with Bohm and Lomanitz of their testimony before the Un-American Activities Committee in 1949.[14]

Four of these items have already been touched on. The remaining three have not, because they assumed no importance at the hearing. The first concerned the meeting in Chevalier's house. In his letter of 4 March 1954, Oppenheimer wrote that he had not recalled the meeting when questioned about it by the FBI in 1946, but that his wife had later remembered it and when

he was asked again in 1950 he said it had taken place as described. This he repeated in his testimony before the Board. The
second related to his refusal to discuss with the FBI the activities
of a friend who had recently died, Dr Thomas Addis. In his
testimony on this matter, which was not pursued by Robb,
Oppenheimer had said that his refusal was on the grounds
that Addis was dead and could not defend himself and that the
interrogators had said it was not important to them. The third
item touched on odd references to figures from the Berkeley
period and Communist meetings held in California during that
time. These references were scattered and fleeting: Oppenheimer's counsel had to scour the transcript to discover them, and
they did not merit the significance which Gray and Morgan
attached to them.[15]

Taken together, however, the incidents indicated to Gray and
Morgan that Oppenheimer had 'repeatedly exercised an arrogance of his own judgment with respect to the loyalty and reliability of other citizens to an extent which has frustrated and at
times impeded the working of the [security] system'. This was
especially serious in view of their earlier insistence that a
public servant must not only understand and support the government's security measures and co-operate with its agents. His
obligation extended to 'a subordination of personal judgment as
to the security status of an individual as against a professional
judgment in the light of standards and procedures when they
have been clearly established by appropriate process'. It also
entailed 'a wholehearted commitment to the preservation of
the security system and the avoidance of conduct tending to
confuse or obstruct'. Oppenheimer had palpably failed to match
up to these exacting standards.[16]

The third reason given by the majority was that they had
found 'a susceptibility to influence which could have serious
implications for the security interests of the country'. Here, three
items were cited: Oppenheimer's intercession on behalf of
Lomanitz in 1943; his public modification of his criticism of
Peters in 1949; and his declared willingness to support Dr
Condon (who had prompted his action on both occasions) when
Condon's own clearance was questioned. The first two of these
items have already been covered. The third cropped up towards
the close of the hearing. Shortly after Oppenheimer's suspension,

Condon had written to him asking for help, and Oppenheimer had given it in the form of a written statement. As his counsel later pointed out, this would have been interpreted by many people as a magnanimous gesture, since Condon had attacked Oppenheimer vehemently in 1949. Gray and Morgan, however, chose to see it differently.[17]

The fourth and final reason for the majority's finding was that 'Dr Oppenheimer has been less than candid in several instances in his testimony before this Board'. Here, what Gray and Morgan had in mind were three aspects of Oppenheimer's testimony on the hydrogen bomb. First they believed that he had said he only opposed a crash programme in the autumn of 1949, and not any kind of thermonuclear development. In fact, they maintained, he had urged that the government should commit itself without qualification to a decision never to produce the bomb. 'Moreover,' they stated, 'the alternatives available to the GAC were not a choice between an "all-out effort" and no effort at all; there was a middle course which might have been considered.' Secondly, they felt that Oppenheimer's influence 'was far greater than he would have led this Board to believe in his testimony before the Board'. Thirdly, they had concluded 'reluctantly' that his candour 'left much to be desired in his discussions with the Board of his attitude and position in the entire chronology of the hydrogen-bomb problem'.[18]

The confusion over all these matters has already been described. It sprang partly from the extreme complexity of the many technical and political issues involved, and partly from Robb's skill in making Oppenheimer appear to be concealing his true role—especially in the affair of Seaborg's letter. The interpretation which Gray and Morgan placed on all these questions cannot, however, be sustained by a close scrutiny of the transcript. They had misunderstood the real nature of the situation, and although they could be forgiven for mistaking Oppenheimer's subtlety for equivocation, it was not difficult to check what he had said against the evidence of many other witnesses. One only has to do this to see that his testimony was sound in practically all respects.

For all the reasons outlined, however, Gray and Morgan did not consider that Oppenheimer should be reinstated. They acknowledged that many had thought Oppenheimer's previous clearances should hold good, particularly the AEC clearance of August 1947, but in their view the objections were overriding. This was the first time that the matter had come up in the form of a hearing, and the only time that all the available evidence had been 'correlated and presented in a package'. Secondly, 'it was necessary to the national security that material information not considered in previous clearances be studied'—a reference, presumably, to the allegations over the H-bomb, tactical atomic weapons and air defence. Thirdly, circumstances in the United States and the world at large had changed, as had the criteria of the security system. In 1947, Oppenheimer had been cleared on the basis of his loyalty and discretion, his service to the country and his indispensability; now, by inference, the standards required of him were even higher than this—and too high for him to reach, and he was no longer essential to the atomic energy programme. Fourthly, 'viewed against the background of earlier history', Oppenheimer's conduct since 1947 had raised large doubts as to his security status.[19]

At the same time, they asked the interesting question : why had not the AEC simply allowed Oppenheimer's consultancy to lapse when his contract expired on 30 June 1954? To have done so would have avoided the need for a hearing altogether. The Board had posed the question to the Commission and had been told it was impossible. In the first place, an AEC clearance was regarded by other agencies as a supreme endorsement and even if Oppenheimer were no longer employed by the AEC, they would continue to use him on the strength of that endorsement. Moreover, 'even though his services were not specifically and currently engaged', he would go on receiving classified reports as a consultant. Finally, AEC contractors could still use him, and most of the Commission's work was carried out by them.[20]

Even given these arguments, Gray and Morgan felt that this would have been the best course to take. This was a very remarkable admission indeed, and it reflected the anguish which punctuated their report. It also reflected the muddled thinking which often underlay it. Both saw the expiry of Oppenheimer's contract as a recommendation which they could have made, when in fact it was beyond their power. President Eisenhower had decided this particular issue when he suspended Oppenheimer's clearance, and although Oppenheimer had chosen to go

through with the hearing, he had no alternative if he were to
answer the charges laid against him. Thus the possibility which
they believed to exist had long since been removed.

Nonetheless, the reasons Gray and Morgan gave for thinking
along these lines were extremely revealing. A recommendation
that the contract should not be renewed would have been possible 'if we were allowed to exercise mature practical judgment
without the rigid circumscription of regulations and criteria
established for us'. As Garrison had feared, a literal interpretation of the rules had triumphed over the broad and flexible
construction which he had pleaded for in his summing-up. On
the issue of security, the majority were as adamant as they were on
the need for the hydrogen bomb. 'Security measures', they declared,

> are for the protection of the country, whose interests should
> never be foreclosed . . . . at no time can the interests of the
> protection of all our people be less than paramount to all
> other considerations. Indeed, action which in some cases may
> seem to be a denial of the freedoms which our security bar-
> riers are erected to protect may rather be a fulfillment of these
> freedoms. For, if in our zeal to protect our institutions against
> our measures to secure them, we lay them open to destruction,
> we will have lost them all, and will have gained only the
> empty satisfaction of a meaningless exercise.[21]

Given a security system as demanding as this, a man charged
with being a security risk had to furnish overwhelming proof that
he was above reproach. The onus lay on him 'to leave no reasonable doubt in the minds of those who are called upon to make a
governmental decision in the case'. The question which had to be
answered was : 'Can an individual who has been a member of the
Communist Party, or closely enough associated with it to make
the difference unimportant at a later time, so comport himself
personally, so clearly have demonstrated a renunciation of interest
and sympathy, so unequivocally have displayed a zeal for his
country and its security as to overcome the necessary presumption of security risk?' It was certainly possible, Gray and Morgan
believed, but not in Oppenheimer's case.[22]

In coming to their recommendation, the majority felt that
they had been able to resolve the interests of national security

and individual freedom. 'We believe', they asserted, 'that it has been demonstrated that the Government can search its own soul and the soul of an individual whose relationship to his Government is in question with full protection of the rights and interests of both. We believe that loyalty and security can be examined within the framework of the traditional and inviolable principles of American justice.' They were also anxious to assure the scientific community that the inquiry did not constitute 'an attack upon scientists and intellectuals generally' and was by no means 'either in fact or in appearance a reflection of anti-intellectualism'. In particular they wished to remove the impression, which, as Conant had indicated, was widespread among his colleagues—namely, that Oppenheimer had been arraigned at least partly because he had expressed strong opinions about the hydrogen bomb. Quite how they reconciled this with their conclusion that Oppenheimer's attitude to the bomb was sincerely motivated but not clearly consistent with the best interests of national security is not immediately apparent.[23]

So Gray and Morgan proposed that Oppenheimer's clearance should not be restored. Evans believed it should be, and outlined his reasons in a short minority report. It was not an impressive document. Less than one-and-a-half pages long, it hardly began to counter the arguments which Gray and Morgan had developed in such detail. The case against Oppenheimer, as Evans saw it, boiled down to the issue of his associations. He had not hindered the hydrogen bomb programme, he was loyal (as Gray and Morgan agreed), and there was nothing wrong with his character. A judgment on his reliability therefore had to turn on his associations. But, Evans asserted, most of the derogatory information on this score was in the possession of the AEC when it cleared Oppenheimer in 1947. In other words, he had been 'investigated twice for the same things' and it was highly disturbing that he should now be denied clearance on the basis of material which had been found to support his clearance seven years earlier. It was even more disturbing if one considered, as Evans did, that Oppenheimer was less of a security risk in 1954 than he was in 1947. 'I personally think', he concluded, 'that our failure to clear Dr Oppenheimer will be a black mark on the escutcheon of our country.'[24]

The majority and minority opinions were delivered to General Nichols at the Atomic Energy Commission on 27 May. The following day he sent copies to Oppenheimer and Garrison, telling them at the same time that they could request a review of the case by the AEC Personnel Security Review Board and submit a brief to support their arguments. The request would have to be in by 7 June and the brief would have to be filed no less than twenty days after the receipt of his letter. Nichols also pointed out that whatever happened, he would be submitting his own recommendation on clearance and that the final decision would be made by the five Commissioners. This was an important change in procedure which the Commission had authorized at a meeting on 18 May; normally the decision would have rested with Nichols as General Manager. In his opinion on the case Commissioner Campbell indicated that he and one other colleague (probably Smyth) had voted against the proposal on the grounds that it would be better to wait until a formal revision could be published in the *Federal Register*. The point of the change is not clear. As we shall see, it would not have altered the outcome if it had not been introduced, and it remains one of the many mysteries of the affair.[25]

At all events, Garrison accepted it. In his reply to Nichols of 1 June, he waived the right to go to the Review Board and asked for a decision by the Commission before 30 June, when Oppenheimer's contract was due to expire. If the issue had not been settled by then, he believed, it would be left in a state of great uncertainty, since, presumably, the AEC would no longer have jurisdiction in the matter. He therefore promised the brief for 7 June and asked to be allowed to support it with oral argument before the Commission. He closed by outlining his objections to the Gray-Morgan report, and by making known his belief that Oppenheimer had suffered by not having had access to documents used against him at the hearing.[26]

At the same time as he wrote to Nichols, Garrison decided to release the Board's reports to the papers, together with Nichols' letter transmitting it and his reply. Indeed, the reply had been written less as an answer to Nichols than as a critique of the majority report, to be published simultaneously with it just as he had published Oppenheimer's letter of 4 March 1954 together with Nichols' allegations of 23 December 1953. The purpose in both instances was the same : to forestall publication of the unfavourable material alone by an unfriendly source and to offset it with Oppenheimer's version of the case. To reinforce Oppenheimer's defence still further, an accompanying statement was given to the press which pointed out the favourable aspects of the Board's findings. Thus, when the documents were published on 2 June, a balanced presentation was available.[27]

The following day Nichols replied to Garrison's letter of 1 June. It was an icy communication. Most importantly, it turned down Garrison's request to make an oral argument before the Commission. At the same time Nichols noted that Garrison had said how anxious he was that there should be no further delay, and claimed that every delay to date had been the fault of Oppenheimer, not of the AEC. He also dismissed the complaint that Oppenheimer had not been given access to material employed against him at the hearing. On 7 June, Nichols too brought the controversy into the open by making the letter public.[28]

The same day, Garrison's brief was filed with the Commission. In it, Garrison and his colleagues attempted to refute the case which Gray and Morgan had made, and suggested that the Commission need not attach too much weight to the 1953 Executive Order, on which Gray and Morgan had clearly based at least two of the four reasons behind their recommendations. They still believed that the final judgment must be one which took all factors into account, and if due note were taken of what Oppenheimer's witnesses had said on his behalf, the only justifiable conclusion would be that he should be reinstated. At the same time, Garrison telegraphed Nichols, asking him whether the Commission could not reconsider its decision not to hear an oral argument. He repeated his request in a letter of 9 June, pointing out that the Commission had already departed from the usual procedure in taking on responsibility for the final determination. No reply was sent from Nichols for more than two weeks, until 24 June, when he answered that the Commission had prescribed 'that further argument, either oral or written, would not be in order'. By that time, as we shall see, the AEC had already come to its decision.[29]

Meanwhile, there had been an intensely hostile reaction to the Gray-Morgan report, or rather to its condemnation of Oppenheimer for not displaying enthusiasm for the hydrogen bomb.

The statement put out by the sociologist Edward Shils typified the bitterness felt in the academic world. 'Unwittingly,' said Shils, 'moderate conservatism has come to accept the postulates of nativistic fundamentalism—of know-nothingism, of crackpot xenophobia, of McCarthyism. . . . American opinion has drifted under the impulsion of unscrupulous or paranoid fanatics to the point where private feelings are more significant than beliefs and actions. The sentiment of active enthusiastic conformity with government policy is now demanded of those who would avoid having their names and reputations darkened as security risks. . . . It used to be said that those who wrestle with pigs are bound to get dirty. The recent experience of the United States shows that those who frivolously permit themselves the luxury of allowing themselves to be led by pigs soon find themselves sliding desperately in the slimy mire created by their leaders.'[30]

The scientists themselves were, of course, most immediately affected. As we have seen, the inclusion of the H-bomb issue in Nichols' allegations had sent a tremor of resentment through the scientific community, and Karl T. Compton was only one of the witnesses at the hearing who expressed his forebodings about the consequences if clearance were refused on this score. 'I believe—and I feel very certain of this,' he had said, 'that there would be a shock, there would be a discouragement, there would be confusion. I think the result would be very bad'.[31]

This was no doubt what the Board had in mind when it sought to give reassurances that Oppenheimer was not being tried for his opinions, but virtually in the same breath it had found against him precisely on those grounds. It was hardly surprising, then, when the scientists rose in protest. The most devastating broadside came from Bush, writing in *The New York Times* on 13 June. It was Bush who had helped to forge the partnership between government and science during the Second World War as director of the Office of Scientific Research and Development. In his opinion, it had now been gravely damaged and was in the process of being gradually destroyed. If it were to be restored, it meant 'that there should be no insistence that any individual cease his thinking at any time, or that he suppress his honest opinions in order slavishly to follow a policy arbitrarily laid down'. It did not mean 'that a citizen who is cognizant of the facts should not protest loudly and persistently any time he feels that decisions are being rendered without full consideration of all sides of an important question'. Dr James R. Killian echoed him when he spoke before a congressional hearing four days later. There was a current feeling, he said, 'that the present security procedures can be handled and administered in a manner to damage creative activity and if they are, the feeling that the giving of an unbiased and objective judgment can be, under certain conditions, dangerous to the giver because this unbiased judgment does not accord with somebody's policy'. This was greatly discouraging to scientists working on government projects.[32]

This outcry was the background to two very important developments, and although it cannot be said to have caused them, it is difficult to believe that they would have taken place without it. The first was the AEC's decision to publish the transcript of the hearing. It came about in the following way. On 7 June the question of whether or not to release the transcript was raised at a meeting of the Commission. It was argued that publication was acceptable now that Oppenheimer had released the text of the Gray Board findings and recommendations. Nothing was done, however, until the following weekend. On Friday, 11 June, Commissioner Eugene M. Zuckert lost a highly confidential summary of the FBI file and the transcript which had been prepared in the AEC. This, needless to say, set off an enormous commotion, and Strauss called an emergency meeting of the Commission the next day. It now seemed inevitable that the transcript should be made public in one way or another. Strauss, according to one account, proposed that the press should be invited to look at the few typescript copies at the AEC building, and, to help them find their way through the mass of words, that the 'most interesting' passages be marked. This suggestion was rejected, for what should have been obvious reasons, and instead the transcript was sent to the Government Printing Office to be set up in type so that it could be released quickly if need be. On Monday, 14 June, the Commission met again and voted four to one for immediate publication, although the summary had been found in the interim; the sole objector was Commissioner Henry D. Smyth.[33]

The release itself had several noteworthy features. One was

the sheer speed of the operation. The 992-page document was printed in something less than 72 hours, a fact which one needs to bear in mind when one comes across its numerous errors. In the circumstances, it was a near-miracle there were not more. This rush into print meant, among other things, that there was no time to secure approval in advance from the witnesses at the hearing, who had been assured by Gray that the AEC would not take the initiative in publishing the proceedings. Although they were, apparently, asked whether they had any objections, in effect it was impossible for them to refuse. It also meant— unaccountably—that Garrison was given no notice by the AEC. He first learned that publication was being contemplated from Oppenheimer's witnesses and from the *New York Times* columnist, Reston.[34]

Reston telephoned Garrison on 13 June to try to persuade him to release the transcript first (as Oppenheimer's counsel, he had been allowed a copy). Garrison, however, refused, for fear of offending the Commission while the matter was still in their hands. So publication by the AEC alone went ahead, and at six o'clock in the evening of 15 June, printed copies were distributed to the press corps in Washington, for publication at noon on 16 June. Accompanying each one was a hand-out which singled out aspects of the case which the AEC apparently wished to draw to the public's attention. Among them were Oppenheimer's relationship with Chevalier, his admission to having lied to the security forces in 1943, and his confession that he had spent the night with Jean Tatlock during his visit to San Francisco that summer. This was comparable with the hand-out which Oppenheimer's counsel had produced at the time they published the Gray Board report a fortnight earlier, but in Garrison's view it served an entirely different purpose. He had wanted the press to make a balanced consideration of the material released; the aim of the AEC was precisely the reverse.[35]

If this was the Commission's objective, it most certainly achieved it. The popular reaction was now extremely unfavour- able to Oppenheimer. The lead was given by Fulton Lewis, Jr, the pro-McCarthy broadcaster, who immediately broke the dead- line imposed on the media and launched into a sensational attack based mainly on the excerpts provided by the AEC. He was followed by most of his colleagues. The right wing seized the

9 President Eisenhower, who ordered the erection of 'a blank wall between Dr Oppenheimer and any secret data'

10 Senator Joseph McCarthy, who almost certainly influenced the instigation of the case

11–12 Gordon Gray and Thomas A. Morgan, the anti-Oppenheimer majority of the AEC Personnel Security Board

13 Ward V. Evans, the only member of the Board to recommend Oppenheimer's reinstatement

14 General Kenneth D. Nichols, the AEC General Manager, who called for the denial of Oppenheimer's clearance

opportunity avidly. Thus to the *Tribune* columnist David Law-rence, 'the most charitable interpretation which can be placed on the strange and complicated behavior of Dr Oppenheimer as revealed in the evidence is that he was never intentionally disloyal but that his actions, as disclosed in the official record, permit the inference by the board that he might unwittingly become involved in disloyalty because of his peculiar standards of judgment when there is a conflict between loyalty to a friend and loyalty to his own government.' Lawrence spoke for ultra-conservative opinion, but there can be no doubt that even the most liberal commentators felt a distinct sense of unease. The wave of support for Oppenheimer which had followed the publication of the Gray Board's reports now subsided, and the instinctive fears which had been aroused when the news of the hearing first broke were sharply revived. Even before the issue was settled, a good many people seemed to have drawn the conclusion that Oppenheimer had deservedly lost the trust of the government he had served so long.[36]

The second major development which took place at this junc-ture was the submission of General Nichols' recommendations on 12 June. Indeed, Nichols' report was so important as to be one of the turning-points in the case. Its primary significance was that it removed the question of the hydrogen bomb from consideration and thus deprived Oppenheimer of his strongest remaining advantage. This was no accident. Nichols' report was not the dispassionate survey of all the evidence which was re-quired by the AEC Procedures. It was, instead, a summary of the case for the prosecution which concentrated almost exclusively on presenting Oppenheimer in the worst possible light. Its tone was implacable, and it clearly looked to a condemnation by the Commission.

To begin with, Nichols disregarded the Gray Board's findings that Oppenheimer was loyal and discreet. In a sub-section headed *Dr Oppenheimer's Communist activities,* he stated merely that 'the record contains no direct evidence that Dr Oppenheimer gave secrets to a foreign nation or that he is disloyal to the United States'. Similarly, he brushed aside the finding that Oppenheimer had given unparalleled service to the country. While he acknowledged that 'through World War II he was of tremendous value and absolutely essential', since then

G

his value had declined 'because of the rise in competence and skill of other scientists and because of his loss of scientific objectivity probably resulting from the diversion of his efforts to political fields and matters not purely scientific in nature'. So much for eight years of public achievement which few men in the United States could match. Finally, like Gray and Morgan, Nichols pointed out that Oppenheimer had been used on only a handful of occasions by the AEC since leaving the General Advisory Committee.[37]

Turning to the hydrogen bomb, Nichols took up a totally different position from Gray and Morgan. For them it had been a cardinal issue; for him it was irrelevant. 'It should be emphasized', said Nichols, 'that at no time has there been any intention on my part or the Board's to draw in question any honest opinion expressed by Dr Oppenheimer. Technical opinions have no security implications unless they are reflections of sinister motives. . . . In reviewing the record I find that the evidence establishes no sinister motives on the part of Dr Oppenheimer in his attitude on the hydrogen bomb, either before or after the President's decision.' Forestalling the question as to why he had included the charge in his letter of notification, he stated that it had been put in to test Oppenheimer's good faith.[38]

This sudden dropping of the H-bomb issue was almost certainly brought about by the furore among the scientific community. As both Robb and Garrison had maintained, it was only relevant if Oppenheimer's motivation was suspect, and to have persevered in it would doubtless have produced the breakdown of the partnership between government and science which Bush had prophesied. In this respect, the AEC's position was now untenable. There were compensations, however. For one thing, the decision to omit the issue could be taken as an affirmation of the principle of freedom of expression. More importantly, it removed the major weakness in the Commission's case and at the same time deprived Oppenheimer of what had become a key item in his defence. It may even be that the AEC could afford to dispense with the hydrogen bomb allegations at this stage. In this writer's opinion, their real value may well have lain in setting the machinery of investigation in motion, and once that had been achieved, they were of considerably less importance. At all events, the Commission lost nothing by discarding them.

Nichols' conclusion that clearance should be denied was therefore based on his appraisal of Oppenheimer's character and associations, and here once again he parted company from Gray and Morgan, who had not seen the associations as a controlling factor, and had not included them in their final considerations. Both the associations of the pre-war and the post-war period raised 'serious questions' as to his eligibility for clearance, in Nichols' view. In the years 1936–42, he stated, Oppenheimer was not 'a mere "parlor pink" or student of communism as a result of immaturity and intellectual curiosity, but was deeply and consciously involved with hardened and militant Communists at a time when he was a man of mature judgment.... Dr Oppenheimer was a Communist in every respect except for the fact that he did not carry a party card.' Since the war he had associated with Chevalier 'on a rather intimate basis', and he had been in touch with Peters, Lomanitz and Bohm 'under circumstances which, to say the least, are disturbing'.[39]

His main criticisms, however, were directed at Oppenheimer's character, or, as Nichols put it, his veracity. Here, the Chevalier incident was central, and Nichols interpreted it in such a way as to give Oppenheimer no escape. Either he had lied to the security officers in 1943, as he himself had said, or he had told the truth then and lied later, as Pash had claimed at the hearing. Nichols was inclined to agree with Pash. If he had lied in 1943, then he had committed a felony under section 80, title 18 of the United States Code. If his story in 1943 had been true, it showed that both he and Chevalier were to some degree involved in a criminal espionage conspiracy. Moreover, as Nichols implied but did not state, if Oppenheimer had lied to the Gray Board, he was guilty of perjury, since he had given evidence under oath. These were criminal offences. So far as the offences against the security system were concerned, Oppenheimer's behaviour over the incident was covered by three parts of Executive Order 10450. It had shown he was 'not reliable or trustworthy'; that he had made 'deliberate misrepresentations [and] falsifications'; and it had constituted 'criminal ... dishonest ... conduct'.[40]

Nichols went on to develop the theme of veracity by reference to six examples. Four were taken from the Gray-Morgan report: the failure to give details of Communist party meetings to the FBI; the intervention on behalf of Lomanitz in 1943; the apparent about-face over Peters in 1949; and the contention that he had only opposed a crash programme for the H-bomb in 1949. Two were new. These were the affair of the Seaborg letter of October 1949, and Oppenheimer's indication to the FBI in 1950 that he had not known Weinberg was a Communist until it was made public (when in fact he had told Lansdale on 12 September 1943 that he knew Weinberg was a member of the Party). All raised a question 'as to the credibility of Dr Oppenheimer in his appearance before the Personnel Security Board and as to his character and veracity in general'.[41]

Nichols' final point was closely related to the issue of veracity. It was Oppenheimer's 'consistent disregard of a reasonable security system'. Here, only two items were explicitly mentioned —the Chevalier incident and the refusal to answer questions about people he knew to be Communists. The issue was also touched on in the section on past associations, however. On this subject, said Nichols, 'it appears that he is not inclined to disclose the facts spontaneously, but merely to confirm those already known'. All told, Oppenheimer's actions were 'wholly inconsistent with the obligations necessarily imposed by an adequate security system on those who occupy high positions of trust and responsibility in the Government'.[42]

Finally came the *coup de grâce*. On 4 June 1954, DuBridge had written to Strauss in his capacity as chairman of the Science Advisory Committee in the Office of Defense Mobilization. He had requested Oppenheimer's clearance so that he could work on the committee. His participation, in DuBridge's view, would be 'of very critical importance'. Nichols was not persuaded, for two reasons. 'Dr Oppenheimer', he wrote, 'could of course make contributions [to the atomic energy programme] but he is far from indispensable.' Moreover, he added in a footnote, 'Dr DuBridge to my knowledge has never had access to the complete file or the transcript of the hearing.' He could not know that Oppenheimer was someone who had to be eliminated from classified work as a matter of national concern.[43]

The savagery of Nichols' verdict was breathtaking, and the picture it presented was one-sided to the point of absurdity.

Few people would have recognized that the man Nichols was describing had been one of the most eminent figures in governmental circles since the end of the war, or that his standing in the scientific world was immensely high. Moreover, in one instance, Nichols had even gone so far as to make two assertions that were completely at variance with each other. In the first place, he said that Oppenheimer had given his current version of the Chevalier incident to the FBI in 1946. In the second place, he maintained that the complete record on the incident was not considered by the AEC in 1947. The implication of this second remark was that the Commission had not known of Oppenheimer's reversal in 1946 when it came to consider his case the following year, but it was made clear at the hearing that it did have this information, and approved Oppenheimer in spite of it. According to Nichols, however, there was no consideration of the full record, nor a cross-examination of Oppenheimer under oath—another thrust at his credibility—until the hearing before the Personnel Security Board.[44]

It is obvious that there were a great many questionable things in Nichols' report. Oppenheimer was allowed no opportunity either to expose them or to refute them, however, since he was not given a copy of the text. Doubtless the AEC did not wish to repeat the experience which had followed after Nichols had transmitted the Gray Board's findings and recommendations. This time, the possibility of stimulating another outburst of pro-Oppenheimer feeling was ruled out in advance. So too was the chance for Garrison to counter Nichols' arguments as he had met those of Gray and Morgan. This was extremely important. In many ways, Nichols had transformed the case. He had restructured the charges so completely that Garrison's brief to the Commission—which had, of course, addressed itself to the Gray-Morgan conclusions—was now largely irrelevant. Garrison, however, was not to know this, and he had no means of finding out. Even the possibility of discovering what Nichols had said during an oral argument before the Commission was foreclosed when his plea for the argument was rejected. Whether it would have made any difference to the outcome if he had been kept informed is highly uncertain, but it was a mockery of the Commission's procedures that he was not.[45]

Nichols' recommendations were significant in yet another sense, in that they set the framework for the Commissioners when they approached their decision in the last two weeks of June. The Chairman of the Commission, Mr Strauss, considered them so important, in fact, that he reprinted them verbatim in his memoirs, and their influence can be seen clearly in each of the majority opinions which were published soon after the decision was reached.[46]

Once Nichols had reported, five men held Oppenheimer's future in their hands. The Chairman of the AEC, Lewis L. Strauss, had had a long political career. As a young man, he had served on Herbert Hoover's Commission for Relief in Belgium during the First World War and had subsequently become one of Hoover's closest advisers. During the Second World War he had risen to the rank of Rear-Admiral in the Naval Reserve, and in 1946 he became an original member of the Atomic Energy Commission. As we have seen, he had taken the opposite side to Oppenheimer in the debate on the H-bomb, and he had resigned once the issue was decided. In March 1953, he had been appointed as President Eisenhower's special assistant on atomic energy affairs, an appointment he retained when he became Chairman of the Commission in July of that year.

The next most senior member of the Commission was Henry D. Smyth, who had been appointed in 1949 and who had also taken part in the H-bomb debate, in sympathy with Oppenheimer and the GAC. A physicist, he had been closely associated with the atomic bomb project during the war, and he was the author of the so-called Smyth Report, a detailed account of the project published in August 1945.

The three remaining members were Thomas E. Murray, Eugene M. Zuckert and Joseph Campbell. Murray had been nominated to the Commission in 1950 and, as has been noted, successfully opposed Oppenheimer on the issue of the second weapons laboratory. Zuckert became a Commissioner in 1952 after serving as Assistant Secretary of the Air Force. Campbell joined in July 1953, at the same time as Strauss became Chairman; he had formerly been Vice-President of Columbia University, New York.

As Garrison had rightly observed, in his letter to Nichols of

1 June, a decision had to be reached by the end of the month, when Oppenheimer's contract expired. The final alignment was already settled by 22 June, however, and it was heavily un- favourable to Oppenheimer. Strauss, Murray, Zuckert and Campbell were against the reinstatement of clearance; only Smyth was for it. A formal vote was taken on 28 June. For the third and last time, Oppenheimer was condemned as a security risk and debarred for ever from access to government secrets.[47]

The condemnation took a complicated form. It consisted of a majority opinion signed by Strauss, Zuckert and Campbell, and written by Strauss; a concurring opinion by Murray; and explanatory statements by Zuckert and Campbell.

Like Nichols' report, the majority opinion makes ugly reading. On Oppenheimer's loyalty, about which the Gray Board had made a positive finding, there was no explicit conclusion and one is left to infer that he was not considered disloyal. On his dis- cretion and his years of service to the government, there was total silence. Whereas Nichols had at least mentioned Oppen- heimer's Second World War achievement, Strauss, Zuckert and Campbell had not one single favourable word to say from start to finish.[48]

What were the grounds on which the opinion was based? It was not based on Oppenheimer's associations up to 1942. Like Gray and Morgan, the Commission majority did not regard these as a controlling factor, even though Oppenheimer had been in contact with Communist Party officials 'some of whom had been engaged in espionage'. Nor was it based on Oppen- heimer's attitude to the hydrogen bomb, or to be more precise, on his attitude during the 1949 debate—the periods before and after the debate were not mentioned, and here again one could only infer that they were relevant. The majority attached no importance to Oppenheimer's opinions as expressed during the debate. Nor, they said—a statement which was quite simply untrue—had the Personnel Security Board. 'Dr Oppenheimer', they concluded blandly, 'was, of course, entitled to his opinion.'[49]

Strauss, Zuckert and Campbell had thus dismissed the bulk of the charges preferred against Oppenheimer in December 1953, charges which they themselves had all approved. Their decision rested instead on the issues of character and associations—the only indication that Oppenheimer's loyalty was not in question.

In the first place, Oppenheimer was 'not entitled to the continued confidence of the Government and of this Commission because of the proof of fundamental defects in his "character" '. In the second place, the majority found that 'his associations with persons known to him to be Communists have extended far beyond the tolerable limits of prudence and self-restraint which are to be expected of one holding the high positions that the Government has continuously entrusted to him since 1942. These associations have lasted too long to be justified as merely the intermittent and accidental revival of earlier friendships.'[50]

On the score of character, the majority cited six items, five of them taken from Nichols' list of proofs of Oppenheimer's doubtful veracity. They comprised the Chevalier incident; the support given to Lomanitz in 1943; the Peters episode of 1949; the affair of the Seaborg letter of October 1949; and the alleged lie over Weinberg's membership of the Communist Party. The charge of dissembling over the issue of an H-bomb crash programme was dropped, and replaced by the following. During his interview with Lansdale on 12 September 1943, Oppenheimer had been asked whether he knew a man called Rudy Lambert. He had replied that he was not sure and asked Lansdale what Lambert looked like. Under cross-examination by Robb at the hearing, however, he said that he had met Lambert half-a-dozen times and that he knew he was a Party official. He also gave a good description of him. It was obvious when the transcript of the Lansdale interview was introduced into the proceedings the next day that Oppenheimer had been trapped on a small detail, but few could have expected that this exposure would be one of the most prominent features of the final judgment on him. One is not sure whether to put it down to heavy-handedness or cynicism, but whatever the motive, the inclusion of this fragment is astounding.[51]

These six examples were not all, stated Strauss, Zuckert and Campbell. Military Intelligence, the FBI and the AEC 'all, at one time or another have felt the effect of his falsehoods, evasions and misrepresentations'. In particular, Oppenheimer's 'persistent and willful disregard for the obligations of security' was betrayed by his behaviour over the Chevalier incident. He had first of all waited for eight months before approaching the authorities and then delayed for nearly four months before giving the name of the man who had contacted him. It was not clear which version of the incident was the true one, but, echoing Nichols, either way he had committed a crime.[52]

Chevalier also loomed large when the majority turned to the question of associations since the war. These were described as 'persistent and continuing association with Communists', and two items were singled out—the help he had given to Chevalier in February 1950 and the visit he had paid to him in December 1953, when again he had helped him on a matter involving Chevalier's clearance. The contacts with Chevalier were given additional significance by the fact that Chevalier was described as 'the same individual who had been intermediary for the Soviet Consulate in 1943'. In other words, it was all but stated that he and Oppenheimer had been involved in a genuine espionage attempt on the Radiation Laboratory, although it had just been said that it was not clear whether or not Oppenheimer had been telling the truth about Chevalier in 1943. Yet wherever the majority really stood on this issue, they believed that either together or separately, the episodes of 1950 and 1953 presented 'a serious picture'. 'It is clear', they concluded, 'that ... Dr Oppenheimer had defaulted not once but many times upon the obligations that should and must be willingly borne by citizens in the national service.'[53]

In coming to their decision, the majority were anxious to stress the fairness of the procedure which had led up to it, and to point out the superiority of the hearing over all previous determinations of Oppenheimer's status. The hearing, they claimed, had done three things. It had introduced sworn testimony which was used to test the value of the derogatory information in the secret dossier, and this had never been done before. By implication, therefore, the material in the dossier had been validated, even by Oppenheimer's witnesses, who had provided the great majority of the evidence. It had brought out 'significant information' on Oppenheimer's character and associations hitherto unknown to the Commission and presumably unknown to his witnesses. Finally, it had 'established as fact many matters which previously had only been allegations'. Precisely what the 'significant information' was, and just what the said allegations were, they did not choose to say. There was, apparently, no need of justification.[54]

Oppenheimer, said Strauss, Zuckert and Campbell, had held

positions of great trust and responsibility, and they had carried with them correspondingly weighty obligations. 'A Government official having access to the most sensitive areas of restricted data and to the innermost details of national war plans and weapons must measure up to exemplary standards of reliability, self-discipline, and trustworthiness.' Oppenheimer, they concluded, had 'fallen far short of acceptable standards'. He had 'consistently placed himself outside the rules which govern others'. He had 'falsified in matters wherein he was charged with grave responsibilities in the national interest'. In his associations, he had 'repeatedly exhibited a willful disregard for the normal and proper obligations of security'. For these reasons, his clearance should not be reinstated.[55]

Strauss did not provide a gloss on his opinion, although he, more than anyone else, should have given one, since he was the only Commissioner who had also cleared Oppenheimer in 1946 and 1947. It was not until his memoirs came out eight years later that he chose to explain why he had changed his mind. In 1947, Strauss wrote, the AEC knew that Oppenheimer had 'informed on a professional colleague at the University of California as being involved in an attempt to obtain secret information on the atomic project for the Soviet espionage organization'. The Commission did not know until the hearing that Oppenheimer had continued to see this man (Chevalier), nor that he had met him as recently as December 1953. In the second place, the AEC in 1947 had not known that Oppenheimer had 'fabricated a "tissue of lies" to tell to American security officers'. In the third place, 'there was other information not before the Commission or known to it in 1947'.[56]

There were several remarkable features about this statement. The third item presumably did not refer to the hydrogen bomb allegations, since the Commission had ruled them out, but to the incidents involving Peters, Weinberg, the Seaborg letter and Lambert. If so, this was unexceptionable. What was extraordinary (and, perhaps, revealing) was Strauss' description of Oppenheimer's disclosure of the Chevalier incident as informing. What other conclusion could be drawn except that Oppenheimer had acted out of malice, and that it would have been more honourable for him to have kept silent? Equally extraordinary was the assertion that the AEC had not known of Oppenheimer's contacts with Chevalier between 1947 and 1953 (the Paris visit possibly excluded), when he was under constant scrutiny and when, as Dean had testified, FBI reports kept coming in from time to time. But most surprising of all was the claim that the AEC in 1947 had been unaware of Oppenheimer's lying in 1943. It was clearly established at the hearing that the Commission *had* known that Oppenheimer had changed his story since 1943; the distinction which Strauss would no doubt draw—that it had not known of the so-called tissue of lies—is academic. There is finally the discrepancy between Strauss's apparent acceptance of Oppenheimer's original story as a lie, and the majority's conclusion in 1954 that it may or may not have been true. All told, this was a peculiar piece of self-justification, to say the very least.[57]

The statement attached by Zuckert attempted to explain his position as follows. He had felt that none of the instances which he, Strauss and Campbell had cited in support of their conclusion would have been decisive in themselves. 'But when I see such a combination of seriously disturbing actions and events as are present in this case,' Zuckert stated, 'then I believe the risk to security passes acceptable bounds.' He appeared to take it for granted that the appraisal should be made solely on the basis of the derogatory information, and should not take into account the favourable evidence before the Commission. In other words, he had focussed his attention exclusively on the worst aspects of the case, and ignored the rest. On this basis, Oppenheimer was a security risk, but not disloyal (Zuckert was the only member of the majority to say this explicitly). Moreover, given the seriousness of the allegations presented to them at the outset, the Commission had had no alternative but to accept that they raised the possibility of security risk. They could not, therefore, merely allow Oppenheimer's contract to lapse as this would only have postponed the issue.[58]

Campbell justified his decision on two main grounds. The first was the fairness of the procedure, which he dwelt on at some length. The second was his view that the Commission held a purely appellate responsibility in the case. 'If the security system of the United States is to be successfully operated,' wrote Campbell, 'the recommendations of personnel security boards must be honored in the absence of compelling circumstances. If the

General Manager of the Atomic Energy Commission is to function properly, his decisions must be upheld unless there can be shown new evidence, violations of procedures, or other substantial reasons why they should be reversed.' The validity of this reasoning was questionable, to say the least (and Commissioner Campbell's tenuous grasp of legal principles was indicated by his description of the brief which Garrison had submitted to the Commission. This, he said, was 'argumentative' and contained 'no new evidence'. In other words, he was unaware that the purpose of a brief is to present an argument and that it may do so only on the basis of evidence which has already been furnished); nonetheless, it was as a result of this interpretation of the procedure that he made up his mind.[59]

Commissioner Murray's concurring opinion was a remarkable document. It contained an affirmation of intellectual freedom which, as one commentator has rightly put it, would have done justice to the American Civil Liberties Union. 'However stringent the need for a security system,' wrote Murray, 'the system cannot be allowed to introduce into American jurisprudence that hateful concept, the "crime of opinion." The very security of America importantly lies in the steady guaranty, even in a time of crisis, of the citizen's right to freedom of opinion and of honest and responsible utterance.' This referred to Oppenheimer's stand on the hydrogen bomb, and it was undoubtedly meant as a message of reassurance to the scientific community. It could with equal justification have applied to his left-wing beliefs during the period between 1936 and 1942.[60]

Having said this, however, Murray went on to find that Oppenheimer was disloyal, a finding shared by none of his colleagues. He came to this conclusion by setting up a criterion of loyalty which he defined as follows. 'The American citizen', he wrote,

'recognizes that his Government, for all its imperfections, is a government under law, of law, by law; therefore he is loyal to it. Furthermore, he recognizes that his Government, because it is lawful, has the right and the responsibility to protect itself against the action of those who would subvert it. The cooperative effort of the citizen with the rightful action of American Government in its discharge of this primary responsibility also belongs to the very substance of American loyalty. This is the crucial principle in the present case.'[61]

Measured against this exacting standard, Oppenheimer had failed. He had failed through maintaining his past associations and they were 'incompatible with obedience to the laws of security ... however innocent in fact'. He had failed in his attitude to the security system. 'The record proves Dr Oppenheimer to have been seriously deficient in his cooperation with the workings of the security system', Murray stated. This too was 'a defect of loyalty to the lawful government', and Oppenheimer's lapses took on additional significance in the light of the Communist conspiracy against a tradition based on the rule of law. 'Revolutionary Communism', wrote Murray, 'has emerged as a world power seeking domination of all mankind. ... It uses all the methods proper to conspiracy, the methods of infiltration and intrigue, of deceit and duplicity, of falsehood and connivance.' It was therefore even more necessary for democracy to insist on loyalty to its principles, and it could accept nothing less than absolute loyalty from men who were national figures. 'Where responsibility is highest,' Murray proclaimed, 'fidelity should be most perfect.' Oppenheimer was not perfect and so he was disloyal.[62]

The sole dissenter from these views was Smyth. Before examining Smyth's opinion, note must be taken of two aspects of the preliminaries leading up to it. According to one recent account, Smyth prepared his appraisal with the help of two AEC employees, Clark C. Vogel and Philip Farley. Farley was responsible to General Nichols, and when Nichols heard that he was about to help Smyth, he summoned him to his office. He told Farley that he was joining a lost cause, and 'made very clear what would happen to Farley's career if he chose to take on this assignment'. Farley went ahead nonetheless. The second item also relates to the preparation of Smyth's dissent and comes from the same source as the first. The dissent was written as a rebuttal of what Smyth understood to be the majority opinion, but when the draft was delivered to Smyth on 27 June, it was quite different from what he had expected. At the meeting of the AEC on 28 June, he therefore made a formal request that the final version of the majority decision be given to him no less than twenty-four hours before it was publicly released. That evening, however, when he was handed his colleagues' opinions he was told that his draft would have to be available by the next morning. He was able to meet the deadline only by working throughout the night.[63]

Smyth began by defining the issue as he saw it. It was to discover 'whether there is a possibility that Dr Oppenheimer will intentionally or unintentionally reveal secret information to persons who should not have it'. This was what was meant by 'security risk', and character and associations were important only as pointers to a conclusion on this score. That is to say, they were not significant in their own right, as the majority had argued. Loyalty, as expressed through discretion in the keeping of secrets, was the decisive factor. A finding which accepted the fact of loyalty and yet denied clearance on the basis of character and associations—as the majority had done—was bound to be invalid.[64]

Oppenheimer, in Smyth's view, had passed the acid test. The past fifteen years of his life had been investigated over and over again, and for most of the last eleven years he had been under close surveillance, with his movements watched, his conversations noted, his correspondence and his telephone calls monitored. This professional scrutiny, moreover, had been 'supplemented by enthusiastic amateur help from powerful personal enemies'. In spite of all this, there was no indication in the entire record that Oppenheimer had ever passed on information to anyone unauthorized to have it.[65]

This left the allegations set out by Nichols in December 1953. The most important of these, in Smyth's view, were in the section relating to the hydrogen bomb, and he was not surprised to find that the evidence did not support them in any way. As for the remainder—the items on Communist associations—there was extremely little that was new in them, and they had been known for years to administration officials. They had never been seen as a bar to Oppenheimer's government service until now, when they were being held up as the main reason for refusing clearance.[66]

Smyth then set out to refute the charges levelled by the majority, taking first the Chevalier incident, which he admitted was inexcusable. Nevertheless, he believed, as Rowe had done, that Oppenheimer would not make the same mistake twice. Nor did he attach significance to the post-war contacts with Chevalier, particularly during the Oppenheimers' visit to Paris in December 1953. As for the other post-war associations, they had been 'limited and infrequent . . . nothing more than occasional incidents in a complex life, and . . . not sought by Dr Oppenheimer'. The remaining episodes cited by the majority, relating to Lambert, Weinberg, Peters, Lomanitz, the Seaborg letter and the obstruction of security officers, were all equally unimportant. Moreover, they constituted the whole of the evidence against Oppenheimer. 'Any implication that these are illustrations only and that further substantial evidence exists in the investigative files to support these charges is unfounded.' If one set aside the Chevalier incident, the evidence was 'thin', whether considered separately or in combination. If one included the Chevalier incident, it was 'singularly unimpressive when viewed in the perspective of the 15 years of active life from which it is drawn.' 'Few men', wrote Smyth, 'could survive such a period of investigation and interrogation without having many of their actions misinterpreted or misunderstood.'[67]

Smyth's reading of the evidence was over-generous to Oppenheimer in many respects. For example, he simply repeated Oppenheimer's testimony that he had told Groves in December 1943 there had not been three contacts, when it was all too clear that Oppenheimer had not done so. Again, he said that Oppenheimer had stated he still considered Chevalier a friend, when Oppenheimer had put their friendship in the past tense at the close of the hearing. He also maintained that the charges of lying about Lambert and Weinberg were partly dependent on a garbled transcript of the interview with Lansdale; the transcript is garbled, but there is no room for ambiguity on these two points. His account of the Peters episode omitted to point out just how vigorously Oppenheimer had criticized Peters in his absence, and there were other instances of what was described as obstruction apart from the one which he claimed to be unique. Two more had in fact been invoked by Gray and Morgan.[68]

Even so, these are not sufficient reasons to reject Smyth's overall appraisal. 'In my opinion,' wrote Smyth, 'the conclusion drawn by the majority from the evidence is so extreme as to endanger the security system. If one starts with the assumption that Dr Oppenheimer is disloyal, the incidents which I have recounted may arouse suspicion. However, if the entire record is read objectively, Dr Oppenheimer's loyalty and trustworthiness emerge clearly and the various disturbing incidents are shown in their proper light as understandable and unimportant.'[69]

As far as the alleged disregard of the security system was concerned, Smyth said, 'I would suggest that the system itself is nothing to worship. . . . Its sole purpose, apart from the prevention of sabotage, is to protect secrets. If a man protects the secrets he has in his hands and his head, he has shown essential regard for the security system. . . . [It] has neither the responsibility nor the right to dictate every detail of a man's life.' An adverse finding on these grounds not only stretched the concept of security risk beyond what was legitimately justifiable but constituted a dangerous precedent.[70]

The failure to use men of outstanding talent could well damage the country's interests, Smyth ended. He could accept this in Oppenheimer's case if he believed that he was disloyal or indiscreet, but he did not. Oppenheimer's advice would continue to strengthen America's position in the world, and his clearance should therefore be reinstated.[71]

But Smyth stood alone in his opinion, and a few hours after it had been delivered to the AEC, the majority's decision was made public. Less than two days before his consultancy expired, Oppenheimer was told that his long career as a public servant was over.

In the evening of 29 June he put out a statement, after conferring with Garrison. His comment on the case itself was brief, no more than that Smyth's 'fair and considered statement, made with full knowledge of the facts, says what needs to be said'. The remainder was addressed to the scientific community. 'Our country', said Oppenheimer, 'is fortunate in its scientists; in their high skill and their devotion. I know that they will work faithfully to preserve and strengthen this country. I hope that the fruit of their work will be used with humanity, with wisdom and with courage. I know that their counsel, when sought, will be given honestly and freely. I hope that it will be heard.'[72]

This was Oppenheimer's last word on the subject. There was

no question of an appeal to the courts. Indeed, as Garrison has recently made clear, this had been ruled out at a very early stage, and for two main reasons. In the first place, the political atmosphere was highly unpropitious. The Cold War was passing through an intense phase, and public fears of treason and Communist infiltration into the government were being constantly exploited by McCarthy and others. In this climate of opinion, 'the courts would scarcely be in a mood to reverse a commission charged with so acutely sensitive a role as that which had been assigned to the Atomic Energy Commission'. In the second place, a court would not reverse the findings of an administrative agency if they were supported by substantial evidence. The most that could be expected would be a re-hearing because of procedural errors, and it seemed most unlikely that the Board would reverse itself after a second inquiry. Moreover, the basis for an appeal would disappear as soon as Oppenheimer's contract expired on 30 June.[73]

There was also the possibility of an appeal to the President, but this too was excluded. Eisenhower, it seemed to Garrison, was in no position to reverse the AEC's decision. He could not spare the time for a close analysis of the case, and he would have to reach his conclusion on the basis of someone else's recommendations. Even if he were willing to intervene, Garrison believed, the most he could do would be to state his personal view, and it was unrealistic to think that he would differ from his subordinates. 'It seemed to us', said Garrison, 'that the necessities of government would compel a statement upholding the Commission, whatever the merits might be, and that this would simply compound the injury suffered by Dr Oppenheimer.'[74]

Garrison was not right if he supposed that Eisenhower was unable to act. He had done so in suspending Oppenheimer's clearance in December 1953, although there was no provision in the AEC Procedures for presidential action, and he could well have taken a hand again after the Commission had pronounced sentence. He did not, however. When the question of an appeal was raised at his press conference on 30 June, he merely replied that if Oppenheimer wanted to make an appeal, 'of course he would be listened to'. Oppenheimer, understandably, did not take up this insubstantial offer, and with good reason. Although he did not say so in so many words, it was clear that Eisenhower had endorsed the Commission's findings, and he makes this explicit in his memoirs. He did not, of course, lend colour to the suggestion that he had given his approval because of *raison d'état*. This had to remain a matter for speculation. What was certain was that, as far as the administration was concerned, the case was closed, once and for all.[75]

Chapter Seven

'An Inquiry and not a Trial'

The Commission's decision, unlike the recommendations of Gray and Morgan, met with widespread approval in the American press, and hardly any editorial comment favoured Oppenheimer. 'Dr Oppenheimer', wrote *The New York Post,* 'is clearly guilty of arbitrariness and deceit.' In the view of *The Chicago Sun-Times* 'a nation's security cannot be risked by trusting one— even one as great as Oppenheimer—who has been guilty of monumental carelessness and whose tongue has been guilty of falsehoods'.[1]

The AEC position, in the opinion of *The New York Herald Tribune,* was the only one it could have taken, given that America was 'confronted by an enemy as implacable as resourceful, adopting every means of infiltration and subversion, taking advantage of the smallest carelessness or weakness to work its fatal poison'. 'In this field, so highly secret and so fundamental to the nation's security,' wrote *The New York World-Telegram and Sun,* 'the only wise course for the public is to accept the decision of those who have the most responsibility—even though it may have tragic and painful aspects.' Even *The New York Times,* which had done so much to publicize Oppenheimer's view of the case, felt it had to note that 'the solid weight of the judgment of four experienced and able Commissioners . . . is on one side'.[2]

Moreover, *The New York Post* asserted, 'there can be no question of the fairness of the procedures'. This was a point which the majorities of both the Board and the Commission (but not General Nichols) had been at some pains to stress. Commissioner Campbell, indeed, gave it as one of his reasons for sustaining the recommendations of Gray, Morgan and Nichols, and Strauss was later to draw attention to it in his memoirs.[3]

Yet were the hearing procedures really as equitable as they were made out to be? A close examination of the Oppenheimer case indicates that they were not. We have already touched on three disturbing features—the distortion of the minutes of the AEC meeting at which Oppenheimer was granted clearance in August 1947, the manner of the publication of the transcript and the concealment of Nichols' report—and they were all too typical of the general way in which the case was handled from start to finish. This is a disagreeable conclusion, but it is the only one that can be reached from the evidence available.

Garrison had objected to certain aspects of the procedure on several occasions: in his summation on 6 May; in his brief to the Board; and in his letters to Nichols of 1 and 9 June. He has also developed his criticisms at some length in a recent book. These criticisms will now be examined, as well as others which Garrison has not brought forward.[4]

The first, and perhaps the most important question to be raised was whether the AEC had to go through the formality of a hearing to settle the issue of Oppenheimer's clearance. The most straightforward thing to have done, in the view of Oppenheimer's supporters, was simply to have let his contract expire or to have terminated it. As Garrison pointed out on the very first day of the hearing, 'there has been no disposition on Dr Oppenheimer's part to hold onto a job for the sake of a job. It goes without saying that if the Commission did not wish to use his services as a consultant that was all right [sic] with him.' In his brief to the Commission, he noted that 'the Commission is under no obligation either to ask his advice or to continue his employment'. Moreover, he argued in his letter to Nichols of 1 June, when the contract expired on 30 June, Oppenheimer's clearance would automatically expire with it.[5]

This viewpoint was taken up by several others. At the hearing, Rabi declared that Oppenheimer's suspension was 'a very unfortunate thing and should not have been done. . . . he is a consultant, and if you don't want to consult the guy, you don't consult him, period. Why you have to then proceed to suspend clearance and go through all this sort of thing, he is only there when called, and that is all there was to it.' In the *Tribune* on 7 June, Lippmann asserted that there was 'no legal obligation to use [Oppenheimer] at all, and if the Administration had exercised its right with firmness and tact, they would not have involved themselves and this country in this inglorious mess'.[6]

The two former chairmen of the Commission agreed. On 22

June, Lienthal discussed the situation with Dean. 'There was a clear and sensible alternative', said Dean. 'Lewis [Strauss] could have called Oppie in and said: "Now, Oppie, we don't want to consult with you any more, because of differences of views about how useful your advice will be; we will cancel the [consulting] contract. And since without the contract you won't need access to classified information, we will not continue that clearance." That would have settled it. It wouldn't have pleased Oppie, but he would have appreciated the fact that his advice wasn't wanted, and that would have been that. Having that clear and simple way out, to use the "security risk" proceeding to get rid of him means that there was no other motive than to punish him for his opinions, and nothing could be more dangerous than that.'[7]

The AEC's reasons for initiating the procedures had been outlined in the Gray-Morgan report, and they have already been mentioned. It had then been stated that if Oppenheimer's contract had simply been allowed to lapse, his clearance would still have been maintained. The issue of his security status could therefore not be resolved 'without the positive act of withdrawal of access' (or—something which Gray and Morgan curiously and perhaps significantly omitted to say—without a clear-cut finding in his favour). Otherwise, he would continue to receive classified AEC reports and his services would still be available to AEC contractors and other government agencies. But since only one of Oppenheimer's nine judges had questioned his loyalty, and since none of them had disputed his discretion, this only lent force to the argument that he had been denied clearance so as to make it impossible for him ever to give advice to the government again.[8]

At least two of Oppenheimer's adversaries pointed out that it was he, and not the AEC, who had instigated the hearing procedure. 'If the government didn't want my advice and wanted to withdraw my clearance for whatever reason,' Teller said, 'I would not raise a peep.' Withdrawal of clearance was a normal occurrence as Lawrence saw it, and there was no stigma attached to it. Oppenheimer should have kept quiet, but since he had chosen to take the matter further, 'he had asked for it'. Lawrence and Teller were right in a narrow technical sense, in that the choice of whether or not to go ahead with a hearing lay entirely in Oppenheimer's hands, but they failed (or refused) to see the essential point. This was that the AEC had presented him with the choice by preferring the charges set out in Nichols' letter. If Oppenheimer had accepted the termination or the expiry of his contract, the charges would have remained on the record uncontested, and the clear implication would have been that he dared not contest them. He therefore had no real choice if he believed he was innocent, and in requesting the hearing he was not making an unreasonable fuss, as Teller and Lawrence both implied. He was taking the only honourable course left open to him, and even Lawrence was bound to say, with astonishing inconsistency: 'How much less complicated it would have been just not to have called him for consultation!'[9]

What seems like one of the real reasons for the suspension of clearance began to emerge in the months leading up to the opening of the hearing in April. The material before the Board at the start of the hearing consisted partly of the huge FBI dossier and partly of documents relating to Oppenheimer's work for the Commission, the State Department and the Defense Department. According to the AEC Procedures, FBI reports were not to be disclosed to an employee or his lawyer, so these were quite definitely out of reach. There was no ruling as to any other documents, but very many of these too were withheld, and largely because Oppenheimer's clearance was in abeyance. On 31 December 1953 his file copies of all classified AEC documents were removed from his possession at the Institute for Advanced Study and placed in the hands of the AEC. Moreover, his suspension also made it impossible for him to go through all this material at the AEC and report back to Garrison on it.

Garrison tried to surmount these latter handicaps by requesting clearance for himself, Marks and Silverman, during and shortly after his first conference with AEC officials on 18 January. On 27 January Nichols replied to the request by saying that Marks and Silverman could not be allowed to apply for clearance, but that 'a limited clearance' might be granted to Garrison. This was not acceptable, and on 3 February, after a further meeting at the AEC, Garrison withdrew the request. He did so for several reasons. In the first place, it would make the preparation of the defence impossible if one lawyer had to conceal material from his uncleared colleagues. Secondly, there was the possibility that

Oppenheimer might at some point publish the transcript, and he foresaw interminable difficulties with the Commission over what should and should not be deleted. Thirdly, he feared that clearance might lead to an excessive concentration on the technical aspects of the hydrogen bomb question and cloud the central issue of Oppenheimer's motivation. In addition, he had been told by Strauss that there might well be considerable delay in achieving clearance, and that it might not even come through until the hearing was well under way. At the same time, Strauss had said that the Commission reserved the right 'to decide what documents were relevant and what portions thereof counsel might examine'. Finally, even if clearance were granted, this would still not enable him to know 'the facts in the possession of the Personnel Security Board which will be used in the Board's final judgment', that is, what was in the FBI dossier.[10]

Garrison was therefore compelled to change his tack, and he ended his letter by asking Strauss instead for access to documents which might be declassified, in particular the GAC report of 30 October 1949. Nichols' reply came on 12 February. The Commission, he said, was willing to make documents available, but must reserve the right to decide 'whether particular documents to which you request access are relevant and whether your access to such documents or parts thereof, would be consistent with the national interest'. It was almost certain, he added, that the GAC report of 30 October 1949 could not be produced, and in view of this Garrison might want to reconsider his decision not to ask for clearance. The AEC was 'willing to expedite the process to the extent possible', and even to 'consider the question' of clearing Marks and Silverman as well.[11]

Garrison, however, did not revert to his original approach, and the same day he asked Strauss for copies of documents which, he believed, would throw light on Oppenheimer's attitude to the hydrogen bomb and on the nature of the 1947 clearance. These, he was convinced, would show that in 1947 the Commission had granted clearance on the basis of practically all the charges in Nichols' letter, except for those relating to the H-bomb, and that there was nothing sinister in Oppenheimer's attitude to the H-bomb programme. The following were the documents requested:

1. the minutes and reports of the General Advisory Committee during Oppenheimer's membership between 1947 and 1952;
2. the transcript of Oppenheimer's testimony before the Joint Committee on Atomic Energy on 30 January 1950 regarding the GAC position on the H-bomb;
3. an itemization of the charges in Hoover's letter to Lilienthal received in the AEC on 8 March 1947;
4. the minutes of the meeting in August 1947 at which the Commission recorded Oppenheimer's clearance;
5. the letters sent to Lilienthal in March 1947 from Patterson, Groves, Bush and Conant regarding Oppenheimer's loyalty;
6. AEC memoranda of the period March-August 1947 regarding the action to be taken on Oppenheimer's clearance.

In addition, Marks submitted a list of nineteen questions asking for clarification of various parts of Nichols' letter. This had been extremely loosely drafted in places and it was difficult to know how to reply to it as it stood. As Oppenheimer remarked at the hearing, in reply to a request from Robb for 'categorical answers' to Nichols' statements on the H-bomb, 'to questions that are badly phrased, categorical answers are not always possible'.[12]

The response from the AEC was almost completely negative. None of Marks' questions was answered, and on 19 February the General Counsel of the Commission, William Mitchell, wrote to Garrison denying all his requests for documents, with two partial exceptions. In the first place, he supplied a stipulation which purported to state what action the AEC had taken over Oppenheimer's clearance in August 1947. In the second place, he said that Oppenheimer was free to go to the AEC and read the GAC report of 30 October 1949 (but no other GAC material). These were not real concessions, however. The stipulation, indeed, was a deliberate travesty of the truth, designed to give a completely misleading picture of what had happened. As for the offer to view the GAC report, this was so framed as to make it acutely embarrassing for Oppenheimer to take it up, and it is not surprising that he did not. So he could not refresh his memory as he prepared his reply to Nichols' allegations, on this or any other issue. Nevertheless, he hoped that when it came to the hearing, the testimony of his many witnesses would make up for what the AEC had been unwilling to supply.[13]

As the hearing drew closer, however, Garrison became increasingly worried about the prospects, and especially about his decision not to ask for security clearance. He could foresee times during the inquiry when he would be required to leave Oppenheimer 'unrepresented and alone' while classified testimony was given. Therefore on 26 March he wrote to Nichols telling him that he now wished to have clearance for himself, but not for his colleagues. On 29 March Nichols replied that Garrison's application was being dealt with as quickly as possible but that the hearing could not be postponed until clearance had been granted. In the event, no decision on clearance came through before the hearing ended, that is, for nearly six weeks. Robb, on the other hand (according to Stern), was given an emergency 'Q' clearance—the highest possible—in no more than eight days, and a permanent 'Q' clearance in only twenty-two days, as opposed to the usual sixty to ninety.[14]

This meant that Garrison was forced to retire on four occasions during the proceedings, when Kelly discussed the report of the 1950 panel on the military uses of the recent discoveries in fission, when Dean referred to the report of the group set up to evaluate the evidence of the Soviet test of August 1949, when Lilienthal spoke of a particular aspect of the hydrogen bomb debate, and when Gray conferred with the other members of the Board and the AEC counsel on the materiality of Borden's letter. On none of these occasions, Garrison believed, were Oppenheimer's interests damaged, yet it made nonsense of the claim of Gray and Morgan that he had been represented 'at all times in the course of the proceedings', and it was still one more illustration of the basic weakness of Oppenheimer's position vis-à-vis his accusers.[15]

Garrison's difficulties grew no less as the opening of the hearing approached. On 5 April, a week before it began, the Board met at the AEC headquarters to study the FBI reports and the other documentary evidence. Here again, the procedure differed drastically from that of a court of law, where a judge enters a trial with no previous knowledge of the case. In an attempt to offset the prejudice which would inevitably arise in their minds, Garrison asked if he might meet them and discuss the substance of the material before them. He was refused. He then asked if he might meet the Board at its first session and present Oppenheimer's viewpoint, and if he might ascertain the procedure which was going to be followed. These requests too were turned down. In the resultant absence of any preliminary contact with the defence, Garrison felt, 'a cloud of suspicion hung over Robert Oppenheimer at the outset which was never quite dissipated in the minds of the majority; even when they became convinced by the testimony that he could not be charged with disloyalty or want of patriotism, we had the impression that an uneasy feeling about him remained which may have been just enough to tip the scales against his clearance.'[16]

Thus, when the hearing began on 12 April, Oppenheimer's defence was already operating at an overwhelming disadvantage as compared with the Board, and Robb and Rolander. The initiative lay entirely with them, and all Oppenheimer's counsel could do was to respond as best they might. Oppenheimer's files had been seized by the Commission, and, as Garrison later recalled, 'we never knew what there might be in them of a derogatory character which could have been rebutted, or of a helpful character which could have been utilized'. The same held true of the FBI dossier, which in no circumstances would he or Oppenheimer have been allowed to see. For all they knew, the material in it could have been highly questionable, but they had no opportunity of testing it themselves and they were compelled to rely on the Board's appraisal of its value.[17]

Gray and Robb, for their part, were fully aware of their superiority, and issued reminders about it from time to time. Thus Gray, when he cross-examined Conant, told him that the Board had 'to take into account all the material which seems to be substantiated which is before us, perhaps some of which you are not at all familiar with'. Immediately afterwards, Robb put it to Conant that in considering the Chevalier incident he must surely agree that 'any opinion about a given problem, to be reliable, must be based on all the relevant facts and all the relevant evidence'. In questioning Rabi about the incident, he told him that 'perhaps the board may be in possession of information which is not now available to you', and in consequence was better placed to assess it. The implication was clear: how could any of the testimony given on Oppenheimer's behalf stand up against such omniscience?[18]

As the hearing progressed, moreover, Robb was able to use this advantage as a weapon against Oppenheimer and his witnesses. This was made possible by Gray, who, as chairman of the Board, interpreted the regulations and gave rulings on points at issue. At the very outset Gray was to say, echoing the language of the Procedures, that 'this proceeding is an inquiry and not in the nature of a trial'. He expanded on this shortly afterwards when he told Marks that 'very considerable latitude' was being allowed, and that he was 'not trying to conform to rigid court procedures'. This again repeated the words of the Procedures, and it seemed to indicate that Oppenheimer's defence would not suffer from the restrictions which would be placed on it in a trial. In practice, it meant the reverse: it was Robb who was free of any restrictions, and Garrison and his associates who were denied the safeguards they would have had in a judicial proceeding. At one of the many contentious moments in the hearing, Garrison said to Gray that he supposed that 'a fortiori, what is proper in a court of law would be accorded to us here in an inquiry'. It was not.[19]

Robb was therefore able to take up the role of prosecutor free of almost all restraint. Throughout the hearing he was described in the transcript as 'counsel for the board', and in the Procedures the members of the Board were enjoined to 'avoid the attitude of a prosecutor'. Gray at first appeared to adopt this view of Robb's function, when he said that he did not think it was his purpose 'to develop anything beyond what the facts are in this case'. Later, however, he said that as far as the summoning of witnesses was concerned, the Board considered Garrison the attorney for Oppenheimer and Robb the attorney for the AEC. Robb's witnesses were called by him and not by the Board, and Gray was extremely anxious that the Board should in no way be identified as part of a prosecution. In other words, he was now regarding the Board not as an administrative tribunal but as a trio of judges presiding over an adversary proceeding with a prosecution on one hand and a defence on the other. As Garrison immediately pointed out, the resemblance was only superficial. No proper trial could have taken place when one lawyer was in possession of evidence which his opponent was not entitled to see. Gray, however, did not alter his view.[20]

Robb, then, emerged, as Mrs Trilling has described him, as 'a prosecuting attorney with a single-minded purpose, to achieve Dr Oppenheimer's defeat'. He accepted this description. Speaking in an interview given years later, he said that Oppenheimer's lawyers 'were there to introduce all the favorable things about him and my job was to bring out the evidence on the other side'. There can be no question as to the efficiency with which he executed his assignment. Robb took up his appointment only in February and he had a huge amount of material to assimilate. Yet he did so, and his mastery of the evidence comes out time and time again in a reading of the transcript.[21]

There can also be no doubt about the ruthlessness of his tactics. Lilienthal, who suffered particularly at his hands, wrote in his journal that the charges against Oppenheimer had been 'handled in such a way as to make them *seem* synonymous with treachery'. Robb had not been engaged in 'a quiet search for the facts and the truth'. Instead, he had evoked 'the atmosphere and methods of a criminal trial, except that it was *in camera*'. Lilienthal was not exaggerating. When he himself was on the stand, for example, Robb had insinuated that the notes he was reading from had been made by someone else, in other words, that they were not his own testimony. With Bethe, he was more blatant, as the following exchange shows:

Q. Doctor, how many divisions were there at Los Alamos?
A. It changed somewhat in the course of time. As far as I could count the other day, there were 7, but there may have been 8 or 9 at some time.
Q. Which division was Klaus Fuchs in?
A. He was in my division which was the Theoretical Division.
Mr ROBB. Thank you. That is all.[22]

At the close of the first week, Oppenheimer and Garrison were advised to walk out if this sort of thing were repeated, but given the decision to follow a strategy of moderation, they did not. Garrison has recently given his reasons for this. 'If we protested too much,' he has written, 'we might only irritate the board members; if we objected too strongly to a particular line of questioning designed to elicit adverse evidence or admissions, we might only magnify its importance in the eyes of the board. We felt from the outset that we were waging an uphill fight in which undue combativeness would be a hindrance rather than a help.' So whatever protests were made were muted, and Robb went ahead as before.[23]

Robb proceeded to press home his advantage over Garrison in two main ways. In the first place, he introduced into the record documents (or excerpts from documents) which the defence was not able to see because they were classified. The principal examples of these were the transcripts of the interviews Oppenheimer had had with Pash and Lansdale on 26 August and 12 September 1943 respectively; the two letters from Oppenheimer to Dr R. C. Tolman of 20 September and 4 October 1944; an anonymous AEC memorandum on Oppenheimer of 14 March 1947; a memorandum from Teller and Murray of 19 December 1951 on the issue of a second weapons laboratory; and a memorandum on the luncheon meeting between DuBridge, Rabi, Burden, Norton and Griggs on 30 April 1952.[24]

In deploying this material, Robb held the whip hand. He could read out whatever passage he chose, without the defence being able to check whether or not it was being taken out of context. Alternatively, if the defence were to object, he could stop reading and leave it as part of the secret dossier for the Board alone to see. In that case, Garrison and his colleagues would not even have the chance to counter the points he was making.[25]

Robb's supremacy was also demonstrated in the way some of the material was made available to Garrison after it had been introduced. In the case of the Pash and Lansdale interviews, this was not without a struggle. When Garrison asked for the transcript of the Pash interview, Gray did not give him an immediate reply, and when he asked again the next day (when the Lansdale transcript was also brought forward), he was told that he could see them both, but only after Robb had finished his cross-examination. After a further protest, he was handed a copy of the Lansdale interview. In the case of the letter to Tolman of 4 October 1944, things were very different. This had already been declassified on 13 April, three weeks previously, and there was no reason why it should not have been made available then if Robb's aim was, as he had agreed, to develop no more than the facts. It was not, however. The documents cited, and many others, were introduced to reinforce the case for the prosecution, and they had a powerful surprise value. Only when they had achieved their effect were they released, and by then, of course, it was too late to do the defence much good.[26]

Robb's second gambit was to use his material in such a way as to cast doubt on the testimony of Oppenheimer and his witnesses. Thus, on his second appearance before the Board, Bush was shown the original of the Nichols letter of 23 December 1953 (which he had not seen before and which differed in lay-out from the version he had read in *The New York Times*) in an attempt to refute his assertion that Oppenheimer was being tried for his opinions. When Dean was cross-examined, both the Teller-Murray memorandum and a letter he himself had written on 9 January 1952 were introduced to point up the fact that his recollection was incomplete on the question of the second laboratory. Shortly afterwards, Bethe was asked about a report he had prepared in May 1952 on the history of the thermonuclear programme at Los Alamos. He testified that he had not discussed it with Oppenheimer, but he was almost immediately confronted with a copy of a letter he had written to Oppenheimer on 28 May 1952 which showed that they had in fact talked about the report. In this way, what could well have been a lapse of memory on Bethe's part was given the appearance of dissimulation.[27]

The most conspicuous example of the use of this technique, however, came when Lilienthal took the stand, and it related to his testimony on Oppenheimer's 1947 clearance. In this instance, a wealth of documentation was produced. First of all, there were the references written by Bush, Conant and Patterson. These (together with Groves' reference, which had already been read into the record), it should be remembered, were among the documents which Garrison had asked for on 12 February, and which the AEC had refused to let him have. Later, four items were introduced with the express purpose of undermining Lilienthal's evidence on the clearance. First, there was the covering letter from Hoover which had accompanied the summaries sent to the AEC on 8 March 1947, and which was used to refute Lilienthal's assertion that the full file on Oppenheimer had been sent across. Second, there was an AEC memorandum of 12 March 1947 which showed he had been wrong in claiming that the files of the Manhattan District (the name of the atomic energy project prior to its take-over by the AEC) had been kept at the Commission's headquarters. Third, there was the record of the Commission's meetings of 10 and 11 March 1947 which corrected many errors in Lilienthal's testimony, in particular his statement that he had not suggested that the President should set up a review board to investigate the matter. Fourth, there was a memorandum dictated by Lilienthal on 12 March 1947 and recounting a telephone conversation he had just had with Truman's special counsel, Clark M. Clifford. This was also used to show that he had in fact proposed a presidential review board.[28]

Although Lilienthal had seen the letters from Bush, Conant, Patterson and Groves when he had gone through the documents at the AEC the previous day, these last four documents had been abstracted from the file. As he wrote in his journal, 'vital parts of these records had been removed without my knowledge. These very documents—which I had been prevented from reviewing—were used by the AEC counsel prosecuting Dr Oppenheimer ... to try to trap me into factual errors and inconsistencies in testimony, with the purpose of minimizing or even casting doubt on the truthfulness and trustworthiness of the testimony I gave.' Both he and Garrison at once protested at what Robb had done, but Robb only replied that 'it is an entirely fair comment to make that it is demonstrated that the memory of the witness was not infallible'. He was upheld by Gray.[29]

Oppenheimer was subjected to the same treatment, although on a much more extensive scale. His testimony on every aspect of his past was repeatedly challenged by the production of documents; points he had neglected to make were made for him, and, as in the case of Bethe and Lilienthal, statements he had been led to give under cross-examination were shortly afterwards countered by the material which Robb drew from the secret file. The impact was extremely significant. Of the thirteen derogatory items featuring in the Gray-Morgan report, five derived from the bad impression Robb had thus succeeded in creating. In Nichols' findings, they numbered six out of eleven, while *all* the Commission's final considerations stemmed from this source.

Thus, in respect of his pre-war associations, a Lansdale

memorandum of 14 September 1943 was twice introduced in an attempt to show that his alleged remark that he had 'probably belonged to every Communist front-organization on the west coast' was not, as he had described it, 'a half-jocular overstatement'. More tellingly (for the Commission majority, at least), the transcript of the interview with Lansdale on 12 September 1943 was used to indicate that he had been evasive about Lambert —whom he described to Robb in some detail.[30]

His relations with Chevalier were also placed in a sinister perspective by documentary evidence and by Robb's tendentious use of it. Here, the key material was the transcript of the interview with Pash of 26 August 1943, which, more than any other item, threw doubt on his credibility. Immediately afterwards, the three telegrams of 12 and 13 December 1943 were produced to show that he had also lied to Groves when ordered to tell the truth about the Chevalier incident. The continuity of his associations with Chevalier was underlined by the display of his letter of 24 February 1950, offering help to Chevalier in his search for a job, and by the exchange of correspondence between Chevalier and Wyman which had followed the Oppenheimers' visit to Paris in December 1953.[31]

The relationship with Lomanitz and Weinberg, which also figured so prominently in his downfall, was portrayed mostly in the transcripts of the Pash and Lansdale interviews. In the Pash transcript, it was shown that he had known that Lomanitz had revealed information about the Radiation Laboratory; in his testimony he had said only that he knew Lomanitz had been indiscreet. It also established that his mention of the Chevalier incident on 25 August 1943 was made in connection with his apprehensions about Lomanitz; under cross-examination he had not said so in so many words. The Lansdale transcript was used to prove that he knew by that time (September 1943) that both Lomanitz and Weinberg were members of the Communist Party; earlier he had told Robb he did not then know this. It was also exploited, much less convincingly, to suggest that Oppenheimer had laid down explicit rules for Lomanitz's political behaviour when Lomanitz began work at the Radiation Laboratory in June 1942; this too Oppenheimer had denied to Robb.[32]

Further documentation used to demonstrate the supposedly

16 Oppenheimer and his counsel, Lloyd K. Garrison, after the announcement of the Commission's decision to withhold his clearance, June 1954

17 President Johnson presents Oppenheimer with the Fermi Award, 2 December 1963

15 The Strauss Commission, summer 1953: (l to r) Zuckert, Smyth, Strauss, Murray, Campbell, and the General Manager, Mr Boyer. (The AEC wishes to point out that Mr Boyer was *not* General Manager at the time of the Oppenheimer hearing)

close relations between Oppenheimer and his pupils was also brought in at this point. Oppenheimer's letter to Lansdale of 19 October 1943, in conjunction with the letter which Lomanitz had just written to him on 15 October, could equally well have been taken to indicate extreme security-mindedness on Oppenheimer's part, but it was reinforced by two items discovered in Oppenheimer's own file on Lomanitz. These were two telegrams sent by Oppenheimer on 31 July 1943, one to the Manhattan District office in New York, the other to Lomanitz himself, and both showing Oppenheimer's urgent interest in prolonging Lomanitz's deferment. Ironically enough, they were offered to the Board by Garrison when the issue arose. Finally, three items from the early months of 1944 were produced to convey the impression that Oppenheimer was seeing more than he should of Bohm, whom he had recently described as a 'truly dangerous' person. These too, however, could just as easily have been interpreted as evidence of Oppenheimer's cooperativeness with the security officers on the project.[33]

Also covering this period was a large group of documents, nine altogether, which set out to prove that Oppenheimer's clearance in 1943 had only been granted because of his indispensability and that military intelligence continued to have the gravest doubts about him. In conjunction with the material on Chevalier, Weinberg, Lomanitz and Bohm, they built up a picture of a man utterly disdainful of security, a man whose word could not in any circumstances be trusted. Coupled with Oppenheimer's own testimony, as developed by Robb, this picture was to remain fixed in the minds of his judges.[34]

Coming to the post-war years, Robb brought forward an exchange of correspondence between Groves and Lilienthal in an effort to show that Oppenheimer fell within the category of suspects who deserved to be removed from government service. Following on from this, his presentation of the 1947 clearance was designed to show that the Commission had not handled the case properly, and that it could only have been determined by a review board acting according to well-defined procedures. Now, he seemed to imply, Gray, Morgan and Evans could rectify the error which had been made seven years before.[35]

On the issue of political associations, Robb's last items related to Peters. Here, he was not using secret documents but news-

H

paper articles. The effect, however, was the same. Once again, Oppenheimer was made out to be a man for whom the distinction between truth and falsehood was a matter of expediency, and who was still all too clearly under the influence of his left-wing past.[36]

This, too, was the image created by the documentation on the hydrogen bomb. The letters to Tolman showed that he had been solidly behind thermonuclear research in 1944, and yet he had evidently changed his mind by 1949. The affidavit from Lawrence indicated the distrust supposedly surrounding him in military circles, and an excerpt from Vandenberg's testimony to the Joint Committee on Atomic Energy on 14 October 1949 was introduced to throw doubt on his assertion that there had been no military demand for the bomb. Alvarez' diary underscored the depth of his influence in the political and scientific communities, and Griggs' memorandum to Finletter of 21 June 1952 pictured a man who would not scruple to use any weapon available to him in a controversy over policy.[37]

The most telling items on the H-bomb, however, were the Seaborg letter of 14 October 1949, and the material which purported to show that Oppenheimer had deliberately concealed its existence. In his testimony, Oppenheimer had said there was no communication from Seaborg prior to the GAC meeting of 28–30 October 1949. After a suitable pause, he was confronted with the letter, and with a letter he had written to Conant on 21 October, saying that he had heard from Seaborg. Later, a further letter from Oppenheimer to Lilienthal of 14 October 1949 was introduced, confirming that Seaborg had been asked to send his views in writing. Thus, Oppenheimer was represented as a liar.[38]

Robb went beyond this, however. At a hearing before the Joint Committee on 30 January 1950, he alleged, Oppenheimer had said that Seaborg had not expressed himself on the subject of the H-bomb *before* the meeting at the end of October. Moreover, he claimed that Oppenheimer had admitted this at that morning's session, a few hours earlier. This was either a rare lapse on Robb's part or a misguided attempt to exploit the situation beyond what it was worth. He had in fact said during the morning session that Oppenheimer had testified on 30

January 1950 'that there was unanimity but that Dr Seaborg was not heard there [*at* the October meeting]'.[39]

Oppenheimer and his counsel quickly pointed out the discrepancy, and asked that the matter be cleared up by getting hold of the transcript of the Joint Committee hearing. Otherwise, it would be impossible to place Oppenheimer's statement in context. He could well have been stating the literal truth, that is, that Seaborg had not been physically present at the GAC meeting to make his views heard. Equally possibly, he could have forgotten about the letter, just as he said he had forgotten about it in 1954. If he had concealed it, it was difficult to see what he had to gain from doing so on either occasion. In 1954 he must have known the letter had been handed over to the Commission, along with all his other AEC documents, and on 30 January 1950 he knew that the hydrogen bomb decision was as good as made and that he could hardly hope to change the Joint Committee's mind by anything he said to them.[40]

The transcript of the 1950 hearing was not forthcoming, however. As Robb explained it, it could not be released without the express authorization of the Committee, and Gray was later to say that 'this board does have the power to produce such a document'. Both these statements seem odd when regarded in the light of the fact that Robb's witness, General Wilson, had been given permission to quote from Vandenberg's testimony to the Committee of 14 October 1949, but they had to be accepted none the less, and Garrison was compelled to make do with a paraphrase supplied by Gray. The Board understood, said Gray, 'from a source it believes to be reliable', that Oppenheimer had been asked about the extent of unanimity in the GAC with regard to the proposed crash-programme. Oppenheimer had answered that the view had been 'pretty unanimous', that Seaborg had been away when the question came to be discussed and that he had 'not expressed himself on it'. This, while it at least had the merit of dismissing the allegation which Robb had introduced, did not allow the defence to penetrate to the heart of the matter. The result was that the initial doubt over Oppenheimer's behaviour was allowed to remain unresolved, and the Seaborg letter incident became one of the principal elements in the adverse case made out by Nichols and the majority of the Commission when they came to bring in their verdicts.[41]

In all these instances, Robb held the advantage of surprise, and he was able to achieve surprise in other ways as well. He could, for example, introduce new items into the hearing not covered by the Nichols indictment, and this he did a number of times. Those relating to Oppenheimer's Communist associations were very minor and were not dwelt on. Those relating to the hydrogen bomb issue, on the other hand, were extremely important—nothing less than the questions of tactical atomic weapons and continental air defence—and they were explored in depth. Yet whether significant or trivial, all were sprung on the defence without warning, in spite of the assurance given by Gray at the outset that notice would be given so as to allow Garrison and his assistants enough time to prepare a reply. This was not done, and Garrison never knew what to expect from one moment to another.[42]

The surprise was maintained when it came to the witnesses. At the start of the hearing, Garrison gave the Board a full list of the witnesses he intended to call, as well as indicating the order of their appearance. Early in the second week, he once again told the Board whom he was going to summon. His courtesies were not reciprocated. When he asked Gray for a schedule of the Board's witnesses, Gray replied that it was not ready, and the following day he gave a similar non-committal answer. At the end of the week Garrison had still not been told, and so he was constrained to make a formal request for the names. Even then he did not get them.[43]

The manner of the refusal was interesting, and possibly significant. It came not from Gray, as it had done before, but from Robb. Robb declared that he would not identify his witnesses 'unless ordered to do so by the board', because he could not trust Garrison to keep the names confidential, and because once they were known he feared that pressure might be exerted on them by Oppenheimer's sympathizers. There was thus 'a serious danger that the orderly presentation of testimony, the truthful presentation of testimony would be impeded'. In rejoinder to Garrison's complaint that he could not prepare for cross-examination without knowing who was going to appear, moreover, Robb had the audacity to claim that 'my only advance preparation . . . was a thorough knowledge of this case'.[44]

Gray then attempted to make his position clear. His explanation has already been touched on. It was that the Board as such did not intend calling any witnesses, although it had the power to do so. Witnesses would be summoned either by Robb, as counsel for the government, or by Garrison, as counsel for Oppenheimer. The Board was neutral in the matter, and since it had a duty to balance the public interest against the interest of the individual, he had to rule that the names of Robb's witnesses should not be disclosed. At the same time, he was anxious to assure Garrison that 'we wish to hear you at any time that you think you are at a disadvantage by not having had the names of the witnesses'.[45]

Gray had thus completely reversed himself. For one thing, he had promised at an earlier stage to give Garrison an indication of whom to expect. For another, he had always spoken so far in terms of the Board's witnesses and not Robb's, and he had even told Garrison that the Board would have called some of his witnesses if he himself had not called them. This was now described as a contingency so remote as to be unforeseeable. Finally, he stated that Garrison's provision of a schedule 'was not something that was required by the board', although on two occasions he had made a point of asking Garrison for it.[46]

Whatever hopes Garrison may have placed in Gray as a protector of Oppenheimer's interests in this respect were therefore destroyed, and Robb was allowed to keep his intentions to himself. When Garrison asked him whether or not he was going to call Mr and Mrs Crouch, he merely toyed with him. He was not considering calling them at the moment, he said, 'but as you realize, I can't project myself into the middle of next week. I don't know what will develop.' The Crouchs were not summoned, not surprisingly, perhaps, since they were paid government informers, but Garrison was never told. Why should he be, when it profited Robb to keep him dangling in uncertainty?[47]

At this juncture, then, all pretence that the hearing was an impartial inquiry was effectively dropped. The AEC witnesses, when they appeared, were all hostile to Oppenheimer. After the case was over Rolander attempted to justify this and at the same time to present it as the Board's responsibility. 'Many of the witnesses called by Dr Oppenheimer', he said, echoing Gray, 'would have been called by the Board.' The Board (not Robb), 'felt compelled' to produce additional witnesses, firstly 'to determine the merits of the Government's case', and secondly 'to provide Dr Oppenheimer with an opportunity for cross-examination'. The Alsops, however, at whom this statement was directed, maintained that not one of Oppenheimer's witnesses had in fact been approached by the AEC, apart from Lansdale, whose agreement was sought to the use of the transcript of his interview with Oppenheimer.[48]

The AEC's witnesses, then, by Gray's own definition, were prosecution witnesses. Given that fact, it was extraordinary, to put it at its lowest, that two of Oppenheimer's judges should do their utmost to marshal them. Pitzer stated that he had appeared 'only at the very specific and urgent request of the general manager', that is, Nichols, and Lawrence's biographer writes of the 'insistent request' of Strauss for witnesses from Berkeley who did not wish to see Oppenheimer's clearance reinstated. Such intervention in a criminal suit would have been intolerable, but, as the Procedures indicated, this was 'an inquiry and not a trial', and the Commission was evidently a law unto itself.[49]

The pressure of Strauss and Nichols was brought to bear partly because Robb's fears about the possible dissuasion of his witnesses were being realized. At a weekend conference of AEC Laboratory Directors on 24 and 25 April, Lawrence was urged not to testify at the hearing, where he was scheduled to appear shortly. Lawrence decided not to go, but according to his biographer gave as his main reason a severe attack of ulcerative colitis which had made him lose a lot of blood. At the same time, however, he telephoned Alvarez in Berkeley and asked him not to testify either. Alvarez agreed, and sent off a telegram to the AEC saying that he would not be coming. He was made to change his mind after an urgent telephone call from Strauss in Washington. Strauss believed that both Lawrence and Alvarez were evading their responsibility to the government, and said so in no uncertain terms. Compelled by the force of Strauss' appeal, Alvarez took the stand. Lawrence, who by then was almost certainly extremely ill, did not.[50]

The final factor which Oppenheimer and Garrison had to contend with was Gray. Throughout the hearing, in spite of his repeated assurances that their interests would be safeguarded in every possible way, it was perceptible that he was biassed in favour of the government. Garrison does not make this feature in his criticisms of the procedure, and for obvious reasons he did not do so at the time. At the beginning of his summation, indeed, he paid a tribute to 'the fairness which the members of the board have displayed in the conduct of these hearings, and the sincere and intense effort which I know you have been making and will make to come to a just understanding of the issues'.[51]

Lilienthal, however, at the time he discussed the case with Dean in June, had written in his journal of 'the lack of impartial attitude of Gray, something I had felt but hardly dared admit even to myself'. Three weeks earlier, when the Board's recommendations were published, he wrote that he had not expected a favourable finding since he did not think there was 'ever the slightest chance that Gray would have been selected if he had been the kind of man who would put the President and the AEC-ers in that kind of box'.[52]

This may have been going too far, but a scrutiny of the transcript indicates that Gray leaned almost exclusively towards the side of authority. Lilienthal himself knew how severe the pressures were to do this. In May 1947 the Commission had granted clearance to Condon on an interim basis, but, Lilienthal wrote, it was quite likely that they would deny him full clearance later. 'The worst part', he confided to his journal, 'is that we will feel impelled to do these things rather than "take chances" or subject ourselves to criticism for having taken chances, and thus decide very important matters affecting people and events on a basis of caution, not justice.' His point was later reiterated by the writer on science and government, Don K. Price. 'Everyone dealing with security affairs', wrote Price, 'has an overwhelming motive to play it safe.' Security boards in particular were fearful that Congressional committees would take over if they consistently upheld the rights of the individual, and this could be disastrous, since the committees often acted arbitrarily and considered themselves bound by few constitutional restraints.[53]

What Price said almost certainly applied to the Oppenheimer hearing, which was without much doubt instituted at least partly so as to keep the affair out of the hands of Senator McCarthy. In this the government was, of course, successful, but only at the cost of allowing many of the same flagrant breaches of lawful procedure which characterized Congressional investigations. Indeed, it is not too much to suggest that Oppenheimer might well have fared a good deal better in a confrontation with Mc-Carthy. After all, McCarthy's intended victims succeeded in turning the tables on him in his televised clash with the Army, thanks to the skilful tactics of the Army's lawyer, Joseph Welch, and to the Senator's failure to realize that he had overreached himself. Oppenheimer could probably have done the same. Instead, he was faced with a secret inquisition, and its many lapses from impartiality were not revealed until weeks after it was over. This is not to say that these considerations weighed heavily in a decision to pre-empt McCarthy. McCarthy's Subcommittee had no jurisdiction in the matter and the administration was bound to follow the AEC Procedures. Nevertheless, the advantages to the government of an inquiry *in camera* over a Congressional investigation held in public were very real, and the argument that Oppenheimer was lucky to have escaped McCarthy's attentions is by no means so convincing as it may seem at first sight. It is invalidated by the way in which the hearing was conducted, and for this, Gray, as chairman of the Board and therefore as director of the proceedings, must bear the greatest share of the responsibility.

As the hearing progressed, no one could doubt Gray's extreme respect for order. At one point, he declared there had been an inclination among witnesses 'to be impatient with procedures and regulations and things of that sort'. 'Men of great stature and eminence', he admonished Winne, '... have been inclined to treat very lightly these matters which we have been discussing here, I think with sincerity and conviction, on the ground that what they think they know of Dr Oppenheimer ... washes out anything that happened in the past.' Later, when cross-examining McCloy, he asked him 'when the paramount concern is the security of the country ... can you allow yourself to entertain reasonable doubts?'[54]

This was the background to his handling of the procedure, and to the strikingly different treatment he accorded the defence and the prosecution. Relations between Gray and Garrison were damaged at the outset by Oppenheimer's publication of the Nichols letter of indictment and his reply to it. Gray was very angry indeed: 'I think', he said, 'these stories are very prejudicial to the spirit of inquiry that I tried to establish as an atmosphere for this hearing as we started yesterday. I would very much regret what would appear to be to the board possible lack of cooperation in conducting these proceedings in the press if that were prejudicial to what are the basic fundamental issues involved.' Moreover, the episode continued to rankle. When Lilienthal was giving evidence, he observed that the question of the 1947 clearance was considered as settled in some quarters and that this was a direct result of Oppenheimer's decision to bring the case into the open. When Bush raised the subject of the phrasing of Nichols' letter, he told him that he could not blame the Board for the fact that it had become public knowledge.[55]

Gray's irritation at the disclosure spilled over into other areas as well. On the first day of the hearing, Garrison had presented extracts from Oppenheimer's speeches and writings over the past decade. Gray now asked Garrison who had prepared them, and he was patently unsatisfied when Garrison told him that he and Ecker had worked on them in New York. He also told Garrison that his schedule of witnesses was unacceptable, that witnesses were to be called to suit the convenience of the Board, and that they would probably be required to state on oath that they could not appear at any other time. Soon afterwards, in questioning Kelly about the 1950 panel on nuclear weapons, he suggested that the report of the panel 'could have reflected discussions which the committee did not actually engage in'. This was an aspersion on Oppenheimer, the author of the report, and it produced a sharp response. Gray, said Oppenheimer, had suggested 'that I was the only person competent to judge and that I sneaked a conclusion into the report that had not been thoroughly hashed out'. It was not a happy moment.[56]

Thereafter, feelings subsided, but the potential for friction remained, and more trouble followed. Thus, at one point, Gray went so far as to say that Lilienthal had perjured himself, even though the question at issue was insignificant. Later, he was to interrupt McCloy during a particularly long piece of exposition—whereas he did not cut into the testimony of Griggs and Alvarez when they too began to ramble. Similarly, he broke in on Silverman during his cross-examination of Pitzer, although he did not cut short Robb when he seemed to be dwelling on Oppenheimer's fabrication to Pash. Again, he had an extremely heated exchange with Garrison over the issue of the withholding of documents, but at no time did he cross swords with Robb. All told, therefore, Gray's attitude to the defence can hardly be described as cordial, and it may not be too fanciful to suggest that it was made no more sympathetic by Garrison's emphasis in his summation on the clearance of Dr Frank Graham in December 1948. Graham had been Gray's predecessor as President of the University of North Carolina, and given Gray's intense security-mindedness, it was probably jarring for him to be reminded of the connection, innocent though it was.[57]

The contrasting relationship between Gray and the counsel for the AEC has already been mentioned, and further evidence of it is not lacking. All told, it gives the impression of a man at best nominally in charge of the inquiry and prepared on all disputable points to place himself in the hands of Robb and Rolander. Thus, when Garrison asked for a copy of the FBI summaries of 8 March 1947 (on the ground they had been made a subject of discussion), Gray replied that he would 'have to be guided by the security officer and the attorneys in this'. Again, when Garrison requested to see the minutes of the Commission's meeting of 6 August 1947, Gray answered that he would have to rely on Rolander for advice. In both instances, not surprisingly, he was led to make a negative ruling, although the minutes were later made available.[58]

He once more took his cue from the AEC when Garrison asked to see a copy of the Lansdale interview transcript as Robb read it. Only after Robb had indicated that he was agreeable did Gray grant the request. Then, when Garrison towards the close of the hearing asked to have either an outline description of the items on which the Commission had based its 1947 decision or information on which of the items then before the Board were previously before the Commission, he again allowed Robb to make the running. Robb immediately declared that it would 'fly right in the face of the rule', and Gray was left to follow suit.[59]

There were several other times when Robb demonstrated his commanding position. When Garrison asked for the hearing transcripts at the end of the first week, his question was addressed to Gray, but it was Robb who answered it in the first instance. Then, when he went on to ask for the transcripts of the Pash and Lansdale interviews, it was Robb who gave his acquiescence, leaving Gray to second him later. On two further occasions Robb removed Gray completely from the dialogue by answering for him, and Gray said nothing. The first was when Project Vista entered the discussion. When Garrison queried its relevance, Robb replied that he thought it was relevant and without referring the matter to Gray, went on with his questioning. The second arose when Garrison objected that Robb was misleading Bacher. 'I don't think the Doctor is misled', said Robb, and moved straight on with his cross-examination. Finally, Gray even allowed him to ignore a question he himself had put. This was during the testimony of Lilienthal, and just after Garrison had objected to the surprise production of documents. 'You are not going to confront the witness with any more documents?' asked Gray. Robb did not bother to reply, but Gray did not call him to account for it.[60]

In all these ways, therefore, the odds had been heavily weighted against Oppenheimer from start to finish. Perhaps the decisive disadvantage which he faced, however, was in the criteria he had to meet. 'It is not a case of proving that the man is a danger', said General Groves when he came to testify before the Board. 'It is a case of thinking, well, he might be a danger, and it is perfectly logical to presume that he would be.' On the basis of that interpretation, he would not clear Oppenheimer if he were a member of the Commission. Groves' statement need not be taken as an endorsement of the criteria but as a criticism of them. In other words, he felt that they were so restrictive that someone of Oppenheimer's background could not possibly hope to measure up to them, even though he had done so much in the way of positive service to the government. This is undoubtedly what Winne meant when he told Gray that 'it may be possible that you have no alternative but to make a certain finding here. ... You may, because of the wording of the law, be forced to make a decision adverse.' This too is what lay behind the reference in the Gray-Morgan report to 'the rigid circumscription of regulations and criteria established for us.'[61]

The prosecution had no quarrel with this view; it naturally

welcomed what its opponents shrank from. In March 1955, Robb described the advantages that such criteria conferred on the government and the disabilities they placed on the individual. 'Since a decision in a security case has to with risk or danger—the chance of harm to come—it necessarily looks to the future. It is prospective, an opinion or prediction as to future conduct. In the language of the medical profession, it is a prognosis. It is not a judgment or conviction for past misdeeds: such a judgment is the business of the criminal law under appropriate statues.'[62]

Clearly, a yardstick such as this set a premium on caution, and since the verdict had to be reached from a presumption of guilt, not innocence, the slightest doubt was technically enough to tip the scales against the accused. In other words, Oppenheimer's judges were required to give him not the slightest benefit of the doubt and to base their conclusions on the most pessimistic forecast of his future behaviour. In his memoirs, Kennan writes that American defence policy in the Cold War was based on an assessment of Soviet capabilities rather than Soviet intentions. Thus the huge strength of the Red Army on the ground was held to demand a response based on mass destruction with nuclear weapons; nothing less would serve. There is a close parallel in the security field. Oppenheimer was assessed as a personality of maximum potential danger, and what mattered according to the standards of the security system was not whether he wished to do his country harm but whether he was capable of it. Manifestly he was. In the words of Commissioner Zuckert, 'I doubt that there have been contemporaneously more than a handful of people at the highest levels who have possessed the amount of sensitive information which was given to Dr Oppenheimer.' Once it was accepted that he might conceivably use this information to undermine the national interest, then he had to be deprived of access to it. The system left no other choice.[63]

At the same time, there was another side to the question. When he spoke of the formulation of defence policy, Kennan also pointed out that the estimates of Soviet conventional power were what he called 'highly inflated' and that they were never 'seriously considered or discussed'. In other words, there was a strong element of self-interest at work in American military circles as well as a genuine fear of Communist ambitions. The same held true of the Oppenheimer case. Oppenheimer was not denied security clearance simply because he could not conform to a series of regulations. Much more was involved, as we shall now see.[64]

Chapter Eight

Origins

In April 1955, the *Bulletin of the Atomic Scientists* published a special issue on the security system. A great deal of it naturally focussed on the Oppenheimer case and on why Oppenheimer's public career had been destroyed. For Raymond Aron, the explanation which seemed 'least offensive' was that Oppenheimer was 'the victim of the mechanical application of the rules of the AEC regarding the type of conduct obligatory on all employees of the AEC, great or obscure'. It is not difficult to see, however, that Aron was implying there was another and more disturbing reason for what had happened and there was a lot more to the affair than the leading figures on either side had so far indicated.[1]

Others besides Aron were not so chary of voicing their suspicions openly. As early as the first week of the hearing, an unnamed nuclear physicist had been reported as saying that Oppenheimer was 'the victim of vindictive treatment' and that 'the atmosphere of suspicion, misunderstanding, and outright fear has allowed an accusation of bad judgment to be turned into a charge of implied treason'. Bush developed this argument in his article in *The New York Times* on 13 June. Many scientists, he wrote, had come to the conclusion that Oppenheimer had fallen foul of 'a group so obsessed with the utter necessity for maximum progress toward a single goal that they have been willing to brush aside or push aside any opinions which would tend to emphasize other matters in connection with the country's defense'. Discussion over defence policy had been 'at times so intense that the decencies of normal controversy and argument have been disregarded and men have been publicly criticized and even their motivation questioned when their only fault was that they had the temerity to disagree'.[2]

As another commentator reported it, most of the senior members of the scientific community believed that Oppenheimer had been 'destroyed' by the Air Force 'as part of a studied campaign to muzzle independent criticism of the Armed Forces'. The action taken against Oppenheimer had been intended to warn scientists 'against expressing their independent personal convictions about Armed Forces research and development programs'. Writing in *The Christian Science Monitor* on 8 July, Roland Sawyer declared that 'it is probable that the case against Dr Oppenheimer would never have been pressed if the personalities had been different'. But both Oppenheimer and Conant had clashed with Lawrence and Teller, and Oppenheimer had had serious disagreements with Strauss. He could have been dropped as a consultant but he was not. 'The case was pressed by Chairman Strauss—that is what most nuclear scientists and informed correspondents believe—and the Lawrence-Teller group. It was not, therefore, a test of security in a vacuum. It was a test of security in an atmosphere charged with personal conflict.'[3]

The most detailed accusations, however, came from the columnists Joseph and Stewart Alsop. In the *Tribune* on 4 June they wrote that the majority of scientists had been convinced 'that this sacrifice has been made to satisfy the personal spite of the chairman of the Atomic Energy Commission, Admiral Lewis Strauss'. Some three months later, they elaborated this viewpoint in a long article, 'We Accuse!', published in the October 1954 issue of *Harper's Magazine*. This is how it began:

> We accuse the Atomic Energy Commission in particular, and the American government in general, of a shocking miscarriage of justice in the case of Dr J. Robert Oppenheimer.
>
> We accuse Oppenheimer's chief judge, the chairman of the Atomic Energy Commission, Admiral Lewis Strauss, and certain of Oppenheimer's accusers, of venting the bitterness of old disputes through the security system of this country.
>
> And we accuse the security system itself, as being subject to this kind of ugliness, and as inherently repugnant in its present standards and procedures to every high tradition of the American past.[4]

These were extremely grave charges, but in the opinion of this writer they had already been given some substance in the way the hearing had been conducted, and in the evidence which had been presented to it. We must now look at the long-term origins of the hearing, and at the aspects of Oppenheimer's career which had not been developed there, so as to see what further significance can be attached to them.

In a statement put out on 13 April 1954, the two senior members of the Joint Committee on Atomic Energy, Representative Cole and Senator Bourke B. Hickenlooper described the Oppenheimer case as something which had evolved 'over the past several years'. These were the years when the United States began to exercise its responsibilities as the most powerful state in the world, a process accompanied by convulsive changes in many areas of American life. This was the period marked, in the eloquent words of Adlai Stevenson, by 'a coincidence of crises ... that brought together the flames of war, the atom's unlocking, and the emergence of aggressive Communism that created dangers—at first imperfectly perceived—of insidiously organized disloyalty'. It is against this background that we have to view both Oppenheimer's sudden rise to eminence and his equally swift fall from grace.[5]

The world in which Oppenheimer moved was signalized by two main features: the predominance of the military and the high emphasis placed on secrecy. These were two sides of the same coin, the positive and negative elements of the defence policy on which America depended for survival. Both acted as the terms of reference by which he and his fellow-scientists were bound to operate, and it is only if they are borne in mind that his eventual predicament can be understood.

The issue of what place the military should hold in the atomic energy programme was one which came up again and again in the immediate post-war period. As we have seen, the wartime project had been put under Army control, and when peace came in the summer of 1945, the Army and its supporters in Congress seemed intent on preserving that control. The first bill setting up an Atomic Energy Commission was drafted by lawyers in the War Department, and it proposed an authority which bore a remarkable resemblance to the Manhattan District of General Groves. When published in October 1945, it triggered off a vehemently hostile reaction in the scientific community, many of whom had detested being subordinated to the military during the war. To them, the bill appeared no more than a device whereby the Army would maintain its monopoly of atomic energy and continue to use it for purely military purposes. After a strenuous campaign against the bill, they succeeded in having it replaced by the alternative scheme introduced by Senator Mc-Mahon in December. On 1 August 1946, this became the country's Atomic Energy Act.[6]

The McMahon Act did not give the military the influence which its admirers wanted, and the Military Liaison Committee which it established had no powers of decision. In this, McMahon had been able to reject an amendment by Senator Arthur H. Vandenberg, which would have given the Committee a virtual veto over the Atomic Energy Commission which became the policy-making body by the terms of the Act. Nonetheless, the pressure for greater military participation was kept up. In January 1947, at the start of the hearings on the confirmation of the Commission, Vandenberg insisted that the Military Liaison Committee should be present at all the Commission's meetings. Strauss, when asked how close the relationship between the Commission and the Committee should be, replied that they ought to 'live in the same suit of clothes'. In 1947 and 1948 no less than seven bills were brought in to increase military involvement, and in May 1949 a measure was sponsored which would have set up an AEC consisting of eight military men and one scientist.[7]

At the same time, there was a continual struggle over the custody of nuclear weapons. In December 1946, as the movement for the take-over by the Commission approached, Groves and his right-hand man Nichols fought hard to retain military possession of all weapons and weapon facilities. They were unsuccessful, but the demand persisted. In November 1947 Lilienthal received a formal request that the stockpile be transferred to the armed services 'at the earliest practicable date', and during the following summer, as the crisis over the Berlin blockade developed, the issue was taken to the President. Truman decided against military custody, and he re-affirmed his decision in April 1949 when the matter was raised again by Senator Millard E. Tydings. In July 1950, however, soon after the outbreak of the Korean War, two transfers of non-nuclear components were made to the Air Force, and in April 1951 a number of complete weapons were handed over. In September 1952 the armed forces were given control of a much larger share of the stockpile. The Commission held what remained, but it was a clear victory for the military, and for men like Nichols and Lawrence who believed that nothing less would guarantee national security.[8]

The issue of secrecy was intimately related to the issue of military control, and it was to have a tremendous impact on Oppenheimer's fortunes. One of the principal objections to the initial atomic energy bill had been on the grounds of its intense preoccupation with security, and McMahon's original bill had declared that basic information in non-military fields was to be made freely available. In February 1946, however, the news broke of the discovery of a Soviet espionage ring in Canada, which had been associated with the wartime project. This brought about a substantial change of approach, and the relevant section of the McMahon bill, which had been headed 'Dissemination of Information' was now entitled 'Control of Information', and became much more negative in character.[9]

Even then, the measure was unacceptable to several members of the House of Representatives, and it was strongly criticized during the debate there in July. The remaining statements urging the free exchange of information were struck from the draft, and amendments inserted requiring investigation of all AEC employees by the FBI, and the adoption of the death penalty for the worst violations of security. These changes, which recalled the severity of the initial bill, were accepted by the Senate at the House-Senate conference at the end of the month.[10]

Congressional zeal over security went on making itself felt in the Joint Committee on Atomic Energy set up under the Act. During the confirmation hearings which began at the end of January 1947, the Committee went so far as to ask for the FBI and Military Intelligence reports on Truman's nominees to the Commission on the grounds that it was privileged to see the dossiers on other AEC personnel. It was rebuffed by the President, and so Senator William F. Knowland introduced a bill making provision for a mandatory FBI investigation of all the Commissioners and the General Manager; this was vetoed by Truman in May 1948. Late in 1947 the Commission came under criticism from the chairman of the Committee, Senator Hickenlooper, for not having pronounced on many doubtful security cases. Among these he no doubt included Dr Condon, whom the

Commission had given provisional clearance in May 1947, but the matter was momentarily taken out of the hands of the Joint Committee by the Committee on Un-American Activities, headed by Lilienthal's inveterate enemy, Representative J. Parnell Thomas. On 1 March 1948 Condon was described by the HUAC as 'one of the weakest links of our atomic security', and he was to be persecuted by it for years to come. His FBI file was denied, however, although it took a presidential Executive Order to do so.[11]

The attack on Condon could well have been intended as an indirect thrust at Lilienthal. At all events, it was the prelude to an open campaign against Lilienthal and his policies which began that spring and went on until the late summer of 1949. Most of it centred around the security issue, but the first offensive concentrated on Lilienthal himself. The Atomic Energy Act had given all five Commissioners two-year terms which expired on 1 August 1948. Truman proposed to reappoint them on a staggered basis, giving Lilienthal the five-year term. Senator Hickenlooper, on the other hand, proposed that since this was an election year, the term of each Commission member simply be extended until 30 June 1950. His scheme was aimed particularly at Lilienthal, for whom he nourished a profound distrust, and Truman—uncertain of re-election—felt compelled to accept it. The compromise avoided a battle over confirmation such as there had been in 1947, but it was damaging to Lilienthal's personal position nonetheless.[12]

As the deal over re-appointment was being hammered out, the Commission was coming under fire for awarding an AEC fellowship to a student who was a member of the Communist Party. Lilienthal argued that since the man would not have access to restricted data, there was no security problem. The Joint Committee did not agree, and several times during the next twelve months the issue was brought up as evidence of his laxness in security matters. So too was the fifth semi-annual report of the Commission, published in January 1949, which was seized on as an allegedly monumental piece of indiscretion. 'Why is it necessary,' asked Senator Tom Connally, 'because you spend public money, to go out and blah, blah all over the country about these bombs?' In fact, the report had been highly circumspect and nothing it disclosed could have been unknown in either Britain or Russia. The Committee, however, did not believe this.[13]

The biggest onslaught on Lilienthal's administration came soon afterwards, in May, with the accusation from Hickenlooper of 'incredible mismanagement' in the AEC. Hickenlooper's charges were entirely unfounded, as his fellow-Republican Senator Vandenberg told Lilienthal when the furore had died down. Yet it was politically impossible to admit it. 'If we say that,' said Vandenberg, 'it will just kill Hickenlooper. He's a nice fellow, very nice fellow. He thinks he and he alone stands between the security of the nation and disaster.... So ... we'll have to write a report ... that will say that Hickenlooper has rendered a great public service by his actions, that it has un-covered some things in the way of laxity that have since been corrected due to his charges, etc. Then, in a very small P.S. down at the bottom ... we'll have to say there has been no "incredible mismanagement".'[14]

Lilienthal was reassured, but the investigation Hickenlooper had launched had succeeded in eroding his position to a con-siderable degree. It had also undermined Oppenheimer, al-though no one could tell this at the time. The issue in question was the export of radioactive isotopes for research purposes, and once again the principle of the dissemination of information was at stake. One member of the Commission was adamantly op-posed to such information being offered to foreign countries even though they might be allies. This was Strauss. The isotopes issue had already come up as early as the spring of 1947, and Strauss had gone so far as to bring it to a vote. He had been defeated, but had threatened to take the matter further, to the State Department and the Pentagon. Relations within the AEC were badly strained in consequence. In the summer of 1948 he had been anxious to prevent Cyril S. Smith of the General Advisory Committee from discussing the metallurgy of plutonium while on a projected trip to Britain. Now, in a public session of the Joint Committee on 9 June 1949, he once again criticized the isotopes shipments, bringing his disagreement right out into the open.[15]

It was Oppenheimer who was brought forward to explain the case for releasing the material. He was a passionate advocate of a liberal information policy. In a letter written to Truman on behalf of the GAC on 31 December 1947, he had spoken of 'how adverse the effect of secrecy, and of the inevitable misunderstanding and error which accompany it, have been on progress, and thus on the common defense and security'. He had also referred specifically to the benefits which he and his colleagues believed would flow from the export of isotopes for biological and medical research, and he developed his point before the Joint Committee four days after Strauss' appearance, on 13 June. It was to be one of the most fateful moments of his career.[16]

'No one', declared Oppenheimer, 'can say that you cannot use [isotopes] for atomic energy development. You can use a shovel for atomic energy development. In fact, you do. You can use a bottle of beer for atomic energy development. In fact, you do. But to get some perspective, the fact is that during the war and after the war these materials have played no significant part, and in my own knowledge, no part at all.' Then, in reply to a question on the general value of isotopes, he stated: 'My own rating of the importance of isotopes in this broad sense is that they are far less important than electronic devices, but far more important than, let us say, vitamins—somewhere in between.' 'The positive arguments for making isotopes available', he concluded, 'lie in fostering science; they lie in making cordial relations with the scientists and technical people in Western Europe; they lie in assisting the recovery of Western Europe; they lie in doing the decent thing.'[17]

In giving his scathing testimony, Oppenheimer was displaying a side of his character little-known outside his own circle. As one man who knew him reasonably well has written: 'Oppenheimer did not willingly suffer people whom he considered wrong. He was a devastating critic, sometimes not sparing the victim's sensibilities. How one reacted depended to a certain extent on one's sense of self-importance.' Lawrence's biographer has spoken about 'a certain arrogance ... directed after Los Alamos toward security people, even toward some colleagues, and felt by many nonscientists'. The Alsops, putting it more bluntly, described it as 'Dr Oppenheimer's regrettable tendency to be contemptuous of government flatfeet'. As they also put it: 'He has impossibly high intellectual standards. He insists on them, with more than a trace of intellectual snobbery and sometimes with cold scorn for those who fall short. He has a good deal of the arrogance of the brightest boy in the class; he is not patient with obtuseness, and his tongue can be very cutting.'[18]

In this particular instance, the rebuke was clearly aimed at Strauss, and Volpe, who was sat nearby, later recalled watching Strauss' face cloud with anger. He also remembered the remarks he exchanged with Oppenheimer at the close of the session. 'Joe,' said Oppenheimer, 'how did I do?' 'Robert,' Volpe answered, 'you did much too well for your own good.' Volpe could not possibly guess the full significance of this comment, but it was clear by the summer of 1954, at least to the two former chairmen of the AEC, Lilienthal and Dean. Recounting a conversation with Dean on 22 June, Lilienthal wrote : 'I went on to say that in a good many quarters there was a feeling that the whole Oppenheimer mess began with a declaration on Lewis' part to punish Oppenheimer. Dean said, "Yes, of course, that is what they believe, and there is no other good explanation for what happened." ' The root of the affair, in Lilienthal's view, lay in the 'offhand way' in which Oppenheimer had dismissed Strauss' objections to the export of isotopes. 'I had feared from that time on,' he wrote, 'that this would be a thing for which Oppenheimer might have to pay in Strauss' enmity, though, of course, I never had the faintest idea how things would actually turn out, in this outrageous and shaking episode.'[19]

In arguing as he did, Oppenheimer was doing no more than affirming his belief in the fullest possible exchange of information, which as one commentator has written, had been for the scientific community 'a firm article of faith and a foundation for personal security ... almost unquestioned so far as any important public issue was concerned until World War II'. One of the most explicit statements of this belief was made by the editor of the *Bulletin of the Atomic Scientists,* Eugene Rabinowitch. It read as follows :

Whoever places outside considerations, whether of ideological purity or political expediency, above scientific truth, is a traitor to the world community of scientists. For him, science is but a handmaiden of the politic il or economic powers he favors, and her set of ethical values is subordinated to the different (and from the point of view of a scientist, inferior) set that dominates political and economic controversies in the world. Advantage to a certain political camp becomes more important than the advancement of truth; compliance with a doctrine more important than freedom of thought; hatred of national or ideological enemies more important than tolerance of dissenters.[20]

During and after the Second World War, however, several scientists had come to equate their cosmopolitanism with the revolutionary internationalism preached by the Soviet Union. It did not seem to occur to them that the Soviet appeal to internationalism veiled a hard dedication to Russian national interests which in practice perverted the beliefs the USSR claimed to stand for. By 1949, some of them had committed espionage in the name of their idealism—Weinberg at Berkeley, the English physicist, Nunn May, in Canada—and others were soon to be uncovered—Klaus Fuchs in 1950 and Bruno Pontecorvo in 1951.

This repeated *trahison des clercs* could only serve to intensify the misgivings felt about scientists in society at large. 'Scientists', Rabinowitch wrote, 'have always been suspicious characters— members of an international brotherhood, a freemasonry with a secret language of symbols and equations they alone understand.' In *The Meaning of Treason,* Rebecca West spoke for popular opinion when she said the scientists appeared to be 'animated by a feeling, for which psychiatrists have a name, that they form an elect class which should be allowed to do as they liked'. Their mistaken assumption was that 'because a man has scientific gifts he is likely to be superior to his fellows in all intellectual respects, including that kind of general far-seeing ability, tender towards the future of the individual and the race, which we call wisdom'.[21]

This assumption was not shared by all the members of the American scientific community. Lawrence, for example, was actuated by the same high-pitched nationalism which drove the critics of science, and, curiously enough, by their anti-intellectualism as well. At Berkeley in the late thirties he had been extremely intolerant of Oppenheimer's 'dilettante humanitarianism' and he had actively opposed his attempts to politicize the campus. As his biographer has written: 'Ernest had little

sympathy with the tendency among scientists to consider themselves superior to businessmen, military leaders and security
people, and the rules and regulations lesser men must respect;
the assumption that, because one was a good scientist, he automatically knew best the directions in which lay the welfare of the
nation—and, indeed, the world. This was, Ernest thought, the
supreme arrogance of which too many scientists were guilty:
that because they had split and controlled the atom, built a most
powerful weapon, and acquired increased understanding of
nature's forces, they were thereby a chosen people, more capable
than others of directing affairs of state, defense, and even the
economic uses of power.'[22]

This was the spirit which was to infuse the campaign for the
hydrogen bomb, and with the subsequent rise of McCarthy the
call among scientists to rally round the flag became more and
more strident, not least, perhaps, out of sheer self-preservation.
At the annual conference of the American Physical Society which
was taking place at the same time as Oppenheimer's hearing in
1954, physicists like Lawrence, Teller and Alvarez were reported
to be declaring 'that their country is in peril and that the best
solution is to build its physical strength as rapidly as possible.
They say they can see no wisdom in tolerating anything or
anyone that even remotely looks like a threat to this objective.'[23]

Oppenheimer and those who thought like him were therefore
more open to attack than perhaps they realized, and they were
particularly vulnerable because they possessed so many secrets.
As one observer put it, the scientists were 'today's supermen' and
their specialized knowledge was 'a prime source of military
strength'. But, he also pointed out, 'it is also a prime threat to
this strength. In the ominous language of the underworld, "They
know too much".... they are at once the most valued and
the most distrusted members of contemporary society.' For
Oppenheimer, as the trustee of more classified information than
any other scientist in Washington, this was especially true.[24]

Moreover, the scientists were also vulnerable in an institu-
tional sense. The Office of Scientific Research and Development
set up in 1941 had been a power in its own right. It had its own
funds, and its director, Bush, had direct access to the President.
With the abolition of the OSRD in 1946, however, the scientist
in government was no longer in such a secure and privileged

position. He was indispensable as an adviser on controversial questions of defence policy because no one else was competent to deal with the technicalities involved. In giving the scientist this role, however, the country's political leaders were often evading their ultimate responsibility. As Huntington has written, strategic issues were 'subjected to relentless study and investigation in an effort to resolve conflicts over goals by research into data and to solve by experts problems which require politicians'. This meant, in turn, that whenever controversy placed the scientist under attack, his political masters were not disposed to defend him. The scientist was in a constitutional limbo, with no official niche in the edifice of government. He had no recognized status in the Executive branch, and he was rarely on easy terms with Congress. If he came under fire, he was liable to be unsupported.[25]

In Oppenheimer's case, there is no doubt that his enemies were actively at work to discredit him from 1947 onwards, beginning with the major effort to remove his clearance in March and continuing with the first public exposure of the Chevalier incident in October. Attacks on his brother were also taking place. On 12 July 1947 *The Washington Times-Herald* made a big story of the fact that Frank Oppenheimer had been a member of the Communist Party and had worked on the atomic bomb at Berkeley, and the timing of the disclosure may well have been significant. The question of Oppenheimer's clearance was just about to come before the AEC for a decision, and this could clearly have influenced its thinking, although the paper issued an italicized disclaimer that '*the official report on Frank Oppenheimer in no way reflects on the loyalty or ability of his brother, Dr J. Robert Oppenheimer*'. Then, nearly two years later, on 14 June 1949, the day after Oppenheimer's testimony on the isotopes issue, Frank and his wife were exposed as former Communists by the Un-American Activities Committee. They had admitted to membership of the Party at a closed session of the Committee, but later in the day they were made to repeat the admission before the press.[25]

As an historian of the Committee saw it, it was difficult to avoid the conclusion that the Committee 'was primarily motivated by a desire to embarrass the Oppenheimers and, through them, J. Robert Oppenheimer'. The assertion that the latter was being victimized may be doubted when one remembers that only a week beforehand Oppenheimer had been congratulated by the members of the Committee over the fullness of his testimony on Peters and other related subjects. The doubts are reinforced by the tone of the Committee's report, published at the end of September. The hearings had concerned themselves largely with the Soviet attempt to penetrate the Radiation Laboratory during the war, and Frank Oppenheimer had been probed on his relationship with Steve Nelson, the intermediary for Weinberg. Both the Communist Party and the Soviet government, the report stated, had known of Nelson's acquaintance with 'one of the leading physicists engaged in the development of the atomic bomb', and had tried to use this 'as a medium of infiltration'. Oppenheimer was thus not named, and, the report concluded, 'an investigation of the aforementioned scientist disclosed that neither he nor his wife engaged in any subversive activities and that their loyalty has never been questioned by the government. Nelson later reported that neither the physicist nor his wife were sympathetic to Communism.' This was a tribute, not a condemnation.[27]

So far, then, Oppenheimer had survived comparatively unscathed. The odds against him were mounting, however, and in January 1950 he was defeated on the crucial issue of the H-bomb, which, as we have seen, was to be used so tellingly against him nearly four years later. Yet instead of the full-scale onslaught which might have been expected in the aftermath of the hydrogen bomb decision, he was faced only with the sniping of the Crouches in May. This concentrated on only one small episode, and it was aimed not from the platform of the Un-American Activities Committee in Washington, but from the comparative obscurity of the state legislature of California. The question then arises: why, when they possessed almost all the evidence which was to be used against him in 1953 did his enemies not make their bid sometime in 1950? The answers offered here are speculative, but they may suggest some reasons why the later attack was successfully initiated.

The atmosphere of 1950 certainly seems to have favoured Oppenheimer's destruction in many ways. At home, anti-Communism had become by far the most outstanding political issue. In January Alger Hiss was convicted of perjury in having denied passing secrets to the Soviet Union. Less than three weeks later Senator Joseph McCarthy made his début as the hammer of all left-wing subversives, and in September the stringently anti-Communist McCarran Act was passed over President Truman's veto. Abroad, the outbreak of the Korean War in June appeared to herald a vigorous Communist attempt to overthrow the entire Western position in the Far East. Finally, two distinguished nuclear physicists had subordinated their countries' interests to those of the USSR. At the end of January the head of the theoretical physics division of the British research establishment at Harwell, Klaus Fuchs, confessed that he had been passing information to Moscow since 1942. Early in April, the High Commissioner of the French Atomic Energy Commission, Frédéric Joliot-Curie, gave equally startling proof of his attachment to Russia. A fervent Communist, he took the rostrum of the Party's National Convention to declare that 'never will progressive scientists, never will Communist scientists give a particle of their knowledge for a war against the Soviet Union. And we shall stand fast, upheld by our conviction that by so doing we are helping France and all humanity.' In addition to this, he endorsed a Party resolution calling on workers to refuse to manufacture or to transport nuclear weapons.[28]

The response of the state in each case was immediate and decisive. On 1 March, Fuchs was sentenced to fourteen years' imprisonment. On 28 April, Joliot-Curie was relieved of his functions. In view of this, why was no large-scale investigation of Oppenheimer set in train? The answer is twofold. In the first place, he was able to satisfy the requirements of the current presidential security system, which were, essentially, loyalty and discretion. He had betrayed no secrets, as Fuchs had, and he had not proclaimed any devotion to the Soviet Union, as Joliot-Curie had. It is true that he failed to meet some of the existing AEC Criteria, which were practically identical with those which prevailed in 1953, but it seems clear that in the event of a conflict between the two sets of regulations it was the presidential system which took precedence. In the second place, as far as the hydrogen bomb was concerned, Oppenheimer was still comparatively unassailable. The breakthrough in fission development in the summer of 1950 strengthened the position of the opponents of the bomb considerably, and Korea greatly enhanced the attractiveness of tactical nuclear weapons. Moreover, the H-bomb had not yet been proved feasible, and it would have been futile to launch an attack on Oppenheimer for opposing it if it turned out that it could never be made. All told, therefore, he was still out of reach of whomever may have wanted to bring him down.[29]

The sniping continued during 1951 and 1952, as we have seen, with the new disputes over the second weapons laboratory, the H-bomb test, tactical atomic weapons and continental air defence. At the same time, there was the occasional burst of fire from other quarters. For example, early in 1951, Representative Harold Velde of the Un-American Activities Committee disclosed that the hitherto anonymous scientist so often mentioned in the hearings on Communist wartime espionage was in fact Oppenheimer. In April 1951, the extreme right-wing *American Mercury* published an article which focussed on the espionage of Nelson and Weinberg and spoke of 'the possibility that Nelson may have gotten some of the secrets from the Oppenheimer family'. A year later came the Weinberg perjury case, and with it the possibility that Oppenheimer's name might be dragged in the mud. So far, however, there was no concerted drive to finish him once and for all.[30]

It was not until the advent of the Eisenhower régime in January 1953 that the situation began to change significantly, and the campaign against Oppenheimer mounted to its climax. Once again, it was given impetus by a controversy over nuclear policy, and a controversy which had Oppenheimer at its heart. In April 1952, as we have noticed, Oppenheimer was appointed chairman of a State Department panel on disarmament, which included Bush and Allen Dulles; it reported early in January 1953. On 17 February, Oppenheimer revealed the declassifiable findings of the report in an address to the Council on Foreign Relations in New York, entitled 'Atomic Weapons and American Policy'. It was not published until the summer, when it appeared in the July issue of the Council's journal, *Foreign Affairs,* but the gist of it was clearly made known in political circles well before then. It amounted to nothing less than a challenge to the existing basis of the government's approach to the problem of nuclear weapons and nuclear strategy.[31]

'The rule for the atom', Oppenheimer began, 'was: "Let us

keep ahead. Let us be sure that we are ahead of the enemy."
Today it would seem that, however necessary these considerations and these policies may be, they are no longer nearly
sufficient.' Nuclear weapons had brought the United States to a
crisis. 'It is generally known we plan to use them,' wrote Oppenheimer. 'It is also generally known that one ingredient of this
plan is a rather rigid commitment to their use in a very massive,
initial, unremitting strategic assault on the enemy.' 'We may
anticipate a state of affairs', he went on, 'in which the two
Great Powers will each be in a position to put an end to the
civilization and life of the other, though not without risking its
own. We may be likened to two scorpions in a bottle, each
capable of killing the other, but only at the risk of his own
life.'[32]

There were, however, a number of initiatives the government
could take to end this grim impasse. The first was to give the
American public a fuller knowledge of the dangers of a nuclear
arms race. 'We do not operate well when the important facts, the
essential conditions, which limit and determine our choices are
unknown', Oppenheimer wrote. 'We do not operate well when
they are known, in secrecy and in fear, only to a few men.'
What could and should be imparted was information about
'the characteristics and probable effects of our atomic weapons'.
This had to be done in spite of the concern that the Soviet Union
might learn something and that 'public knowledge of the situation might induce in this country a mood of despair, or a too
ready acceptance of what is lightheartedly called preventive
war.'[33]

The second recommendation was that the government should
share information on weapons capabilities and delivery systems
with its major allies, that is, with Britain, France and Japan. In
October 1951, Section 10 of the Atomic Energy Act had been
amended so as to enable some information to be given to
Britain. But this did not include information on weapons, and
America's allies remained totally in the dark about the workings
of the deterrent, even though they were entirely dependent on it.
However, given America's intense security-mindedness on the
one hand, and the behaviour of Nunn May, Fuchs and Joliot-
Curie on the other—not to mention the more recent defection

of Burgess and Maclean—it was improbable that change would come easily or soon.[34]

The third proposal was that the country's air defence should be strengthened. This would serve several purposes: it would be a disincentive to the Russians to attempt a first strike; it would raise allied morale; and it would be a useful complement to any future agreements on arms regulation. That is to say, it would be possible to detect an infringement of the agreement such as a surprise attack if the machinery of an early warning system were already in place. For all these reasons, the government must bring to bear all the many technical developments that lay to hand and that had not yet been pushed intensively.[35]

As evidence that all three aims should be pursued, Oppenheimer cited Truman's recent statement (of 26 January) that the Soviet Union did not have the atomic bomb, and the declaration by a high-ranking officer of the Air Defense Command that it was America's policy to protect the Strategic Air Command 'but that it was not really our policy to protect this country, for that is so big a job that it would interfere with our retaliatory capabilities'. 'Such follies', he wrote, 'can occur only when even the men who know the facts can find no one to talk to about them, when the facts are too secret for discussion, and thus for thought.'[36]

Oppenheimer's plea could not be disregarded, coming as it did from one of the government's most senior advisers on nuclear policy, and it was especially significant in that it fused two of the most important issues of recent years, secrecy and air defence. The call for governmental candour had already been made at the time of the debate on the hydrogen bomb, and on 20 September 1949 Oppenheimer had told Lilienthal that he believed the administration had been presented with a chance 'to end the miasma of secrecy'. The chance was not taken, and shortly after Truman's decision he was to say this:

> There is grave danger for us in that these decisions have been taken on the basis of facts held secret. This is not because the men who must contribute to the decisions, or must make them, are lacking in wisdom; it is because wisdom itself cannot flourish, nor even truth be determined, without the give and take of debate or criticism. The relevant facts could be of

little help to an enemy; yet they are indispensable for an understanding of questions of policy.[37]

Oppenheimer was far from alone in this. Shortly after his departure from the AEC, Lilenthal urged a freer information policy on the government, and he was accompanied by some of the most distinguished scientists in the country, including Harold C. Urey and Leo Szilard. 'Neither the President nor the Atomic Energy Commission', said Szilard, 'have explained to the American people what the decision to develop hydrogen bombs will involve, what the meaning of the "hydrogen bomb" is, or what the cost of the indispensable defense measures will be. Yet these are things the American people must know.' 'Americans', wrote the *Bulletin of the Atomic Scientists,* 'must be given the opportunity to decide whether, and under what conditions, they want to embark on this course [the manufacture of thermo-nuclear weapons]. Furthermore, only in the light of full knowledge of what a future war may be like, can the American people decide to what lengths they are prepared to go to make our country less vulnerable in war, and how much of our national resources, sovereignty, and living standards they are willing to sacrifice for the sake of making war less likely.'[38]

The administration's response, however, had been decidedly unsympathetic and the movement for greater candour had subsided. Now, with a new régime in power it revived, in the hope that a fresh start could be made. It was no doubt with this hope in mind that Oppenheimer also pressed the case for air defence. The dying months of the Truman presidency had certainly given him and his co-partners little encouragement. In the autumn of 1952 the Lincoln Summer Study had reported in sombre terms. In its estimate, by 1955 the Soviet Union would have enough aircraft and nuclear weapons to cripple the United States in a surprise attack. Moreover, the current American defence system was only capable of achieving a 20 per cent kill-rate. A kill-rate of between 60 and 70 per cent was attainable, but preparations must be put in hand at once for a system incorporating a distant-early-warning line, an elaborate communications network, and screens of fighter and missile interceptors. Nothing less would serve if the country's defence were to be placed on an adequate footing.[39]

These findings may have been clear enough to the scientists, but they still did not convince the Air Force, which continued to pin its faith on strategic air power. At the same time, it was feared that they might be accepted over the department's head, together with the recommendations of Project Vista, on which a decision had not yet been taken. Therefore, neither Finletter, the Air Force Secretary, nor Lovett, the Secretary of Defense, approved the findings, and they both refused to lay them before the National Security Council. As Berkner saw it, this was a blatant attempt to stifle the Summer Study's work. 'For reasons known only to the Armed Forces,' he later stated, ' . . . many efforts were made to ignore or to suppress the findings of the Lincoln Summer Study and little effort was made to demonstrate how the ideas might work out . . . . the Armed Forces refused to recognize the serious state of the air-defense problem or to admit that it could be improved by radical measures.'[40]

The findings did eventually reach the NSC through the agency of the chairman of the National Security Resources Board, Jack Gorrie, and Gorrie himself urged them on the administration. His arguments were reinforced by a Council policy paper, NSC-141, which called for a big increase in air defence spending, but both Lovett and the Joint Chiefs of Staff were reluctant to have a programme worked out in detail. It was, in fact, unrealistic to expect that the government would take on a firm commitment to this or any other new departure on the eve of a presidential election, and so there the matter lay until Eisenhower and the Republicans came to power the following January.[41]

Oppenheimer's initiative was thus a challenge to Eisenhower to take action on both fronts. By throwing it down, however, he was indicating that he and those who thought like him no longer had the ear of the administration. In other words, Oppenheimer and his companions were now on the margin of the establishment they had once belonged to, and as innovators this was a weak position to be operating from. In this sense they resembled the advocates of the H-bomb during the great debate of 1949–50, since Teller, Lawrence and Alvarez had had to manoeuvre largely from outside the centres of decision. Now, however, the roles were reversed : it was the devotees of the bomb who were on top, resisting the changes which Oppenheimer and the others were anxious to have introduced.

In this too, Oppenheimer calls to mind Sir Henry Tizard, the man who more than any other is associated with the development of air defence in Britain in the late 1930s. In 1940, with Churchill's accession to power, Tizard lost his place as a scientific adviser to the government, and was replaced by Churchill's protégé, Lord Cherwell. In the spring of 1942, they clashed over the value of the policy of area bombing, that is, bombing concentrating purely on civilian targets. Here, many of the same arguments were put forward as were featured in the dispute over the H-bomb after 1949. Tizard, like Oppenheimer, opposed this use of air power; Cherwell, like Teller, believed that it was the key to victory. In both cases, it was the opponents of the strategy who lost, and Oppenheimer, like Tizard, was left on the fringe of events, ignored by the makers of policy.[42]

Unlike Tizard, however, Oppenheimer had a means of offsetting his weakness by making the issues he was campaigning for public, that is, by briefing selected journalists and having details disclosed in the press. In Britain, even in peacetime, this would have been impossible because of the Official Secrets Act, but in the United States no such legislation was in force. It is true that silence could be imposed by the President if need be, and Truman had been able to maintain secrecy for the greater part of the hydrogen bomb debate. In this case there was no presidential intervention. Indeed, it was with White House approval that the address to the Council on Foreign Relations was published in the summer. By then, an open (and ferocious) controversy was in progress.[43]

The first sign that the fight was being taken to the country came in two articles by Stewart Alsop in *The New York Herald Tribune* early in September 1952. They covered the question of air defence and, as we shall see, they aroused a great deal of comment in Washington. A long lull followed, and it was not until March 1953 that the public was once again made aware that new policies were being urged on the government. On 1 and 2 March, the defence correspondent of *The New York Times,* Hanson Baldwin, published articles on the secrecy issue which echoed much of what Oppenheimer had had to say to the Council on Foreign Relations. Two weeks later, between 16 and 20 March, the Alsops brought out no less than five articles on air defence. On 1 May, Berkner gave a public address in which

1

he said that 'the United States has acquired a terrific punch with which to meet an all-out war; but it has at the same time acquired a "glass jaw", because of its own vulnerability to atomic attack'. There was, therefore, an urgent need for defensive measures to be taken, but Berkner believed that there was 'ample evidence that really significant undertakings will not be sponsored by the military except in the event of dire emergency'. The trouble was, however, Berkner declared, that 'when the emergency arrives in this atomic age, it will be too late'.[44]

All these developments touched off a furore in Air Force circles. Shortly after Alsop's articles of September 1952 came out, Finletter is reported as having had a conversation with one of his aides, Charles J. V. Murphy, who was serving in the Air Force Reserve. 'Oppenheimer may not be a Communist,' Finletter is supposed to have said, 'but he is the cleverest conspirator in America.' No outright response was made, however, until after the appearance of Baldwin's articles on secrecy, and the Alsops' extended comment on air defence. It came in the form of an anonymous article in *Fortune* magazine, which had in fact been written by Murphy and which was clearly based on a considerable amount of inside information. Here, for the first time, the virulent hostility of the Air Force towards Oppenheimer was given public expression.[45]

The article was entitled 'The Hidden Struggle for the H-Bomb', and sub-titled 'The story of Dr Oppenheimer's persistent campaign to reverse US military strategy'. 'A life-and-death struggle over national military policy has developed', the writer began, 'between a highly influential group of American scientists and the military.' It revolved round the question of 'whether a strategy shaped around the "retaliatory-deterrent" principle embodied in the Strategic Air Command shall be discarded, or at least drastically modified, in favour of a defensive strategy wherein the US atomic advantage would be confined to short-range tactical forces, designed to engage other military forces in the field.' The 'prime mover' among the scientists was none other than Oppenheimer. 'He and his followers', wrote Murphy, 'have no confidence in the military's assumption that SAC as a weapon of mass destruction is a real deterrent to Soviet action. On the contrary, they believe that, by generating fear in the Kremlin, it has been a goad to Soviet development of counter-atomic weapons. They argue that it has aroused misgivings in Western Europe; and that a renunciation of atomic-offensive power by both major adversaries is essential to an easement of world tension.'[46]

There followed a highly distorted account of the events of the past few years, beginning with the H-bomb debate of 1949 and ending with the Lincoln Summer Study. The conflict was still unresolved, wrote Murphy, but meanwhile, 'the development of thermonuclear and fission weapons continues apace. And SAC, under General LeMay, retains its mighty mission.' He concluded by giving what was described as Finletter's view of the issue. The scientists, according to Finletter, 'hold no exclusive option on the belief that war is evil; for the US, at this juncture in world history, to throw away its strongest weapon merely because it is an offensive weapon is a naïve way to go about ridding the world of war.' America's nuclear superiority constituted 'a "shield" behind which the American people can work steadily for peace—until Mr Eisenhower's proposals for world disarmament are universally accepted'. For the present, Murphy ended, there was 'a serious question of the propriety of scientists' trying to settle such grave national issues alone, inasmuch as they bear no responsibility for the successful execution of war plans'.[47]

The *Fortune* article marked the most determined bid to discredit Oppenheimer since the Crouch episode three years beforehand. It was extremely damaging in that its allegations could not be refuted unless Oppenheimer were prepared to answer them publicly and in great detail. In view of the extreme secrecy surrounding all the issues in question, it was a foregone conclusion that he would not do so. Thus the highly inaccurate version of events set out by Murphy remained on the record and Oppenheimer's silence could be taken for consent.

At the same time, the article provided a superb opening for interested Congressional investigators, above all, of course, their doyen Senator McCarthy. As we know, McCarthy was not allowed to seize it, and the administration remained in control of the situation. It paid a price for doing so, however, in the form of the assurances it gave that the matter would be given a thorough examination, and it knew that if it went back on its promise, the Senator and his powerful following would not take it lightly. This was to be an important factor when the issue was broached once again later in the year.

Meanwhile, the government was faced with the need to make some response to the twin campaigns for the reduction of official secrecy and for a vastly improved system of air defence. On the secrecy issue its concessions were marginal. This was in spite of the fact that Eisenhower himself was apparently ready to share the nation's confidence. One of his speech-writers, C. D. Jackson, was instructed to draft a presidential address on the subject, and he worked on this throughout the summer. As he did so, some highly distinguished advocates of greater public candour came forward. Dean made it one of the themes of his last press conference on 25 June, and his predecessor, Lilienthal, brought out a long article in *The New York Times* on 4 October in which he urged the administration to adopt a less restrictive policy.[48]

By the time Lilienthal's article appeared, however, the struggle had been lost. The opponents of candour had not been slow in making their views publicly known. In the August issue of *Fortune*, an article by Murphy (signed this time) attacked the suggestion on the grounds that it undermined national security. Disclosing secrets to the American public could well give a big advantage to an enemy, he argued, and he quoted Strauss as saying that 'in a shooting war it would be a short-lived commander who announced how many rounds he had in his locker'. 'An authority of wide experience' was also quoted as saying that the United States was 'in a poker game with a dangerous adversary. Does it make sense for us to play our hand with a mirror over our shoulder?' There was some room for a relaxation of secrecy, but it should not involve 'giving away the last critical magnitudes of national strength'. As for the proposal to share information with America's allies, this too entailed unacceptable risks and must be rejected if security were to be maintained.[49]

The views Murphy had put forward predominated within the administration, and the Alsops were wrong when they wrote in the *Tribune* on 16 September that Eisenhower had approved plans for reports to the public on various aspects of the nuclear arms race. The policy had indeed been considered at length, but it was rejected for a number of reasons. There might well be a panic-stricken popular reaction, and intensified pressure for an expanded military budget; America's allies would be alarmed, it was said, and so would the neutral states. Above all, it would most probably cause 'glee in Moscow'. At his press conference on 8 October, therefore, Eisenhower stated that the government did not intend 'to disclose the details of our strength in atomic weapons of any sort'. Instead, partly at the instigation of Strauss, he opted for the policy of 'Atoms for Peace', which concentrated on the peaceful applications of atomic energy and steered well clear of mentioning the horrors of thermonuclear warfare. It is true that in his State of the Union message on 7 January 1954, the President asked Congressional approval for the disclosure of some information about nuclear weapons to the European allies, but the concessions embodied in the new Atomic Energy Act of 1954 were not substantial.[50]

The campaign for air defence fared much better. In December 1952, Lovett had referred the Lincoln Summer Study proposals to a committee headed by Mervin J. Kelly, who had sat with Oppenheimer on the 1950 panel on military uses, and who was to be his opening witness at the hearing. In May 1953 Kelly submitted the committee's report to the new Secretary of Defense, Wilson. It was broadly favourable to the adoption of an improved system, but the administration could not make up its mind. After disagreement in the National Security Council, the issue was referred to yet more advisory groups. Even then, there was indecision.[51]

The deadlock was broken by a momentous event, the explosion of a thermonuclear bomb by the Russians on 12 August. The reaction was typified by Representative Cole, speaking in a radio interview shortly afterwards. The Russian bomb, Cole pointed out, could be delivered by air—unlike the device which the AEC had tested at the end of 1952, which weighed some sixty tons. 'We need more civil defense,' said Cole, 'more continental defense, and since we are a God-fearing people, I hope a prayer. I think the condition is that desperate.'[52]

The urgency of the situation was also emphasized by the way in which Murphy suddenly changed his tune. In the attack on Oppenheimer in the May issue of *Fortune,* he had dismissed air defence almost out of hand. Now he went into reverse. In May he had written that 'the whole panoply' set out by the Lincoln

Summer Study 'suggested a jet-propelled, electronically-hedged Maginot line'. In the November issue, on the other hand, he stated that the conflict between the scientists and the Air Force was not 'a crude argument between Maginot-minded exponents of the defensive and the fire-eating bombardiers who want to stake everything on a frightful counter-blow at Russia, and never mind what is happening to the American civilians. For SAC to get off the ground, after all, it needs warning from the same radar installations that might notify the citizens of Chicago to take cover; ADC's [Air Defense Command's] fighter squadrons help defend the B-36 bases as well as the big cities of the US. The debate is about the right *balance* of defensive and offensive investment.'[48]

By the time Murphy's article came out, the administration had decided to throw large resources into an air defence programme. In August, Eisenhower's new Chiefs of Staff conferred together in the aftermath of the news of the Soviet H-bomb, and came to the conclusion that the two most vital requirements for the country were improved air defence and a strengthened strategic strike force. On 6 October the planning board of the National Security Council, in the policy paper NSC-162, recommended virtually all the Lincoln proposals at a cost of $20 billion over the next five years. Although there was still some resistance from the Air Force in the form of a public statement by the Vice-Chief of Air Staff that to neglect the SAC 'because of preoccupation with last-resort defenses' would be 'suicidal', on 18 October Wilson announced that the policy had been adopted. This was confirmed at a meeting of the National Security Council on 30 October, at which it was decided to allocate no less than 10 per cent of the defence budget for the coming financial year to launching the improved system which the Summer Study had called for. At this same meeting, it was also decided to accept tactical atomic weapons as part of the defence of Western Europe against Soviet invasion.[54]

As the debate reached its climax, a further article attacking Oppenheimer was published in *Time* magazine on 21 September. It depicted him and Lilienthal as naïve and confused idealists under whose influence the Atomic Energy Commission had drifted irresolutely, particularly during the H-bomb dispute. Strauss, the main subject of the article, was, on the other hand, portrayed as the decisive and dedicated man who had saved the Commission from their 'hand-wringing and baseless hope'. Like Murphy's piece of the previous May, this was plentifully sprinkled with half-truths and inaccuracies. To Lilienthal it was 'slimy, wicked, and damaging', and in *The New York Times* on 4 October he attempted to set the record straight. The general public, however, had no means of telling whose version could be trusted.[55]

It was at this point that Borden entered the situation and changed it decisively with his letter to J. Edgar Hoover. As the executive secretary of the Joint Committee on Atomic Energy, Borden had been an advocate of maximum security in every field. He has been described as a man 'who would defend an official secret with his life, if necessary, and who could not help expecting others to comport themselves likewise'. As we have seen, he was one of the leading figures in the H-bomb lobby in 1949, and as a former Air Force officer, he was pledged to the cause of strategic air warfare. Moreover, since the JCAE conceived of itself as the watchdog of the Commission, Borden and his staff were ever-vigilant for lapses from the standards which they set for the atomic energy programme. In Borden's view there were many such lapses, and it was not difficult to see who was to blame for them. 'The entire time I spent working for the Committee', he said, 'was spent fighting the paralysis which gripped the Atomic Energy Commission and the Pentagon. The more I looked, the more it appeared to me that J. R. Oppenheimer was responsible for this paralysis—not merely as to the H-bomb but as to each new type of A-bomb which was proposed, each plant expansion, raw materials step-up, detection of Soviet test explosions, each reactor project, each step designed to strengthen the military and industrial power position of the US. We won all our battles, but in each case J. R. Oppenheimer's influence delayed us from one to four years.'[56]

In view of this, it seems strange that it was not until November 1950, that is, almost two years after his appointment, that he first examined Oppenheimer's FBI file. Needless to say, it reinforced his misgivings, and when in the summer of 1952 Oppenheimer's term with the General Advisory Committee expired, Borden was determined it should not be renewed. Commissioner Murray went even further, according to this account, in raising the question of whether not only Oppenheimer's committee membership should be continued but his security clearance as well. In the event, the clearance issue was not raised, but Oppenheimer was not asked to stay on the GAC.[57]

Borden was still not satisfied, however. In July 1952, a former FBI agent, Francis Cotter, joined the Joint Committee staff, and Borden asked him to investigate the possibility of whether Oppenheimer might have been an accomplice of Fuchs. Cotter eventually came to the conclusion that the suspicion was unfounded, but Borden grew increasingly convinced that Oppenheimer had been, and still was, a Soviet agent. So he came to draw up his mammoth list of 400 questions on Oppenheimer's activities since the late 1930s, not, he let himself be quoted, 'to leave a legacy of political trouble' but 'merely to acquaint the future staff of the Joint Committee with his concern about Oppenheimer'. This done, he handed over to his successor.[58]

As Borden left Washington, Strauss returned. In March 1953 he had been made Eisenhower's special assistant on atomic energy affairs, and on 3 July he succeeded Dean as Chairman of the AEC. As we have seen, Strauss and Oppenheimer had clashed head-on in 1949, and like Borden, he had queried Oppenheimer's loyalty. Indeed, they had both discussed the matter in August 1951. Now he was in a position to do something about it, if, like Borden, his suspicions were still alive.[59]

The accounts we have of Strauss' behaviour, from himself and from other sources, indicate that they were. According to Stern, little more than an hour after taking over at the AEC, he sent for the file on the export of radio-active isotopes, the topic on which he had had such a bitter disagreement with Oppenheimer four years before. A few days later, Herbert Marks received a telephone call from someone at the Commission with the warning that: 'You'd better tell your friend Oppy to batten down the hatches and prepare for some stormy weather.'[60]

Strauss took no immediate action, however, although it was later claimed that he had done so. In the statement put out by the AEC on 13 April 1954, the Commission was described as having 'initiated steps' as early as 7 July 1953 to 'organize the removal' of classified AEC documents from Oppenheimer's custody at Princeton. This had been done at Strauss' request, and the implication was that Strauss had foreseen the danger

Oppenheimer represented as soon as he had become Chairman, and had taken the first of the necessary counter-measures. In fact, there is no evidence that any such action was taken at this time. In December 1952, following Oppenheimer's departure from the GAC, Dean had ordered GAC documents to be transferred from him to Rabi, his successor as chairman of the Committee. Nothing further was done until after the suspension of Oppenheimer's clearance in December 1953, when all classified AEC material was taken from Oppenheimer's possession and sent to the Commission's headquarters in Washington.[61]

The statement of 13 April 1954 also asserted that Oppenheimer's file 'underwent preliminary study' by the AEC and the FBI some time between July and November 1953. This was in accordance with Section 4 of the new Executive Order 10450, which required all agency heads to review the cases of all employees with derogatory information in their dossiers. The assertion was repeated in Reston's column in *The New York Times* on 11 June, and it has been suggested that his information was supplied by Strauss. According to Stern, however, Commission records contain no mention of such a review, and this part of the AEC statement, like the other referred to above, seems very much open to question.[62]

The decisive move against Oppenheimer, then, does not seem to have been made until November, when Borden's letter was despatched to Hoover and when, as the statement of 13 April 1954 put it, the file 'had been brought up for definitive examination and appraisal'. Until this moment, Oppenheimer's enemies could be said to have been 'willing to wound, and yet afraid to strike'. They now struck, and with devastating effect.

Borden's letter produced the desired reaction within the administration for several reasons. In the first place, new and very much more stringent security criteria were now in force. The criterion established by Truman was severe enough. In April 1951 it had been altered from 'reasonable grounds . . . for belief that the person involved is disloyal to the Government of the United States' to the much broader standard of 'a reasonable doubt as to the loyalty of the person involved to the Government of the United States'. The Executive Order introduced by Eisenhower in April 1953, however, was even more exacting. The overriding criterion was that government employment should be 'clearly consistent with the interests of the national security', and loyalty was no longer to be the only factor, as it had been under Truman. Henceforth, all those 'privileged to be employed' in government were to be 'reliable, trustworthy, [and] of good conduct and character' as well as 'of complete and unswerving loyalty to the United States'. Oppenheimer had survived the test of the old system, but could he meet the requirements of the new, indeterminate and wide-ranging as they were?[63]

In the second place, Borden had raised an issue of the utmost gravity which had not been considered before—the hydrogen bomb. If his letter had simply reiterated the charges about Oppenheimer's past affinity with Communism, it is unlikely that it would have made a big impact. It had to include an allegation so serious as to make it imperative for the government to investigate it. The hydrogen bomb served the purpose because it had become the symbol of national power and because it appeared to be the guarantee of national survival. Therefore anyone accused of obstructing its development was in effect being accused of high treason, and statements like this, as Strauss put it, 'could not be brushed aside'.[64]

At the time of the hearing and later, Eisenhower claimed that the question of the H-bomb had not influenced him. As we have seen, on 7 April 1954 he had answered McCarthy's charges of an eighteen-month delay in the programme by saying that he had never heard of any such delay. Then, in his memoirs he said that he had given no weight to the hydrogen bomb allegations. 'Professor Oppenheimer's opposition to the hydrogen-bomb project', he wrote, 'could well have been a matter of conscience; it could have been his belief that, as a practical matter, the world would be better off if this development was stifled before birth.' He himself, he revealed, had been opposed to dropping the atomic bomb on Japan.[65]

These were puzzling remarks. As Lilienthal pointed out in his journal, if the H-bomb issue really was as insignificant as Eisenhower made out on 7 April, why had he appeared to attach so much importance to it the previous December when he ordered Oppenheimer's suspension? As we shall see, Eisenhower realized that the other charges relating to Communist associations were well-known and had already been examined at length, so that they alone could not have triggered off such an emphatic response.[66]

The answer may well lie in the circumstances surrounding the sending of Borden's letter. It was dated 7 November. On 6 November, Eisenhower's Attorney-General, Herbert Brownell, Jr, had accused Truman of nominating one of his officials, Harry Dexter White, to be director of the International Monetary Fund when he knew he had been a Communist spy. The FBI had reported White's alleged activities to Truman in December 1945, but he had gone on to nominate him in January 1946, and had allowed the Senate to confirm the nomination in February in spite of a second FBI report. When Hoover received Borden's letter, therefore, it is reasonable to suppose that he was especially concerned to see that the allegations were placed before the President, and it is equally reasonable to suppose that Eisenhower himself felt he had to react positively to Hoover's report, so as not to lay himself open to the same charge which his senior legal officer had levelled against Truman.[67]

This argument is reinforced when one remembers that this was precisely the moment when Senator McCarthy launched his first major offensive on the Eisenhower régime, with a speech on 24 November widely interpreted as a declaration of war. 'Over the past few months', McCarthy said, 'I have been becoming somewhat disturbed that my party might also fall victim to the same evil which beset the Democratic Party and did so much toward destroying this nation.' This attack was considered so serious that no less a figure than the Secretary of State was brought forward to reply to it on 1 December, and Eisenhower himself countered it the next day.[68]

The theme of Eisenhower's speech was that subversives would be uprooted by means of the security system he had set up in the spring. In saying this, he was asserting the primacy of the Executive branch over Congress as represented by McCarthy and his Subcommittee. He had done so on many occasions since assuming office. In his State of the Union message on 2 February 1953 he had proclaimed that 'the primary responsibility for keeping out the disloyal and the dangerous rests squarely upon the executive branch'. The first purpose of the security regulations he proposed to bring in was 'to make certain that this Nation's security is not jeopardized by false servants'. The second was 'to clear the atmosphere of that unreasoned suspicion that accepts rumor and gossip as substitutes for evidence'. In making the latter point, Eisenhower was directing an oblique blow at McCarthy and at the whole paraphernalia of congressional inquisition, and he repeated his intention at a Cabinet meeting on 5 March. 'Fairness, justice, and decency must characterize all the procedures that are set up to handle personnel', he is reported to have said; 'we cannot defeat Communism by destroying Americanism. We must observe every requirement of law and of ethics.'[69]

This, then, was the background to the events which took place after Hoover transmitted copies of his report on Oppenheimer and of Borden's letter to the White House, the Pentagon and the AEC on 30 November. On 2 December, the same day that he replied to McCarthy, Eisenhower was telephoned by Wilson, who asked him at once to 'terminate Oppenheimer's clearance to military installations'. McCarthy, Wilson added, was aware of Hoover's report and the Borden letter.[70]

The following afternoon, that is, on 3 December, Eisenhower summoned a meeting in his office. Present were Wilson, Brownell, Strauss, the President's Special Assistant for National Security Affairs, General Robert Cutler, the Director of the Office of Defense Mobilization, Dr Arthur S. Flemming, and a presidential aide, General Wilton B. Persons. As a result of their discussion, Brownell was ordered to place 'a blank wall between Dr Oppenheimer and any secret data', and to get the entire file from Hoover with a view to 'a thorough and prompt recommendation as to what further action should be taken'. As he understood it, wrote Eisenhower in his diary, 'this same [security] information, or at least the vast bulk of it, has been constantly reviewed and re-examined over a number of years, and . . . the over-all conclusion has always been that there is no evidence that implies disloyalty on the part of Dr Oppenheimer.' 'However,' he concluded, 'this does not mean that he might not be a security risk.'[71]

That Eisenhower himself intervened testifies to the importance which he attached to the Hoover report. There was no provision in any of the security statutes, orders or regulations for action of this kind on the part of the President, and it was clearly an emergency measure. Eisenhower later described it as 'almost compulsory under the circumstances'. It is so far impossible to say categorically that the initiative was taken in order to forestall Senator McCarthy, and in his memoirs Eisenhower goes out of his way to deny this, as did Vice-President Nixon on 16 April 1954. Nevertheless, all the evidence we have points in this direction, and it may be significant that in *Mandate For Change,* Eisenhower cites a letter sent him by the writer Robert E. Sherwood, in which Sherwood praised the instigation of the hearing as 'an entirely proper and wise action which will deprive McCarthy of a great deal of the headline thunder to which I am sure he was looking forward eagerly'.[72]

It is worth pointing out that the step was taken to protect the government and not Dr Oppenheimer. It requires little imagination to envisage how McCarthy would have exploited the case if the administration had not reacted as it did, and the dangers which it faced from this quarter were certainly real. It therefore appears to have considered it had no choice but to move, because of the fear—as Bush later put it—that inaction might be construed as complacency. This is exactly what the anti-Oppenheimer forces must have been banking on. If so, they calculated rightly, but it did not speak highly for the government that they should have been right. As one anonymous observer commented in the *Tribune* on 3 May 1954 :

> It is hard to suppress a question whether public officers have lost confidence in themselves and in the dependability of support from their superiors [a reference, presumably, to Hoover]; and whether their superiors, in turn, have lost confidence in their ability to face a possible storm of frightened and bewildered public feeling, fomented by reckless and unscrupulous political opportunists. Have they all felt drawn to play it safe? If so, it could mean that there exists in high places fear and inertia of a kind calculated to encourage the further growth of the elements of hysteria and recklessness which the Administration genuinely wants to curb.[73]

Seen in this light, Eisenhower's action does not seem as wise as Sherwood supposed; nor was it so proper as he believed, since it was taken without the knowledge of the Atomic Energy Commission as a whole. The point is important because the Commission held a collective responsibility and the Chairman alone could not represent it. Indeed, the Act providing for the summary suspension of government employees vested the power of suspension in the Commission and not in the Chairman. Therefore, all five Commissioners, and not just Strauss, should have been present when a decision of such gravity was in the making. That they were not was a serious breach of orderly procedure.[74]

According to Rolander, writing in a subsequent debate with the Alsops, there was no need for Strauss to consult his colleagues, and Strauss himself relates that he left it to the acting General Manager to tell them of the President's intervention. He could not do so as he was flying to Bermuda first thing the following morning for the summit conference which had been arranged with the French and British Prime Ministers, Laniel and Churchill. When he returned, he convened a meeting of the full Commission on 10 December and here the AEC procedures were set in motion by a unanimous vote, with the aim of determining the truth or falsity of the charges made by Borden. According to the AEC's official records, the other four Commissioners had still not seen either the FBI report or the Borden letter (although Strauss claims to have circulated copies as soon as he received them), and some of them apparently took the view that they had been 'ordered to proceed' by Eisenhower's directive. At least two of them, if this account is accurate, had no knowledge even then of precisely what had happened on 3 December.[75]

Such was the way in which the hearing was launched, but stranger things were still to come. Late in the afternoon of 11 December, Harold P. Green, a lawyer on the staff of the AEC General Counsel, William Mitchell, was given the assignment of drafting the formal charges against Oppenheimer. The Commissioners, Mitchell explained, were unhappy about bringing charges, and Strauss had been so troubled that he had 'sought divine guidance as to the proper course of action'. However, Eisenhower's suspension of Oppenheimer and the AEC regulations themselves left no alternative. He ended the conversation by giving two specific instructions. In the first place, Green was told not to include the allegations on the hydrogen bomb, as the Commission felt it would be inappropriate to seem to be trying Oppenheimer for his opinions. In the second place, he was enjoined to keep the matter entirely to himself, both for fear that there might be 'a scientists' strike' if it became public knowledge, and because, if Oppenheimer really were a Soviet agent (as Borden had asserted), it might prompt him to leave the country and make for Russia.[76]

Green began work on the draft at six o' clock in the morning of 12 December. As he worked, he was interrupted from time to time by Nichols, who, according to this account, talked to him at length about Oppenheimer, about his 'miserable attitude toward security', about the bad advice he had given the government, and about his arrogance. This, as Green knew, was coming from the same man who was scheduled to make the final decision on Oppenheimer's clearance.[77]

Green had finished his task by noon on 13 December, but as he waited for Mitchell to come in to look the draft over, he added something more. He had already inserted charges aimed at testing Oppenheimer's veracity, since he knew that this was often the decisive factor in security cases. He therefore put in additional charges on the hydrogen bomb, framed in such a way as to stress the issue of veracity, and these were accepted by Michell in spite of his previous insistence that they should be left out. They were also accepted by Nichols and by the Commission when it met the next day to approve the draft.[78]

This was the offhand way in which the H-bomb issue was injected into the hearing. In view of its importance, it seems extraordinary to say the least that it was not introduced with much greater care and after much lengthier deliberation. It is equally extraordinary that it should have been thought of only as providing material for a straightforward test of veracity when there was clearly much more at stake. The juxtaposition of the H-bomb charges with the charges relating to Communist sympathies at once brought up the matter of Oppenheimer's motivation, and the letter stated that the allegations as a whole raised questions not only as to his veracity but as to his conduct and even as to his loyalty. Nichols, in his report to the Commission of 12 June 1954, said explicitly that the section on the hydrogen bomb had been put in to test the good faith of Oppenheimer's opinions. Finally, it is astounding that not one of the five Commissioners who accepted the inclusion of the H-bomb charge on 14 December 1953 considered it of any consequence when they came to reach their verdicts six months later.[79]

All told, the sequence of events which began with the sending of Borden's letter and culminated with the approval of Nichols' letter of notification is a damning indictment of the American security system and of the Eisenhower administration. It is almost inconceivable that no one appears to have remarked on the venomous tone of Borden's letter or to have queried the accuracy of his facts in relation to the hydrogen bomb. If anyone's veracity and motivation were to be scrutinized, they should have been Borden's, yet even Smyth (according to Strauss) stated in a memorandum of 15 December that he believed the letter was important. This was 'not because it brings forward new evidence of any consequence but because of the position he has held as head of the staff of the Joint Congressional Committee on Atomic Energy'. So this outrageous document was allowed to be taken so seriously as to cause Oppenheimer's immediate suspension by the highest authority in the land. With that, the anti-Oppenheimer forces had achieved perhaps their most difficult objective, that is, setting the machinery of investigation in motion. The rest, given the nature of the security regulations and given the personalities involved, was comparatively simple.[80]

In short, the developments of the period 7 November–14 December were extremely disturbing if one remembers that they were supposed to be the prelude to an inquiry and not a political trial. Moreover, the unease one feels is heightened by two incidents which are said to have taken place on 14 December. In the first place, Green was telephoned by a special agent from the FBI with an offer of help in drawing up the indictment. This was very unusual indeed, since the FBI normally only responded to requests put to it by other agencies and rarely took such an initiative itself. In the second place, as Nichols was about to sign the papers to open the hearing procedures, he is said to have asked those present (including the Commission): 'Do we really have to go through with this? Why don't we just turn the file over to McCarthy?' It is scarcely credible that he should have dared to say this openly, but if he did, it is an indication of his supreme confidence that the matter was already virtually decided.[81]

The next step was to confront Oppenheimer with the news of his suspension, and a meeting was arranged in Strauss' office for the afternoon of 21 December. The previous day, however,

Strauss was telephoned by Marks—or, as he describes him, 'a man named Herbert Marks', a curious description in view of the fact that he must have known Marks reasonably well during his term as General Counsel of the AEC in 1947. Marks asked to see Strauss immediately, but was persuaded to wait until the morning of 21 December. When he met Strauss, he told him that he had heard that Oppenheimer was about to be publicly investigated by the Senate Internal Security Subcommittee headed by Senator William Jenner. The investigation, he said, should be stopped because it would be embarrassing to the AEC and to Vice-President Nixon, who had endorsed Oppenheimer at the time of the Crouch episode in May 1950. Strauss, who did not know of any such development, declined to pursue the matter further, and Marks left.[82]

When Oppenheimer arrived for his interview with Strauss, Nichols was also present. He was first of all asked whether he had known of Marks' visit, and said he had not. He was then told that his case had had to be re-evaluated under the terms of the new Executive Order, and that 'a former Government official who had occupied a responsible position in the preceding administration' had 'made a statement concerning him'. This had brought about a special report to the President by the FBI, and his clearance had been suspended pending a hearing.[83]

At this point, the accounts of the meeting diverge. Oppenheimer was handed a copy of Nichols' letter, and according to Strauss he read it carefully and then said that there many statements in it that were correct and others that were not. Oppenheimer himself, however, in the letter he wrote to Strauss the next day, said that he had 'paged through the letter quite briefly', and that Strauss and Nichols had told him that the charges in it were 'familiar charges'. This latter remark is one which it is difficult to imagine Strauss and Nichols making, and it is not surprising that it does not figure in the memorandum which Nichols dictated some time after the meeting and which forms the basis of Strauss' account.[84]

The second item on which Oppenheimer and the others conflict is the issue of whether Oppenheimer should resign rather than face a hearing. According to Strauss and Nichols, it was Oppenheimer who first raised the question and said that resignation would not look good if the Jenner Subcommittee

L

were in fact about to launch a public investigation. Oppenheimer, on the other hand, stated in his letter of 22 December
that Strauss had put it to him 'as a possibly desirable alternative'
that he should resign 'and thereby avoid an explicit consideration of the charges'. This Strauss has subsequently denied, but
Nichols states that he showed Oppenheimer a memorandum
which had been drawn up to notify AEC Laboratory Directors
in case Oppheimer did choose to resign; it even included a
sentence which said that he wished the matter to be kept secret.
It may well be that Strauss would have preferred Oppenheimer
to go quietly, but, as he himself has said, resignation would have
left all the charges on the record, and that is something he can
hardly have expected Oppenheimer to accept.[85]

The interview ended at 3.35, according to Nichols, and
Oppenheimer told Strauss that he was going to consult with
Marks at his nearby office. Instead, he went to the office of Volpe
and outlined what had just happened, to him and to Marks, who
joined the group soon after Oppenheimer's arrival. Since he had
been refused a copy of Nichols' letter, they had no opportunity
of examining the charges in detail. As they spoke, if we are to
believe one later account of their conversation, their words were
being recorded by a monitoring device. If this is true, it could
represent a remarkable feat on the part of the responsible government agents, since Oppenheimer had not indicated he was going
to see Volpe and since he entered Volpe's office less than half an
hour after he left the AEC. Alternatively, of course, Volpe's
chambers could already have been wired long before. Yet
whether or not eavesdropping did take place on this occasion, it
is significant that throughout the hearing Garrison and Oppenheimer behaved as though their telephones were being tapped
and as if there were listening devices hidden in the room set
aside for them in the AEC. The real centre of their work was
the Washington house of Garrison's partner, Randolph Paul,
where they believed they would be free from the attentions of
the secret service. Whether they were, we do not know.[86]

After lengthy discussions, Oppenheimer sent his reply to
Strauss on 22 December. He really had only one choice.

I have thought most earnestly of the alternative suggested
[resignation]. Under the circumstances, this course of action

would mean that I accept and concur in the view that I am not fit to serve this Government, that I have now served for some 12 years. This I cannot do. If I were thus unworthy I could hardly have served our country as I have tried, or been the Director of our Institute in Princeton [to which Strauss had nominated him in 1947], or have spoken, as on more than one occasion I have found myself speaking, in the name of our science and our country.[87]

The reply was received in the AEC on 23 December, and Nichols' letter was dispatched at once, thus initiating the hearing procedures. So Oppenheimer's enemies had at last succeeded in calling him to account, and in little more than six months they were to succeed in driving him out of public life beyond hope of return.

Chapter Nine

Aftermath

The aftermath of the Oppenheimer case was no less acrimonious than anything that had gone before. 'Great as the public controversy has been,' wrote Robert J. Donovan of the affair, ' . . . it pales by comparison with the impassioned bitterness below the surface. Few who were deeply involved in it on either side came out of this conflict without a mark, and some carry scars that will never heal in their lifetimes.'[1]

One of the first reverberations was the upheaval in the scientific community. Early in July 1954, when Strauss went to Los Alamos to present a presidential citation to the laboratory for its work on both fission and fusion weapons, he was met by a chorus of protest from many of the personnel on the site. Later in the month, at a conference at Los Alamos, Teller was snubbed and insulted by Rabi, and it was nine years before he visited the laboratory again.[2]

Feeling among the scientists was intensified towards the end of September, with the publication in the magazine *U.S. News & World Report* of extracts from the forthcoming book *The Hydrogen Bomb* by the journalists James R. Shepley and Clay Blair, Jr. This followed much the same lines as Murphy's anonymous *Fortune* article of May 1953, that is, it combined a detailed attack on Oppenheimer and his sympathizers with an extravagant eulogy of Strauss, Borden, McMahon and the remainder of the pro-H-bomb group. On 6 October, it was characterized by Representative Cole as 'a misleading portrayal', marked by 'omissions, part-truths and oversimplifications'. Gordon Dean, in his review for the *Bulletin of the Atomic Scientists*, was less restrained. 'This', he wrote, 'is a vicious book. And it is an untrue book . . . the publisher (with no attempt at humor, I am sure) has noted quite accurately that the book was "manufactured in the United States of America." Believe me, it was!' One man interviewed by Shepley and Blair had told him: 'It was clear from the time they entered the room that they were out to do an axe job. When I attempted to supply a few facts which would introduce perspective into their account, they were frankly uninterested.'[3]

In the light of this appraisal by a former Chairman of the Atomic Energy Commission, eminently well fitted to judge the accuracy of the book, it is interesting to note that the manuscript was passed by the AEC before publication. As Strauss recollects in his memoirs, this was to see whether it contained 'any information which might not be published without violating the law'. It passed the AEC review office in that respect,' he writes, with scrupulous qualification. At the same time, Strauss offered to buy the manuscript from Shepley and Blair to prevent the controversy it was bound to stir up among the scientists. This, at least, was the motivation ascribed to Strauss by Shepley in a television interview on 26 September. Lilienthal was less charitable. The following day he wrote in his journal that 'the real point is: he read the MS; he didn't try to get the falsities corrected, and the implication of trying to suppress it is that the story is true, but embarrassing to those who opposed him.'[4]

Strauss was right in thinking that the book would touch off uproar in the scientific world. Once again, a wave of protest welled up, especially over the implied claim that it had been Livermore, and not Los Alamos, which had perfected the hydrogen bomb. This had already provoked comment at the hearing. Bethe, when he gave evidence, remarked that the second weapons laboratory 'has been getting all the credit for thermonuclear development, which is unjustified'. Rabi had gone so far as to say that it was a lie to assert that Livermore had produced the bomb. These reactions were renewed in the autumn. On 24 September, Bradbury issued a statement on behalf of Los Alamos in which he declared that the laboratory had developed every successful thermonuclear weapon then in existence. Ten days later, he was followed by Fermi, in what was to be the last public utterance of his life—he died on 28 November. Both testified to the widespread sense of outrage among the physicists.

Yet more fuel was added to the fire by the publication in the October issue of *Harper's Magazine* of a long article by the Alsop brothers, entitled 'We Accuse!'. In it, the case for Oppenheimer and against Strauss was developed in detail, and it confirmed the suspicions of those who believed that Oppenheimer had been the victim of a personal vendetta. Just as *The Hydrogen Bomb* could be said to have been a brief for the prosecution, so the Alsops' article could be described as a case for the defence, and one unbound by the restraints which had marked Garrison's conduct at the hearing. Aggressive in tone and unashamedly partisan, it provided an immediate and effective rejoinder to Shepley and Blair and made some self-justification by the AEC imperative.[6]

The AEC's response to these developments was twofold. In the first place, Strauss was anxious to remove the impression which was still current among the scientists, namely, that they were now liable to dismissal as security risks for the advice they gave to the government. Early in July, he wrote to one Los Alamos employee : 'The Atomic Energy Commission does not believe that any government servant—scientist, engineer or administrator— should slant his advice or temper his professional opinion because of apprehension that such advice or opinion might be unpopular now or in the future.' Interviewed in December, he said that in the H-bomb debate of 1949, the GAC 'may have influenced some of the people on the Commission. That is what an adviser is supposed to do.' 'I can't believe you intend', he went on, 'that the fact that a man is a scientific adviser disqualifies him from expressing an opinion on a moral issue or on a political issue.'[7]

Strauss also appeared to be pursuing conciliation in other ways. Von Neumann's appointment to the Commission in October 1954 was seen as an effort to reassure the scientific community. So too was the departure of his personal assistant, David S. Teeple, the former aide of Senator Hickenlooper. Finally, Strauss was quick to turn down Lawrence's suggestion that Borden should succeed Nichols as General Manager when the latter announced his intention to resign at the end of 1954. This would undoubtedly have brought the crisis in the relations between the AEC and the scientists to a head, and it was something which Strauss could not afford to accept.[8]

At the same time, Teller attempted to soothe the feelings of those of his colleagues such as Fermi who rejected the assertion made by Shepley and Blair that he alone had been the progenitor of the H-bomb. His disclaimer was published in the February

1955 issue of *Science,* in an article significantly entitled 'The Work of Many People'. Here, Teller gave an extremely full account of the progress of the bomb from its theoretical beginnings to the successful test of November 1952. The bomb, he wrote, was 'the work of many excellent people who had to give their best abilities for years and who were all essential for the final outcome'. The picture presented of its being the achievement of a single individual was 'both untrue and unjust'. The development of the bomb, he concluded, 'should not divide those who in the past have argued about it but rather should unite all of us who in a close or distant way, by work or by criticism, have contributed toward its completion. Disunity of the scientists is one of the greatest dangers for our country.'[9]

The second aspect of the AEC's response was quite different. In October, a summary of the Alsops' article was included in, of all things, the monthly *Periodical Digest* put out by the Commission's Division of Public and Technical Information. This was an indication of a serious rift within the AEC, and the inclusion of the summary in the *Digest* seems to have been sanctioned by the Director of the Division, Morse Salisbury. At all events, the pro-McCarthy commentator, Fulton Lewis, Jr, reported that the AEC was reprimanding 'a top official' who had been 'brought in under Lilienthal' and who was 'a person of decided left-wing tendencies'.[10]

To counter the impact of the summary, Rolander, Robb's assistant at the hearing, drew up a list of excerpts from the Alsops' article which it seemed to him had taken serious liberties with the facts. These excerpts he rebutted with what, according to him, was the truth. On 25 October he sent the end-product to Nichols, and on 2 November Nichols asked Salisbury to circulate Rolander's memorandum to everyone on the distribution list for the *Digest*. On 10 November, Teeple's successor sent two copies of the memorandum to Roscoe Drummond, the columnist of *The New York Herald Tribune*. The Alsops' article was shortly to be published as a book, and Drummond was asked to send a copy of the memorandum to the *Tribune* reviewer. The Alsops themselves were not given the document, nor were they allowed to know who had received it. This decision, they were told, had been made 'at the very top', that is, by Strauss himself.[11]

Nonetheless, the Alsops eventually gained access to the memorandum, and in the 24 December issue of *US News & World Report,* all the arguments were set out: in the excerpts taken from their article; in Rolander's rebuttal; and in the Alsops' replies to Rolander's criticisms. All this was prefaced by a statement from the Alsops in which Rolander's memorandum was described as being 'more marked by bias than veracity'. 'The whole tone of the document', they wrote, 'constitutes the final proof that the Oppenheimer case was in no sense the judicial inquiry it was supposed to be, but a blindly partisan prosecution.' It was also introduced by a reply to the Alsops from Robb, who dismissed what he called their 'shrill abuse and malicious insinuations', and in which he defended himself against their charges of unfair behaviour at the hearing. In this connection, a critique of the hearing published by Professor Harry Kalven in the *Bulletin of the Atomic Scientists* was condemned with the comment that the *Bulletin* was 'a magazine which lists Dr J. Robert Oppenheimer as Chairman of its Board of Sponsors'. Clearly Robb had not lost his talent for innuendo.[12]

The exchange settled nothing one way or the other, and by this time attention was beginning to focus less on the details of the Oppenheimer case itself than on the broader issue of the security system as a whole. During Strauss' visit to Los Alamos in July 1954, he had been met by a deputation from the local branch of the Federation of American Scientists and handed a list of suggestions as to how the system might be improved. In the first place, the scientists proposed, the burden of proof should be taken off the employee and placed on the government. In the second place, the criteria of what constituted a security risk should be limited, and clearance should only be withheld if a man were 'demonstrably disloyal to our Constitution, clearly indiscreet in his protection of classified matters, dishonest, or susceptible to coercion to treason'. Thirdly, associations should not be one of the determinants of a finding. Fourthly, opinion should not fall within the scope of the security regulations, and lastly, there should be safeguards for the right to dissent after an administrative decision had been taken.[13]

In all these ways, the scientists hoped to protect themselves against what they saw as a system that had begun to get out of control. Three years beforehand, one writer had commented that in the current anti-Communist hysteria it was perfectly feasible for a foreign agent to deprive the country of its most distinguished scientists 'by a few words craftily spoken before some legislative committee or whispered anonymously to an FBI investigator!' In his article in *The New York Times*, Bush had seen this nightmare coming true. 'Are we to think', he asked, 'that some Communist who wishes to bring about confusion in Government can do so by merely filing under one name or another allegations against individuals in important positions? If so, the system offers an unbelievable opportunity to effect shutdowns of our efforts on various fronts.'[14]

The experience of others besides Oppenheimer seemed to bear out these speculations. In the spring of 1953, the Director of the National Bureau of Standards, Dr A. W. Astin, was suspended by the Secretary of Commerce, Sinclair Weeks, apparently on the grounds that the advice he had given on a certain battery additive had been hostile to small business interests. He was reinstated in August. Between July 1953 and September 1954, a hydrographer in the Navy Department, Abraham Chasanow, suffered lengthily at the hands of the system. Clearance was recommended by his personnel security board, but denied by the appeal board. After his case had been taken up, however, he was granted clearance following a second hearing. In July 1954, Condon was recommended for clearance by the appropriate security board, but two days after this was reported in the press, the Secretary of the Navy announced that he had asked the board to reconsider its decision and had again suspended clearance. Late in 1954, Wolf Ladejinsky, an expert on agrarian reform, was denied clearance by the Department of Agriculture when he was transferred there under a government reorganization. Hitherto he had been employed in the State Department and there he had enjoyed clearance. In this case, however, Eisenhower intervened beneficently, and through the Director of the Foreign Operations Administration, Harold Stassen, he was assigned to a post in South Vietnam. Six months later, in July 1955, he was cleared by the Secretary of Agriculture, Ezra Taft Benson.[15]

The fact that Ladejinsky had been reinstated was evidence of the concern that was being felt in some quarters at the working of the system. On 15 January 1954, Dulles is reported to have told the Eisenhower cabinet that the derogatory information in the files of some security risk cases in his department included such items as drunkenness, the existence of a pacifist in the family, or membership of the United World Federalists. In April 1954 it was revealed that one of the FBI reports on Charles E. Bohlen, Eisenhower's ambassador to Moscow, contained material from an informant who claimed to have a sixth sense. As described by Senator Guy M. Gillette, the informant had said that thanks to this attribute, he could 'look at a man and determine whether there was something immoral about him, or something pertaining to moral turpitude in the man's makeup, or some tendency on his part to take action that would not be accepted in good society as moral action'. Having looked at Bohlen, 'he determined that Mr Bohlen was a man who did have in the back of his mind such a tendency toward immorality as to make him unfit'. The following year a study of the system showed that the security dragnet had even been used to haul in a government meat inspector, and that indictments included such allegations as: 'you indicated a definite interest in Communist history and economics'; 'you displayed unreasonable sympathy toward Russia'; 'you were in close and continuing association with your parents with whom you resided until 1948'. It is easy to laugh these things off as absurdities, but for those who were penalized as a result it was to be no joke.[16]

Eisenhower's immediate reaction to the situation was to introduce a number of revisions to the programme, published on 4 March 1955. First, the statement of charges was to be drawn up as specifically as possible, and the senior legal officer in the agency in question was always to be consulted. The statement was to be given to the employee at the time he was told of his suspension. Second, the greatest possible care was to be exercised over suspension. A personal interview with the employee before suspension was proposed, and the legal officer responsible was to be asked whether in his view the material in the file justified suspension. Third, a legal officer was to be present at hearings to advise the security board on procedure and to inform the employee as to his rights if he were not represented by counsel. Fourth, to offset the fact that hearings could not be bound by the same restrictions as trials, agencies were to be sure that their security boards were composed of men of the highest integrity, ability and good judgment. Fifth, in the event of conflicting evaluations by two departments (such as there had in the case of Ladejinsky), there was to be full consultation, with the assistance of the Justice Department if need be. Sixth every effort was to be made to produce government witnesses so that the employee could confront them. This, however, was subject to the critical proviso that it would not endanger national security. Seventh and last, all violations of law under the system were to be reported to the Justice Department's Division of Internal Security.[17]

These modifications affected only the presidential programme, but the AEC procedures too were altered, in spite of the impression Strauss gives in his memoirs. On 17 January 1955, he writes, he brought together all the Laboratory Directors to review the security regulations. 'No material changes were suggested and the regulations were commended as eminently fair.' In May 1956, however, the new Procedures published in the *Federal Register* unmistakably reflected the experience of the Oppenheimer hearing and the additions they incorporated were by no means insignificant. In the first place, the counsel to the Board was instructed to 'avoid the attitude of a prosecutor' and always to 'bear in mind that the proceeding is an administrative hearing and not a trial'. This injunction had hitherto been confined to the Board, and it had clearly been inserted as the result of Robb's behaviour in the spring of 1954. Secondly, in the event that a government witness could not be produced for security reasons, the Board was to take this into account, and if it chose to do so, it could summon the witness for a thorough private examination. In this way, presumably, the value of the evidence of informers such as the Crouchs and others could be tested at first hand.[18]

Thirdly, in coming to its recommendation, the Board was to take notice of the fact that the employee might have been handicapped by the inability to confront confidential witnesses or by the non-disclosure of confidential information. This, of course, called to mind Robb's continual use of classified documents which Garrison had not been able to see. At the same time, the Board was allowed to take into consideration other things which had previously not been mentioned—the employee's past record with the atomic energy programme, and the nature and sensitivity of the jobs he might be expected to undertake. If these regulations had been in force at the time of the Oppenheimer hearing, they could not but have inclined the Gray Board in a more favourable direction.[19]

Fourthly, in the section relating to the Security Review Board it was stated that this board could take additional testimony from witnesses and could request additional briefs if it believed this was appropriate. The point of this could well lie in the situation which obtained in June 1954, when the Review Board's place was taken by the Commission, and when Garrison had not been able to present a brief to the Commission which was relevant to the General Manager's report. It still left the initiative with the Review Board, but at least it offered an opportunity to avoid a repetition of the injustice which had been committed at that stage of the case.[20]

Finally, the new Procedures stipulated that where clearance had been granted, an individual's case should only be reconsidered if 'new substantially derogatory information' were brought up, or if there were a significant increase in the scope or in the sensitivity of the restricted data to which he had access. Conversely, where clearance had been denied, a case might be reconsidered if there were a bona fide offer of employment and if at the same time either new evidence were introduced or the employee could submit 'convincing evidence of reformation or rehabilitation'. A great deal here naturally depended on interpretation, but it was at least possible under these regulations that Oppenheimer's 1947 clearance would have held good in the face of Borden's accusations, and the possibility would no doubt have been even stronger if the second of Eisenhower's revisions of 4 March 1955 had been in force at the time Borden's letter reached the administration.[21]

Taken together, both the modifications in the presidential programme and those in the AEC Procedures marked a considerable advance, but they did not answer the call for a fundamental review of the security system which was going up from about the end of 1954. Indeed, the government took great pride in the statistics of dismissals under Executive Order 10450 which were issued in July 1955. During the period between 28 May 1953, when the Order came into force, and 31 March 1955, when the investigations it required were deemed to have been completed, 3,432 people were said to have been dismissed and 5,447 to have resigned. This was out of a total of some 2.3 million Federal employees.[22]

The real value of this purge was very much open to doubt, however. As the editor of the *Bulletin of the Atomic Scientists* had pointed out in 1951, if the truly dangerous Communists took care to keep quiet and avoid a formal Party commitment, they were unlikely to be spotted by checks on loyalty. There was also the risk that in its zeal to leave no stone unturned, the government was defeating its own object. Every security case was apparently being treated as if it were of the same importance, when it was obvious that some were very much more important than others. In this undiscriminating quest for purity, what was crucial could well be overlooked, with disastrous consequences.[23]

The response was the setting-up of a commission in August 1955. Its terms of reference were to examine the operation of the Federal security programmes and of Congressional investigations. Meanwhile, a private study of the Federal programmes was already in progress under the auspices of the Association of the Bar of the City of New York. Its report, issued in July 1956, made several recommendations for drastic changes. Among other things, a single criterion was urged, to replace the numerous criteria set up by Executive Order 10450, namely, 'whether or not in the interest of the United States the employment or retention in employment of the individual is advisable'; associations were to be taken into account but not if they did not appear to be substantive. The charges against an employee were to be drawn up, not by the agency in which he worked, but by a Central Screening Board in the Civil Service Commission. Indeed, the whole programme was to be fully centralized under a Director in the Executive Office of the President. In this way, it was hoped, the confusion arising from the extreme de-centralization of the system established by Eisenhower could be avoided. As for the hearing procedures, it was suggested that the attorney for the government should not be present during the deliberations of the hearing board (as Robb had been), and that whenever witnesses could not be produced for security reasons, the inability of the employee to confront them should be taken into consideration. Finally, the programme was to apply to those in sensitive positions only, and not to all Federal employees, and as far as possible successive determinations of security risk were to be avoided if the evidence had not changed. If new evidence were brought forward, a case should only be re-opened with the joint agreement of the Central Screening Board and the head of the agency involved.[24]

None of these proposals was taken up by the White House, although they would undoubtedly have improved the security system to a very significant extent. On the other hand, Eisenhower also chose to ignore the proposals of the governmental Commission which reported in June 1957. These, if implemented, would have widened the scope of the system still further, by requiring the investigation of *every* Federal employee, that is, civil servants in the Legislative and Judicial branches besides those in the Executive branch. The Commission also proposed that evidence culled from wire-tapping should become admissible, and that the disclosure of classified information by those outside as well as inside government should be penalized. It upheld the distinction between loyalty and security which the Eisenhower system had drawn, and it accepted criteria for the programme as wide-ranging as those listed in Executive Order 10450. It also accepted that the final decision on security should lie with the departmental head, although the preliminary stages of hearings and appeals were to be placed in the hands of a central security office.[25]

Such further changes as did take place in the security system came about at the instance of the Supreme Court, which, under its new Chief Justice, Earl Warren, was emerging as the country's principal guarantor of individual liberties. In June 1955, the Court upheld the appeal of Dr John Peters of Yale University against his dismissal by a review board in 1953, on the grounds that the board had exceeded its competence in reaching the decision on dismissal itself. In April 1956, the Court ordered a case decided after a hearing before the Subversive Activities Control Board to be returned to the Board for another hearing, because of the 'tainted evidence' of several witnesses, among them none other than Paul Crouch, Oppenheimer's accuser in 1950. In June 1956, the Court ruled that government employees could only be dismissed for security reasons if they occupied sensitive posts; this was in the case of a former food and drug inspector removed two years previously because of his political associations.

Four days later Brownell ordered the immediate reinstatement of all such workers in accordance with the Court's directive. Finally, a year later, the Court prescribed that in criminal prosecutions confidential FBI reports must be made available to the defence. This arose from the case of a man sentenced to five years in gaol partly on the basis of reports from an FBI informer, Harvey Matusow, who subsequently recanted his testimony and was convicted of perjury. How much evidence of this calibre lay in Oppenheimer's dossier can only be guessed at, but it is probably safe to assume that it contained some. Whatever the proportion, it undoubtedly influenced his judges against him.[26]

Valuable as these reforms were, however, none of them affected Oppenheimer's position. He was to be excluded from public service for the rest of his life, and it hit him hard. As Garrison has written, 'the blow was a lasting one, which he took with him to his grave'. In Bethe's words, 'he was a changed person, and much of his previous spirit and liveliness had left him'.[27]

In one important respect his standing was undiminished. On 1 October 1954 he was unanimously reelected by the trustees as head of the Institute for Advanced Study. Among them were Garrison and Strauss. As Strauss later presumptuously described it: 'I retained him in the academic position he holds by virtue of the fact I had invited him to take it.' Strauss' action may seem strange in view of his recent vote against Oppenheimer's clearance, but, as one commentator has written, 'apparently to Strauss, Oppenheimer out of a responsible position in government was not the same man that he was in a responsible position out of government, or to be judged by the same standards'.[28]

Others were less certain than Strauss that Oppenheimer could be trusted to hold a place in the academic world. In February 1955, the President of the University of Washington, Dr Henry Schmitz, vetoed an invitation which had been extended to Oppenheimer to lecture in the university for three months. It was, he believed, 'not . . . in the best interests of the university'. Two years later, an invitation to Oppenheimer to deliver the William James lectures at Harvard was also opposed, but this time unsuccessfully.[29]

Caution also marked the government's attitude to Oppenheimer, even after his dismissal. In mid-July 1954, he had taken his family cruising off the Virgin Islands and before leaving had gone to the trouble of informing J. Edgar Hoover of his destination, presumably so as to reassure the authorities he was not about to leave the country. He need not have bothered to do so. In March 1955 Lilienthal was on holiday in the Virgin Islands and discovered that the FBI were still shadowing Oppenheimer, who had recently been there on a further visit. How much longer the surveillance was kept up we do not know, but it was clear that the administration were taking no chances that he might make a bid to defect to the Soviet Union.[30]

By this time, Oppenheimer had regained a great deal of the sympathy he had lost when the transcript and the verdict of the AEC were published. This was with at least one significant exception: Chevalier. When the transcript came out in June 1954, Chevalier had naturally been shocked to find what Oppenheimer had done to him by the cover story he had concocted in 1943. There followed an agonized correspondence with Oppenheimer which lasted the rest of the year, and an open letter to Oppenheimer published in the Paris magazine *France-Observateur* early in December. Chevalier believed, with a good deal of justification, that Oppenheimer had inflicted serious damage on his career, and when he accused him of doing this Oppenheimer could not offer a convincing reply. With Chevalier's final letter to him of 13 December, their long friendship can be said to have come to an end.[31]

Shortly after this, Oppenheimer's name dropped out of the headlines, and he entered comparative obscurity. Public interest in him was revived dramatically, however, in the autumn of 1957, when the Soviet Union placed its first artificial satellites, Sputnik I and Sputnik II, in orbit round the earth. By this achievement, Russia appeared to have gained an enormous and possibly decisive lead over the United States in a field which could be critical to national security. At once the call went up for a mobilization of scientific effort, and several leading figures came out in support of the idea that Oppenheimer should be allowed to return at once to government service.

In November, for example, the former Assistant Secretary for the Air Force, Trevor Gardner, suggested that the President's Special Assistant for Science and Technology, Dr James R.

Killian, might 'ask himself' whether Oppenheimer should not be brought back as a consultant and Senator Henry M. Jackson of the Joint Committee considered it 'entirely proper' for the AEC to arrange for a re-hearing of the case. Early in December, nine of the seventeen members of the new presidential Scientific Advisory Committee were said to feel that Oppenheimer should be used again, while Rabi was quoted as saying that 'American scientists would look upon it as elementary justice for a man who was smeared to be restored'.[32]

The most notable comment came, however, from the erstwhile Commissioner Murray, who, it will be remembered, had not only found Oppenheimer a security risk in 1954 but disloyal into the bargain. Asked on 21 November what his views on Oppenheimer now were, Murray had replied that 'I would not be at all displeased if he were to be reinstated'. A decision for reinstatement 'would simply be a new decision taken within the context of the national interest, to be judged on its own merits'. The decision taken by the Commission in 1954 had been made 'within the context of the exigencies of the moment'. In other words, it had been formed on political grounds rather than on grounds of principle, and now that political circumstances had changed, a different verdict could be rendered.[33]

This, coming from a man who had worded his 1954 opinion in the most abstract and philosophical terms, was nothing short of amazing. Murray's new-found flexibility was not, however, shared by Chairman Strauss. On 8 January 1958 Strauss stated that the AEC had no plans to re-open the Oppenheimer case. The onus lay on Oppenheimer to re-apply for clearance or to submit 'substantial new evidence'. If such evidence existed, it would be considered, but Strauss himself was not aware there was any. It did not take much perspicacity to see that Oppenheimer had nothing to hope for from this quarter, and it is hardly surprising that no initiative from Oppenheimer was forthcoming. He remained in his exclusion, in spite of continued protests from the scientific community.[34]

At the same time, it should be noted that although Oppenheimer personally recovered no ground, the recommendation he had made in 1953 for greater official candour in the nuclear sphere at last began to be taken up vigorously by the administration. In the wake of the Sputniks, Eisenhower made two important speeches in which he took the public into the government's confidence to an extent so far unprecedented. Equally significantly, there was an immediate relaxation of the restrictions on sharing secret information with America's allies. On 25 October 1957, Eisenhower and the British Prime Minister, Harold Macmillan, issued a 'Declaration of Common Purpose' which envisaged much closer collaboration in the nuclear field. On 27 January 1958 Strauss proposed amendments to the 1954 Atomic Energy Act to enable the release of both information on weapons and of weapons material to an allied power, and on 2 July 1958 the Act was so amended, with the United Kingdom being the first country to benefit. It was an unmistakable victory for Oppenheimer's school of thought.[35]

By the same token, it was a defeat for advocates of a tightly restrictive information policy such as Strauss, and during 1958 and 1959 Strauss was to suffer further setbacks. In the spring of 1958, with his five-year term as AEC Chairman drawing to a close, Strauss was offered re-appointment by Eisenhower, but foresaw a bitter fight in the Senate over his confirmation and so resigned. Strauss' fears about his stock in the Senate had a real basis. The following year, having been designated as Secretary of Commerce by the President, he was refused confirmation after three months of hearings, and left public life that summer, like Oppenheimer, never to return.

Since confirmation is very rarely denied to a presidential nominee, this was a bitter blow for Strauss, and he himself has admitted that the Oppenheimer affair had a part in it. He was, for example, confronted by two Los Alamos scientists, David R. Inglis and David L. Hill, and accused by Inglis of having been motivated by 'personal vindictiveness' in 1954. 'It is he', said Inglis, quoting Strauss' condemnation of Oppenheimer back at him, 'who, because of "substantial defects of character" ... is unfit to serve on the President's cabinet.'[36]

There were many other echoes of the Oppenheimer case, among them the appearance of Teller to testify on Strauss' behalf and the introduction of the issue of the export of radio-isotopes, which had caused such a rift between Strauss and Oppenheimer ten years earlier. The most striking similarity, however, came in the tactics and the material used by his opponents to discredit Strauss. On one occasion, he was cross-examined about a letter written several years before, and his lapses of memory presented as lying; how often had Robb used the same device against Oppenheimer! At the same time, documentation was brought forward equally as dubious (if Strauss' account is to be believed) as some featured during the Oppenheimer case. One item was 'a document containing many assertions at second hand by persons who were not identified and also a number of untrue statements'. Another was 'a prepared statement containing allegations, many introduced by such expressions as "It is believed", "It is reported", "It is generally credited", "The impression was" and an assortment of innuendoes'. Another was an anonymous memorandum. The descriptions of the first and second could just as well apply to Nichols' letter of notification, while the third has its exact equivalent in the anonymous AEC memorandum of 14 March 1947 used during Bacher's testimony. So Strauss was subjected to the same techniques which had helped to destroy Oppenheimer five years before.[37]

He too was wrecked, as Oppenheimer had been, although his confirmation was recommended by a majority of the Senate Commerce Committee. The minority, on the other hand, found him to be 'lacking in the degree of integrity and competence essential to proper performance of the duties of the office to which he has been nominated', and it was their view which prevailed in the Senate when a vote came to be taken. Strauss was rejected by 49 to 46, and he departed from office less than a fortnight afterwards.[38]

Oppenheimer meantime remained in the wilderness, but with the advent of the Kennedy administration he enjoyed at least a partial rehabilitation. On 5 April 1963 it was announced that he was to receive the Enrico Fermi Award, given annually by the AEC in memory of Fermi. The recommendation by the General Advisory Committee had been unanimous, as had been the acceptance by the Commission.[39]

This was the culmination of years of effort on the part of Oppenheimer's sympathizers. In 1958, shortly after Strauss left the Commission, the chairman of the Joint Committee, Senator Anderson, had asked for the case to be reviewed. Strauss' successor, John A. McCone, had directed the General Counsel, Loren K. Olson, to do so, and Olson had found that there was 'a messy record from a legal standpoint, that the charges kept shifting at each level of the proceedings, that the evidence was stale and consisted of information that was twelve years old and was known when a security clearance was granted during World War II, and that it was a punitive, personal abuse of the judicial system'. This was precisely what Oppenheimer's supporters had been saying since 1954, and when Olson was appointed to the Commission in 1960 he tried to devise an arrangement whereby Oppenheimer's clearance could be restored.[40]

Nothing came of this, as might have been expected while Eisenhower was still in office, and it was not until after Kennedy had become President in 1961 that the government began to change its attitude. The impetus came from the Federation of American Scientists, which in October 1961 petitioned the AEC to re-open the case. The Federation was supported in this by Volpe and by several members of the Joint Committee, and Olson proposed in March 1962 that Oppenheimer be appointed as a consultant and cleared by the Commission after the usual investigation.[41]

In the event, however, the Commissioners took no decision, on the curious grounds that the matter was beyond their competence, and it was left to Kennedy to take the first gingerly step towards making amends. At the end of April 1962, Oppenheimer was among the guests at a White House dinner for Nobel Prize-winners (although he himself was not one). There, apparently, he was asked whether he wanted another hearing by the AEC Chairman, Seaborg, his former colleague on the General Advisory Committee. The answer was an emphatic 'no', and the administration was left to resume the initiative. Eventually, it was decided to adopt the solution of the Fermi Award.[42]

This, it should be remembered, was at best a conciliatory gesture and it did not restore Oppenheimer's security clearance. As *The New York Herald Tribune* described it, it was 'an honor, not an indemnity'. There was to be no revision of the judgment issued in 1954, and Oppenheimer remained immured behind the 'blank wall' which Eisenhower had set up to cut him off from the secrets of state. In 1957 Rabi had written that 'only when he [Oppenheimer] is returned to more active Government service will it indicate that a change of heart has occurred'. Kennedy's action gave no such indication.[43]

Indeed, the administration approached the issue with the most extreme circumspection. In the first place, it delayed making an announcement until after the mid-term elections of November 1962 for fear of a hostile public reaction. Then, as the date for the presentation of the prize drew close, *The New York Times* reported that it was 'not insensitive to the possible political repercussions of giving an award to Dr Oppenheimer'. There were even doubts about 'the political desirability of having the President present the award personally at a public ceremony in the White House'.[44]

This cautiousness was in part a response to the criticisms being voiced in some Republican circles. In July 1963 Representative Craig Hosmer of California demanded that Kennedy should make it clear that the bestowal of the prize 'does not condone the recipient's actions which lost him his security clearance'. Senator Hickenlooper for his part announced that he would introduce legislation giving Congress control over future selection policy, and on 27 November he sent a letter to the AEC opposing the choice of Oppenheimer outright. 'I fail to see how anyone who has any respect for the security system of the United States could support this award,' he wrote. 'I have been unable to find convincing evidence of any outstanding contribution to atomic science such as could be attributed to other recipients of the Fermi Award that could be credited to Dr Oppenheimer other than the fact that he is a scientist and was engaged in organization and coordination activities during the Manhattan Project.'[45]

Hickenlooper's astonishing statement was a reminder that the old hatreds still smouldered. So too was the conspicuous absence of the Republican members of the Joint Committee from the presentation ceremony which took place on 2 December, the anniversary of Fermi's pioneering chain reaction. Strauss also had declined an invitation to be there, but Teller, who had received the 1962 prize, was among the gathering and shook hands with Oppenheimer before the photographers. The award was handed over by President Johnson, who had so recently succeeded to the White House after the assassination of Kennedy on 22 November. 'I think it just possible, Mr President,' said Oppenheimer, 'that it has taken some charity and some courage for you to make this award today. That would seem to me a good augury for all our futures.'[46]

The following day, *The New York Times* wrote that the occasion 'served to write *finis* to the controversy surrounding Dr Oppenheimer'. It could not and it did not. Oppenheimer was still banned from government employment on the basis of the decision arrived at in 1954, and the AEC was still insistent that the first move for a reconsideration of his clearance must come from him. This was a condition which no man of any pride could be expected to agree to, and it was a foregone conclusion that Oppenheimer should refuse to make such an approach. When he died in February 1967, the interdict pronounced on him so long before remained in force, and he had not recovered the confidence of the state he had served with such distinction.[47]

Oppenheimer was destroyed by two of the most powerful forces of his time—an uncompromising anti-Communism, and the cult of weapons of mass destruction as the embodiment of American national strength. As we have seen, anti-Communism in the United States became a major political issue in the decade after the Second World War, with the emergence of the Soviet Union as a rival super-power and with the installation of a Communist régime in China. Democrats and Republicans, Congress and the President vied strenuously with each other to prove their Americanism with a flood of statutes, orders and investigations, all aimed at stamping out Communist influences in every quarter. At the same time, nuclear weapons were given pride of place in the American response to the Communist challenge on the international plane. The monopoly of the atomic bomb seemed to put the United States in an unassailable position, and even when the monopoly was lost, possession of the hydrogen bomb was seen as the best guarantee of the country's security. This feeling was reinforced by the heavy losses sustained in Korea, and reliance on the bomb was given the status of a doctrine in Dulles' announcement of the policy of 'massive retaliation' in January 1954.

It was not a healthy climate for a man with Oppenheimer's political background and strategic concepts. His pro-Communist period condemned him in a number of ways. He had been closely associated with the Communist Party for several years, associated, moreover, at a time when the barbarities of Stalinism were becoming widely known and when the USSR was aligned with its supposed arch-enemy, Nazi Germany. Oppenheimer was certainly unfortunate in the timing of his relationship with the Communist movement. If it had begun at the outset of the Depression and ended in the late 'thirties, he would have been much better placed later on. As it was, he laid himself open to the suspicion that his disengagement was merely a tactical man-oeuvre brought about by the need to infiltrate himself into a key position in the American war effort. This in turn lent colour to the charge of attempting to promote the interests of his Communist friends and acquaintances during the war, and to the belief that his Communist sympathies were maintained in the post-war years.

It is not difficult to modify this picture and to point out the things that offset it. Oppenheimer, it should be remembered, was never a member of the Communist Party, and his connection with it (like that of many others) seems to have been determined largely by his admiration for Communism as a force for social justice. It is also worth noting that it was the Soviet Union and not the democracies which came actively to the defence of Spain and China at the close of the 'thirties, and this did a great deal to preserve its good image in non-Communist circles. As for the war and the post-war period, there is every evidence that Oppenheimer was determined to put his career before his politics and to dissociate himself from any feature of his past which could act as a stumbling-block to his future as a servant of the state.

None of this made any impression on Oppenheimer's critics, however. Nor did the arguments he deployed against the hydrogen bomb. Probably after Alamagordo and certainly after Hiroshima and Nagasaki, Oppenheimer knew that the forces he had helped to unleash could well bring about a world catastrophe; this was why he became wedded to policies that would restrain them by every possible means. The proposals he set out were not perfect, nor was it pretended that they were. The introduction of tactical atomic weapons and continental air defence might only serve to postpone the outbreak of a full-scale nuclear war. To disclose the predictable facts about such a war might only stimulate widespread panic. To pass on top-secret material to America's allies might only foster the spread of nuclear weapons. Yet in all these ways, Oppenheimer and those who thought like him were plainly trying to reduce to tolerable proportions the huge element of risk involved in living in the atomic era.

By doing so Oppenheimer was placing himself in the extremely difficult position of advising moderation when severe pressures were being exerted for an unqualified response to the country's problems. It was inevitable that he should cross those who were convinced that the security of the United States must and could be made absolute in every respect. Oppenheimer, on the other hand, took the view that security was consistent with solutions that were less than total, and that extremism could easily be self-defeating, even disastrous. It was a cogent argument, and the policies it underlay were certainly more practical and less dangerous than those supported by Oppenheimer's opponents. To men who equated loyalty with unreserved acceptance of their own point of view, however, they were not far short of treasonable.

The fact that Oppenheimer had made enemies is not remarkable. High politics are marked by an endless series of such bitter controversies. What is astonishing is that the accusations levelled against him were taken seriously by the responsible authorities. That they were was due principally to two men, Senator McCarthy and President Eisenhower. McCarthy's influence in paving the way for the instigation of the hearing was very significant, without much doubt, and here luck played a great part. Eight months later, after his defeat by the Army, McCarthy was a spent force and any initiative taken against Oppenheimer then would almost certainly have failed. Yet even given McCarthy's indirect assistance, it was to President Eisenhower that the anti-Oppenheimer camp had most cause to be grateful. Only a few weeks before, Eisenhower had sanctioned major policy-changes promoted by Oppenheimer. He knew that his pro-Communist past had not so far caused his dismissal. He professed to attach no importance to his attitude to the hydrogen bomb. Nonetheless, he suspended Oppenheimer's security clearance.

This, and everything that followed, was an act of the deepest injustice to Dr Oppenheimer. There was to be no real reparation, however, either from Eisenhower or from his successors, even when it was realized that a wrong had been done and that Oppenheimer still had an important contribution to make as a policy adviser. Governments rarely admit their mistakes, particu-

larly over issues as momentous as those raised here. So infalli-
bility was preserved, but at a high price to America's good name
as well as to Oppenheimer himself. From start to finish the Oppenheimer case did grave damage to the principles the United States
claims to cherish. Above all, perhaps, it indicated that the
interests of the state could not be reconciled with the freedom of
an individual. It may, of course, be that they are irreconcilable,
even in a democracy professing full respect for individual rights.
If so, then Oppenheimer's experience is an ominous pointer to the
future for us all.

References

CHAPTER 1
1 J. R. Shepley and C. Blair, Jr, *The Hydrogen Bomb* (London, Jarrolds, 1955), 193. Hereafter cited as Shepley & Blair
2 R. Cohn, *McCarthy* (New York American Library, 1968), 110–30
3 *Bulletin of the Atomic Scientists*, 10 (1954), 163–4. Hereafter cited as *BAS*. *Public Papers of the Presidents of the United States. Dwight D. Eisenhower. 1954* (Washington, DC, United States Government Printing Office, 1960), 372–81. Hereafter cited as *Public Papers 1954*
4 *US News & World Report*, 16 April 1954, 39. Hereafter cited as *USN & WR*
5 *The New York Times*, 8 April 1954. Hereafter cited as *NYT*
6 *Public Papers 1954*, 382, 389. *USN & WR*, 15 August 1960, 72. Senator Bourke B. Hickenlooper was not reassured by the President. On 16 April he was to say that the bomb had been delayed 'several years' because 'important people' had 'definite and powerful objections'. *NYT*, 17 April 1954
7 *NYT*, 13 April 1954
8 Text in United States Atomic Energy Commission, *In the Matter of J. Robert Oppenheimer. Transcript of Hearing Before Personnel Security Board. Washington, DC April 12, 1954, through May 6, 1954* (Washington, DC, United States Government Printing Office, 1954), 3–7. Hereafter cited as *Tr*.
9 Text in *Tr*., 7–20
10 Text in *BAS*, 10 (1954), 187
11 *The Christian Science Monitor*, 13 April 1954 and *The New York Herald Tribune*, 13 April 1954. The latter hereafter cited as *NYHT*. P. M. Stern, *The Oppenheimer Case* (New York, Harper & Row, 1969), 516–7. Hereafter cited as Stern. The former AEC Chairman, David Lilienthal, had forecast McCarthy's attack more than six months previously when he wrote in his journal that 'one of these days McCarthy or some similar rabble-rouser would see the pay-dirt in a sensational to-do about the H-bomb and the devils who were "against it"'. D. E.

Lilienthal, *The Journals of David E. Lilienthal. Volume III. The Venturesome Years 1950–1955* (New York, Harper & Row, 1966), 424. Hereafter cited as Lilienthal III.

12 *NYT*, 14 April 1954
13 *NYHT*, 14 and 16 April 1954
14 *NYT*, 17 April 1954
15 *Tr.*, 501–3
16 *NYT*, 13 April 1954. Stern, 507
17 *BAS*, 10 (1954), 189, 173
18 *Manchester Guardian*, 14 April 1954. Cooke was, of course, wrong in inferring that Oppenheimer was charged with Communist Party membership

CHAPTER 2

1 The text of Public Law 733 of 26 August 1950 is at 64 STAT. 476, and in D. B. Bonsal (chairman), *Report of the Special Committee on the Federal Loyalty-Security Program of the Association of the Bar of the City of New York* (New York, Dodd, Mead & Company, 1956), 227–9. See also ibid., 84. Hereafter cited as Bonsal. The text of the Atomic Energy Act of 1 August 1946 is at 60 STAT. 755 and in *BAS*, 2/3 & 4 (1946), 18–25

2 United States Atomic Energy Commission, *Security Clearance Procedures;* the text is at 15 Federal Register 6241. Hereafter cited as *Procedures*. United States Atomic Energy Commission, *Personnel Security Clearance Criteria for Determining Eligibility;* the text is at 15 Federal Register 8093. Hereafter cited as *Criteria*

3 The text is at 18 Federal Register 2489

4 Text in *Tr.*, 837–8

5 Ibid., 834, 835, 839. Borden later stated that he had more evidence to back up his charges, but that he was not allowed to present it. See Stern, 353

6 *Public Papers 1954*, 435. United States Atomic Energy Commission, *In the Matter of J. Robert Oppenheimer. Texts of Principal Documents and Letters of Personnel Security Board, General Manager, Commissioners. Washington, DC May 27, 1954, through June 29, 1954* (Washington, DC, United States Government Printing Office, 1954), 57. Hereafter cited as *Texts*

7 *Tr.*, 3–7

CHAPTER 3

1 This account relies largely on Oppenheimer's letter of 4 March 1954 (the relevant section is in *Tr.*, 8–11) and partly on H. Chevalier, *Oppenheimer* (London, André Deutsch, 1966), 13–46. Hereafter cited as Chevalier

2 D. Trilling, 'The Oppenheimer Case: A Reading of the Testimony', *Partisan Review*, 31 (1954), 620

3 *Tr.*, 327, 440–1, 113–4, 885

4 Ibid., 266

5 Ibid., 11, 582

6 R. G. Hewlett and O. E. Anderson, Jr., *The New World, 1939–1946* (University Park, Pa., Pennsylvania State UP, 1962), 46, 54, 61, 103. Hereafter cited as *New World*. See also *Tr.*, 11

7 *New World*, 74, 81–2, 229–30 and *Tr.*, 12, 561

8 *BAS*, 7 (1951), 364 and *Tr.*, 165, 260. See also H. Childs, *American Genius: The Life of Ernest Orlando Lawrence* (New York, Dutton, 1968), 338–9. Hereafter cited as Childs

9 Childs, 320. *New World*, 228–32. *Tr.*, 12, 29–31, 325, 262

10 *Tr.*, 260–1

11 Pash's memorandum of 29 June 1943 is in ibid, 821–3. The same day, Oppenheimer was sent a personal letter from Roosevelt, stressing the need for tight security! Ibid., 29–30

12 Ibid., 170, 736, 261, 823. L. R. Groves, *Now It Can Be Told* (London, André Deutsch, 1963), 141. Hereafter cited as Groves.

13 See W. B. Huie, 'Who Gave Russia the A-Bomb?, *The American Mercury*, April 1951, 416–8

14 *Texts*, 8–9. *Tr.*, 573–6, 13, 119–20, 122–3, 124–8, 878. For the probable reason why Weinberg was allowed to be taken on by the Radiation Laboratory, see above, p. 60

15 *Tr.*, 172, 268, 275–6, 263

16 Ibid., 847, 880, 277, 117–8, 134

17 Ibid., 876, 883, 277. In March 1944, Oppenheimer referred a request from Bohm for transfer to Los Alamos to Pash's assistant, DeSilva, who turned it down. Ibid., 149–50

18 Ibid., 14, 263, 136, 130, 875

19 Ibid., 14, 136, 848

20 Ibid., 137, 813. The text of the Pash interview is in ibid., 845–53

21 Ibid., 846–7

22 Ibid., 845–6

23 Ibid., 845, 847, 851

24 Ibid., 845, 848, 852

25 Ibid., 850, 852, 820, 814, 815

26 Ibid., 816

27 Ibid., 273–5. At the close of the hearing, Silverman read out a letter of 11 April 1945 from DeSilva to Oppenheimer, thanking him for 'the support and encouragement which you have personally given me'! Ibid., 961

28 Ibid., 273

29 Ibid., 277–8, 263, 270–1

30 Ibid., 872, 874
31 Ibid., 882, 876, 881, 879
32 Ibid., 876–8, 883–4, 880, 882–3, 886
33 *USN & WR,* 1 April 1955, 93. *Tr.,* 137–8, 141, 144–7, 148–9, 888. Oppenheimer's counsel counted eleven admissions of lying; in fact there were fourteen. See L. K Garrison, H. S. Marks, and S. J. Silverman, *Brief On Behalf Of Dr. J. Robert Oppenheimer. Filed with the Atomic Energy Commission's Personnel Security Board: Gordon Gray, Chairman; Dr. Ward V. Evans; Thomas A. Morgan. May 17, 1954* (Privately printed), 55. Hereafter cited as *Brief to PSB*
34 C. Strout, 'The Oppenheimer Case: Melodrama, Tragedy, and Irony', *The Virginia Quarterly Review,* 40 (1964), 274
35 *Tr.,* 138, 149, 823–4, 888, 14, 251, 830
36 Ibid., 817–20
37 Ibid., 167–8, 253, 264–5. Nichols' letter alleged that Chevalier had approached Oppenheimer either directly or through his brother; ibid., 5
38 Ibid., 168. *New World,* 160–1. *Tr.,* 176. Groves, 138, 141. If this were Groves' strategy, it was, of course, neutralized by Fuchs, though Groves could not know it.
39 *Tr.,* 277, 168, 152–3, 889, 904
40 Chevalier, 171, 116–7, 194
41 *Tr.,* 168
42 Chevalier, 57–8, 60–1
43 Ibid., 62–8
44 Ibid., 53–4
45 Ibid., 54–5
46 Ibid., 68
47 Ibid., 69–70 and *Tr.,* 209
48 *Tr.,* 192, 209, 380
49 D. E. Lilienthal, *The Journals of David E. Lilienthal. Volume II. The Atomic Energy Years 1945–1950* (New York, Harper & Row, 1964), 69–70. Hereafter cited as Lilienthal II
50 *Tr.,* 15, 35, 332, 45, 327, 344, 470, 378, 385. See also ibid., 252
51 Ibid., 104–7. R. Jungk, *Brighter Than A Thousand Suns* (Harmondsworth, Penguin Books, 1964). 218–9. Hereafter cited as Jungk. Chevalier, 73–4
52 *Tr.,* 210–5, 120–2
53 Ibid., 120, 150, 211
54 Ibid., 211–5. See also *NYT,* 16 April 1954
55 *Tr.,* 214–5, 252
56 Ibid., 151–2, 180–1, 573–6
57 Chevalier, 76–9. *NYT,* 31 October 1947

58 *NYT*, 7 November 1947. Stern, 116
59 Stern, 120. Chevalier, 81–3. *Tr.,* 141–2
60 Chevalier, 83–4. *Tr.,* 142–3
61 *Tr.,* 140, 920. According to Oppenheimer, Chevalier had been told the Oppenheimers were coming to Europe by the eminent Danish physicist, Niels Bohr
62 *NYT*, 30 June 1954. *Tr.,* 141, 920–1, 969, 971
63 Chevalier, 68–9, 72, 80–1, 82–3, 86–8. *Tr.,* 920, 140, 141. Stern, 518
64 *Tr.,* 971, 14, 140, 888, 916–7, 919. Wyman's affidavit is referred to by Smyth in *Texts*, 65
65 *Tr.,* 23, 170, 179, 168–70
66 L. L. Strauss, *Men and Decisions* (London, Macmillan, 1963), 272–3. Hereafter cited as Strauss. 60 STAT. 757. *New World,* 648. *Tr.,* 25
67 Lilienthal II, 105
68 Ibid., 156. *Tr.,* 374, 411–2
69 Lilienthal II, 157. 60 STAT. 766–7. *Tr.,* 416, 417
70 *Tr.,* 41, 343, 344–6. R. G. Hewlett and F. Duncan, *Atomic Shield, 1947–1952* (University Park, Pa., Pennsylvania State UP, 1969), 268. Hereafter cited as *Atomic Shield*
71 *Tr.,* 417–8
72 Lilienthal II, 157. *Tr.,* 418. Stern, 103
73 *Tr.,* 418–9, 967
74 Ibid., 379, 415, 419–20, 422
75 The text of Executive Order 9835 of 21 March 1947 is at 12 Federal Register 1935 and in Bonsal, 231–8. Lilienthal II, 163, 176
76 *Tr.,* 379–81
77 *Atomic Shield*, 24–6, 88, 101. *Tr.,* 424–5
78 Lilienthal II, 233. *Atomic Shield,* 101
79 W. Gellhorn (ed.), *The States and Subversion* (Ithaca, NY, Cornell UP, 1952), 42–3
80 Ibid., 43–4. *Tr.,* 103–4
81 Gellhorn, 45–6
82 Ibid., 44–5, 46–7
83 Ibid., 48. *NYT*, 11 May 1950. *Tr.,* 178–9
84 *Tr.,* 306, 308. Oppenheimer contended that he was in New Mexico at the time of the meeting, and this was supported by Bethe; it is also confirmed by Chevalier. See ibid., 16–7, 103–4, 216–9, 335–6, 921, and Chevalier, 42
85 *Tr.,* 495
86 Ibid., 499–500, 506, 507
87 Ibid., 976, 987

88 Ibid., 317–8, 411–2, 413, 415, 416–7, 431, 610, 613, 424
89 Ibid., 25, 612, 677, 678. Stern, 528–9. Belsley was Secretary to the Commission
90 *Tr.*, 412, 805–8
91 Ibid., 417, 434, 630, 678, 808, 968, 963, 976
92 Ibid., 465, 472, 414, 280, 393
93 Ibid., 279, 270. E. Bontecou, *The Federal Loyalty-Security Program* (Ithaca, NY, Cornell UP, 1953), 15. *Tr.*, 391. See also *BAS*, 7 (1951), 157 and Earl Browder's letter in *NYT*, 29 April 1954
94 *Tr.*, 368–9, 365, 368, 372
95 Ibid., 468, 522
96 Ibid., 558–9, 736, 741–2
97 Ibid., 741, 559
98 Ibid., 553–4, 555, 559, 566, 739
99 Ibid., 8–11, 13–14, 24, 101–8, 980–3, 987–8. *Brief to PSB*, 46–71
100 *Brief to PSB*, 46–8
101 *Tr.*, 522. *Time*, 8 November 1948, 29
102 *Tr.*, 188, 285–99
103 Stern, 360, 280, C. P. Curtis, *The Oppenheimer Case* (New York, Simon & Schuster, 1955), 79. Chevalier, 106. The comment of Alan Simpson is apt: 'Possibly the feature of these days which will seem most humiliating to a later and saner generation is the impossibility of offering anything but an abject apology for the offense of having held left-wing opinions ten or twenty years ago.' *BAS*, 10 (1954), 388. The reviewer of Chevalier's book in *The Times Literary Supplement* (Professor Brogan?) suggests that 'I was an idiot' was intended to be taken in the sense of the Greek ἰδιώτης, that is, a clumsy amateur (as opposed to the skilled professionals of military security). It is an ingenious suggestion, but I do not think Oppenheimer was in any state to display such finesse at this moment. *TLS*, 25 June 1966
104 Chevalier, 114–6

CHAPTER 4

1 *Tr.*, 11, 28, 325. *New World*, 104
2 *Tr.*, 28–9, 452, 771–2, 804. Stern, 36. *Tr.*, 325
3 Shepley & Blair, 45. E. Teller, 'The Work of Many People', *Science*, 121 (1955), 269
4 *New World*, 240, 164. *Tr.*, 949
5 *Tr.*, 954–5, 956
6 *New World*, 329, 356. Strauss, 221. *Tr.*, 6, 227–8
7 *Tr.*, 711. E. Teller and A. Brown, *The Legacy of Hiroshima* (London, Macmillan, 1962), 41. Hereafter cited as Teller & Brown

8   *Tr.*, 32, 949, 33, 950. *New World*, 417

9   *Tr.*, 33–4, 949–50. Letter to the author from Dr Richard C. Hewlett, 12 November 1969

10 *Tr.*, 712–3, 714, 786

11 Shepley & Blair, 99–100. *Tr.*, 233. *New World*, 631–2. *Science*, 121 (1955), 270–1

12 *Tr.*, 341, 69

13 *Atomic Shield*, 30–32. *Tr.*, 18. *BAS*, 10 (1954), 344. *Tr.*, 478, 337

14 *Tr.*, 18, 72, 492, 333, 654–5, 485, 492. *Science*, 121 (1955), 270–1. *Tr.*, 640–2

15 *Tr.*, 658–9

16 Ibid., 838. Stern, 325n

17 *Tr.*, 660, 662–3, 666

18 D. Masters and K. Way (eds.), *One World or None* (London, Latimer Press, 1947), 100, 105. *Tr.*, 47

19 *The Times*, 19 August 1966. *BAS*, 23 (1967), 15

20 *Atomic Shield*, 362–6

21 *BAS*, 9 (1953), 43, 45. Anon., 'The Hidden Struggle for the H-Bomb', *Fortune*, 47/5 (1953), 109

22 *Tr.*, 951, 692, 787, 910, 969, 970

23 *BAS*, 23/12 (1967), 9. *NYT*, 27 January 1953. *Public Papers of the Presidents of the United States. Harry S. Truman. 1949* (Washington DC, United States Government Printing Office, 1964), 485

24 H. S. Truman, *Years of Trial and Hope 1946–1953* (London, Hodder & Stoughton, 1956), 395. Hereafter cited as Truman

25 *Tr.*, 660

26 *BAS*, 6 (1950), 108. *Tr.*, 774

27 *Tr.*, 435. B. Brodie, 'Nuclear Weapons: Strategic or Tactical?', *Foreign Affairs*, 32 (1953–54), 222–3

28 *Atomic Shield*, 584, 593. Strauss, 220

29 *USN & WR*, 17 December 1954

30 *Tr.*, 716. *Science*, 121 (1955), 273

31 *Tr.*, 683

32 S. T. Possony, *Strategic Air Power* (Washington, DC, Infantry Journal Press, 1949), 196

33 *Tr.*, 803, 774. Childs, 471. *Atomic Shield*, 394. Strauss, 220. As Lilienthal later remembered it, McMahon had expressed himself even more pungently on the subject. 'I recall', he wrote in 1953, 'that when Senator McMahon was hot on the trail four years ago, he said: "Why, a President who didn't approve going ahead on the H-bomb all-out would be hanged from a lamp-post if the Russians should get it and we hadn't." ' Lilienthal III, 424

34 The remaining five pre-H-bomb witnesses were Alvarez, Latimer, Teller, Kenneth S. Pitzer and General Roscoe C. Wilson. Another could be added to the list – Bethe – but he did not decide to support the bomb until after the outbreak of the Korean War in June 1950. He nevertheless testified on Oppenheimer's behalf

35 Truman, 325. *Tr.*, 242, 434, 228, 80

36 *Atomic Shield*, 415

37 Ibid., 183, 365, 380. *Tr.*, 432, 453, 469, 546, 565

38 *Atomic Shield*, 372, 164, 175–6, 178–9. *Tr.*, 242, 400

39 H. A. Bethe, 'The Hydrogen Bomb', *BAS*, 6 (1950), 101. *Tr.*, 432, 400

40 *BAS*, 6 (1950), 104. *Tr.*, 564–5

41 *Tr.*, 400, 77, 682, 447, 407, 432. *Atomic Shield*, 387. W. R. Schilling, 'The H-Bomb Decision', *The Political Science Quarterly*, 76 (1961), 33. According to the brothers Alsop, in 1948 both Strauss and Nichols 'joined in recommending that only the then current level of effort be maintained in the thermonuclear program.' *USN & WR*, 24 December 1954, 101

42 *Tr.*, 360

43 Ibid., 360, 361

44 Ibid., 79, 959, 326, 328. *BAS*, 4 (1948), 66. Lilienthal II, 581

45 *Tr.*, 235, 236

46 Ibid., 242–3, 366, 367, 404, 423–4

47 Ibid., 250, 80, 87, 249–50, 409–10. H. A. Bethe, 'Oppenheimer: "Where He Was There Was Always Life and Excitement" ', *Science*, 155 (1967), 1083. G. F. Kennan, *Memoirs 1925–1950* (London, Hutchinson, 1968) 470. Strauss in his statement on the H-bomb test of 1 March 1954, said that there was 'good reason to believe that they [the Russians] had begun work on this weapon substantially before we did'. *BAS*, 10 (1954), 163

48 Strauss, 216–7, *Atomic Shield*, 373–4

49 *Tr.*, 775–8, 245, 460–1. *Atomic Shield*, 375–8

50 *Tr.*, 682–3. *Atomic Shield*, 380

51 *Tr.*, 778–81. *Atomic Shield*, 379–80

52 *Tr.*, 437, 715, 783–4. *Science*, 121 (1955), 271. *Atomic Shield*, 380–1

53 Strauss, 217. *Tr.*, 401

54 *Atomic Shield*, 380

55 *Tr.*, 18–19, 76, 400

56 Ibid., 402, 433, 518. Truman, 325

57 *Tr.*, 238–9, 778

58 Ibid., 19, 77–8, 462, 896. Strauss, 221. *Atomic Shield*, 383

59 *Tr.*, 19, 79, 228. *Atomic Shield*, 383

K

60 *Tr.,* 78, 79. *Atomic Shield,* 383–4
61 *Tr.,* 80, 895. *Atomic Shield,* 384
62 *Tr.,* 79–80, 395, 455. *Atomic Shield,* 384. Lilienthal II, 582
63 *Tr.,* 896–7
64 Ibid., 237, 895–7, 80, 87, 464, 469. *Atomic Shield,* 385. Lilienthal II, 582
65 *Tr.,* 640, 707
66 Ibid., 526–7, 243, 237, 894, 896. See also Pike at ibid., 436
67 Ibid., 606–7. *Atomic Shield,* 396
68 *BAS,* 10 (1954), 190
69 *Tr.,* 784, 786
70 Ibid., 6, 232
71 Ibid., 714, 659, 802. Teller & Brown, 232, Childs, 466, 471
72 *Tr.,* 793, 781–2, 778, 783, 785. *Atomic Shield,* 381–2
73 *Tr.,* 707, 715, 328–9
74 Ibid., 66, 461, 518
75 Ibid., 240, 241, 239, 233, 237, 462, 240, 234. *Atomic Shield,* 642–3
76 *Tr.,* 241
77 Teller & Brown, 44. *Tr.,* 716, 717–8. *Atomic Shield,* 388, 643
78 *Tr.,* 6, 716. Teller & Brown, 44
79 *Tr.,* 90–1, 481
80 *Atomic Shield,* 402, 385–6. Lilienthal II, 584–5
81 *Atomic Shield,* 386, 391–4, 395. Childs, 472. Strauss, 222–3
82 Strauss, 225. N. Moss, *Men Who Play God* (London, Gollancz, 1968), 31. W. R. Schilling, 'Scientists, Foreign Policy, and Politics', *The American Political Science Review,* 56 (1962), 290
83 Lilienthal II, 582. *Atomic Shield,* 360–1, 386, 389
84 *Atomic Shield,* 386–8
85 Ibid., 388–90. *Tr.,* 244, 242
86 *Atomic Shield,* 390–1
87 Ibid., 394. Truman, 326
88 *Atomic Shield,* 395–6, 402–3. *Tr.,* 81
89 *BAS,* 10 (1954), 359. *Atomic Shield,* 399–400, 401–2
90 *Atomic Shield,* 403–4. *The Political Science Quarterly,* 76 (1961), 38–9
91 R. Lapp, *Atoms and People* (New York, Harper & Brothers, 1956), 106. *Atomic Shield,* 394, 400. *The Times,* 13 January 1950. *Public Papers of the Presidents of the United States. Harry S. Truman. 1950* (Washington, DC, United States Government Printing Office, 1965), 134. Hereafter cited as *Public Papers 1950.* See also L. W. Nordheim 'Fear and Information', *BAS,* 10 (1954), 344. Senator Johnson's disclosure is usually thought of as a gaffe; I am not so sure.
92 *Atomic Shield,* 404–5

93 Stern, 153. J. Mason Brown, *Through These Men* (New York, Harper & Brothers, 1956), 250. D. Whitehead, *The F.B.I. Story* (New York, Random House, 1956), 308. Lilienthal II, 634–5. *Atomic Shield*, 312–3, 412. The evidence provided by these sources is conflicting. Stern says that the Foreign Office told the State Department about Fuchs's treason on 27 January, Mason Brown that it was discussed by the GAC on 30 January. Whitehead indicates that the FBI were informed on 31 January and that Hoover 'notified the government's top echelon [presumably Truman] of the turn of affairs.' Lilienthal and the official history of the AEC state that the AEC was only informed on 2 February. The Foreign Office did not tell the State Department until 2 February according to information received from the UK Atomic Energy Authority. I am satisfied, however, that both Hoover and Truman knew about Fuchs before the decision was made on 31 January

94 Lilienthal II, 623–32. *Atomic Shield*, 406–8

95 Lilienthal II, 624, 631. *Tr.*, 86

96 Lilienthal II, 624

97 Ibid., 625, 630, 627–8, 631–2

98 Ibid., 632–3. Shepley & Blair, 84. *Public Papers 1950*, 138. Truman, 326

99 *Atomic Shield*, 411–3. *Tr.*, 435. In spite of his proposals, Pike was still not trusted, and in June 1950 his re-appointment by the Senate was delayed partly because of the stand he had taken on the bomb. *Atomic Shield*, 448

100 *Atomic Shield*, 400, 415–6. Truman, 327

101 *Atomic Shield*, 417. D. G. Acheson, *Present at the Creation* (New York, Norton, 1969), 751. Truman, 327–8. *The Political Science Quarterly*, 76 (1961), 43–6

102 *Tr.*, 363, 367. Lilienthal II, 581

103 *Tr.*, 367, 302

104 Lilienthal II, 633

105 *Tr.*, 700–1

106 Ibid., 83, 86, 307, 898, 704. *Science*, 155 (1967), 1083

107 Shepley & Blair, 85

108 *BAS*, 6 (1950), 72

109 *Tr.*, 719, 310. *Atomic Shield*, 415, 416, 440. Shepley & Blair, 98, 103, 90

110 *Tr.*, 19, 645, 330–1, 962

111 *BAS*, 6 (1950), 137–8. *NYT*, 19 April 1954

112 *Tr.*, 19, 82, 232, 719–20, 481, 83, 646, 655, 701–2, 705. Strauss, 274

113 *Tr.*, 897, 898–9. Stern, 161

114 *Atomic Shield*, 424–30, 522–9
115 Ibid., 527–8. *Tr.*, 304
116 *Atomic Shield*, 530
117 Ibid., 530
118 Ibid., 530–1
119 Ibid., 530. *Tr.*, 46, 62–3
120 *Tr.*, 788
121 Ibid., 797–8. *Atomic Shield*, 530–1
122 *Tr.*, 788–9
123 Ibid., 951–2. *Atomic Shield*, 536
124 *Atomic Shield*, 536–7
125 Ibid., 542–6. *Science*, 121 (1955), 273. See also *BAS*, 10 (1954), 344
126 *Tr.*, 251, 81, 232, 480
127 Jungk, 266. M. Thomas, *Atomic Energy and Congress* (Ann Arbor, Mich., University of Michigan Press, 1956), 110. Stern, 180
128 *Atomic Shield*, 535–6, 539–41
129 Ibid., 528, 554–6. *Science*, 121 (1955), 274. *Tr.*, 85. The transcript reads 'anomalous' for 'omelette'.
130 *Atomic Shield*, 562, 569–71. *Tr.*, 313
131 *Tr.*, 755. *Atomic Shield*, 581–2. See also Bethe's comment on Griggs in *Tr.*, 338–9
132 *Tr.*, 755. Teller & Brown, 60–1. *Atomic Shield*, 582–3. Shepley & Blair, 127–30. The relevant part of the Atomic Energy Act is Section 6(a)
133 *Atomic Shield*, 582–4
134 Ibid., 590–3. *Tr.*, 247–8, 561, 592, 525–6, 749
135 *Tr.*, 247–8. *Fortune*, 47/5 (1953), 110. The proposal attributed by *Fortune* to Oppenheimer was later attributed by the Alsops to Fermi and Rabi's minority annex of 30 October 1949. See *USN & WR*, 24 December 1954, 101
136 *Tr.*, 463, 704
137 Ibid., 384–5
138 Ibid., 565–7
139 Ibid., 566. Stern, 510. Von Neumann, a supporter of the bomb, believed Oppenheimer had acted sincerely. *Tr.*, 644–5
140 *Tr.*, 567, 385. Brief to PSB, 9. *Partisan Review*, 21 (1954), 615
141 *Tr.*, 567. Stern, 106

CHAPTER 5

1 *Tr.*, 22, 447, 886. Stern, 541
2 B. Brodie, *Strategy in the Missile Age* (Princeton, NJ, Princeton UP, 1959), 71–144, and 'Some Notes on the Evolution of Air Doctrine', *World Politics*, 7 (1954–55), 349–70

3 HC Deb., fifth series, 270 (1931–32), col. 632

4 W. L. Borden, *There Will Be No Time* (New York, Macmillan, 1946), 119, 220

5 W. W. Rostow, *The United States in the World Arena* (New York, Harper & Row, 1960), 223–4

6 D. Masters and K. Way (eds.), *One World Or None* (London. Latimer Press, 1947), 61. S. T. Possony, *Strategic Air Power*, (Washington, DC, Infantry Journal Press, 1949), 307–8. *Atomic Shield*, 183

7 C. E. LeMay, *Mission With LeMay* (New York, Doubleday, 1965), 482, 561

8 H. Kissinger, *Nuclear Weapons and Foreign Policy* (New York, Harper & Brothers, 1957), 25. *Atomic Shield*, 150, 152. *The Political Science Quarterly*, 76 (1961), 27–8. United States Bureau of Statistics. *Historical Statistics of the United States* (Washington, DC, United States Government Printing Office, 1960), 718. A. P. de Seversky, *Air Power*, (London, Jenkins, 1952), 297

9 *One World Or None*, 53, 60

10 *Tr.*, 46–7

11 *The Annals of the American Academy of Political and Social Science*, 299 (1955), 36

12 *Tr.*, 47

13 Ibid., 690. M. B. Ridgway, *Soldier* (New York, Harper & Brothers, 1956), 273

14 *Tr.*, 46

15 Ibid., 953, 46, 75

16 O. N. Bradley, 'This Way Lies Peace', *The Saturday Evening Post*, 15 October 1949

17 *Tr.*, 58, 497–8

18 *BAS*, 7 (1951), 44–5

19 *Tr.*, 498, 684, 694

20 Ibid., 684–5

21 H. P. Green and A. Rosenthal, *Government of the Atom* (Englewood Cliffs, NJ, Prentice Hall, 1963), 242. See also *Tr.*, 46, 75

22 D. G. Acheson, *Present At The Creation* (New York, Norton, 1969), 478

23 *Atomic Shield*, 535, 563–4, 672–3, 557–8. *Keesing's Contemporary Archives*, 8 (1950–52), 11903A

24 *Tr.*, 584–5, 891

25 Ibid., 763, 747, 532, 590

26 Ibid., 616–7, 635, 747, 900, 584

27 Ibid., 759. *Fortune*, 47/5 (1953), 110

28 G. F. Kennan, *Memoirs 1925–1950*, 471–4. The policy was adopted by the Kennedy government in 1962; *Survival*, 4 (1962), 195

29 *BAS*, 6 (1950), 75. Italics in text
30 *Tr.*, 891, 893. *Brief to PSB*, 96
31 *Tr.*, 594–5, 891–4
32 Ibid., 893
33 Ibid., 760, 759, 900, 960
34 Shepley & Blair, 157, 159. *Fortune*, 47/5 (1953), 110
35 Stern, 182–3
36 *Tr.*, 905, 892–3, 901
37 Ibid., 940. *NYT*, 5 June 1952
38 *There Will Be No Time*, 220. V. Bush, *Modern Arms and Free Men* (London, Heinemann, (1950), 112–3
39 *BAS*, 6 (1950), 107
40 *The United States in the World Arena*, 249. C. J. V. Murphy, 'The US as a Bombing Target', *Fortune*, 48/5 (1953), 247. *Atomic Shield*, 487. *Tr.*, 585
41 Don K. Price, *Government and Science* (New York, Oxford UP, 1962 edition), 136
42 N. Frankland, *The Bombing Offensive Against Germany* (London, Faber & Faber, 1965), 40, 43, 45
43 E. M. Emme, *The Impact of Air Power* (Princeton, NJ, Van Nostrand, 1959), 429. Italics in text
44 *Tr.*, 458–9. *The United States in the World Arena*, 313
45 *Tr.*, 598, 923
46 Ibid., 935–6
47 Ibid., 924
48 Ibid., 768
49 Ibid., 749, 760–1. This last allegation, like the allegation over the renunciation of first strike, was false, according to Garrison. *Brief to PSB*, 46
50 *Tr.*, 749–50, 751
51 Shepley & Blair, 163, 165. *Fortune*, 47/5 (1953), 230. *Historical Statistics of the United States*, 718
52 *Tr.*, 952–3, 59, 458, 600
53 *Air Power*, 255. *Tr.*, 599
54 *Tr.*, 504–5, 525–6, 751–2
55 Ibid., 752–4, 757–8. The authors of *The Hydrogen Bomb* have kindly supplied the missing number of bombs – seven. Shepley & Blair, 129
56 *Tr.*, 763–5
57 Ibid., 925–7, 937–9, 941–2. *Atomic Shield*, 519
58 *Tr.*, 750, 769
59 Ibid., 96, 600, 922–3, 927–8, 929, 936
60 Ibid., 721. Garrison interviewed Teller with a view to calling him as a witness, but did not do so because his feelings on

Oppenheimer's judgment and his dislike of Oppenheimer were so intense. Stern, 516
61 Ibid., 710, 726
62 Ibid., 710, 726

CHAPTER 6
1 *Tr.,* 972
2 Ibid., 972–3
3 Ibid., 974
4 Ibid., 976–83
5 Ibid., 982–9
6 Ibid., 987, 989–90
7 *Texts,* 13, 20, 17–18
8 Ibid., 3–11, 19
9 Ibid., 11–13, 19
10 Ibid., 19
11 *Tr.,* 385. *Texts,* 12
12 *Texts,* 13
13 Ibid., 19–20, 18, 21
14 Ibid., 20–1
15 *Tr.,* 10, 191–3, 220, 903, 915, 155, 183–5, 825, 102, 139, 156, 191–2
16 Texts, 20–1, 15
17 Ibid., 20–1. *Tr.,* 904–5. L. K. Garrison, H. S. Marks, S. J. Silverman, A. B. Ecker, and J. W. Davis, *Brief On Behalf Of J. Robert Oppenheimer. Filed with the Atomic Energy Commission. June 7, 1954* (Privately printed), 54–5. Hereafter cited as *Brief to AEC*
18 *Texts,* 21, 13, 19
19 Ibid., 16
20 Ibid., 13–14
21 Ibid., 13, 1
22 Ibid., 14
23 Ibid., 1–2, 17
24 Ibid., 21–3. According to Stern, the final draft of Evans' report was partly the work of Robb! Stern, 379–80
25 *Texts,* 27, 58
26 Ibid., 31–6
27 Stern, 518–20
28 *Texts,* 39–40
29 *Brief to AEC,* 3–4. Stern, 536–7, 542–4
30 *BAS,* 10 (1954), 242, 256
31 *Tr.,* 258

32 V. Bush, 'If We Alienate Our Scientists—', *NYT*, 13 June 1954. *BAS*, 10 (1954), 374
33 Stern, 387–9
34 *Tr.*, 20. Stern, 520–1
35 Stern, 389–92, 521–2
36 *NYHT*, 21 June 1954
37 *Texts*, 44, 47
38 Ibid., 44, 47
39 Ibid., 44, 46
40 Ibid., 45
41 Ibid., 46
42 Ibid., 46–7
43 Ibid., 47–8
44 Ibid., 45–6
45 Garrison is not certain whether or not he and his colleagues asked for a copy of Nichols' report. At all events, the AEC took no steps to make it available to them. Stern, 538
46 Strauss, 281–91
47 Stern, 404–5
48 *Texts*, 51–4
49 Ibid., 54, 51
50 Ibid., 51
51 *Tr.*, 877, 139–40
52 *Texts*, 52–3
53 Ibid., 54
54 Ibid., 52
55 Ibid., 52
56 Strauss, 294
57 *Tr.*, 306, 381
58 *Texts*, 54–7
59 Ibid., 57–60
60 Ibid., 62–3
61 Ibid., 61
62 Ibid., 63, 61, 62
63 Stern, 403–5
64 *Texts*, 64
65 Ibid., 64
66 Ibid., 64
67 Ibid., 65–6
68 *Tr.*, 152–3, 888, 877, 875. *Texts*, 20
69 *Texts*, 67
70 Ibid., 67
71 Ibid., 67

72 *NYHT*, 30 June 1954
73 Stern, 541–2, 523
74 Ibid., 523
75 *Public Papers 1954*, 608. D. D. Eisenhower, *Mandate for Change 1953–1956* (London, Heinemann, 1963), 313. Hereafter cited as Eisenhower

CHAPTER 7

1 *NYT*, 2 July 1954
2 Ibid., 2 July 1954 and *NYHT*, 1 July 1954
3 *NYT*, 2 July 1954. *Texts*, 1–2, 55, 57–8, 59. Strauss, 278, 292–3
4 *Tr.*, 971–2. *Brief to PSB*, 2–3. *Texts*, 34–5. *BAS*, 10 (1954), 270–1
5 *Tr.*, 22. *Brief to AEC*, 70. *Texts*, 31
6 *Tr.*, 468. *NYHT*, 7 June 1954
7 Lilienthal III, 522
8 *Texts*, 14
9 Stern, 336. Childs, 468, 472–3
10 Stern, 509–11
11 Ibid., 512–3
12 Ibid., 526–7. *Tr.*, 227
13 Stern, 526–7
14 Ibid., 513–4, 245
15 *Tr.*, 62, 316, 4–7, 834. *Texts*, 2. Garrison faced an additional problem arising out of the fact that he was not cleared, namely, that he was not allowed to see the transcript of the hearing until classified portions had been deleted. This meant that, during the first week, he had to wait until Saturday for his copy. See *Tr.*, 148, 160, 223, 281, 346–7, 438–9. On top of this, the AEC declassification authority at the hearing was his opponent, Robb's assistant, Rolander!
16 Stern, 527–8
17 Ibid., 515
18 *Tr.*, 391, 393
19 Ibid., 20, 143, 202. *Procedures*, 4.15(a) and (g)
20 *Procedures*, 4.15(a). *Tr.*, 201, 539, 541
21 *Partisan Review*, 21 (1954), 605. Stern, 318n
22 Lilienthal III, 506. *Tr.*, 399, 331
23 Stern, 300, 542
24 *Tr.*, 143–9, 199–209, 953–5, 618–24, 312, 526
25 Ibid., 201, 619–20. Stern, 285–6
26 *Tr.*, 148, 200, 203, 955
27 Ibid., 912–4, 313, 338–9
28 Ibid., 179, 376–8, 412, 417–9, 420. Six more documents relative to the 1947 clearance were also placed in the record in

whole or in part, four during Lilienthal's testimony and two
during Bacher's. See *Tr.*, 380–1, 424–5, 611, 618–24. The last of
these was an anonymous analysis of the FBI reports on Oppenheimer, and it constituted double hearsay evidence which
would have been inadmissible in a court of law. Stern, 322–3

29 Lilienthal III, 505n. *Tr.*, 420–2
30 *Tr.*, 9, 159, 277–8; 140, 205
31 Ibid., 143–9, 152–3, 142, 969
32 Ibid., 118, 119, 128, 136, 143; 14, 36, 143; 118–9, 194, 200–1;
123, 126–7, 208–9
33 Ibid., 117–8, 123, 133, 149–50
34 Ibid., 170, 273–6, 814–23
35 Ibid., 168–9, 179–80, 374–82, 387–9, 390, 406–7, 411–22, 424–5,
609–13, 618–24, 629–30
36 Ibid., 210–11, 213–4
37 Ibid., 953–5, 969, 682–3, 774–86, 757–8
38 Ibid., 233–4, 237–9, 402
39 Ibid., 239–40, 234
40 Ibid., 239–41
41 Ibid., 239, 240, 682
42 Ibid., 181–3, 191–2, 201–2, 212; 447; 22
43 Ibid., 24, 48, 352, 460, 537
44 Ibid., 537–8
45 Ibid., 539–40
46 Ibid., 352, 541, 539, 48, 352
47 Ibid., 541–2
48 *USN & WR*, 24 December 1954, 96
49 *Tr.*, 702. Childs, 470
50 Childs, 473. Stern, 347–8. Strauss, when interviewed in 1967,
did not recollect getting in touch with any witnesses during the
hearing. Stern, 411–2. See also *Tr.*, 679
51 *Tr.*, 972
52 Lilienthal III, 521, 510
53 Lilienthal II, 180–1. Don K. Price, *Government and Science*
(New York, OUP, 1962), 113
54 *Tr.*, 559, 555, 739
55 Ibid., 55, 421, 565
56 Ibid., 54–5, 56, 64, 66
57 Ibid., 411, 736, 755, 799, 690–1, 903, 677–9, 972–3
58 Ibid., 412, 612
59 Ibid., 203, 808
60 Ibid., 223, 447, 621–2, 422
61 Ibid., 171, 555. *Texts*, 13. According to the Alsops, Groves
telephoned Oppenheimer after the Commission's decision was

published to express his 'shocked regret'. See *USN & WR*, 24 December 1954, 90
62 *USN & WR*, 1 April 1955, 92
63 G. F. Kennan, *Memoirs 1925–1950* (London, Hutchinson, 1968), 474–5. *Texts*, 56–7
64 Kennan, 474–5

CHAPTER 8
1 *BAS*, 11 (1955), 112
2 *The Christian Science Monitor*, 17 April 1954. *NYT*, 13 June 1954
3 *BAS*, 10 (1954), 285. *The Christian Science Monitor*, 8 July 1954
4 *NYHT*, 4 June 1954. *Harper's Magazine*, 209/4 (1954), 25
5 *NYT*, 14 April 1954. J. Mason Brown, *Through These Men* (New York, Harper & Brothers, 1956), 243
6 *New World*, 412–5, 428–55, 482–530
7 Ibid., 504–13. Lilienthal II, 135. M. Thomas, *Atomic Energy and Congress* (Ann Arbor, Mich., University of Michigan Press, 1956) 13–14, 44–9. Lilienthal II, 134
8 *New World*, 642–4, 651–5. *Atomic Shield*, 150, 165–70, 521–2, 524–5, 537–9, 539, 579–80, 585. Lilienthal II, 262, 311–2, 373–5, 377, 388–92, 502, 527–8
9 *New World*, 432, 444, 493, 512, 514
10 Ibid., 524, 526–7, 529
11 H. P. Green & A. Rosenthal, *Government of the Atom* (Englewood Cliffs, NJ, 1963), 80–2. M. Thomas, *Atomic Energy and Congress*, 34–43. *Atomic Shield*, 324–6. Lilienthal II, 321, 324, 329, 331, 336–7, 341
12 *Atomic Shield*, 326–32. Lilienthal II, 304–7, 314, 319–20, 322–5, 326–9, 331, 333, 334–5, 337, 339–40, 341, 357, 359–60, 362–4, 367
13 *Atomic Shield*, 340–2, 352, 356, 450–1. Lilienthal II, 360–1, 453, 528–9, 530–1, 533, 556, 558
14 *Atomic Shield*, 358–61. Lilienthal II, 533–47, 561–4
15 *Atomic Shield*, 81–2, 109–10. Lilienthal II, 234–5, 238–9, 400, 544, 541
16 Truman, 317–8
17 Stern, 128–30. *BAS*, 5 (1949), 227
18 *The New Yorker*, 10 May 1969, 162. Childs, 467. *NYHT*, 4 June 1954. *Harper's Magazine*, 209/4 (1954), 35–6
19 *Harper's Magazine*, 209/4 (1954), 36. Lilienthal III, 522. Strauss went to the lengths of making a reply to Oppenheimer in the form of a letter to McMahon which was read into the record at a JCAE hearing on 24 June 1949. See *NYT*, 25 June 1949

20　D. K. Price, *Government and Science*, 97. *BAS*, 9 (1953), 42

21　*BAS*, 7 (1951), 354. R. West, *The Meaning of Treason* (Harmondsworth, Penguin Books, 1965), 188

22　Childs, 266–7, 319, 468

23　*The Christian Science Monitor*, 1 May 1954

24　A. Barth, *The Loyalty of Free Men* (New York, Viking Press, 1951), 193

25　W. W. Rostow, *The United States in the World Arena*, 247–8. D. K. Price, *Government and Science*, 43–6, 108, 147–8, 151. S. P. Huntington, *The Common Defense* (New York, Columbia UP, 1961), 289

26　Stern, 107, 130–1, Lilienthal II, 224

27　R. K. Carr, *The House Committee on Un-American Activities 1945–1950* (Ithaca, NY, Cornell UP, 1952), 181. Stern, 122, 153

28　L. Scheinman, *Atomic Energy Policy in France under the Fourth Republic* (Princeton, NJ, Princeton UP, 1965), 41

29　The AEC Criteria in operation before the revision of November 1950 are at 14 Federal Register 42. They are also reproduced in *BAS*, 11 (1955), 159–60

30　R. K. Carr, *The House Committe on Un-American Activities 1945–1950*, 181. W. B. Huie, 'Who Gave Russia the A-Bomb?', *The American Mercury*, April 1951, 417

31　J. R. Oppenheimer, 'Atomic Weapons and American Policy', *Foreign Affairs*, 31 (1952–53), 525–35

32　Ibid., 526, 528, 529

33　Ibid., 531, 532

34　Ibid., 532. *Atomic Shield*, 479–83

35　*Foreign Affairs*, 31 (1952–53), 532

36　Ibid., 531

37　Lilienthal II, 572. *BAS*, 6 (1950), 75

38　*BAS*, 6 (1950), 126, 67

39　S. P. Huntington, *The Common Defense* (New York, Columbia UP, 1961), 329–30

40　Ibid., 330, 335

41　Ibid., 330–1

42　C. Webster and N. Frankland, *The Strategic Air Offensive Against Germany 1939–1945. Volume I: Preparation* (London, Her Majesty's Stationery Office, 1961), 331–6

43　*Tr.*, 95

44　*NYHT*, 3 and 5 September 1952, and 16–20 March 1953. *NYT*, 1 and 2 March 1953. *BAS*, 9 (1953), 154, 155

45　Stern, 193–4

46　*Fortune*, 47/5 (1953), 109

47　Ibid., 109, 110, 230

48 R. J. Donovan, *Eisenhower: The Inside Story* (New York, Harper & Brothers, 1956), 184–5. *BAS*, 9 (1953), 348. D. E. Lilienthal, 'The Case for Candor on National Security Policy', *NYT*, 4 October 1953

49 *Fortune*, 48/2 (1953), 97, 202

50 *NYHT*, 16 September 1953. W. W. Rostow, *The United States in the World Arena* (New York, Harper & Row, 1960), 318–9. R. Gilpin, *American Scientists and Nuclear Weapons Policy* (Princeton, NJ, Princeton UP, 1962), 127–9. *Public Papers of the Presidents of the United States. Dwight D. Eisenhower. 1953* (Washington, DC, United States Government Printing Office, 1960), 645. Hereafter cited as *Public Papers 1953*. *Public Papers 1954*, 10–11

51 *BAS*, 9 (1953), 229. S. P. Huntington, *The Common Defense*, 331–3

52 *BAS*, 9 (1953), 351

53 *Fortune*, 47/5 (1953), 230. Ibid., 48/5 (1953), 219

54 G. H. Snyder, 'The "New Look" of 1953' in W. R. Schilling, P. Y. Hammond and G. H. Snyder, *Strategy, Politics and Defense Budgets* (New York, Columbia UP, 1962), 414–5, 420–6, 438. S. P. Huntington, *The Common Defense*, 333–4, 338–9

55 *Time*, 21 September 1953, 13–15. *NYT*, 4 October 1953. Lilienthal III, 423

56 Stern, 214. *Atomic Shield*, 372. M. Thomas, *Atomic Energy and Congress*, 115. Shepley & Blair, 186

57 Stern, 168–9, 190–1

58 Ibid., 191–2, 196, 205

59 Ibid., 178–9

60 Ibid., 206

61 *NYT*, 14 April 1954. *Tr.*, 320. Stern, 206–7, 564–5

62 *NYT*, 14 April & 11 June 1954. Bonsal, 240. Stern 207

63 Bonsal, 236, 238, 239

64 N. Chiaromonte, 'State Reason and Individual Reason', *Confluence*, 5 (1965), 162. Strauss, 268

65 *Public Papers 1954*, 382, 389. Eisenhower, 312–3

66 Lilienthal III, 500. Eisenhower, 311

67 *Keesing's Contemporary Archives*, IX (1952–1954), 13245–8

68 Ibid., 13313–5

69 *Public Papers 1953*, 24–5. Donovan, 253

70 Eisenhower, 310

71 Ibid., 310–11. Strauss, 267–8

72 *Public Papers 1954*, 609. See also ibid., 437. *NYT*, 17 April 1954. Eisenhower, 314

73 *NYT*, 13 June 1954. *NYHT*, 3 May 1954; this sounds remarkably like Lilienthal

74 *The Christian Science Monitor*, 7 June 1954. Lilienthal III, 515 Bonsal, 228
75 *USN & WR*, 24 December 1954, 91. Strauss, 275. *Texts*, 57. Stern, 223, 220. *NYT*, 14 June 1954
76 Stern, 223–5
77 Ibid., 225–6
78 Ibid., 226–8
79 *Texts*, 47
80 Strauss, 275
81 Stern, 228–9
82 Strauss, 275–6
83 Ibid., 276–7, 443–4
84 Ibid., 277, 444. *Tr.*, 22
85 Strauss, 277–8, 444–5. *Tr.*, 22
86 Strauss, 278, 445. Stern, 231–2, 518
87 *Tr.*, 22

CHAPTER 9

1 R. J. Donovan, *Eisenhower: The Inside Story*, 297
2 *The Christian Science Monitor*, 26 July 1954 and Stern, 446–8
3 *USN & WR*, 24 September 1954. *BAS*, 10 (1954), 368, 357
4 Strauss, 293–4, 445–6. Lilienthal III, 563
5 *Tr.*, 339, 457–8. *BAS*, 10 (1954), 358–9
6 *Harper's Magazine*, 209/4 (1954), 25–45
7 *NYHT*, 14 July 1954. *USN & WR*, 17 December 1954, 59, 61
8 N. P. Davis, *Lawrence and Oppenheimer* (London, Jonathan Cape, 1969), 311
9 *Science*, 121 (1955), 267, 275
10 Stern, 430
11 *USN & WR*, 24 December 1954, 87, 88–9. Stern, 430–1. *NYT*, 20 December 1954
12 *USN & WR*, 24 December 1954, 86–103
13 *The Christian Science Monitor*, 26 July 1954
14 A. Barth, *The Loyalty of Free Men* (New York, Viking Press, 1951), 201. *NYT*, 13 June 1954
15 D. K. Price, *Government and Science*, 103. R. J. Donovan, *Eisenhower: The Inside Story*, 287–8. *The Times*, 17 January and 4 July 1955. *BAS*, 11 (1955), 66
16 Donovan, 289. *USN & WR*, 16 April 1954, 94–5. A. Yarmolinsky (ed.), *Case Studies in Personnel Security* (Washington, DC, Bureau of National Affairs, 1955), 30, 199, 45
17 Department of Justice Press Release, 6 March 1955
18 Strauss, 293. 21 Federal Register 3107
19 21 Federal Register 3108

20 Ibid., 3108
21 Ibid., 3109
22 *The Times*, 29 July 1955. See also the figures in Bonsal, 220
23 *BAS*, 7 (1951), 140
24 Bonsal, 113, 195, 7–17, 137–88
25 *The Times*, 24 June 1957. Bills incorporating several of the Commission's proposals were placed before Congress in 1958 and 1959, but they were not enacted
26 Ibid., 7 June 1955. *NYT*, 1 May 1956. *The Times*, 12 and 16 June 1956, and 4 June 1957. A useful summary of post-war developments in the security system can be found in *Congress and the Nation 1945–1964* (Congressional Quarterly, Inc., Washington, DC, 1965), 1645–70
27 Stern, 504. *Science*, 155 (1967), 1084
28 N. P. Davis. *Lawrence and Oppenheimer*, 347. J. M. Brown, *Through These Men*, 238
29 *NYT*, 15 February 1955
30 Stern, 428. Lilienthal III, 615
31 Chevalier, 102–12
32 *The Washington Post*, 26 December 1957. Gardner had actively sympathized with Oppenheimer at the time of the hearing; see *Tr.*, 527–9. As a result, his confirmation as Assistant Secretary of the Air Force was held up at the request of Senator Hickenlooper; see *BAS*, 10 (1954), 334
33 *NYT*, 9 December 1957
34 Ibid., 9 January 1958. Strauss was presumably referring to Part 4.33(b) of the revised AEC security procedures. See 21 Federal Register 3109
35 *Public Papers of the Presidents of the United States. Dwight D. Eisenhower. 1957* (Washington, DC, United States Government Printing Office, 1958), 789–99, 807–16, 768–72
36 Stern, 441–6
37 Strauss, 380–94
38 Ibid., 394–403
39 *NYT*, 5 April 1963
40 Ibid.
41 Ibid.
42 Ibid.
43 *NYHT*, 8 April 1963. *The Washington Post*, 26 December 1957
44 *NYT*, 5 April 1963 and 22 November 1963
45 Stern, 455n. *NYT*, 30 November 1963
46 *NYT*, 3 December 1963
47 Ibid.

Select Bibliography

A. *Primary Sources (in chronological order)*

The Atomic Energy Act of 1 August 1946. 60 STAT. 755

Public Law 733 of 26 August 1950. 64 STAT. 476

United States Atomic Energy Commission, *Security Clearance Procedures* [12 September 1950]. 15 Federal Register 6241

United States Atomic Energy Commission, *Personnel Security Clearance Criteria for Determining Eligibility* [17 November 1950]. 15 Federal Register 8093

Executive Order No. 10450 of 27 April 1953. 18 Federal Register 2489

United States Atomic Energy Commission statement of 13 April 1954. *Bulletin of the Atomic Scientists*, 10 (1954), 187

Lloyd K. Garrison, Herbert S. Marks and Samuel J. Silverman, *Brief on behalf of Dr J. Robert Oppenheimer. Filed with the Atomic Energy Commission's Personnel Security Board: Gordon Gray, Chairman; Dr Ward V. Evans; Thomas A. Morgan. May 17, 1954.* Privately printed. [Xerox copy in the Library of the University of Hull]

Lloyd K. Garrison, Herbert S. Marks, Samuel J. Silverman, Allan B. Ecker, and John W. Davis (of counsel), *Brief on behalf of J. Robert Oppenheimer. Filed with the Atomic Energy Commission. June 7, 1954.* Privately printed. [Xerox copy in the Library of the University of Hull]

Letter from Lloyd K. Garrison to General Kenneth D. Nichols of 9 June 1954. *Bulletin of the Atomic Scientists*, 10 (1954), 270

United States Atomic Energy Commission, *In the Matter of J. Robert Oppenheimer. Transcript of Hearing Before Personnel Security Board. Washington, DC. April 12, 1954, through May 6, 1954.* United States Government Printing Office, Washington, DC, 1954

United States Atomic Energy Commission, *In the Matter of J. Robert Oppenheimer. Texts of Principal Documents and Letters of Personnel Security Board, General Manager, Commissioners. Washington, DC. May 27, 1954, through June 29, 1954.* United States Government Printing Office, Washington, DC, 1954

Letter from the Attorney-General, Herbert Brownell, Jr, to President Eisenhower of 4 March 1955 regarding changes in the Employee Security Programme. Department of Justice press release of 6 March 1955. [Xerox copy in the Library of the University of Hull]

United States Atomic Energy Commission, *Criteria and Procedures for Determining Eligibility for Security Clearance* [7 May 1956]. 21 Federal Register 3103

B. *Secondary Sources (in alphabetical order by author)*

Acheson, Dean G. *Present at the Creation.* New York, Norton, 1969

Adams, Sherman. *Firsthand Report.* New York, Harper & Row, 1961

Alsop, Joseph and Alsop, Stewart. 'Project Lincoln', *The New York Herald Tribune,* 16 to 20 March 1953

Alsop, Joseph and Alsop, Stewart. 'We Accuse!', *Harper's Magazine,* 209/4 (1954), 25

Anon. 'The Hidden Struggle for the H-Bomb', *Fortune,* 47/5 (1953), 109

Baldwin, Hanson W. 'Project Vista', *The New York Times,* 5 June 1952; 'Atomic Secrecy', ibid., 1 and 2 March 1953

Barth, Alan. *The Loyalty of Free Men.* New York, Viking Press, 1951

Berkner, Lloyd V. 'Science and National Strength', *Bulletin of the Atomic Scientists,* 9 (1953), 159; 'Science and Military Power', ibid., 9 (1953), 359

Bethe, Hans. 'The Hydrogen Bomb', ibid., 6 (1950), 99

———— 'Oppenheimer: "Where He Was There Was Always Life and Excitement" ', *Science,* 155 (1967), 1080

Bonsal, Dudley B. (chairman) *Report of the Special Committee on the Federal Loyalty-Security Program of The Association of the Bar of the City of New York.* New York, Dodd, Mead, 1956

Bontecou, Eleanor. *The Federal Loyalty-Security Program.* Ithaca, NY, Cornell UP, 1953

———— President Eisenhower's "Security Program" ', *Bulletin of the Atomic Scientists,* 9 (1953), 215

———— 'Due Process in Security Dismissals', *The Annals of the American Academy of Political and Social Science,* 300 (1955), 102

Borden, William L. *There Will Be No Time.* New York, Macmillan, 1946

Brodie, Bernard. 'Nuclear Weapons: Strategic or Tactical?', *Foreign Affairs,* 32 (1953–54), 217

———— 'Some Notes on the Evolution of Air Doctrine', *World Politics,* 7 (1954–55), 349

———— *Strategy in the Missile Age.* Princeton, NJ, Princeton UP, 1959

Brown, Ralph S. 'The Operation of Personnel Security Programs', *The Annals of the American Academy of Political and Social Science*, 300 (1955), 94

Bulletin of the Atomic Scientists. Special issue on internal security, April 1955. 11 (1955), 105–68

Bush, Vannevar. *Modern Arms and Free Men*. New York, Simon & Schuster, 1949

——— 'If We Alienate Our Scientists—', *The New York Times*, 13 June 1954

Chevalier, Haakon. *Oppenheimer*. London, André Deutsch, 1966

Chiaromonte, Nicola. 'State Reason and Individual Reason', *Confluence*, 5 (1956), 158

Childs, Herbert. *American Genius: The Life of Ernest Orlando Lawrence*. New York, Dutton, 1968

Cohn, Roy. *McCarthy*. New York, The New American Library, 1968

Curtis, Charles P. *The Oppenheimer Case*. New York, Simon & Schuster, 1955

Davis, Nuel P. *Lawrence and Oppenheimer*. London, Cape, 1968

Dean, Gordon. *Report on the Atom*. London, Eyre & Spottiswoode, 1954

Donovan, Robert J. *Eisenhower: The Inside Story*. New York, Harper & Brothers, 1956

DuBridge, Lee A. 'Policy and the Scientists', *Foreign Affairs*, 41 (1962–63), 571

Dupré, J. S. and Lakoff, S. A. *Science and the Nation*. Englewood Cliffs, NJ, Prentice-Hall, 1962

Eisenhower, Dwight D. *Mandate for Change 1953–1956*. London, Heinemann, 1963

Emme, E. M. *The Impact of Air Power*. Princeton, NJ, Van Nostrand, 1959

Finletter, Thomas K. *Power and Policy*. New York, Harcourt, Brace, 1954

Finney, Nat S. 'The Threat to Atomic Science', *Bulletin of the Atomic Scientists*, 10 (1954), 285

Frankland, Noble. *The Bombing Offensive Against Germany*. London, Faber & Faber, 1965. See also Webster, Charles

Gellhorn, Walter. *Security, Loyalty and Science*. Ithaca, NY, Cornell UP, 1950

——— (ed.). *The States and Subversion*. Ithaca, NY, Cornell UP, 1952

Gilpin, Robert. *American Scientists and Nuclear Weapons Policy*. Princeton, NJ, Princeton UP, 1962

Glasstone, Samuel (ed.). *The Effects of Nuclear Weapons*. Washington, DC, United States Atomic Energy Commission, 1962 edn.

Graebner, Norman. *The New Isolationism.* New York, Ronald Press, 1956

Green, Harold P. 'The Unsystematic Security System', *Bulletin of the Atomic Scientists*, 11 (1955), 118

―――― and Rosenthal, A. *Government of the Atom.* Englewood Cliffs, NJ, Prentice-Hall, 1963

―――― See also Stern, Philip M.

Groves, Leslie R. *Now It Can Be Told.* London, André Deutsch, 1963

Hewlett, Richard G. and Anderson, Oscar E., Jr. *A History of the United States Atomic Energy Commission. Volume I. The New World 1939–1946.* University Park, Pa., Pennsylvania State UP, 1962

―――― and Duncan, Francis. *A History of the United States Atomic Energy Commission. Volume II. Atomic Shield 1947–1952.* University Park, Pa., Pennsylvania State UP, 1969

Hughes, Emmett. *The Ordeal of Power.* London, Macmillan, 1963

Huntington, Samuel P. *The Common Defense.* New York, Columbia UP, 1961

Johnson, Robert N. 'The Eisenhower Personnel Security Program', *The Journal of Politics*, 18 (1956), 625

Jungk, Robert. *Brighter Than A Thousand Suns.* Harmondsworth, Penguin Books, 1964

Kalven, Harry, Jr. 'The Case of J. Robert Oppenheimer before the Atomic Energy Commission', *Bulletin of the Atomic Scientists*, 10 (1954), 259

Kennan, George F. *Memoirs 1925–1950.* London, Hutchinson, 1968

Killian, James R. Jr and Hill, Albert G. 'For a Continental Defense', *The Atlantic Monthly*, 194 (1954), 37

Kissinger, Henry. *Nuclear Weapons and Foreign Policy.* New York, Harper & Brothers, 1957

Lapp, Ralph E. 'Atomic Candor', *Bulletin of the Atomic Scientists*, 10 (1954), 314

―――― *Atoms and People.* New York, Harper & Brothers, 1956

Lee, Asher. *Air Power.* London, Duckworth, 1955

Leghorn, Richard S. 'No Need to Bomb Cities to Win War', *US News & World Report*, 28 January 1955, 78

LeMay, Curtis E. *Mission With LeMay.* New York, Doubleday, 1965

Lilienthal, David E. 'The Case for Candor on National Security Policy', *The New York Times*, 4 October 1953

―――― *The Journals of David E. Lilienthal. Volume II. The Atomic Energy Years 1945–1950.* New York, Harper & Row, 1964

―――― *The Journals of David E. Lilienthal. Volume III. The Venturesome Years 1950–1955.* New York, Harper & Row, 1966

Mason Brown, John. *Through These Men.* New York, Harper & Brothers, 1956

Masters, D. and Way, K. (eds.). *One World Or None*. London, Latimer Press, 1947

Moss, Norman. *Men Who Play God*. London, Gollancz, 1968

Murphy, Charles J. V. 'The Atom and the Balance of Power', *Fortune*, 48/2 (1953), 97

——— 'The U.S. as a Bombing Target', ibid., 48/5 (1953), 118

Nieburg, H. L. 'The Eisenhower AEC and Congress', *The Midwest Journal of Political Science*, 6 (1962), 115

Nordheim, L. W. 'Fear and Information', *Bulletin of the Atomic Scientists*, 10 (1954), 344

O'Brian, John L. *National Security and Individual Freedom*. Cambridge, Mass., Harvard UP, 1955

Oppenheimer, J. Robert. 'Comments on the Military Value of the Atom', *Bulletin of the Atomic Scientists*, 7 (1951), 43

——— 'Atomic Weapons and American Policy', *Foreign Affairs*, 31 (1952–53), 525

——— *The Open Mind*, New York. Simon & Schuster, 1955

——— 'An Inward Look', *Foreign Affairs*, 36 (1957–58), 209

——— *The Flying Trapeze*. London, OUP, 1964

Possony, Stephan T. *Strategic Air Power*. Washington, DC, Infantry Journal Press, 1949

Potts, Ramsay D., Jr. 'National Policy and Air Defense', *Bulletin of the Atomic Scientists*, 9 (1953), 253

Price, Don K. *Government and Science*. New York, OUP, 1962 edn.

——— *The Scientific Estate*. Cambridge, Mass., Harvard UP, 1965

Public Papers of the Presidents of the United States. Harry S. Truman. 1949 Washington, DC, United States Government Printing Office, 1964

——— *Harry S. Truman. 1950*. Washington, DC, USGPO, 1965

——— *Dwight D. Eisenhower. 1953*. Washington, DC, USGPO 1960

——— *Dwight D. Eisenhower. 1954*. Washington, DC, USGPO, 1960

——— *Dwight D. Eisenhower. 1955*. Washington, DC, USGPO, 1959

——— *Dwight D. Eisenhower. 1957*. Washington, DC, USGPO, 1958

Rabinowitch, Eugene. 'The Narrowing Way', *Bulletin of the Atomic Scientists*, 9 (1953), 295

——— 'Fortune's Own "Operation Candor" ', ibid., 9 (1953), 372

Rostow, W. W. *The United States in the World Arena,* New York, Harper & Row, 1960

Rouzé, Michel. *Robert Oppenheimer*. London, Souvenir Press, 1964

Santillana, Giorgio de. 'Galileo and J. Robert Oppenheimer', *The Reporter*, 26 December 1957, 10

Sawyer, Roland. 'More Than Security', *Bulletin of the Atomic Scientists*, 10 (1954), 284

——— 'The H-Bomb Chronology', ibid., 10 (1954), 287

Scheinmann, Lawrence. *Atomic Energy Policy in France under the Fourth Republic.* Princeton, NJ, Princeton UP, 1965

Schilling, Warner R. 'The H-Bomb Decision', *The Political Science Quarterly,* 76 (1961), 24

―――― 'Scientists, Foreign Policy, and Politics', *The American Political Science Review,* 56 (1962), 287

Schlesinger, Arthur M., Jr. 'The Oppenheimer Case', *The Atlantic Monthly,* 194 (1954), 29

Seitz, Frederick. 'Offensive or Defensive Weapons?', *Bulletin of the Atomic Scientists,* 9 (1953), 325

Seversky, Alexander P. de. *Air Power.* London, Jenkins, 1952.

Shepley, James R. and Blair, Clay, Jr. *The Hydrogen Bomb.* London, Jarrolds, 1955

Shils, Edward. *The Torment of Secrecy.* London, Heinemann, 1956

Smith, Alice K. *A Peril and a Hope.* Chicago, Chicago UP, 1965

Snyder, Glenn H. 'The "New Look" of 1953' in Schilling, Warner R., Hammond, Paul Y. and Snyder, Glenn H. *Strategy, Politics and Defense Budgets.* New York, Columbia UP, 1962

Stern, Philip M. (with the collaboration of Harold P. Green) *The Oppenheimer Case.* New York, Harper & Row, 1969

Strauss, Lewis L. *Men and Decisions.* London, Macmillan, 1963

Strout, Cushing (ed.). *Conscience, Science and Security.* Chicago, Rand, McNally, 1963

―――― 'The Oppenheimer Case: Melodrama, Tragedy, and Irony', *The Virginia Quarterly Review,* 40 (1964), 268

Teller, Edward. 'The Work of Many People', *Science,* 121 (1955), 267

―――― and Brown, A. *The Legacy of Hiroshima.* London, Macmillan, 1962

Thomas, Morgan. *Atomic Energy and Congress.* Ann Arbor, Mich., University of Michigan Press, 1956

Time. 'The Atom'. 21 September 1953, 13

Trilling, Diana. 'The Oppenheimer Case: A Reading of the Testimony', *Partisan Review,* 21 (1954), 604

Truman, Harry S. *The Memoirs of Harry S. Truman. Volume Two. Years of Trial and Hope 1946–1953.* London, Hodder & Stoughton, 1956

Unna, Warren. 'Dissension in the AEC', *The Atlantic Monthly,* 199 (1957), 36

U.S. News & World Report. 'Can The H-Bomb Be Stopped?', 16 April 1954, 17

―――― 'New Debate on the Oppenheimer Case', 24 December 1954, 86

Webster, Charles and Frankland, Noble. *The Strategic Air Offensive Against Germany. 1939–1945. Volume I: Preparation*. London, Her Majesty's Stationery Office, 1961

West, Rebecca. *The Meaning of Treason*. Harmondsworth, Penguin Books, 1965

Wharton, Michael (ed.). *A Nation's Security* [an abridgement of the transcript]. London, Secker & Warburg, 1955

White, Leonard D. 'The Loyalty Program of the United States Government', *Bulletin of the Atomic Scientists*, 7 (1951), 363

Yarmolinsky, Adam (ed.). *Case Studies in Personnel Security*. Washington, DC, Bureau of National Affairs, 1955

Index

Acheson, Dean G., 74, 126, 127, 128, 132, 143
Addis, Thomas, 36, 183
Adelson, David, 37, 39
Aircraft, nuclear-powered, 31, 155, 156–7
Air defence, 105, 147, 164–74, 182, 185, 228, 254, 255–9, 260, 261–2
Air Force. *See* Department of the Air Force, Secretary of the Air Force *and* Strategic Air Command
Air power, doctrine of. *See* Strategic air power, doctrine of
Alsop, Joseph W.; 270, accusations against AEC, 239, 277–8, 279–80; air defence, 257, 258; Groves, 314–5; H-bomb, 305, 308; Mc-Carthy, 15; Oppenheimer, 245–6; secrecy, 260; witnesses at hearing, 230
Alsop, Stewart J. O., *see* Alsop, Joseph W.
Alvarez, Luis W.; H-bomb, &., 91, 94–5, 99, 100, 102–3, 110, 111, 112, 113, 119, 120, 134, 226, 248, 256; tactical atomic weapons, &., 137–8; witness at hearing, 230, 233, 305
American-Russian Institute of San Francisco, 35, 36
American Committee for Democracy and Intellectual Freedom, 34
Anderson, Clinton P., 291
Anderson, Orville, 157
Army. *See* Department of the Army *and* Military, influence of the
Arnold, Henry H., 150–1, 152
Aron, Raymond, 238
Associations. *See* Oppenheimer, J. Robert: Communist associations
Astin, Allen V., 281
Atomic bomb: custody of, 241–2; detection of tests, 98–9, 156–7, 217, 263; diffusion, gaseous, 49, 60, 142; electromagnetic process, 32, 49, 56, 60, 61, 136, 142; fissionable material, 31, 49, 56, 92, 97, 104, 114, 136; Hiroshima, 31, 69, 93, 95, 99, 105, 107, 149, 161, 295; isotope separation, 49, 56; Los Alamos, 13, 20, 31, 38, 40, 46, 47, 49, 50, 51, 52, 53, 56, 57, 58, 60, 61, 64, 66, 70, 88,

94, 95, 96, 137; military value of, 104–5; Nagasaki, 93, 107, 149, 153, 161, 295; neutrons, 104, 110, 112, 136; Oak Ridge, 56, 92; plutonium, 56, 97, 104, 112, 114, 130, 136; post-war development of, 94, 95, 96, 104, 105, 114, 136–8, 153, 154–5, 157–8; Radiation Laboratory, 39, 49, 50, 53, 56, 60, 61, 66, 67, 80, 201, 250, 300; reactors for, 97, 110, 112, 113, 114, 120, 130, 136, 142; Second World War, in, 12, 49, 56, 60, 91–3; strategic weapon, as, 105, 149–54, 155–6, 158, 160–4; tactical weapon, as, 105, 114, 136–7, 138, 154, 157–60, 217, 233, 251–2, 258; tested, 157–8; uranium, 31, 97, 263
Atomic Energy Act of 1946, 21, 34, 72, 73–4, 86, 141–2, 241, 242, 243, 253
Atomic Energy Act of 1954, 261, 290
Atomic Energy Commission: Criteria and Procedures for Determining Eligibility for Security Clearance, 283–4
Atomic Energy Commission, General, Advisory Committee: 13, 19–20, 72, 74, 81, 83, 144, 158, 194, 244, 292; Fermi Award to Oppenheimer, votes for, 292; H-bomb, &., 11, 40, 95–6, 103, 106, 112–9, 121, 122–3, 124, 125, 126, 128, 131–2, 133, 134, 135, 139–40, 161, 171–2, 180, 184, 198, 215, 216, 226–7, 278; Oppenheimer, influence on, 97, 120–1; Oppenheimer leaves, 263–4, 265; second laboratory, &., 140–1; secrecy, &., 245; tactical atomic weapons, &., 114, 136
Atomic Energy Commission: Military Liaison Committee, 129, 241
Atomic Energy Commission: Personnel Security Clearance Criteria for Determining Eligibility, 21, 22, 23–6, 41, 41–2, 86–7, 251
Atomic Energy Commission: Security Clearance Procedures, 14, 21–3, 28–9, 41, 41–2, 87, 147, 193, 209, 214, 219, 230, 232, 270
Atomic weapons. *See* Atomic bomb
Bacher, Robert F., 82, 83, 120, 134, 137, 235, 291, 314

Baldwin, Hanson W., 164, 257, 258
Beckerley, James G., 19
Belsley, G. Lyle, 83, 303
Berkeley, University of California at:
45, 51, 52, 53, 58, 59, 63, 97, 230;
A-bomb, &, 30, 32, 39, 46, 49, 50,
54, 55, 56, 66, 77, 247, 249; H-bomb,
&, 91, 109, 110, 111, 142; Oppenheimer at, 12, 47, 57, 88, 89
Berkner, Lloyd V., 166, 168, 256,
257–8
Bethe, Hans A.: 20, 45, 302; H-bomb,
and, 96, 105, 107, 109, 111, 113,
120, 134, 139, 141, 143, 161, 222,
305; Los Alamos, at, 91; Oppenheimer, on, 47, 132, 287; Peters, &,
66; Robb, &, 220, 223; second
laboratory, &, 277; Soviet A-bomb,
&, 98
Blair, Clay C., Jr., 169, 170, 276–7,
278, 310
Bohlen, Charles E., 282
Bohm, David, 38, 49, 51, 67, 145,
182, 195, 225, 300
Bohr, Niels, 302
Borden, William L.: air defence, &,
164; allegations against Oppenheimer, 29–33, 97, 217, 263–4,
265–8, 270, 271, 272, 284, 299;
General Manager of AEC, proposed
as, 278; H-bomb, &, 100, 110, 120,
123, 133, 140, 276; strategic air
power, &, 150
Bradbury, Norris E.: H-bomb, &,
20, 94, 96, 103, 110, 122, 123, 126,
128, 135, 139, 140, 141, 277
Bradley, Omar N., 106, 108, 124, 126,
155
Brownell, Herbert, Jr., 267, 268, 287
Buckley, Oliver E., 103, 115, 118
Bulletin of the Atomic Scientists, 17–18,
133, 238, 246, 255, 276, 280, 285
Burden, William A. M., 171, 221
Burgess, Guy F. M., 254
Bush, Vannevar, 20, 248; air defence,
&, 164–5; detection of tests, 86,
98, 99; H-bomb, &, 92, 104, 105,
143, 252; H-bomb allegations, &,
144–5, 176, 181, 190–1, 194, 222,
233, 238; Oppenheimer's appointment (1942–3), &, 46; Oppenheimer's clearance of 1947, &, 75,
76, 216, 223; Oppenheimer's suspension, &, 269; Oppenheimer's
victimisation, &, 238; security systems, &, 281
Byrnes, James F., 94
California Institute of Technology, 45,
120, 137, 158
California Labor School, 35, 36
California Senate Fact-Finding Com-

mittee on Un-American Activities,
37, 68, 79–80
California, University of. *See* Berkeley,
University of California at
Campbell, Joseph, 188, 198, 199–202,
203–4
Chasanow, Abraham, 281
Cherwell, Lord, 257
Chevalier, Haakon M.: 145, 192, 225,
302; AEC allegations, &, 37, 39;
'Chevalier Incident', &, 39, 51–4,
56–64, 68–9, 202, 224; end of
relationship with Oppenheimer, 71,
288; post-war association with
Oppenheimer, 65, 68–71, 88, 201,
202–3, 207, 302; view of Oppen-
heimer at hearing, 89–90; witness,
possible, 89. *See also* 'Chevalier
Incident'
'Chevalier Incident', 39, 51–4, 56–64,
68–9, 77, 80, 84, 178, 182, 195,
196, 197, 200–1, 202, 206–7, 218,
224, 249, 303
Civil defence, 112, 165, 166, 261
Clifford, Clark M., 76, 223
Cole, W. Sterling: air defence, &, 261;
H-bomb, &, 10, 134; *Hydrogen Bomb,
The,* &, 276; Oppenheimer case,
statements on, 9–10, 16, 240
Communism, 9, 10, 24, 25, 28, 76, 85,
177, 205, 237, 240, 243, 249, 251
267, 285, 294–5. *See also* Oppent
heimer, J. Robert: Communis-
associations *and* Espionage, Soviet
Compton, Arthur H., 91, 93
Compton, Karl T., 103, 190
Conant, James B.: 20, 108, 226;
'Chevalier Incident', &, 84; H-bomb,
&, 92, 103, 115, 117, 132, 133, 181,
239; H-bomb allegations, &, 144–5,
187; Oppenheimer's appointment
(1942–3), &, 46; Oppenheimer's
clearance of 1947, &, 75, 76, 216,
222, 223; Oppenheimer, view of, 65;
Robb &, 218
Condon, Edward U., 50, 66, 183–4,
231, 242–3, 281
Consumers' Union, 34
Cooke, A. Alistair, 18, 299
Cotter, Francis, 264
Crouch, Mrs. Sylvia, 79–80, 180, 229,
250, 259, 273, 283, 302
Crouch, Paul, 79–80, 180, 229, 250,
259, 273, 283, 286, 302
Cutler, Robert B., 268
Dallett, Joseph, 35, 45, 49
Davis, John W., 20
Dean, Gordon E.: 19, 173, 231, 264;
detection of tests, &, 217; H-bomb,
&, 100, 103, 123, 125, 131, 132,
133, 135, 136, 139; Oppenheimer,
confirms clearance of, 80–1, 178,

203; removes documents from, 265; on suspension of clearance of, 213; second laboratory, &, 140, 141, 142, 222; secrecy, official, &, 260; tactical atomic weapons, &, 158
Defense Department. *See* Department of Defense
Defense Secretary. *See* Secretary of Defense
Department of Defense: 244, 263; air defence, &, 172; Borden, &, 268; H-bomb, &, 11, 110, 124, 126, 128, 129, 130; Oppenheimer, &, 13, 16–17, 29, 81, 136–8, 142–3, 154–6, 214, 268; second laboratory, &, 142; strategic air power, &, 153; tactical atomic weapons, &, 136, 154, 155, 163
Department of Defense, Research and Development Board, 29, 81, 154, 163
Department of State: 53, 244; H-bomb, &, 108–9, 127, 160; Oppenheimer, &, 13, 29, 142, 169, 214, 252
Department of the Air Force: 198, 263, 288, 319; A-bomb, &, 96–7, 241; air defence, &, 165–6, 167, 168–71, 172–4, 254, 256, 258–9, 262; detection of tests, &, 98–9; H-bomb, &, 102, 106, 110–11; Oppenheimer, victimisation of, &, 239; second laboratory, &, 140, 141–2; strategic air power, 150–2, 154; tactical atomic weapons, &, 155, 156–7, 159–64
Department of the Army: 21, 85, 138; A-bomb, &, 46, 47, 64, 240–2; McCarthy, &, 10, 232, 296; Oppenheimer, &, 48–9, 54–6
DeSilva, Peer, 55–6, 66, 300
Douhet, Giulio, 148, 151
Doyle, Bernadette, 37
Drummond, Roscoe, 279
DuBridge, Lee A.: air defence, &, 171, 221; H-bomb, &, 103, 113, 115, 117, 120–1; Oppenheimer, Communist associations of, 88; government service of, 86; pleads for, 196; Strauss, on, 246; tactical atomic weapons, &, 158, 159, 163
Dulles, Allen, 252
Dulles, John Foster, 267, 281–2, 294
Ecker, Allan B., 20, 233
Einstein, Albert, 133
Eisenhower, Dwight D.: 252, 259, 292; air defence, &, 262; appeal to, question of, 209–10; H-bomb allegations, 11, 266; McCarthy, &, 9, 259–60, 267–8, 296; Oppenheimer, suspension of, 12, 14, 33, 185, 209, 266, 268–70, 296; secrecy, official, &, 256, 260, 261, 289–90; security programme of, 265–6, 267–8, 281,

282–3, 284–6; Strauss, &, 198, 264, 290; tactical atomic weapons, 163, 262
Eltenton, George, C., 39, 51, 52, 53, 54, 55, 57, 58, 59, 61, 62, 63, 68, 69. *See also* 'Chevalier Incident'
Espionage, Soviet, 30, 31, 32, 36, 39, 48, 49, 51, 52, 54, 55, 56, 58, 60, 61, 62, 66, 67, 77, 195, 201, 202, 242, 247, 250, 252
Europe, Western, defence of, 106–7, 127, 150, 154, 159, 160–4, 259, 262
Evans, Ward V., 21, 179, 187, 225, 311
Executive Order 10450, 14, 26–8, 34, 35, 36, 41–2, 81, 178, 189, 195, 265–6, 273, 284, 285, 286
Fanelli, Joseph, 69
Farley, Philip J., 205
Federal Bureau of Investigation: 30, 68, 264; AEC, &, 21, 73–4, 242; AEC allegations, drafting of, &, 272; Chevalier, &, 62–3; Director of, 29, 64, 73, 77–8, 146; Oppenheimer, &, 31, 36, 37, 38, 46, 47, 63, 73–4, 75, 77–8, 79, 80, 182, 183, 196, 197, 200, 265, 288; reports of, 22, 28, 71, 73, 74, 76, 78, 81, 82, 83, 191, 203, 214, 215, 217, 218, 234, 243, 263, 268, 270, 273, 282, 287, 314; White, Harry Dexter, &, 267
Federation of American Scientists, 280, 292
Federation of Architects, Engineers, Chemists, and Technicians (FAECT), 51, 52, 57
Fermi, Enrico: 20; Fermi Award, 291, 293; H-bomb, &, 93, 103, 111, 115–6, 122, 161, 308; Los Alamos, &, 277, 278
Finland, Soviet invasion of, 30, 37, 44
Finletter, Thomas K.: 171; air defence, 179, 256, 259; H-bomb, &, 172, 226; Oppenheimer, views on, 169, 258; second laboratory, &, 141; strategic air power, &, 152; tactical atomic weapons, &, 163
'First Strike', policy of, 106–7, 109, 160–4, 253, 310
Fission weapons. *See* Atomic bomb
Flemming, Arthur S., 268
Folkoff, Isaac, 36
Fortune, 15, 160, 170, 174, 258–9, 260, 261–2, 276, 308
France, fall of, 45
Friedman, Max B., 38
Friends of the Chinese People, 34
Fuchs, Klaus E., 32, 95, 128, 130, 220, 247, 251, 253, 264, 301, 307
Fusion weapons. *See* Hydrogen bomb
Gardner, Trevor, 288, 319
Garrison, Lloyd K.: 17, 116, 208; AEC allegations, publishes, 13, 15,

188, 232–3; AEC Criteria, &, 86–7; air defence, &, 147, 310; appeal, issue of, &, 209; associates of, 20; background, 20; Borden allegations, &, 33; brief to AEC, 188, 189, 197, 204, 212, 284; brief to PSB, 88, 161, 179, 212; Communist associations, &, 71, 88–9, 177–8, 301; clearance, requests, 214–5, 217, 313; criticism of tactics of, 88–9; documents, forbidden access to, 33, 215–8, 221, 227, 283; Gray, &, 230–1, 232–4; H-bomb allegations, 144–5, 146, 178, 180, 194; hearing, during, 219, 220–1, 227, 228–9, 230–1, 232–3, 234–5, 274, 278, 283; Nichols, correspondence with, 188–9, 197, 212, 214, 215, 217, 312; Nichols recommendations, refused sight of, 197, 312; Oppenheimer, 1947 clearance of, &, 82, 83, 84, 178; oral argument, refused, 189; procedures, criticism of, 179, 186, 188, 189, 212–30 *passim*; PSB, attempts to meet, 217–8; PSB recommendations, publishes, 188; Robb, &, 221–2, 227–9; summation of, 88, 177–9, 212, 231, 234; tactical atomic weapons, &, 147; transcript, publication of, &, 192, 214–5

General Advisory Committee. *See* Atomic Energy Commission, General Advisory Committee

Germany, Nazi, 43, 45, 49, 145, 149, 166, 295

Gorrie, Jack O., 256

Graham, Frank P., 177, 234

Gray, Gordon: air defence, &, 182; background, 20–1; bias, 230–1, 232; broadening of allegations, &, 147, 161, 162, 163; classified documents, &, 218, 227; 'Chevalier Incident', &, 58–9, 84, 182; Communist associations, &, 85, 180, 182–3, 195, 199; Garrison, &, 230–1, 232–4; Graham, &, 177, 234; H-bomb allegations, &, 109, 116, 117, 118, 180, 180–2, 189, 190, 194; Oppenheimer, attitude to security system, 182–3; candour of, 184; clearance of 1947, 82, 83–4, 185; discretion, 179, government service, 179–80, loyalty, 179, 180, motivation, 175–6, 180–2, susceptibility to influence, 183–4, suspension, 185–6, 213, 217, value, 194; procedures, fairness of, 211, interpretation of, 87, 186, 219, 235; recommendations to AEC, 179–87, 188, 189–91, 192, 193, 194, 195, 197, 199, 207, 211, 213, 217, 223, 235; Robb, &, 219–20, 223, 225, 234–5; scientists,

reassurance to, 190; security system, &, 182–3, 186–7; tactical atomic weapons, &, 182; witnesses, question of, &, 228–30

Green, Harold P., 270–1, 272

Griggs, David T., air defence, &, 168–9, 171–4, 221, 226; second laboratory, &, 141, 142; tactical atomic weapons, &, 160, 162, 168–9; witness, as, 233

Groves, Leslie R.; 19, 31, 51, 78; AEC decision, &, 314–5, 'Chevalier Incident', &, 54, 56, 59–62, 207, 224, 301; H-bomb, &, 93–4; Lawrence, &, 50; military influence, &, 240, 241; Oppenheimer, clearances of, &, 46–7, 48–9, 71–2, 75, 76, 80, 178, 216, 222, 223, 225, 235; Oppenheimer, influence of on, 97; tactical atomic weapons, &, 154

Hafstad, Lawrence R., 111

Harper's Magazine, 239, 277–8

Hawkins, David, 38, 48

Hickenlooper, Bourke B.: 278; criticism of AEC, 242, 243, 244; criticism of Gardner, 319; criticism of Oppenheimer's Fermi Award, 293; H-bomb, &, 298; statement on Oppenheimer case, 240

Hill, Albert C., 168, 173

Hill, David L., 290

Hiskey, Clarence, 36

Hiss, Alger, 250–1

Hoover, J. Edgar: 146, 288; Borden allegations, &, 29, 263, 265, 267, 268, 269; 'Chevalier Incident', &, 64, 77; Fuchs, &, 307; Oppenheimer's clearance of 1947, &, 73–4, 77–8, 83, 216, 222

House Committee on Un-American Activities, 34–5, 65–7, 68–9, 80, 182, 243, 249–50, 252

Hydrogen bomb: AEC consider, 124–6; armed forces and, 96–7, 105–6, 110–11, 124, 126, 129–30, 140–2, 159, 226; atom bomb as trigger for, 96, 100; atomic weapons programme and, 93–6, 104–5, 112–3, 114, 130, 137–8, 155; breakthrough achieved, 139–40; computers and, 96, 135; 'crash programme' for, 110, 112–3, 116, 117–8, 120, 125, 128–30, 184, 196, 200; decision to develop, 40, 129–30, 131, 132, 133, 134, 135, 143, 159, 161, 165, 181; delay in, 9–12, 13, 136–9, 180, 181; deliverability of, 104–5; deuterium, 91, 92, 93; disarmament, and, 108–9, 115–6, 125–6, 127, 142–3, 169, 172, 252, 254, 259; fall-out from, 10, 101; feasibility of, 39–40, 96, 100, 103–4, 114, 115, 116, 127, 130, 136, 137,

139, 143, 157, 159, 161, 181, 263;
Fuchs and, 95, 128, 130, 220, 307;
GAC consider, 95–6, 113–8; inefficiency of, 105, 114; intellectual
challenge of, 139–40; lithium, 104;
lobby for, 94–5, 100, 109–12, 123–4,
126–8; Los Alamos and, 91, 92,
93, 95, 96, 97, 107, 109, 110, 111,
122, 123, 126, 128, 133, 134, 135,
138, 139, 140, 141, 142, 180, 222,
276, 277; military value of, 100–1,
104–7, 112, 159; moral issue, as,
101, 102, 107–8, 115; MTA, 136,
142; NSC special committee considers, 104, 126, 128–9, 130;
neutrons, 104, 110, 112, 136;
panacea, as, 108, 131, 296; post-war
status of, 93–7; Radiation Laboratory and, 103, 111; reactors and, 97,
110, 112, 113, 114, 120, 130, 136,
142; second laboratory for, 140–2;
Second World War, status in, 91–3;
significance as an allegation, 13, 31,
39–40, 92–3, 96, 103–4, 107–9,
112–5, 116–8, 119, 120–3, 132–6,
137–40, 141, 142–3, 144–6, 178,
180–2, 184, 187, 193, 194–5, 199,
202, 204, 206, 215, 226–8, 233,
266–7, 270, 271, 295–6; Soviet
Union and, 98, 102–3, 106–9, 115,
116, 119, 123, 125, 127, 128, 129,
131, 135, 145, 261, 304, 305; State
Department and, 127; strategic
weapon, as, 100–1, 105, 106–8,
115; tactical weapon, as, 101, 159;
test of, 113, 114, 115, 127, 128,
129, 130, 136, 138, 140, 142–3,
157, 252, 279, 305; tritium, 91, 93,
104, 110, 114, 129, 130, 136
Hydrogen Bomb, The, 92, 133, 163, 169,
276–7, 278, 310
Independent Citizens' Committee of
the Arts, Sciences and Professions
(ICCASP), 39, 65
Inglis, David R., 290
Institute for Advanced Study, 13, 96,
133, 135, 139, 275, 287
International control of atomic energy,
64, 65, 74, 108, 125–6, 127, 152,
156, 174
Ivanov, Peter, 39
Jackson C. D., 260
Jackson, Henry M., 289
Jenner, William E., 16, 273–4
Johnson, Edwin C., 127, 306
Johnson, Louis A., 124, 126, 129, 130
Johnson, Lyall, 52–3, 89
Johnson, Lyndon B., 293
Joint Chiefs of Staff, 106, 111, 113,
124, 130, 256, 262
Joint Committee on Atomic Energy:
AEC, &, 242–5, 315; Borden, &,

29, 263, 264, 272; detection of tests,
&, 99; H-bomb, &, 11, 100, 102,
110, 111, 123, 124, 126, 127, 129,
133, 134, 216; hearing, relationship
to, 16; Oppenheimer, reinstatement
of, &, 289, 291, 292, 293; Seaborg
Incident, &, 121, 216, 226–7;
second laboratory, &, 140, 141;
statement on the case, 10–11, 240
Joliot-Curie, Frédéric, 251, 253
Jones, Thomas O., 77, 82
Kallett, Arthur, 35
Kalven, Harry, Jr., 280
Kelly, Mervin J., 137, 155, 170, 217,
233, 261
Kennan, George F., 19, 85–6, 106–7,
108–9, 113, 127, 131, 236–7
Kennedy, John F., 291, 292–3
Kenney, George C., 167, 170
Killian, James R., 191, 288–9
Knowland, William F., 242
Korean War, 131, 136, 137, 138, 157,
165, 166, 241, 251, 294, 305
Kurchatov, Igor, 98
Ladejinsky, Wolf, 281, 283
Lambert, Rudy, 36, 200, 202, 207,
224
Lansdale, John, Jr., 54, 55; 'Chevalier
Incident', &, 56–7; Communist
associations, &, 84–5, 223–4; Lambert, &, 200, 207; Lomanitz, &,
50–1, 52, 225; Mrs Oppenheimer,
&, 45; Oppenheimer, interrogation
of, 59, 196, 200, 207, 221, 224, 230,
234, 235; Oppenheimer, suspicions
about, 47, 48, 49, 178; Weinberg,
&, 51, 196, 207
Latimer, Wendell M., 97, 100, 110,
119, 174, 305
Lauritsen, Charles C., 45, 137, 143,
158, 160, 161, 163, 165, 168, 169,
174
Lawrence, David, 193
Lawrence, Ernest O.: 66, 245; armed
forces, &, 242; Borden, &, 278;
conservatism of, 47, 247–8; detection
of tests, &, 226; electromagnetic
process, &, 49, 136; H-bomb, &,
93, 100, 103, 110, 111, 113, 124,
239, 256; Lomanitz, &, 50–1;
Materials Testing Accelerator, &,
136, 142; Oppenheimer, sponsors,
45–6; Oppenheimer's suspension, &,
213–4; witness at hearing, 230
LeBaron, Robert, 129, 130, 137, 142
LeMay, Curtis E., 151, 157, 163, 167,
259
Lewis, Fulton J., Jr., 192, 279
Libby, Willard F., 135
Lilienthal, David E.: 81, 279; attacked
by Hickenlooper, 243, 244; attacked
in *Time,* 262, 263; background,

72–3; 'Chevalier Incident', &, 84; Condon, &, 231; confirmation delayed, 73, 78; custody of atomic weapons, 241; Eisenhower, on, 266, 317; Fuchs, &, 307; H-bomb, &, 11, 103, 105–6, 108, 109, 112, 113, 114, 116, 117, 123, 124–5, 126, 128, 129, 131, 154, 217, 226, 304; McCarthy, on, 298; Oppenheimer, &, 64, 132, 288; Oppenheimer's clearance of 1947, &, 73–4, 75–9, 82, 216, 222–3, 233; resigns, 125, 130; Robb &, 83, 220, 222–3, 235; secrecy, &, 243–4, 254, 255, 260; Strauss, on, 213, 246, 277; witness at hearing, 19, 83, 220, 222–3, 233, 235, 313–4

Lincoln Laboratory, 168, 169, 172–3
Lincoln Summer Study, 147, 168–74, 255–6, 257–9, 261–2
Lippmann, Walter, 212
Lomanitz, Giovanni R., 38, 49–51, 52, 57, 67, 89, 145, 182, 183, 195, 196, 200, 207, 224–5
Longmire, Conrad, 135
Los Alamos Scientific Laboratory. *See* Atomic bomb *and* Hydrogen bomb
Lovett, Robert A., 142, 256, 261
Maclean, Donald D., 254
Malraux, André, 70, 90
Manley, Jack, 36, 37
Manley, John H., 113, 122, 123, 125
Marks, Herbert S., 20, 76, 179, 214, 215, 216, 219, 264, 273, 274
Massachusetts Institute of Technology, 165, 168, 173
Matusow, Harvey, 287
May, Kenneth, 36
May, Mrs Ruth, 36
McCarran Act, 251
McCarthy, Joseph R.: H-bomb, accusations on, 9, 10, 11, 13, 266, 298; hearing, influence on, 231–2, 259–60, 267–8, 269, 296; Lewis, &, 192, 279; McCarthyism, 90, 146; Nichols, &, 272; Oppenheimer, view of, 15; political influence of, 209, 248, 251; Stevens, &, 138, Strauss, praise for, 15
McCloy, John J., 19, 49, 86, 87, 232, 233
McCone, John A., 291
McCormack, James, Jr., 96, 103, 104–5, 117, 118, 137, 139, 155, 170
McMahon, Brien: 95, 315; Atomic Energy Act of 1946, &, 241, 242; H-bomb, &, 100, 101, 103, 110, 111, 122, 123–4, 127, 141, 276, 304; tactical atomic weapons, &, 158
Military, influence of the, 240–2
Military Liaison Committee. *See* Atomic Energy Commission: Military Liaison Committee
Mitchell, 'Billy', 148

Mitchell, William, 42, 216, 270–1
Morgan, Thomas A.: air defence, &, 182; background, 21; 'Chevalier Incident', &, 182; Communist associations, &, 180, 182–3, 195, 199; H-bomb allegations, 180, 180–2, 189, 190, 194; Oppenheimer, attitude to security system, 182–3; candour, 184, clearance of 1947, &, 185, discretion, 179, government service, 179–80, loyalty, 179, 180, motivation, 180–2, susceptibility to influence, 183–4, suspension, 185–6, 213, 217, value, 194; procedures, fairness of, 211, interpretation of, 186, 219, 235; recommendations to AEC, 179–87, 188, 189–91, 192, 193, 194, 195, 197, 199, 207, 211, 213, 217, 223, 235; scientists, reassurance to, 190; security system, &, 182–3, 186–7; tactical atomic weapons, &, 182
Morrison, Philip, 88
Mundt, Karl E., 16
Murphy, Charles J. V., 99, 258–9, 260, 276
Murray, Thomas E., 141, 198, 199, 204–5, 221, 222, 263–4, 289
Murrow, Edward R., 9, 10
National Security Council, 29, 110, 142, 172, 256, 261, 262
Nazi-Soviet Pact, 30, 37, 44
Nelson, Steve, 36, 37, 38, 49, 52, 55, 57, 67, 250, 252
New York Herald Tribune, The, 13, 15, 193, 211, 212, 239, 257, 260, 269, 279, 292
New York Times, The, 11, 13, 134, 164, 190, 192, 211, 222, 238, 257, 260, 263, 265, 281, 293, 294
Nichols, Kenneth D.: 13–14, 45, 58, 59, 63, 71, 88, 96, 134, 232, 274–5; A-bomb, &, 137, 155, 241, 242; AEC allegations (Nichols letter), 13, 14, 28, 33–42 (text), 43, 63, 91, 93, 97, 103–4, 119, 122, 134, 144–5, 147, 176, 178, 180–1, 190, 194–5, 199, 206, 214, 215, 216, 222, 228, 232, 270–2, 273–4, 275, 291, 301, drafting of, 271, 272, presentation of, 273–4; Alsops, &, 279, 305; Garrison, &, 188–9, 197, 204, 211, 212, 223, 227, 271, 312; Groves, &, 241; H-bomb, &, 100, 110–11, 137, 305; leaves AEC, 278; Oppenheimer, &, attitude to security system, 196, 271, character, 195–6, 'Chevalier Incident', &, 195, 196, Communist associations, 195, 196, discretion, 193, government service, 193–4, H-bomb, &, 194–5, 271, loyalty of, 193, value as adviser, 194, 196, 271, veracity of, 195–6; recommendations

to AEC, 193–6, 196–8, 199, 204, 211, 212, 223, 227, 271, 312; Smyth's dissent, &, 205; Strauss, &, 273–4; witnesses at hearing, &, 230
Nixon, Richard M., 16, 80, 269, 273
Norstad, Lauris, 163, 164
Norton, Garrison, 171, 221
Nuclear-powered aircraft. *See* Aircraft, nuclear-powered
Nuclear weapons. *See* Atomic bomb
Nunn May, Alan, 247, 253
Office of Defense Mobilization, 14, 196, 268
Office of Scientific Research and Development, 20, 190, 248
Ofstie, Ralph A., 153–4
Olson, Loren K., 291–2
Oppenheimer, Frank F., 13, 30, 35–6, 39, 57, 59, 65, 66, 88, 249, 250, 301
Oppenheimer, J. Robert: aircraft, nuclear-powered, and, 31, 156–7; air defence, and, 147, 165, 169, 170, 171–2, 173–4, 228, 254, 256–7; allegations of AEC against, 13, 14, 28, 33–42, 43, 63, 91, 93, 97, 103–4, 119, 122, 134, 144–5, 147, 176, 178, 180–1, 190, 194–5, 199, 206, 214, 215, 216, 222, 228, 232, 270–2, 273–4, 275, 291, 301; allegations of AEC, reply to, 13-14, 45, 58, 59, 63, 71, 88, 96, 134, 232, 274–5; allegations of Borden against, 29–33, 97, 217, 265–8, 270, 271, 272, 284, 299; arrogance of, 245–6, 271; attacks on (1947–53), 73–4, 79–80, 249–52, 258–60, 262–3; background of, 12–13; candour of, 184 (*see also* veracity of); character of, 175, 177, 187, 195–6, 199–201, 290; 'Chevalier Incident', and, 39, 51–4, 56–61, 63–4, 68–9, 77, 80, 84, 178, 182, 195, 196, 197, 200–1, 202, 206–7, 218, 224, 249, 288, 303; clearances, (1942–3) 46–9, 71–2, 73–4, 178, (1947) 72–9, 81–4, 118, 178, 184–5, 187, 197, 201, 202–3, 215–6, 222–3, 225, 233, 234, 249, 284, 291, 313–4, (1950) 80–1, 178, (1953) 81, 178; Communist associations of, 13, 15, 16, 18, 30, 31, 32, 34–9, 43–71, 84–9, 144, 145–6, 177, 178, 180, 181, 182–3, 186, 187, 195, 199, 200, 201, 202, 205, 206–7, 223–6, 228, 266–7, 294–5, 296, 313–4; Communist Party, non-membership of, 15, 18, 48, 299; consultancy, lapse of, 185–6, 203, 212–4, 239; death of, 294; defection, possible, 271, 288; Defense Department, and, 13, 16–7, 81, 136–8, 142–3, 154–6, 214, 268; detection of nuclear tests, and, 98–9, 156–7; discretion of, 156,

177–8, 179, 185, 193, 199, 206, 208, 213, 251; dissociation from Communism, 44–5, 47, 50–1, 64–7; documents, AEC, taken from, 121, 214, 218, 227, 264–5; FBI and, 31, 36, 37, 38, 46, 47, 63, 73–4, 75, 77–8, 79, 80, 182, 183, 196, 197, 200, 265, 288; Fermi Award, given, 291, 292–4; General Advisory Committee, and, 11, 40, 95–6, 97, 103, 106, 112–9, 120–1, 122–3, 124, 125, 126, 128, 131–2, 133, 134, 135, 136, 139–41, 161, 171–2, 180, 184, 198, 215, 226–7, 245, 263–4, 265, 278, 292; government service of, 14, 18, 29–30, 31, 37–8, 45–61, 75, 80, 86–7, 88, 174–6, 178, 179–80, 185, 193–4, 197, 199, 235; hearing, behaviour at, 89–90, 303; hydrogen bomb, attitude to, 13, 31, 39–40, 91–4, 95–6, 97, 103–4, 105, 106, 107–9, 112–3, 114–5, 116–8, 119–23, 132–6, 137–40, 141, 142–3, 144–6, 178, 180–2, 184, 187, 193, 194–5, 199, 202, 204, 206, 215, 226–8, 233, 266–7, 270, 271, 295–6; influence of, 30, 40, 97, 119–23, 132–6, 137–9, 140, 141, 142–3, 156–7, 159–64, 169, 171–2, 173–4, 184, 225; Institute for Advanced Study, and, 13, 96, 133, 135, 139, 275, 287; international control of atomic energy, and, 64, 65, 74, 108, 125–6, 127, 152, 156, 174; isotopes, export of, and, 244–6, 264, 290, 315; Lincoln Summer Study, and, 168–74; Los Alamos, and, 12, 13, 31, 38, 40, 46–61, 64, 66, 70, 88, 91–4, 95–6, 97, 107, 122–3, 133–4, 134–6, 137–9, 140–2, 174, 180, 222, 300; loyalty of, 40, 55, 56, 66, 81, 156, 157, 169, 172, 175, 177, 178, 179, 180, 185, 187, 193, 199, 203, 204–5, 206, 207–8, 213, 218, 251, 268, 271, 272, 289; opinions of, 144–6, 175–6, 180–2, 187, 189–91, 194, 199, 204, 278; ostracised, 287; rehabilitation of, 291–4; reinstatement called for, 288–9; resignation of, 131–2, 273–5; secrecy, official, and, 242–5, 246–7, 252–5, 260–1, 289–90; security system, attitude to, 47, 53–4, 182–3, 196, 200–1, 202, 205, 207, 225, 271; Soviet agent, alleged, 30, 32, 48, 178, 264, 271; Soviet Union, attitude to, 30–2, 43–5, 65, 74–5, 108–9, 115, 116, 138, 143, 145, 153–4, 160–2, 163–4, 180, 251, 253, 288, 294–5; State Department, and, 13, 29, 142–3, 169, 252; strategic air power, and, 152–7, 161–2, 163–4, 170, 171–4; suspended by Eisenhower, 12, 14, 33, 185, 209, 266, 268–70, 296; suspicions about (1942–4), 46, 47, 48, 50, 54–6, 71; tactical atomic weapons, and, 147, 152–64, 262; value as government adviser, 75, 174–6, 185, 193–4, 196, 225, 271, 293, 296; veracity of, 31, 40, 195–6, 197, 200–1, 202–3, 206–7, 211, 223–7, 271, 301; verdicts, reaction to, 188–9, 208–9; victimisation of, alleged, 206, 238–40, 246, 277–8, 290, 292; Vista, Project, and, 158–64; vulnerability of, 248–9

Oppenheimer, Mrs Jacqueline, 35, 88, 249

Oppenheimer, Mrs Katherine, 13, 30, 35, 45, 57, 69, 70, 71, 182, 250

Oppenheimer Hearing, the: air defence, issue of, 147–8, 167–9, 170–4, 182, 185, 228; AEC allegations — answered, 13–14, 45, 58, 59, 63, 71, 88, 96, 134, 232, drafted, 270–2, featured in hearing, 13, 14, 28, 43, 63, 91, 93, 97, 103–4, 119, 122, 134, 144–5, 147, 176, 180–1, 190, 194–5, 199, 206, 214, 215, 216, 222, 228, 232, 275, 291, 301, presented, 273–4, published, 13, 15, 188, 232–3, sanctioned by AEC, 269–70, 271, text of, 34–42; AEC decision— Campbell's opinion, 203–4, Majority opinion, 199–202, 205–6, 208, 211, 223, 224, 227, Murray's opinion, 204–5, Oppenheimer's reaction, 208, public reaction, 211, scientists' reaction, 276, 277, 278–9, Smyth's dissent, 206–8, Strauss' gloss, 202–3, Zuckert's opinion, 203; appeal, question of, 208–10; brief to AEC, 188, 189, 197, 204, 212, 284; brief to PSB, 88, 161, 179, 212; Communist associations, issue of, 13, 15, 16, 18, 30, 31, 32, 34–9, 43–71, 84–9, 144, 145–6, 177, 178, 180, 181, 182–3, 186, 187, 195, 199, 200, 201, 202, 205, 206–7, 223–6, 228, 266–7, 294–5, 296, 313–4; departures from procedures, 188, 189, 197, 219–20; Eisenhower's role in, 12, 14, 33, 185, 209, 266, 268–70, 296; General Manager's recommendations, 193–8, 212, 223, 312; hydrogen bomb, issue of, 13, 31, 39–40, 92–3, 96, 103–4, 107–9, 112–5, 116–8, 119, 120–3, 132–6, 137–40, 141, 142–3, 144–6, 178, 180–2, 184, 187, 193, 194–5, 199, 202, 204, 206, 215, 226–8, 233, 266–7, 270, 271, 295–6; instigation of, 265–75; legal basis of, 21–8; oral argument, question of, 188, 189, 197; procedures criticised, 179, 186, 188, 189–91, 208, 212–36,

276, 280–1; procedures praised, 186–7, 201, 203, 211; PSB recommendations—Evans' dissent, 187, majority opinion, 179–87, 188, 189–91, 192, 193, 194, 195, 197, 199, 207, 211, 213, 217, 223, 235; Oppenheimer's reaction, 188–9, published, 188, scientists's reaction, 189–91, 194, 197; setting of, 19; summation, 88, 177–9, 212, 231, 234; tactical atomic weapons, issue of, 147–8, 152–7, 158–64, 182, 185, 228; transcript, publication of, 191–3, 212, 215, 288; verdicts, 179–87, 193–7, 199–208; witnesses at, 19–20, 174, 201, 216, 219, 228–30, 233, 314

Osborn, Frederick H., 74

Parsons, William S., 154

Pash, Boris T.: 'Chevalier Incident', &, 52–4, 57–8, 59, 63, 195; Oppenheimer, interrogation of, 50, 52–4, 57–8, 63, 89, 221, 224, 235; Oppenheimer, suspicions about, 48, 54–5, 56

Patterson, Robert P., 216, 222, 223

Paul, Randolph E., 274

Pearl Harbor, 150, 168

Pentagon. *See* Department of Defense

People's Daily World, 36

Personnel Security Clearance Criteria for Determining Eligibility. *See* Atomic Energy Commission: Personnel Security Clearance Criteria for Determining Eligibility

Persons, Wilton B., 268

Peters, Bernard, 66–7, 69, 89, 145, 183, 195, 196, 200, 202, 207, 225–6, 250

Peters, John P., 286

Peters, Mrs Hannah, 37, 66

Pinsky, Paul, 37, 39

Pitzer, Kenneth S., 117, 118, 132, 144, 230, 233, 305

Placzek, George, 120

Poland, Soviet invasion of, 44

Pontecorvo, Bruno, 247

Project Vista. *See* Vista, Project

Public Law 733 of 1950, 21

Rabi, Isidor I.: air defence, &, 167, 169, 170, 172, 174, 221; AEC allegations, &, 144, 178; 'Chevalier Incident', &, 84, 218; GAC documents transferred to, 265; H-bomb, &, 103, 104, 110, 115–6, 116–7, 120, 121, 124, 161, 171, 308; Oppenheimer, government service of, 86; Oppenheimer, suggested reinstatement of, 289, 292; Oppenheimer, suspension of, &, 212; Teller, &, 276, 277

Rabinowitch, Eugene, 246–7

Radiation Laboratory, Berkeley. *See* Atomic bomb *and* Hydrogen bomb

Ramsey, Norman, 45, 103, 106

Reston, James B., 11, 15, 17, 192, 265
Ridgway, Matthew B., 154
Robb, Roger: 83, 99, 175, 177, 178, 279, 285, 313; AEC Criteria, &, 86–7; air defence, &, 147, 174, 228; Alsops, &, 280; background of, 20; Borden allegations, &, 33; 'Chevalier Incident', &, 57–8; clearance of, 217; Communist associations, &, 89, 145, 183, 200; documents, classified, use of, 218–9, 221–5, 226–7, 283, 291; Evans' dissent, &, 311; Garrison, &, 221–2, 227–9; Gray, &, 219–20, 228–30, 232, 234–5; H-bomb allegations, &, 107, 116, 143, 145–6, 176, 180, 184, 194, 216; Oppenheimer's clearance of 1947, &, 82, 84, 222–3; Oppenheimer's influence, &, 119, 226, Oppenheimer's veracity, &, 223–7; prosecutor, as, 219–20, 283; security system, on, 236; tactical atomic weapons, &, 147, 160, 162, 163, 228; witnesses, question of, &, 228–30
Roberts, Owen J., 177
Rolander, C. A.: 20, 218; Alsops, &, 229–30, 270, 279–80; classified documents, &, 83, 313; Gray, &, 234; Oppenheimer, suspension of, &, 270; witnesses at hearing, &, 99, 229–30
Roosevelt, Franklin D., 165, 300
Roosevelt, Mrs Eleanor, 85, 134
Rowe, Hartley, 103, 107, 115
Russell, Louis J., 68
Russia. *See* Soviet Union
Salisbury, Morse, 279
Sandow, Katrina, 37
Schine, David T., 10
Schmitz, Henry, 287
Schneiderman, William, 37
Scientific community, the: Air Force &, 164; Army, &, 47, 240–1; H-bomb, &, 101–2, 107, 247–8; hearing, reaction to, 17–18; Oppenheimer on, 208; Oppenheimer's reinstatement, &, 288–9; Personnel Security Board reports, reaction to, 189–91, 194, 271; reassured, 187, 204, 278–9; secrecy, &, 247, 253, 254–5, 289–90; security system, &, 189–91, 276, 280–1; Strauss, &, 290; suspicions about, 247, 251, 253–4; Teller, &, 278–9; view of case, 239, 276, 277; vulnerability of, 248–9
Seaborg, Glenn T.: AEC programme (1947–9), &, 97; H-bomb, &, 103, 113–4, 121–2, 184, 196, 200, 202, 207, 226–7; offers second hearing to Oppenheimer, 292
'Second strike', policy of, 106, 160–2
Secrecy, issue of, 242–5, 246–7, 252–5, 260–1, 289–90

Secretary of Defense, 14, 16–17, 81, 126, 128, 129, 130, 142, 157, 256, 261, 268
Secretary of State, 126, 267, 281–2
Secretary of the Air Force, 141, 152, 163, 169, 171, 172–3, 256, 258, 259
Secretary of the Army, 10, 21, 138
Security Clearance Procedures. *See* Atomic Energy Commission: Security Clearance Procedures
Security system for Executive Branch of US Government: abuses of, 281–2; Atomic Energy Act of 1946, 21, 34, 72, 73–4, 86, 242; AEC Personnel Security Clearance Criteria for Determining Eligibility, 21, 22, 23–6, 41–2, 86–7, 251, 316; AEC Security Clearance Procedures, 14, 21–3, 28–9, 41, 41–2, 87, 147, 193, 209, 214, 219, 230, 232, 270, 319; AEC praise for, 201, 203, 211; Eisenhower security programme, 26–8, 265–6, 267–8; Executive Order 10450, 14, 26–8, 34, 35, 36, 41–2, 81, 178, 189, 195, 265–6, 273, 284, 285, 286; Garrison's criticisms of, 179, 186, 188, 189, 212–30 *passim*; PSB criticises, 186; PSB praises, 186–7; Public Law 733 of 1950, 21; reforms in, 282–7, 319; scientists' criticisms of, 189–91, 276, 280–1; Second World War regulations, 46; Smyth's criticism of, 208; Truman loyalty programme, 76–7, 265–6
Seitz, Frederick, 98
Senate Internal Security Subcommittee, 16, 273–4
Serber, Robert, 88, 113, 120
Shell Development Company, 51, 62, 80
Shepley, James R., 169, 170, 276–7, 278, 310
Shils, Edward A., 17, 190
Silverman, Samuel J., 20, 179, 214, 215, 233, 300
Smith, Cyril S., 103, 115, 118, 121, 244
Smyth, Henry D.: AEC procedures, &, 188; background of, 198; Borden allegations, &, 272; dissent of, 205–8, & 'Chevalier Incident', 206–7, & Communist associations, 206–7, & H-bomb allegations, 206, & Oppenheimer's character, 206, & Oppenheimer's discretion, 206, 208, & Oppenheimer's loyalty, 206, 207–8, preparation of, 205–6; security system, view of, 207–8; transcript, publication of, 191; Wyman, &, 302
Souers, Sidney W., 110, 129
Soviet consul in San Francisco, 35, 39, 53, 201
Soviet Union. *See* Espionage, Soviet; Hydrogen bomb, Soviet Union &;

Oppenheimer, J. Robert, Soviet Union, attitude to
Spaatz, Carl, 152
Spanish civil war, 35, 44, 45, 85
Sputniks I and II, 288, 289
State Department. *See* Department of State *and* Secretary of State
Stevens, Robert T. B., 138
Strategic Air Command, 150, 151, 155, 156, 158, 159, 160, 162–3, 164, 167, 168, 169, 170, 171, 173, 258, 259, 262
Strategic air power, doctrine of, 148–54, 155–6, 157, 158, 160–4, 166–7, 168–71, 256–9, 261–2
Strauss, Lewis L.: AEC decision, &, 199–203, 290; background, 198; 'Chevalier Incident', &, 199–200; Communist associations, &, 199–200; detection of tests, &, 99; fall-out, &, 10, 101; Fermi Award, &, 293; Garrison, &, 215; H-bomb, &, 11–12, 100, 101, 103, 106, 109–10, 112, 123, 124, 125, 132, 135, 139, 305; *Hydrogen Bomb, The*, &, 277; H-bomb allegations, &, 199; Institute for Advanced Study, &, 275, 287; isotopes, export of, &, 244–6, 264, 315; leaves public life, 290–1; military, &, 241; Nichols' recommendations, &, 198; Oppenheimer, &, attitude to security system, 200, 202, character, 199–202, 290, clearance of 1947, 72, 75, 202–3, discretion, 199, documents, AEC, removal of, 215, 264–5, government service of, 199, loyalty, 199, presents with AEC allegations, 272–5; reinstatement, 289, 319, suspension, 14, 15, 213, 266, 268, 269–70, veracity, 200–2, victimisation, 239, 277–8, 279, 290; praised, 15, 99, 262–3; procedures, belief in fairness of, 211; procedures, reform of, 283–4; Rabi, &, 144, 178; scientists, &, 276, 277, 278, 280; second laboratory, &, 140; secrecy, &, 244–6, 260, 261; transcript, publication of, &, 191–2; witnesses at hearing, &, 230, 314
Supreme Court, United States, 286–7
Szilard, Leo, 165, 255
Tactical atomic weapons. *See* Atomic bomb
Tatlock, Jean, 30, 35, 44, 48, 192
Teeple, David S., 278, 279
Teller, Edward: Fermi Award, &, 293; H-bomb, &, 91–2, 93, 94–5, 100, 101–2, 110, 111–12, 119, 120, 122, 123, 124, 133, 134, 138, 139, 140–2, 159, 163, 221, 222, 256, 257, 278–9; Oppenheimer, suspension of, &, 213–4; Oppenheimer, victimisation of, &, 239; Rabi, &, 276; Strauss, &, 290; witness at hearing, 20,

175–6, 305, 310–11
Thermonuclear weapons. *See* Hydrogen bomb
Thomas, J. Parnell, 243
Tizard, Henry Thomas, 257
Tolman, Richard C., 92, 221, 226
Trilling, Diana, 145, 220
Truman, Harry S: 255; A-bomb, &, 104, 136, 241–2; AEC, &, 72, 243; Fuchs, &, 307; H-bomb, &, 11, 94, 100, 101, 103, 106, 110, 113, 118, 123, 125, 126, 127, 129, 130, 131, 132, 133, 134, 135, 136, 143, 159, 161, 165, 181, 257; loyalty programme, 76–7, 242, 251, 265, 266; Oppenheimer, clearance of 1947, &, 76, 223; secrecy, &, 244–5; Soviet A-bomb, &, 11, 99–100, 254; Truman Doctrine, &, 74, 76, 129; White, Harry Dexter, &, 267
Ulam, Stanislaw M., 139
Un-American Activities Committee. *See* House Committee on Un-American Activities
Urey, Harold C., 255
USSR. *See* Soviet Union
Vandenberg, Arthur H., 241, 244
Vandenberg, Hoyt S., 99, 102, 110–11, 169, 226, 227
Velde, Harold H., 252
Vista, Project, 158–64
Vogel, Clark C., 205
Volpe, Joseph A., Jr., 75, 77, 81, 246, 274, 292
Von Neumann, John, 20, 96, 103, 134, 135, 139, 278, 308
Weapons. *See* Atomic bomb *and* Hydrogen bomb
Weeks, Sinclair, 281
Weinberg, Joseph W., 36, 38, 49, 51, 52, 55, 57, 58, 60, 67, 79, 173, 196, 200, 202, 207, 224, 225, 247, 250, 252, 300
Weisskopf, Victor F., 66, 120
Welch, Joseph N., 232
White, Harry Dexter, 267
Whitman, Walter G.: background, 81; Oppenheimer, recommends clearance for, 81; tactical atomic weapons, &, 155, 156, 163, 171, 178
Wilson, Carroll L., 77, 122—3, 139
Wilson, Charles E., 16–17, 157, 261, 262, 268
Wilson, Roscoe C., 99, 106, 137, 155, 156–7, 174, 227, 305
Winne, Harry A., 87, 104, 232, 235
Wyman, Jeffries, Jr., 70, 71, 302
Zacharias, Jerrold R., 168, 169, 171, 173, 174
Zinn, Walter H., 111, 112
'ZORC', 173–4
Zuckert, Eugene M., 191, 198, 199–202, 203, 236